EIGHT MODERN ESSAYISTS

EIGHT MODERN ESSAYISTS

SECOND EDITION

WILLIAM SMART

SWEET BRIAR COLLEGE

St. Martin's Press, New York

ACKNOWLEDGMENTS

"Notes on the English Character," "My Wood," and "Voltaire's Laboratory," from *Abinger Harvest*, copyright, 1936, © 1964, by E. M. Forster, are reprinted by permission of Harcourt Brace Jovanovich, Inc., and Edward Arnold Ltd.

"Not Listening to Music" and "What I Believe," from *Two Cheers for Democracy*, copyright, 1938, 1939, 1947, 1949, 1951, by E. M. Forster, are reprinted by permission of Harcourt Brace Jovanovich, Inc., and Edward Arnold Ltd.

"The Shadow Across the Page," from Chapter 6 of *A Room of One's Own* by Virginia Woolf, copyright 1929 by Harcourt Brace Jovanovich, Inc.; copyright 1957 by Leonard Woolf. Reprinted by permission of the publishers, Harcourt Brace Jovanovich, Inc., the Author's Literary Estate and The Hogarth Press.

"Lord Chesterfield's Letters to His Son" and "How Should One Read a Book?" from *The Second Common Reader* by Virginia Woolf, copyright, 1932, by Harcourt Brace Jovanovich, Inc., © 1960 by Leonard Woolf, are reprinted by permission of the publishers, Harcourt Brace Jovanovich, Inc. and Leonard Woolf and The Hogarth Press.

"The Strange Elizabethans," from *The Second Common Reader* by Virginia Woolf, copyright, 1932, by Harcourt Brace Jovanovich, Inc., renewed, 1960, by Leonard Woolf, is reprinted by permission of the publishers, Harcourt Brace Jovanovich, Inc. and Leonard Woolf and The Hogarth Press.

"Adolf" and "Nottingham and the Mining Countryside," from

PHOENIX: *The Posthumous Papers of D. H. Lawrence* ed. by Edward McDonald. All rights reserved. Reprinted by permission of The Viking Press, Inc.

"Pan in America" and "Why the Novel Matters," from PHOENIX: *The Posthumous Papers of D. H. Lawrence* ed. by Edward McDonald. Copyright 1936 by Frieda Lawrence, © 1964 by the Estate of the Late Mrs. Frieda Lawrence Ravagli. All rights reserved. Reprinted by permission of The Viking Press, Inc.

"Burlesque Shows," from *The Shores of Light* by Edmund Wilson, copyright 1952, is reprinted by permission of Farrar, Straus & Giroux, Inc.

"Communists and Cops" and "The Old Stone House," from *The American Earthquake* by Edmund Wilson (Doubleday & Co., Inc.), are reprinted by permission of the author. Copyright 1958 by Edmund Wilson.

"Miami," from *Red, Black, Blond and Olive* by Edmund Wilson (Oxford University Press), is reprinted by permission of the author. Copyright 1956 by Edmund Wilson.

"*Upstate*: Epilogue, 1970," from *Upstate: Records & Recollections of Northern New York* by Edmund Wilson, copyright 1971, is reprinted by permission of Farrar, Straus & Giroux, Inc.

"The World of Tomorrow" (May 1939) and "Walden" (June 1939), from *One Man's Meat* by E. B. White, are reprinted by permission of Harper & Row, Publishers, Inc. Copyright 1939 by E. B. White.

"Once More to the Lake" (August, 1941), from *One Man's Meat* by E. B. White, is reprinted by permission of Harper & Row, Publishers, Inc. Copyright 1941 by E. B. White.

"Death of a Pig," from *The Second Tree from the Corner* by E. B. White, is reprinted by permission of Harper & Row, Publishers, Inc. Copyright 1947 by E. B. White.

"The Ring of Time" (Fiddler Bayou, March 22, 1956), pp. 51–55, is reprinted from *The Points of My Compass* by E. B. White. Originally published in *The New Yorker* without its postscript, and reprinted with the permission of Harper & Row, Publishers, Inc. Copyright © 1956 by E. B. White.

"Shooting an Elephant," "Politics and the English Language," "Some Thoughts on the Common Toad," and "Reflections on Gandhi," from *Shooting an Elephant and Other Essays* by George Orwell, copyright 1945, 1946, 1949, 1950, by Sonia Brownell Orwell. Reprinted by per-

mission of Harcourt Brace Jovanovich, Inc., and Martin Secker & War-
burg Limited.

"Democracy and the Search for Style" and "Cities Higher Than
Mountains" from *Cannibals and Christians,* by Norman Mailer, copyright 1966, and "Grandma with Orange Hair," from *Armies of the Night*
by Norman Mailer, copyright 1971, and "Miami Beach" and "The Siege
of Chicago: Chapter 16" from *Miami and the Siege of Chicago* by
Norman Mailer, copyright 1971, are all reprinted by permission of the
author and his agents, Scott Meredith Literary Agency, Inc., 580 Fifth
Avenue, New York, New York, 10036.

"Stranger in the Village" and "Notes of a Native Son," from *Notes
of a Native Son* by James Baldwin, are reprinted by permission of the
Beacon Press, copyright © 1955, James Baldwin.

"Fifth Avenue Uptown: A Letter from Harlem," copyright © 1960
by James Baldwin. From *Nobody Knows My Name* by James Baldwin.
Reprinted by permission of the publisher, The Dial Press. Originally
appeared in *Esquire.*

"On the Fascination of Style" by F. L. Lucas, reprinted by permission
from *Holiday,* Vol. 27, No. 3 (March, 1960).

Preface

    I PUT off doing a revision of this book for several years after it was first suggested to me because, quite frankly, I liked the book as it was. There were a few essays I might have replaced, but in general I was satisfied. However, it has now been seven years since *Eight Modern Essayists* was first published, and both the world and my own interests have changed. The preface to a textbok is not the place for an autobiography, but I suppose that some of the directions in which my interests have changed can be detected in the several new selections from the writings of E. M. Forster, Virginia Woolf, Edmund Wilson, and James Baldwin, and perhaps especially in the writers I have put in place of Max Beerbohm and James Thurber— namely, D. H. Lawrence and Norman Mailer.

    Revising the standard sort of anthology that contains a lot of different writers is, I'm sure, a great deal of work; but I doubt that it is very emotional work. You can always keep your favorites. However, in this book, where the objective is to represent writers in depth and their number must therefore be severely limited, *all* are favorites; the dropping of even one is accompanied by a sense of regret. Even though I have replaced Beerbohm and Thurber, my regard for them as essayists has not diminished. At the same time, I hope that readers of the second edition will find as exciting as I do the new sections by Lawrence and Mailer. The essays reprinted there represent, I believe, not only something of the range but also the dynamic progressions in the work of two of the most original writers of this century.

    Like its predecessor, this second edition holds to the principle that the best way to learn to write is by studying outstanding writers in depth. One then begins to appreciate that good writing is not a matter of following certain strict rules of composition but in fact is as personal and unique as one's signature. In short, good writing arises out of the serious, patient effort of a writer to discover the best way to say whatever he or she wants to say, and it is interesting primarily

because of the particular mind and temper the individual writer
brings to the topic. I have found that students who come to understand these principles become better writers themselves, for they
become bolder, more personal, and more enthusiastic about the
opportunity writing offers them to have their own say.

W. S.

Contents

EIGHT MODERN ESSAYISTS

E. M. FORSTER

EDWARD MORGAN FORSTER was born in London on January 1, 1879. On his father's side he was descended from an important banking family whose wealth and energies had for several generations been devoted to bringing about social reforms in areas such as relief for the poor and the abolition of slavery. They were, according to Forster, pious, respectable people, hard-working and generous, but for whom "poetry, mystery, passion, ecstasy, music" didn't count. "This indifference to the unseen seems to me the great defect in my great-grandfather's set. . . ." On his mother's side, on the other hand, his forebears were both less successful and more spontaneous: "they were devoid of public spirit, and they were averse to piety and quick to detect the falsity sometimes accompanying it." And it was with them and their wit and improvidence that Forster's sympathies always remained.

Two years after his father died in 1880, he and his mother—who had entered the family as a governess—moved to a house in Hertfordshire, and it was there, in rural England, that the happiest years of Forster's childhood were spent. In the background hovered his great-aunt, Marianne Thornton, the *grande dame* of his father's family, who claimed young Morgan as her favorite upon his father's death, and who now gave him the nickname The Important One. When Marianne Thornton died in 1887, she bequeathed her nephew a legacy of £8000, which Forster later called "the financial salvation of my life. Thanks to it, I was able to go to Cambridge—impossible otherwise, for I failed to win scholarships. After Cambridge I was able to travel for a couple of years, and traveling inclined me to write." Indeed, "she and no one else made my career as a writer possible."

Forster disliked Tonbridge, the public school he attended as a day-boy, but at King's College, Cambridge, which he entered in 1897, he found at last the atmosphere that brought out that combination of qualities he most admired: "Body and spirit, reason and emotion, work and play, architecture and scenery, laughter and seriousness, life and art—these pairs which are elsewhere contrasted were there fused into one. People and books reinforced one another, intelligence joined hands with affection, speculation became a passion, and discussion was made profound by love." In 1900 he took a classical degree, and in 1901 a degree in history.

The decade following Cambridge was the most active and productive of Forster's life. For a year and a half he traveled through Italy and Greece, then settled in London and began contributing to *The Independent Review,* a liberal journal founded by a group at Cambridge that included his friends G. Lowes Dickinson and Nathaniel Wedd. In quick succession he published four novels—*Where Angels Fear to Tread* (1905), *The Longest Journey* (1907), *A Room With a View* (1908), *Howard's End* (1910)—and his first collection of short stories, *The Celestial Omnibus* (1911). Also during this period he became associated with those writers and thinkers who would later be known as the "Bloomsbury group": Virginia and Leonard Woolf, Lytton Strachey, John Maynard Keynes, Roger Fry, and Clive and Vanessa Bell. Together they shared that same fusion of qualities—Life and Art—that had made Forster's years at Cambridge so delightful.

In 1913 he spent three months in India in the Hindu native state of Dewas Senior, "an amazing little state," as he wrote home, "which can have no parallel, except in a Gilbert and Sullivan opera." But more than with its comic-opera aspects, Forster was impressed with the mysteries of India and began a novel that he was unable to complete. During World War I he was in Alexandria for three years as a noncombatant, then came back to London to serve for a short while as literary editor of the *Daily Herald.* Then, in 1921, he went back to Dewas State Senior as Private Secretary to the Maharajah and, when he returned to England at the end of a year, was at last able to finish the book he had started nearly twelve years earlier. *A Passage to India* (1924) is not only Forster's most popular novel, but probably his best.

In 1927 Forster gave the Clark lectures at Trinity College, Cambridge; published under the title *Aspects of the Novel,* they have become a minor classic among books of criticism on the techniques of fiction. In the same year he was elected a Fellow of King's. His collected essays appeared in *Abinger Harvest* (1936) and *Two Cheers for Democracy* (1951), and in 1953 he published *The Hill of Devi*, a record of his visits to Dewas State Senior. In 1956 he published *Marianne Thornton*, a biography of his great-aunt. Forster spent the last twenty-five years of his life in Cambridge in rather scholarly seclusion, and died in 1970 at the age of ninety-one. A year later his long-awaited last novel, *Maurice*, written many years earlier, was finally published.

Two main ideas that one finds throughout Forster's novels and essays are that "poetry, mystery, passion, ecstasy, music" do indeed count, and that personal relationships are a good deal more important than public duty. His heroes are spontaneous, passionate, and occasionally cruel, but never cold or hypocritical. What they come in conflict with are members of the English middle classes who possess just the opposite characteristics. In the end neither side is the victor. But, if in nothing more than their juxtaposition, Forster managed to state his theme, which is: "Only connect the prose and the passion, and both will be exalted, and human love will soon be at its height" (*Howard's End*). For love is everything; nothing in the world is substantial but the relationships between people, ideas, and things: "Only connect . . ."

Like Erasmus and Montaigne, his spiritual ancestors, Forster was a true humanist whose plea was not for Heaven or Utopia, but simply "tolerance, good temper, and sympathy." And the modesty of his hopes for mankind can be detected immediately in the casual, off-hand style of his prose. His "unbuttoned manner," as Lionel Trilling once called it, is serious without being solemn. He believes what he says, but is fearful of the way beliefs solidify; therefore, his manner is slightly comic. If a few readers are put off by the voice, it is not because Forster was too urbane, but just the opposite: so civilized he didn't need to seem sophisticated.

NOTES ON THE ENGLISH CHARACTER

FIRST NOTE. I had better let the cat out of the bag at once
and record my opinion that the character of the English is essentially
middle class. There is a sound historical reason for this, for, since
the end of the eighteenth century, the middle classes have been the
dominant force in our community. They gained wealth by the Industrial Revolution, political power by the Reform Bill of 1832; they
are connected with the rise and organization of the British Empire;
they are responsible for the literature of the nineteenth century.
Solidity, caution, integrity, efficiency. Lack of imagination, hypocrisy. These qualities characterize the middle classes in every country,
but in England they are national characteristics also, because only
in England have the middle classes been in power for one hundred
and fifty years. Napoleon, in his rude way, called us "a nation of
shopkeepers." We prefer to call ourselves "a great commercial
nation"—it sounds more dignified—but the two phrases amount to
the same. Of course there are other classes: there is an aristocracy,
there are the poor. But it is on the middle classes that the eye of
the critic rests—just as it rests on the poor in Russia and on the
aristocracy in Japan. Russia is symbolized by the peasant or by
the factory worker; Japan by the samurai; the national figure
of England is Mr. Bull with his top hat, his comfortable clothes,
his substantial stomach, and his substantial balance at the bank.
Saint George may caper on banners and in the speeches of politicians, but it is John Bull who delivers the goods. And even Saint
George—if Gibbon is correct—wore a top hat once; he was an army
contractor and supplied indifferent bacon. It all amounts to the
same in the end.

Second Note. Just as the heart of England is the middle classes,
so the heart of the middle classes is the public school system. This

extraordinary institution is local. It does not even exist all over the British Isles. It is unknown in Ireland, almost unknown in Scotland (countries excluded from my survey), and though it may inspire other great institutions—Aligarh, for example, and some of the schools in the United States—it remains unique, because it was created by the Anglo-Saxon middle classes, and can flourish only where they flourish. How perfectly it expresses their character—far better, for instance, than does the university, into which social and spiritual complexities have already entered. With its boarding-houses, its compulsory games, its system of prefects and fagging, its insistence on good form and on *esprit de corps*, it produces a type whose weight is out of all proportion to its numbers.

On leaving his school, the boy either sets to work at once—goes into the army or into business, or emigrates—or else proceeds to the university, and after three or four years there enters some other profession—becomes a barrister, doctor, civil servant, schoolmaster, or journalist. (If through some mishap he does not become a manual worker or an artist.) In all these careers his education, or the absence of it, influences him. Its memories influence him also. Many men look back on their school days as the happiest of their lives. They remember with regret that golden time when life, though hard, was not yet complex; when they all worked together and played together and thought together, so far as they thought at all: when they were taught that school is the world in miniature and believed that no one can love his country who does not love his school. And they prolong that time as best they can by joining their Old Boys' society; indeed, some of them remain Old Boys and nothing else for the rest of their lives. They attribute all good to the school. They worship it. They quote the remark that "the battle of Waterloo was won on the playing fields of Eton." It is nothing to them that the remark is inapplicable historically and was never made by the Duke of Wellington, and that the Duke of Wellington was an Irishman. They go on quoting it because it expresses their sentiments; they feel that if the Duke of Wellington didn't make it he ought to have, and if he wasn't an Englishman he ought to have been. And they go forth into a world that is not entirely composed of public-school men or even of Anglo-Saxons, but of men who are as various as the sands of the sea; into a world of whose richness and subtlety they have no conception. They go forth into it with well-developed bodies, fairly developed minds, and undeveloped hearts. And it is this undeveloped heart that is largely responsible for the difficulties of Englishmen abroad. An undeveloped heart—not a cold one. The difference is important, and on it my next note will be based.

For it is not that the Englishman can't feel—it is that he is afraid to feel. He has been taught at his public school that feeling is bad form. He must not express great joy or sorrow, or even open his mouth too wide when he talks—his pipe might fall out if he did. He must bottle up his emotions, or let them out only on a very special occasion.

Once upon a time (this is an anecdote) I went for a week's holiday on the Continent with an Indian friend. We both enjoyed ourselves and were sorry when the week was over, but on parting our behavior was absolutely different. He was plunged in despair. He felt that because the holiday was over all happiness was over until the world ended. He could not express his sorrow too much. But in me the Englishman came out strong. I reflected that we should meet again in a month or two, and could write in the interval if we had anything to say; and under these circumstances I could not see what there was to make a fuss about. It wasn't as if we were parting forever or dying. "Buck up," I said, "do buck up." He refused to buck up, and I left him plunged in gloom.

The conclusion of the anecdote is even more instructive. For when we met the next month our conversation threw a good deal of light on the English character. I began by scolding my friend. I told him that he had been wrong to feel and display so much emotion upon so slight an occasion; that it was inappropriate. The word "inappropriate" roused him to fury. "What?" he cried. "Do you measure out your emotions as if they were potatoes?" I did not like the simile of the potatoes, but after a moment's reflection I said, "Yes, I do; and what's more, I think I ought to. A small occasion demands a little emotion, just as a large occasion demands a great one. I would like my emotions to be appropriate. This may be measuring them like potatoes, but it is better than slopping them about like water from a pail, which is what you did." He did not like the simile of the pail. "If those are your opinions, they part us forever," he cried, and left the room. Returning immediately, he added: "No—but your whole attitude toward emotion is wrong. Emotion has nothing to do with appropriateness. It matters only that it shall be sincere. I happened to feel deeply. I showed it. It doesn't matter whether I ought to have felt deeply or not."

This remark impressed me very much. Yet I could not agree with it, and said that I valued emotion as much as he did, but used it differently; if I poured it out on small occasions I was afraid of having none left for the great ones, and of being bankrupt at the crises of life. Note the word "bankrupt." I spoke as a member of a prudent middle-class nation, always anxious to meet my liabilities. But my friend spoke as an Oriental, and the Oriental has behind him a tradition, not of middle-class prudence, but of kingly munifi-cence and splendor. He feels his resources are endless, just as John Bull feels his are finite. As regards material resources, the Oriental is clearly unwise. Money isn't endless. If we spend or give away all the money we have, we haven't any more, and must take the conse-quences, which are frequently unpleasant. But, as regards the resources of the spirit, he may be right. The emotions may be end-less. The more we express them, the more we may have to express.

> True love in this differs from gold and clay,
> That to divine is not to take away,

says Shelley. Shelley, at all events, believes that the wealth of the spirit is endless; that we may express it copiously, passionately, and always; and that we can never feel sorrow or joy too acutely.

In the above anecdote, I have figured as a typical Englishman. I will now descend from that dizzy and somewhat unfamiliar height, and return to my business of notetaking. A note on the *slowness* of the English character. The Englishman appears to be cold and un-emotional because he is really slow. When an event happens, he may understand it quickly enough with his mind, but he takes quite a while to feel it. Once upon a time a coach, containing some Englishmen and some Frenchmen, was driving over the Alps. The horses ran away, and as they were dashing across a bridge the coach caught on the stonework, tottered, and nearly fell into the ravine below. The Frenchmen were frantic with terror: they screamed and gesticulated and flung themselves about, as Frenchmen would. The Englishmen sat quite calm. An hour later the coach drew up at an inn to change horses, and by that time the situations were exactly reversed. The Frenchmen had forgotten all about the danger, and were chattering gaily; the Englishmen had just begun to feel it, and one had a nervous breakdown and was obliged to go to bed. We have here a clear physical difference between the two races—a difference that goes deep into character. The Frenchmen responded at once; the Englishmen responded in time. They were slow and they were also practical. Their instinct forbade them to throw themselves about in the coach, because it was more likely to tip over if they did. They had this extraordinary appreciation of *fact* that we shall notice again and again. When a disaster comes, the English instinct is to do what can be done first, and to postpone the feeling as long as possible. Hence they are splendid at emergencies. No doubt they are brave—no one will deny that—but bravery is partly an affair of the nerves, and the English nervous system is well equipped for meeting a physical emergency. It acts promptly and feels slowly. Such a combination is fruitful, and anyone who possesses it has gone a long way toward being brave. And when the action is over, then the Englishman can feel.

There is one more consideration—a most important one. If the English nature is cold, how is it that it has produced a great literature and a literature that is particularly great in poetry? Judged by its prose, English literature would not stand in the first rank. It is its poetry that raises it to the level of Greek, Persian, or French. And yet the English are supposed to be so unpoetical. How is this? The nation that produced the Elizabethan drama and the Lake Poets cannot be a cold, unpoetical nation. We can't get fire out of ice. Since literature always rests upon national character, there must be in the English nature hidden springs of fire to produce the fire we see. The warm sympathy, the romance, the imagination, that we look for in Englishmen whom we meet, and too often vainly look for, must exist in the nation as a whole, or we could not have this outburst of national song. An undeveloped heart—not a cold one.

The trouble is that the English nature is not at all easy to understand. It has a great air of simplicity, it advertises itself as simple, but the more we consider it, the greater the problems we shall encounter. People talk of the mysterious East, but the West also is mysterious. It has depths that do not reveal themselves at the first gaze. We know what the sea looks like from a distance: it is of one color, and level, and obviously cannot contain such creatures as fish. But if we look into the sea over the edge of a boat, we see a dozen colors, and depth below depth, and fish swimming in them. That sea is the English character—apparently imperturbable and even. The depths and the colors are the English romanticism and the English sensitiveness—we do not expect to find such things, but they exist. And—to continue my metaphor—the fish are the English emotions, which are always trying to get up to the surface, but don't quite know how. For the most part we see them moving far below, distorted and obscure. Now and then they succeed and we exclaim, "Why, the Englishman has emotions! He actually can feel!" And occasionally we see that beautiful creature the flying fish, which rises out of the water altogether into the air and the sunlight. English literature is a flying fish. It is a sample of the life that goes on day after day beneath the surface; it is a proof that beauty and emotion exist in the salt, inhospitable sea.

And now let's get back to terra firma. The Englishman's attitude toward criticism will give us another starting point. He is not annoyed by criticism. He listens or not as the case may be, smiles and passes on, saying, "Oh, the fellow's jealous;" "Oh, I'm used to Bernard Shaw; monkey tricks don't hurt me." It never occurs to him that the fellow may be accurate as well as jealous, and that he might do well to take the criticism to heart and profit by it. It never strikes him—except as a form of words—that he is capable of improvement; his self-complacency is abysmal. Other nations, both Oriental and European, have an uneasy feeling that they are not quite perfect. In consequence they resent criticism. It hurts them; and their snappy answers often mask a determination to improve themselves. Not so the Englishman. He has no uneasy feeling. Let the critics bark. And the "tolerant humorous attitude" with which he confronts them is not really humorous, because it is bounded by the titter and the guffaw.

Turn over the pages of *Punch*. There is neither wit, laughter, nor satire in our national jester—only the snigger of a suburban householder who can understand nothing that does not resemble himself. Week after week, under Mr. Punch's supervision, a man falls off his horse, or a colonel misses a golfball, or a little girl makes a mistake in her prayers. Week after week ladies show not too much of their legs, foreigners are deprecated, originality condemned. Week after week a bricklayer does not do as much work as he ought and a futurist does more than he need. It is all supposed to be so good-tempered and clean; it is also supposed to be funny. It is actually an outstanding example of our attitude toward criticism: the middle-class Englishman, with a smile on his clean-shaven lips, is engaged in admiring himself and ignoring the rest of mankind. If, in those colorless pages, he came across anything that really was funny—a drawing by Max Beerbohm, for instance—his smile would disappear, and he would say to himself, "The fellow's a bit of a crank," and pass on.

This particular attitude reveals such insensitiveness as to suggest a more serious charge: is the Englishman altogether indifferent to the things of the spirit? Let us glance for a moment at his religion—not, indeed, at his theology, which would not merit inspection, but at the action on his daily life of his belief in the unseen. Here again his attitude is practical. But an innate decency comes out: he is thinking of others rather than of himself. Right conduct is his aim. He asks of his religion that it shall make him a better man in daily life: that he shall be more kind, more just, more merciful, more desirous to fight what is evil and to protect what is good. No one could call this a low conception. It is, as far as it goes, a spiritual one. Yet—and this seems to me typical of the race—it is only half the religious idea. Religion is more than an ethical code

with a divine sanction. It is also a means through which man may
get into direct connection with the divine, and, judging by history,
few Englishmen have succeeded in doing this. We have produced
no series of prophets, as has Judaism or Islam. We have not even
produced a Joan of Arc, or a Savonarola. We have produced few
saints. In Germany the Reformation was due to the passionate
conviction of Luther. In England it was due to a palace intrigue.
We can show a steady level of piety, a fixed determination to live
decently according to our lights—little more.

Well, it is something. It clears us of the charge of being an unspiritual nation. That facile contrast between the spiritual East and
the materialistic West can be pushed too far. The West also is
spiritual. Only it expresses its belief, not in fasting and visions,
not in prophetic rapture, but in the daily round, the common task.
An incomplete expression, if you like. I agree. But the argument
underlying these scattered notes is that the Englishman is an incomplete person. Not a cold or an unspiritual one. But undeveloped,
incomplete.

The attitude of the average orthodox Englishman is often misunderstood. It is thought that he must know that a doctrine—say,
like that of the Trinity—is untrue. Moslems in particular feel that
his faith is a dishonest compromise between polytheism and mono-
theism. The answer to this criticism is that the average orthodox
Englishman is no theologian. He regards the Trinity as a mystery
that it is not his place to solve. "I find difficulties enough in daily
life," he will say. "I concern myself with those. As for the Trinity,
it is a doctrine handed down to me from my fathers, whom I
respect, and I hope to hand it down to my sons, and that they will
respect me. No doubt it is true, or it would not have been handed
down. And no doubt the clergy could explain it to me if I asked
them; but, like myself, they are busy men, and I will not take up
their time."

In such an answer there is confusion of thought, if you like, but
no conscious deceit, which is alien to the English nature. The
Englishman's deceit is generally unconscious.

For I have suggested earlier that the English are sometimes hypocrites, and it is now my duty to develop this rather painful subject. Hypocrisy is the prime charge that is always brought against us. The Germans are called brutal, the Spanish cruel, the Americans superficial, and so on; but we are perfide Albion, the island of hypocrites, the people who have built up an Empire with a Bible in one hand, a pistol in the other, and financial concessions in both pockets. Is the charge true? I think it is; but while making it we must be quite clear as to what we mean by hypocrisy. Do we mean *conscious* deceit? Well, the English are comparatively guiltless of this; they have little of the Renaissance villain about them. Do we mean *unconscious* deceit? Muddle-headedness? Of this I believe them to be guilty. When an Englishman has been led into a course of wrong action, he has nearly always begun by muddling himself. A public-school education does not make for mental clearness, and he possesses to a very high degree the power of confusing his own mind. We have seen this tendency at work in the domain of theology; how does it work in the domain of conduct?

Jane Austen may seem an odd authority to cite, but Jane Austen has, within her limits, a marvelous insight into the English mind. Her range is limited, her characters never attempt any of the more scarlet sins. But she has a merciless eye for questions of conduct, and the classical example of two English people muddling themselves before they embark upon a wrong course of action is to be found in the opening chapters of *Sense and Sensibility*. Old Mr. Dashwood has just died. He has been twice married. By his first marriage he has a son, John; by his second marriage three daughters. The son is well off; the young ladies and their mother—for Mr. Dashwood's second wife survives him—are badly off. He has called his son to his death-bed and has solemnly adjured him to provide for the second family. Much moved, the young man promises, and mentally decides to give each of his sisters a thousand pounds; and then the comedy begins. For he announces his generous intention to his wife, and Mrs. John Dashwood by no means approves of depriving their own little boy of so large a sum. The thousand pounds are accordingly reduced to five hundred. But even this seems rather much. Might not an annuity to the stepmother be less of a wrench? Yes—but though less of a wrench it might be more of a drain, for "she is very stout and healthy, and scarcely forty." An occasional present of fifty pounds will be better, "and will, I think, be amply discharging my promise to my father." Or, better still, an occasional present of fish. And in the end nothing is done, nothing; the four impecunious ladies are not even helped in the moving of their furniture.

Well, are the John Dashwoods hypocrites? It depends upon our definition of hypocrisy. The young man could not see his evil impulses as they gathered force and gained on him. And even his wife, though a worse character, is also self-deceived. She reflects that old Mr. Dashwood may have been out of his mind at his death. She thinks of her own little boy—and surely a mother ought to think of her own child. She has muddled herself so completely that in one sentence she can refuse the ladies the income that would enable them to keep a carriage and in the next can say that they will not be keeping a carriage and so will have no expenses. No doubt men and women in other lands can muddle themselves, too, yet the state of mind of Mr. and Mrs. John Dashwood seems to me typical of England. They are slow—they take time even to do wrong; whereas people in other lands do wrong quickly.

There are national faults as there are national diseases, and perhaps one can draw a parallel between them. It has always impressed me that the national diseases of England should be cancer and consumption—slow, insidious, pretending to be something else; while the diseases proper to the South should be cholera and plague, which strike at a man when he is perfectly well and may leave him a corpse by evening. Mr. and Mrs. John Dashwood are moral consumptives. They collapse gradually without realizing what the disease is. There is nothing dramatic or violent about their sin. You cannot call them villains.

Here is the place to glance at some of the other charges that have been brought against the English as a nation. They have, for instance, been accused of treachery, cruelty, and fanaticism. In these charges I have never been able to see the least point, because treachery and cruelty are conscious sins. The man knows he is doing wrong, and does it deliberately, like Tartuffe or Iago. He betrays his friend because he wishes to. He tortures his prisoners because he enjoys seeing the blood flow. He worships the Devil because he prefers evil to good. From villainies such as these the average Englishman is free. His character, which prevents his rising to certain heights, also prevents him from sinking to these depths. Because he doesn't produce mystics he doesn't produce villains either; he gives the world no prophets, but no anarchists, no fanatics —religious or political.

Of course there are cruel and treacherous people in England— one has only to look at the police courts—and examples of public infamy can be found, such as the Amritsar massacre. But one does not look at the police courts or the military mind to find the soul of any nation; and the more English people one meets the more convinced one becomes that the charges as a whole are untrue. Yet foreign critics often make them. Why? Partly because they are annoyed with certain genuine defects in the English character, and in their irritation throw in cruelty in order to make the problem simpler. Moral indignation is always agreeable, but nearly always misplaced. It is indulged in both by the English and by the critics of the English. They all find it great fun. The drawback is that while they are amusing themselves the world becomes neither wiser nor better.

The main point of these notes is that the English character is incomplete. No national character is complete. We have to look for some qualities in one part of the world and others in another. But the English character is incomplete in a way that is particularly annoying to the foreign observer. It has a bad surface—self-complacent, unsympathetic, and reserved. There is plenty of emotion further down, but it never gets used. There is plenty of brain power, but it is more often used to confirm prejudices than to dispel them. With such an equipment the Englishman cannot be popular. Only I would repeat: there is little vice in him and no real coldness. It is the machinery that is wrong.

I hope and believe myself that in the next twenty years we shall see a great change, and that the national character will alter into

something that is less unique but more lovable. The supremacy of
the middle classes is probably ending. What new element the working classes will introduce one cannot say, but at all events they will
not have been educated at public schools. And whether these notes
praise or blame the English character—that is only incidental. They
are the notes of a student who is trying to get at the truth and
would value the assistance of others. I believe myself that the truth
is great and that it shall prevail. I have no faith in official caution
and reticence. The cats are all out of their bags, and diplomacy
cannot recall them. The nations *must* understand one another, and
quickly; and without the interposition of their governments, for the
shrinkage of the globe is throwing them into one another's arms.
To that understanding these notes are a feeble contribution—notes
on the English character as it has struck a novelist.

[1926]

MY WOOD

A FEW YEARS ago I wrote a book which dealt in part with
the difficulties of the English in India. Feeling that they would
have had no difficulties in India themselves, the Americans read
the book freely. The more they read it the better it made them
feel, and a check to the author was the result. I bought a wood
with the check. It is not a large wood—it contains scarcely any
trees, and it is intersected, blast it, by a public footpath. Still, it is
the first property that I have owned, so it is right that other people
should participate in my shame, and should ask themselves, in
accents that will vary in horror, this very important question: What
is the effect of property upon the character? Don't let's touch
economics; the effect of private ownership upon the community as a
whole is another question—a more important question, perhaps, but

another one. Let's keep to psychology. If you own things, what's their effect on you? What's the effect on me of my wood?

In the first place, it makes me feel heavy. Property does have this effect. Property produces men of weight, and it was a man of weight who failed to get into the Kingdom of Heaven. He was not wicked, that unfortunate millionaire in the parable, he was only stout; he stuck out in front, not to mention behind, and as he wedged himself this way and that in the crystalline entrance and bruised his well-fed flanks, he saw beneath him a comparatively slim camel passing through the eye of a needle and being woven into the robe of God. The Gospels all through couple stoutness and slowness. They point out what is perfectly obvious, yet seldom realized: that if you have a lot of things you cannot move about a lot, that furniture requires dusting, dusters require servants, servants require insurance stamps, and the whole tangle of them makes you think twice before you accept an invitation to dinner or go for a bathe in the Jordan. Sometimes the Gospels proceed further and say with Tolstoy that property is sinful; they approach the difficult ground of asceticism here, where I cannot follow them. But as to the immediate effects of property on people, they just show straightforward logic. It produces men of weight. Men of weight cannot, by definition, move like the lightning from the East unto the West, and the ascent of a fourteen-stone bishop into a pulpit is thus the exact antithesis of the coming of the Son of Man. My wood makes me feel heavy.

In the second place, it makes me feel it ought to be larger.

The other day I heard a twig snap in it. I was annoyed at first, for I thought that someone was blackberrying, and depreciating the value of the undergrowth. On coming nearer, I saw it was not a man who had trodden on the twig and snapped it, but a bird, and I felt pleased. My bird. The bird was not equally pleased. Ignoring the relation between us, it took fright as soon as it saw the shape of my face, and flew straight over the boundary hedge into a field, the property of Mrs. Henessy, where it sat down with a loud squawk. It had become Mrs. Henessy's bird. Something seemed grossly amiss here, something that would not have occurred had the wood

been larger. I could not afford to buy Mrs. Henessy out, I dared
not murder her, and limitations of this sort beset me on every side.
Ahab did not want that vineyard—he only needed it to round off
his property, preparatory to plotting a new curve—and all the land
around my wood has become necessary to me in order to round off
the wood. A boundary protects. But—poor little thing—the boundary
ought in its turn to be protected. Noises on the edge of it. Children
throw stones. A little more, and then a little more, until we reach
the sea. Happy Canute! Happier Alexander! And after all, why
should even the world be the limit of possession? A rocket containing a Union Jack, will, it is hoped, be shortly fired at the moon.
Mars. Sirius. Beyond which . . . But these immensities ended by
saddening me. I could not suppose that my wood was the destined
nucleus of universal dominion—it is so small and contains no
mineral wealth beyond the blackberries. Nor was I comforted when
Mrs. Henessy's bird took alarm for the second time and flew clean
away from us all, under the belief that it belonged to itself.

In the third place, property makes its owner feel that he ought
to do something to it. Yet he isn't sure what. A restlessness comes
over him, a vague sense that he has a personality to express—the
same sense which, without any vagueness, leads the artist to an act
of creation. Sometimes I think I will cut down such trees as remain
in the wood, at other times I want to fill up the gaps between them
with new trees. Both impulses are pretentious and empty. They are
not honest movements towards moneymaking or beauty. They
spring from a foolish desire to express myself and from an inability
to enjoy what I have got. Creation, property, enjoyment form a
sinister trinity in the human mind. Creation and enjoyment are
both very very good, yet they are often unattainable without a
material basis, and at such moments property pushes itself in as a
substitute, saying, "Accept me instead—I'm good enough for all
three." It is not enough. It is, as Shakespeare said of lust, "The
expense of spirit in a waste of shame": it is "Before, a joy pro-
posed; behind, a dream." Yet we don't know how to shun it. It is
forced on us by our economic system as the alternative to starvation.
It is also forced on us by an internal defect in the soul, by the

feeling that in property may lie the germs of self-development and of exquisite or heroic deeds. Our life on earth is, and ought to be, material and carnal. But we have not yet learned to manage our materialism and carnality properly; they are still entangled with the desire for ownership, where (in the words of Dante) "Possession is one with loss."

And this brings us to our fourth and final point: the blackberries.

Blackberries are not plentiful in this meagre grove, but they are easily seen from the public footpath which traverses it, and all too easily gathered. Foxgloves, too—people will pull up the foxgloves, and ladies of an educational tendency even grub for toadstools to show them on the Monday in class. Other ladies, less educated, roll down the bracken in the arms of their gentlemen friends. There is paper, there are tins. Pray, does my wood belong to me or doesn't it? And, if it does, should I not own it best by allowing no one else to walk there? There is a wood near Lyme Regis, also cursed by a public footpath, where the owner has not hesitated on this point. He has built high stone walls each side of the path, and has spanned it by bridges, so that the public circulate like termites while he gorges on the blackberries unseen. He really does own his wood, this able chap. Dives in Hell did pretty well, but the gulf dividing him from Lazarus could be traversed by vision, and nothing traverses it here. And perhaps I shall come to this in time. I shall wall in and fence out until I really taste the sweets of property. Enormously stout, endlessly avaricious, pseudo-creative, intensely selfish, I shall weave upon my forehead the quadruple crown of possession until those nasty Bolshies come and take it off again and thrust me aside into the outer darkness.

VOLTAIRE'S LABORATORY

1. How They Weighed Fire

DURING THE spring of 1737 the iron foundries in a remote district of Lorraine were often visited by a thin middle-aged man with a notebook. He would weigh out two pounds of iron, have them heated till they were red-hot, and then weigh them again. He repeated the experiment, increasing the amount until he had weighed up to a thousand pounds. Three cauldrons were next prepared under his directions, they were placed on scales, so that their weight could be estimated, and then molten metal was poured into them from the furnace, a hundred pounds into the first cauldron, thirty-five pounds into the second, twenty-five into the third, and when the cauldrons were cold the mass was weighed again. As the title of this article suggests, the thin, middle-aged man is Voltaire, but what on earth is he doing in an iron foundry? Wait a minute. Here comes a still more remarkable figure.

The newcomer is a lady of about thirty, with a long thin face, a commanding nose, and greenish eyes. Her appearance is masculine but not mannish; in spite of her earnest mien she is gay and charming, she dresses well, and is very kindhearted. It will be easy to make fun of her. For she, too, holds a notebook in her hand, in which she enters the weights of the hot and cold iron. She is quite as keen as Voltaire, and even more serious. She has taken up science, not because it is fashionable and brings her into contact with celebrities, but because she hopes to discover the nature of the universe. Facts, facts! A theory may come later—if there is one. She gives up acting, dancing, games, in order to do experiments. Voltaire calls her "divine Emilie." She is his mistress, Madame du Châtelet, and she owns Cirey, the great house where he is stopping.

On returning to Cirey, the investigators separate, and Voltaire goes to his own suite, which contains half a dozen ground-floor rooms, beautifully furnished; passing through a tiny antechamber, and a bedroom of crimson velvet, he comes to the long gallery, and sits down there. The long gallery is lacquered in yellow, with panels of Indian paper; it is ornamented with statues, one of which, a statue of Love, conceals the stove; there are cupboards full of books and scientific instruments; there are windows opening into the garden or on to the chapel—so that without disturbing himself too much he can hear Mass. At the end is a camera obscura and another room, not yet in order. Voltaire drinks a cup of coffee. Establishing himself at a superb writing-desk, he takes up his pen in despair. For he is going in for a prize competition on the subject of the Nature and Propagation of Fire, and he has been unable to find out whether fire weighs anything. Since fire is an element, one expects it to weigh something, yet the hot iron at the foundry was only occasionally heavier than the cold: sometimes it was the same weight and sometimes actually lighter. Nor is this all: other problems connected with fire are equally obscure. If he shuts up burning coals in a metal box, sometimes they continue to burn, at other times they go out. If he prepares sections of little trees and places them on a red-hot surface, the time in which they are reduced to ashes varies considerably, although they are exactly the same thickness and size, and even come from the same plantation. "I then repeated this experiment with vegetables"; but the vegetables burned unevenly too. An experiment with objects painted different colours had been more satisfactory: black objects got hot quicker than green ones, yellow than white; but even here there were exceptions, and all he can do is to add to the Laws of Fire a supplementary law to the effect that they do not always work.

"My dear Abbé, we are surrounded by uncertainties," he writes to his agent in Paris. "To discover the least scrap of truth entails endless labour," and he implores the Abbé to inquire of people who are likely to know whether fire really does weigh anything; also whether a burning glass has a normal effect on objects in a vacuum; also, is it true that Persian naphtha of the best quality flames under water;

also he wants writing-paper of various sizes, sealing-wax, an astrolabe, two globes on stands, thermometers, barometers, earthenware pans, retorts, crucibles; also a complete sportsman's outfit—gun, costume; also face-powder, hair-powder, scent, nail-scissors, sponges, two very large pots of orange-flower pomatum; also a young priest who will officiate in the chapel, and knows a little chemistry besides; and a young mathematician who knows astronomy; also he does *not* want the publications of the French Academy, but the publications of the Academy of Sciences: the good Abbé has confused the two institutions, and sent the wrong volumes, so that Voltaire feels like the man who ordered eighteen swans for his ornamental water, and received eighteen monkeys by mistake; also—also—the list of wants rolls on; what, meantime, is Madame du Châtelet doing at her end of the house?

She, too, is entering for the prize competition on the Nature and Propagation of Fire, but she has not told her lover this. It is to be a surprise. An indefatigable inquirer, she has visited foundries and scorched vegetables until she is left with very little time for the actual writing, and has to dip her hand constantly in cold water, it aches so. Her suite is even more gorgeous than his: everything matches in blue and yellow, down to the little dog's basket, the bed is covered with blue satin, Veroneses and Watteaus adorn the walls, her writing table, inlaid with amber, was the gift of Prince Frederick of Prussia, her bathroom is tiled, and paved with marble, the chandeliers are exquisite, a looking-glass door leads from the bedroom into the library. Far into the night she writes; so does Voltaire; and between them slumbers the dilapidated central portion of the house, possibly occupied by her husband.

Life at Cirey was certainly comic, but before we have our good laugh at it we had better remind ourselves that Voltaire and Madame du Châtelet were abreast of their age, and their science relatively no more absurd than our own—indeed, it may well prove to be less absurd, for they were highly intelligent. We find them funny because we know more, but if we patronize them for not knowing more it is we who become funny. For example, their difficulties over fire were shared by all their contemporaries. Chemistry now informs us that fire is not an element, but a state through which bodies are passing, and which is likely to be accompanied by certain reactions: under some conditions, when they are heated, they give out gas, and so get lighter; under other conditons they generate solid oxide, and so get heavier. In a hundred years' time chemistry will inform us of something else. The eighteenth century had not discovered even what we know, so the experiments at the foundry seemed to give contradictory results. Moreover, the apparatus was hopelessly inaccurate; however good a pendulum clock the Abbé sent from Paris, and however carefully he packed it, it still could not record the exact times two cauliflowers took to burn. "My dear Abbé, we are surrounded by uncertainties." The uncertainties thrilled him, he dashed hither and thither to put them right and took genuine pleasure in the complexity of the universe.

It has been well said that Voltaire is not a journalist but a newspaper. Every sort of activity gets mentioned in his columns. The literary side is strongest, but science jottings constantly appear, and first become prominent during his exile in England. He picked up in England many scraps that moved his respect or mirth: inoculation; a woman who bore rabbits; an Irishman who saw worms through a microscope in mutton broth. But it was not until he returned to France and fell under Madame du Châtelet's influence that his interests concentrated. She inclined him to the subjects she herself had studied—that is to say to physics and to astronomy—and his chief scientific work, an exposition of Newton's theory, was composed under her protection. He presented the theory accurately, criticized it intelligently, and has the undivided credit of introducing Newton to the French public. Orthodoxy was alarmed; it had invested in the whirlwinds of Descartes as a suitable basis for the physical universe, and resented the possibility of gravitation. On account of gravitation, and on account of other laxities, which included an improper poem on Joan of Arc, Voltaire kept away from Paris. He was not yet the very great Voltaire who quarrelled with Frederick the Great and avenged Calas. But he was a considerable figure, tragedian, poet, wit, philosopher, and now science was to place her metallic wreath a little crookedly upon his brows.

He and his hostess had arrived at Cirey earlier in that same year, 1737. They had driven by night and through the snow, and the wheel had come off the carriage on Voltaire's side, so that Madame du Châtelet, her maid, and a quantity of luggage fell on him. At the same moment, all the menservants fell off the box. It was long before the luggage, the maid, the mistress, and the great man could be progressively extracted, and he uttered a series of short, sharp shrieks. As so often happened, he was enjoying himself. Cushions were spread in the frozen road, and he and Madame du Châtelet sat on them and pointed out to one another the glories of the night sky. "The stars shone brilliantly," one of their servants writes. "Not a tree, not a house disturbed the expanse of the horizon. M. de Voltaire and Madame du Châtelet were in ecstasies: wrapped in furs, they discussed the nature and the orbits of the stars and their destination in space while their teeth chattered. If only they had had a telescope, their joy would have been complete." There they sat, half laughing and wholly serious, until the carriage could be repaired and take them on to their home.

When they got there, they evolved a routine which both impressed and annoyed their visitors. They took themselves seriously, in which they were fully justified, and they were obliged to organize their work, or it would not have got done. Eleven in the morning and nine at night were the only hours in the twenty-four when they were certain to be visible. At eleven there was coffee in Voltaire's gallery; in the evening came the great event—supper—occasionally marred by a quarrel. After supper, if all had gone well, Voltaire showed the magic lantern, or directed a telescope at the moon, or played tricks with prisms, being screamingly funny all the time, or read Joan of Arc aloud in the marble bathroom, or had plays performed in a barn. Science was much discussed, also religion; at no time of his life was he either an atheist or an agnostic, he believed firmly in God, provided God is given nothing to do, and he always insisted that physics must rest upon metaphysics, and that metaphysics are divine. When the party broke up, they retired to their work, and somewhere or other in the house, well looked after but seldom seen, slept her little boy. The variety, the vigour of Cirey is most impressive; the imagination flits from room to room until it wearies, and fails even to reach the huge woods which shut in the domain, and the peasants whose labour supported it. What stands out in the end is the laboratory work. That the experiments were primitive, ill-directed, and unsuccessful did not trouble the investigators, and need not trouble us if we understand what they felt: they saw a new world opening in every direction and asking to be interpreted.

Madame du Châtelet was certainly a most remarkable creature—tiresome, but not too tiresome, and therefore an ideal mate for a very tiresome man. "Venus-Newton," Frederick of Prussia calls her, while Madame du Deffand insinuates that she was only Newton because she could not be Venus, and also accuses her of spending more on her dresses than on her underthings—gravest of charges that one woman of quality can bring against another. Voltaire adored her. She irritated him, but he also irritated her, which he enjoyed doing, and they were too affectionate and gay to subside into sourness. The relationship between them is very odd: it included emotion, and lasted twelve years, yet it cannot be classed among famous love-affairs. He was not a lover—he had all the ingredients that make up love, such as tenderness, pity, lust, selfishness, unselfishness, but they never combined: he was a chemical experiment, which, if love be the desired result, may be said to have failed. Madame du Châtelet was more normal, and it was she in the end who tired of the liaison, or rather tried for an additional one which ended in a ghastly catastrophe. With their tragedy I am not concerned here: at the moment I visualize them they were wholly in accord, and in accord with her husband, and now that the eighteenth century is no longer here to sneer or the nineteenth century to lecture, they are perhaps coming into their own. What kept them together was their interest in outside things—science, the drama, philosophy, art. They can never have said—at least I cannot imagine them ever saying—"What is this? What has brought us so close? We had better not inquire, lest it vanish away." They were held by their common interests, and so the nerve-storms that occasionally swept over them left no wreckage behind.

Neither he nor she obtained the prize for the Nature and Propagation of Fire. The judges complimented him on being a poet and her on being a lady, but appear to have been slightly shocked

by the number of facts they mentioned, and divided the prize
between three other competitors, who confined themselves to theory.
In the opinion of modern authorities, the award ought to have been
made to Madame du Châtelet: her essay is much the best.

2. Troublesome Molluscs

THIRTY YEARS have passed, and Voltaire, now at the height
of his fame, holds a pair of scissors in one hand and a slug in the
other. Let me repeat: in the one hand he holds a large brown slug,
and in the other a pair of scissors. The slug is of Swiss extraction,
and comes off one of his estates, where it has been eating the
lettuces. *Ecrasez l'infame?* But no: he reserves it for another purpose. Looking into its face, he surveys the gloomy unresponsive
snout which is all a slug offers, he compares it with the face of a
snail, so much more piquant, and both with the face of a man. All
three are different, but all are faces, and he does not know whether
he trembles at the edge of a great discovery or of a joke. Beneath
him are the blue waters of the Lake Leman, beyond them the walls
of Mont Blanc, he stands with one foot in Genevan territory to
escape the French, and the other in France, to be safe from the
Swiss. He stands triumphant, all his possessions are around him,
thousands of his trees grow, his contented peasantry work, his invalid cousin dozes, the bells of the church he built chime—and he
cuts off the slug's head.

His niece, Madame Denis, keeps house for him now—or rather
houses, for he possesses three. Awkward and torpid, Madame Denis
holds at bay the ambassadors, savants, mountebanks, princesses, who
have come from all over Europe to see her uncle. He is researching,
he must not be disturbed. The scissors approach again, and a second
slug is decapitated, and a third, until there are twelve. Nor does this
conclude the gruesome tale: in a box hard by seethes a clot of head-
less snails. Voltaire surveys his victims with affability. He does not
like the slugs much, but has great sympathy with the snails, he finds

their courtships gallant if curious, their contours intelligent, and their taste delightful. Nevertheless, he continues to snip off their heads. It is Science. He is trying to find out whether heads grow again.

Once more, the results are conflicting. As in the case of fire, it is as if all nature combines to conceal the truth. Slugs behave differently to snails, which might be expected, but they also behave differently among themselves. All molluscs lack earnestness of purpose, so to speak—sometimes they die when their heads are removed, sometimes they grow fresh heads and live, sometimes they live without heads. Voltaire is delighted, but puzzled. On the whole, slugs grow new heads, snails don't; though snails when mutilated merely between the horns repair the damage more frequently than do slugs whose heads have been removed entirely. What may we deduce from this? Well—not much, and at the end of one of his solemn works (his *Questions on the Encyclopaedia*) he suddenly exclaims, "Retraction! I retract the scissors with which I cut off the snails' heads." For they had grown in 1772 but not in 1773, and what can one build on such creatures? He can only say that Nature is always admirable, and that what we call "Nature" is really an art that we have not yet understood. "All is art, from the Zodiac down to my snails."

To retract and to relinquish are, however, different things, and Voltaire had the happy idea of turning his failures into a joke, and fathering them on the unfortunate clergy. He invents a charming monk, Père l'Escarbotier, who is also a cook, and causes him to pour out his difficulties to Père Elie, who is a Doctor in Theology in another convent. The correspondence between the two is superb. "People used only to talk about Jesuits, but now they are completely occupied with snails," begins Père l'Escarbotier with modest pride, and he goes on to describe his own inconclusive experiments in the kitchen; he has often mentioned them in his sermons: "I could compare certain of my snails only to Saint Denis, who, after his head had been cut off, carried it tenderly for six miles in his arms." Père Elie receives this miracle in silence. In a second letter the reverend cook asks what, when the heads are cut off, happens to the souls. He replies to this readily enough: the question is simple, though it requires a different answer in the case of snails and of slugs, for the souls of snails are in their heads, but slugs have their souls anywhere. But a third letter, raising the question of a "vital germ," from which all species have developed, elicits a sharp rebuke; Père Elie reminds Père l'Escarbotier that "corruption is the mother of all things" and warns him against heretical speculations which lead to no good. "Adieu!" he concludes, on a kinder note. "May the snails who are set beneath you and the insects who accompany you ever bless your reverence." And there is a further conclusion as from the pen of Voltaire himself: "We must marvel and be silent." Gaily and charmingly he has turned his foolish scientific experiments into a humorous pamphlet: he has begun as a goose and ended as a mockingbird.

Since Madame du Châtelet's death he had taken science less seriously. He had never married, and his niece urged him towards the drama, if anywhere, for she enjoyed acting. Now and then the old ardour would break out: he would wonder whether Hannibal had really dissolved the Alps with hot vinegar, as the historian Livy reports, so he heated some vinegar and poured it on a piece of Mont Blanc. As soon as Mont Blanc adequately cracked, his mind was at rest, and he went on to other matters. The fact is that his seriousness was taking another direction: all his wit and wisdom were being marshalled for his struggle against the Church. He believed in God, he even built a church: but he loathed the Church, and the depth of his hatred appears in the extraordinary difficulties into which he got over sea-shells.

Sea-shells do not, to the outsider, seem more troublesome than other molluscs, but Voltaire regarded them from a very special point of view: they were traitors, who attempted to demonstrate the truth of revealed religion instead of advancing the cause of Liberty, as natural objects should. Had they remained in the sea, all would have been well, but straying from their proper element they appeared in large heaps in the middle of Touraine and elsewhere, or in fossil forms, or on the tops of mountains. Why, you may ask, did this disconcert Voltaire? Why, because it suggested that they had

been left when the waters of the Flood subsided, so that Genesis
was true. He could not allow this, and he set out with his usual
energy and ingenuity to put shells in their places. He had not been
trained by the Jesuits for nothing, and the arguments he brought
forward are rather too conclusive to be convincing.

In the first place, he argued that the shells in question are not from
the sea at all, but are either the shells of fresh-water oysters or the
property of his old friends the snails. "In a rainy year, there are
more snails in a space of thirty miles than there are men in the whole
earth," and this being so, the deposits in Touraine and elsewhere
can be easily accounted for. Then he argues that the shells were
engendered spontaneously in the earth, "and grew just as stones do."
A correspondent of his, a gentleman who had property near Chinon,
had actually watched empty shells growing; twice in eighty years a
heavy crop had been produced, they were microscopic at first, and
gradually swelled and stuck against one another until they formed
a soft stone, suitable for building; there were five or six species of
these empty shells, and since the tenants and neighbours of the
gentleman had seen them too, doubt was impossible. Indeed, we
can all of us watch the process for ourselves, for the reason that the
so-called Ammonite fossils vary in size: the curves of their spirals
must obviously increase the longer they lie in the earth. And, finally,
let us grant, for the sake of argument, that all the above arguments
are false, and that the shells which have given such support to
superstition really did originate in the sea. No matter—all is not lost:
they can still be accounted for in three ways. Firstly, since so many
of them are cockles, they may have dropped from the hats of
Palmers who were going to the shrine of St. James at Compostella
in the Middle Ages. Secondly, since so many are edible, they may
be the debris of picnic parties. And thirdly, since so many of them
are different, they may have come from the collections of dead conch-
ologists. To this last argument—which leaves us almost more
breathless than its companions—Voltaire returns more than once.
He was vexed by the bones of a reindeer and of a hippopotamus
which were found near Etampes. "Are we to conclude from this," he
asks, "that the Nile and Lapland once shared the Orleans-Paris

road?" Surely, it is simpler to suppose that the bones once adorned the cabinet of a connoisseur!

His anxiety over shells led him even further than we should expect. He feared that if once a flood was admitted Noah's ark would come sailing in, and consequently had to ridicule all theories of the universe that emphasized water. There was the fish Oannes, who came out of the Euphrates to preach to the Babylonians. There was Thales, who thought that the stars lived on mist. There was Buffon, who ascribes mountains to the action of waves. There was Maillet, who deduced from a heap of shells at Cairo that Egypt had once been under the sea and the Egyptians fish. Voltaire mocks them all indiscriminately. "In spite of the present passion for genealogies, there are not many people who would claim descent from a turbot or a cod." Then the coral insects strike his eye, and seeing that they may give trouble he makes short work of their claims. They must not be allowed to build coral reefs, or the land will appear once to have been under the sea. "Certainly, one does find little insects in coral, but where does one not find little insects? Old walls are full of them, but no one supposes that they build the old walls. So is old cheese—but no one argues that the cheese has been made by the mites." One way and another, the sea is prevented from encroaching on human destiny; not even in the name of science may it cover the earth, lest when the waters decrease Mount Ararat should appear and our race again enter into bondage. Voltaire's attitude here is, in a cruder form, the attitude of certain unorthodox people today, who are disquieted by the work of Eddington and Jeans, because of the support for Christianity that may be extracted from it. He hated religion, having witnessed the misery it caused, and he was not detached enough to admit that because a thing is baneful it is not necessarily untrue. Indeed, he was not detached at all, and if we think he was we misread both him and his age; he loved freedom, not truth, so that when the coral insects appeared to be helping the Jesuits he used casuistry to discredit them. Never, never, if he could help it, should Noah's ark sail over the world again. And if he had lived today, and been told that in the opinion of many biologists all life, including human life, had a marine or intertidal origin, he would once more bring up his armoury and produce arguments which, alas! we should no longer find devastating. For Voltaire, today, would seem a much smaller figure than he was in the eighteenth century; we should admire his personality, fear his tongue, and adore his short stories, but dismiss his "serious" utterances as journalism.

Probably he could have been an eminent scientist if he liked—he was intelligent enough for anything, and while he was under Madame du Châtelet's influence he showed powers of application: his treatise on Newton proves this. But after her death he became desultory and a tease; his mistrust of theories led him to the theory that other people's conclusions must be wrong. He was hampered by his need of fun; both scientists and their pursuits can be irresistibly amusing, and Voltaire was not the man to check his own mirth. He came, he saw, he laughed, and the slugs and snails that might have led a serious anatomist towards the discovery of the pharyngeal ring, suggested instead a correspondence between two comic monks.

Nevertheless, he did science one good turn: he impressed the general public with her importance. This is all that a literary man can do for science, and perhaps only a literary man can do it. The expert scientist is too conscious of the difficulties of his subject; he knows that he can only communicate his discoveries to us by simplifying and therefore falsifying them, and that even when he can state a fact correctly we receive it incorrectly, because we cannot relate it to the thousands of other facts relevant. The literary man has no such misgivings. His imagination is touched by the infinite variety of the natural world; he reads books about it, skipping the statistics, he forgets most of what he does read, and perhaps he performs a few experiments in order to grasp the meaning of research. Then, in the course of his other activities, he writes about science, with a spurious lucidity that makes the expert smile. Spurious, but stimulating; the public does realize, from the remarks of such men as Lucretius, Voltaire, Charles Kingsley, Samuel Butler, Mr. Aldous Huxley, Mr. Gerald Heard, that something is happening. It does get a misty idea of the expanding empire of mankind.

"Certainly, one must admit that Nature is varied," said the traveller.

"Yes, Nature is like a bed of flowers, where—"

"Oh, never mind the bed of flowers!"

"She is," the secretary continued, "like an assemblage of blondes and of brunettes, whose tresses—"

"Oh, bother the blondes and brunettes!"

"Well, she is like a picture gallery, where the features—"

"No, no; Nature is like Nature; why introduce similes?"

"To amuse you!" the secretary replied.

"I don't want to be amused," said the traveller; "I want to learn!"

In this passage—it comes from his charming fantasy *Micromegas*—Voltaire neatly contrasts the literary man and the scientist. The literary man loves images, and as soon as he has found a vivid one, his interest in the truth it is supposed to illustrate is apt to cease. But the scientist knows that Nature is Nature. Voltaire himself was literary, yet he had enough sense of science to perceive his own limitations, and though he amuses us and is amused by hot iron and slugs, he has realized—perhaps through Madame du Châtelet—that the universe has not been created for our stylistic exercises. For what, then, has it been created? He cannot say; *"cultiver son jardin"* is a reaction, not a reply. But he could ask the question, he could cause others to ask it, and if "popular interest in science" has any importance (for my own part, I think it has immense importance), he must be honoured as an early popularizer.

NOT LISTENING TO MUSIC

LISTENING TO MUSIC is such a muddle that one scarcely knows how to start describing it. The first point to get clear in my own case is that during the greater part of every performance I do not attend. The nice sounds make me think of something else. I wool-gather most of the time, and am surprised that others don't. Professional critics can listen to a piece as consistently and as steadily as if they were reading a chapter in a novel. This seems to me an amazing feat, and probably they only achieve it through intellectual training; that is to say, they find in the music the equivalent of a plot; they are following the ground bass or expecting the theme to re-enter in the dominant, and so on, and this keeps them on the rails. But I fly off every minute: after a bar or two I think how musical I am, or of something smart I might have said in conversation; or I wonder what the composer—dead a couple of centuries—can be feeling as the flames on the altar still flicker up; or how soon an H.E. bomb would extinguish them. Not to mention more obvious distractions: the tilt of the soprano's chin or chins; the antics of the conductor, that impassioned beetle, especially when it is night time and he waves his shards; the affectation of the pianist when he takes a top note with difficulty, as if he too were a soprano; the backs of the chairs; the bumps on the ceiling; the extreme physical ugliness of the audience. A classical audience is surely the plainest collection of people anywhere assembled for any common purpose; contributing my quota, I have the right to point this out. Compare us with a gang of navvies or with an office staff, and you will be appalled. This, too, distracts me.

What do I hear during the intervals when I do attend? Two sorts of music. They melt into each other all the time, and are not easy to christen, but I will call one of them "music that reminds me of something," and the other "music itself." I used to be very fond of music that reminded me of something, and especially fond of Wagner. With Wagner I always knew where I was; he never let the fancy roam; he ordained that one phrase should recall the ring, another the sword, another the blameless fool and so on; he was as precise in his indications as an oriental dancer. Since he is a great poet, that did not matter, but I accepted his leitmotiv system much too reverently and forced it on to other composers whom it did not suit, such as Beethoven and Franck. I thought that music must be the better for having a meaning. I think so still, but am less clear as to what "a meaning" is. In those days it was either a non-musical object, such as a sword or a blameless fool, or a non-musical emotion, such as fear, lust, or resignation. When music reminded me of something which was not music, I supposed it was getting me somewhere. "How like Monet!" I thought when listening to Debussy, and "How like Debussy!" when looking at Monet. I translated sounds into colors, saw the piccolo as apple-green, and the trumpets as scarlet. The arts were to be enriched by taking in one another's washing.

I still listen to some music this way. For instance, the slow start of Beethoven's Seventh Symphony invokes a gray-green tapestry of hunting scenes, and the slow movement of his Fourth Piano Concerto (the dialogue between piano and orchestra) reminds me of the dialogue between Orpheus and the Furies in Gluck. The climax of the first movement of the Appassionata (the "più allegro") seems to me sexual, although I can detect no sex in the Kreutzer, nor have I come across anyone who could, except Tolstoy. That disappointing work, Brahms' Violin Concerto, promises me clear skies at the opening, and only when the violin has squealed up in the air for page after page is the promise falsified. Wolf's "Ganymed" does give me sky—stratosphere beyond stratosphere. In these cases and in many others music reminds me of something non-musical, and I fancy that to do so is part of its job. Only a purist would condemn all visual parallels, all emotional labelings, all programs.

Yet there is a danger. Music that reminds does open the door to that imp of the concert hall, inattention. To think of a gray-green tapestry is not very different from thinking of the backs of the chairs. We gather a superior wool from it, still we do wool-gather, and the sounds slip by blurred. The sounds! It is for them that we come, and the closer we can get up against them the better. So I do prefer "music itself" and listen to it and for it as far as possible. In this connection, I will try to analyze a mishap that has recently overtaken the Coriolanus Overture. I used to listen to the Coriolanus for "itself," conscious when it passed of something important and agitating, but not defining further. Now I learn that Wagner, endorsed by Sir Donald Tovey, has provided it with a Program: the opening bars indicate the hero's decision to destroy the Volscii, then a sweet tune for female influence, then the dotted-quaver-restlessness of indecision. This seems indisputable, and there is no doubt that this was, or was almost, Beethoven's intention. All the same, I have lost my Coriolanus. Its largeness and freedom have gone. The exquisite sounds have been hardened like a road that has been tarred for taffic. One has to go somewhere down them, and to pass through the same domestic crisis to the same military impasse, each time the overture is played.

Music is so very queer that an amateur is bound to get muddled when writing about it. It seems to be more "real" than anything, and to survive when the rest of civilization decays. In these days I am always thinking of it with relief. It can never be ruined or nationalized. So that the music which is untrammeled and untainted by reference is obviously the best sort of music to listen to; we get nearer the center of reality. Yet though it is untainted, it is never abstract; it is not like mathematics, even when it uses them. The Goldberg Variations, the last Beethoven Sonata, the Franck Quartet, the Schumann Piano Quintet and the Fourth Symphonies of Tchaikovsky and of Brahms certainly have a message. Though what on earth is it? I shall get tied up trying to say. There's an insistence in music—expressed largely through rhythm; there's a sense that it is trying to push across at us something which is neither an esthetic pattern nor a sermon. That's what I listen for specially.

So music that is itself seems on the whole better than music that reminds. And now to end with an important point: my own performances upon the piano. These grow worse yearly, but never will I give them up. For one thing, they compel me to attend—no wool-gathering or thinking myself clever here—and they drain off all non-musical matter. For another thing, they teach me a little about construction. I see what becomes of a phrase, how it is transformed or returned, sometimes bottom upward, and get some notion of the relation of keys. Playing Beethoven, as I generally do, I grow familiar with his tricks, his impatience, his sudden softnesses, his dropping of a tragic theme one semitone, his love, when tragic, for the key of C minor, and his aversion to the key of B major. This gives me a physical approach to Beethoven which cannot be gained through the slough of "appreciation." Even when people play as badly as I do, they should continue: it will help them to listen.

[1939]

WHAT I BELIEVE

I DO NOT believe in Belief. But this is an age of faith, and there are so many militant creeds that, in self-defense, one has to formulate a creed of one's own. Tolerance, good temper and sympathy are no longer enough in a world which is rent by religious and racial persecution, in a world where ignorance rules, and science, who ought to have ruled, plays the subservient pimp. Toler-ance, good temper and sympathy—they are what matter really, and if the human race is not to collapse they must come to the front before long. But for the moment they are not enough, their action is no stronger than a flower, battered beneath a military jack-boot. They want stiffening, even if the process coarsens them. Faith, to my mind, is a stiffening process, a sort of mental starch, which ought to be applied as sparingly as possible. I dislike the stuff. I do not believe in it, for its own sake, at all. Herein I probably differ from most people, who believe in Belief, and are only sorry they cannot swallow even more than they do. My law-givers are Erasmus and Montaigne, not Moses and St. Paul. My temple stands not upon Mount Moriah but in that Elysian Field where even the immoral are admitted. My motto is: "Lord, I disbelieve—help thou my unbelief."

I have, however, to live in an Age of Faith—the sort of epoch I used to hear praised when I was a boy. It is extremely unpleasant really. It is bloody in every sense of the word. And I have to keep my end up in it. Where do I start?

With personal relationships. Here is something comparatively solid in a world full of violence and cruelty. Not absolutely solid, for Psychology has split and shattered the idea of a "Person," and has shown that there is something incalculable in each of us, which may at any moment rise to the surface and destroy our normal balance. We don't know what we are like. We can't know what other people are like. How, then, can we put any trust in personal relationships, or cling to them in the gathering political storm? In theory we cannot. But in practice we can and do. Though A is not unchangeably A or B unchangeably B, there can still be love and loyalty between the two. For the purpose of living one has to assume that the personality is solid, and the "self" is an entity, and to ignore all contrary evidence. And since to ignore evidence is one of the characteristics of faith, I certainly can proclaim that I believe in personal relationships.

Starting from them, I get a little order into the contemporary chaos. One must be fond of people and trust them if one is not to make a mess of life, and it is therefore essential that they should not let one down. They often do. The moral of which is that I must, myself, be as reliable as possible, and this I try to be. But reliability is not a matter of contract—that is the main difference between the world of personal relationships and the world of business relationships. It is a matter for the heart, which signs no documents. In other words, reliability is impossible unless there is a natural warmth. Most men possess this warmth, though they often have bad luck and get chilled. Most of them, even when they are politicians, *want* to keep faith. And one can, at all events, show one's own little light here, one's own poor little trembling flame, with the knowledge that it is not the only light that is shining in the darkness, and not the only one which the darkness does not comprehend. Personal relations are despised today. They are regarded as bourgeois luxuries, as products of a time of fair weather which is now past, and we are urged to get rid of them, and to dedicate ourselves to some movement or cause instead. I hate the idea of causes, and if I had to choose between betraying my country and betraying my friend, I hope I should have the guts to betray my country. Such a choice may scandalize the modern reader, and he may stretch out his patriotic hand to the telephone at once and ring up the police. It would not have shocked Dante, though. Dante places Brutus and Cassius in the lowest circle of Hell because they had chosen to betray their friend Julius Caesar rather than their country Rome. Probably one will not be asked to make such an agonizing choice. Still, there lies at the back of every creed something terrible and hard for which the worshipper may one day be required to suffer, and there is even a terror and a hardness in this creed of personal relationships, urbane and mild though it sounds. Love and loyalty to an individual can run counter to the claims of the State. When they do—down with the State, say I, which means that the State would down me.

This brings me along to Democracy, "even Love, the Beloved Republic, which feeds upon Freedom and lives." Democracy is not a Beloved Republic really, and never will be. But it is less hateful than other contemporary forms of government, and to that extent it deserves our support. It does start from the assumption that the individual is important, and that all types are needed to make a civilization. It does not divide its citizens into the bossers and the bossed—as an efficiency-regime tends to do. The people I admire most are those who are sensitive and want to create something or discover something, and do not see life in terms of power, and such people get more of a chance under a democracy than elsewhere. They found religions, great or small, or they produce literature and art, or they do disinterested scientific research, or they may be what

is called "ordinary people," who are creative in their private lives,
bring up their children decently, for instance, or help their neighbors. All these people need to express themselves; they cannot do so
unless society allows them liberty to do so, and the society which
allows them most liberty is a democracy.

Democracy has another merit. It allows criticism, and if there is
not public criticism there are bound to be hushed-up scandals. That
is why I believe in the Press, despite all its lies and vulgarity, and
why I believe in Parliament. Parliament is often sneered at because
it is a Talking Shop. I believe in it *because* it is a talking shop. I
believe in the Private Member who makes himself a nuisance. He
gets snubbed and is told that he is cranky or ill-informed, but he
does expose abuses which would otherwise never have been mentioned, and very often an abuse gets put right just by being
mentioned. Occasionally, too, a well-meaning public official starts
losing his head in the cause of efficiency, and thinks himself God
Almighty. Such officials are particularly frequent in the Home
Office. Well, there will be questions about them in Parliament
sooner or later, and then they will have to mind their steps. Whether
Parliament is either a representative body or an efficient one is
questionable, but I value it because it criticizes and talks, and because its chatter gets widely reported.

So Two Cheers for Democracy: one because it admits variety and
two because it permits criticism. Two cheers are quite enough: there
is no occasion to give three. Only Love the Beloved Republic
deserves that.

What about Force, though? While we are trying to be sensitive
and advanced and affectionate and tolerant, an unpleasant question
pops up: does not all society rest upon force? If a government cannot
count upon the police and the army, how can it hope to rule? And
if an individual gets knocked on the head or sent to a labor camp,
of what significance are his opinions?

This dilemma does not worry me as much as it does some. I
realize that all society rests upon force. But all the great creative
actions, all the decent human relations, occur during the intervals
when force has not managed to come to the front. These intervals

are what matter. I want them to be as frequent and as lengthy as possible, and I call them "civilization." Some people idealize force and pull it into the foreground and worship it, instead of keeping it in the background as long as possible. I think they make a mistake, and I think that their opposites, the mystics, err even more when they declare that force does not exist. I believe that it exists, and that one of our jobs is to prevent it from getting out of its box. It gets out sooner or later, and then it destroys us and all the lovely things which we have made. But it is not out all the time, for the fortunate reason that the strong are so stupid. Consider their conduct for a moment in the Niebelung's Ring. The giants there have the guns, or in other words the gold; but they do nothing with it, they do not realize that they are all-powerful, with the result that the catastrophe is delayed and the castle of Walhalla, insecure but glorious, fronts the storms. Fafnir, coiled round his hoard, grumbles and grunts; we can hear him under Europe today; the leaves of the wood already tremble, and the Bird calls its warnings uselessly. Fafnir will destroy us, but by a blessed dispensation he is stupid and slow, and creation goes on just outside the poisonous blast of his breath. The Nietzschean would hurry the monster up, the mystic would say he did not exist, but Wotan, wiser than either, hastens to create warriors before doom declares itself. The Valkyries are symbols not only of courage but of intelligence; they represent the human spirit snatching its opportunity while the going is good, and one of them even finds time to love. Brünnhilde's last song hymns the recurrence of love, and since it is the privilege of art to exaggerate, she goes even further, and proclaims the love which is eternally triumphant and feeds upon freedom, and lives.

So that is what I feel about force and violence. It is, alas! the ultimate reality on this earth, but it does not always get to the front. Some people call its absences "decadence"; I call them "civilization" and find in such interludes the chief justification for the human experiment. I look the other way until fate strikes me. Whether this is due to courage or to cowardice in my own case I cannot be sure. But I know that if men had not looked the other way in the past, nothing of any value would survive. The people

I respect most behave as if they were immortal and as if society was eternal. Both assumptions are false: both of them must be accepted as true if we are to go on eating and working and loving, and are to keep open a few breathing holes for the human spirit. No millennium seems likely to descend upon humanity; no better and stronger League of Nations will be instituted; no form of Christianity and no alternative to Christianity will bring peace to the world or integrity to the individual; no "change of heart" will occur. And yet we need not despair, indeed, we cannot despair; the evidence of history shows us that men have always insisted on behaving creatively under the shadow of the sword; that they have done their artistic and scientific and domestic stuff for the sake of doing it, and that we had better follow their example under the shadow of the aeroplanes. Others, with more vision or courage than myself, see the salvation of humanity ahead, and will dismiss my conception of civilization as paltry, a sort of tip-and-run game. Certainly it is presumptuous to say that we *cannot* improve, and that Man, who has only been in power for a few thousand years, will never learn to make use of his power. All I mean is that, if people continue to kill one another as they do, the world cannot get better than it is, and that since there are more people than formerly, and their means for destroying one another superior, the world may well get worse. What is good in people—and consequently in the world— is their insistence on creation, their belief in friendship and loyalty for their own sakes; and though Violence remains and is, indeed, the major partner in this muddled establishment, I believe that creativeness remains too, and will always assume direction when violence sleeps. So, though I am not an optimist, I cannot agree with Sophocles that it were better never to have been born. And although, like Horace, I see no evidence that each batch of births is superior to the last, I leave the field open for the more complacent view. This is such a difficult moment to live in, one cannot help getting gloomy and also a bit rattled, and perhaps short-sighted.

In search of a refuge, we may perhaps turn to hero-worship. But here we shall get no help, in my opinion. Hero-worship is a dangerous vice, and one of the minor merits of a democracy is that it does not encourage it, or produce that unmanageable type of citizen known as the Great Man. It produces instead different kinds of small men—a much finer achievement. But people who cannot get interested in the variety of life, and cannot make up their own minds, get discontented over this, and they long for a hero to bow down before and to follow blindly. It is significant that a hero is an integral part of the authoritarian stock-in-trade today. An efficiency-regime cannot be run without a few heroes stuck about it to carry off the dullness—much as plums have to be put into a bad pudding to make it palatable. One hero at the top and a smaller one each side of him is a favorite arrangement, and the timid and the bored are comforted by the trinity, and, bowing down, feel exalted and strengthened.

No, I distrust Great Men. They produce a desert of uniformity around them and often a pool of blood too, and I always feel a little man's pleasure when they come a cropper. Every now and then one reads in the newspapers some such statement as: "The coup d'état appears to have failed, and Admiral Toma's whereabouts is at present unknown." Admiral Toma had probably every qualification for being a Great Man—an iron will, personal magnetism, dash, flair, sexlessness—but fate was against him, so he retires to unknown whereabouts instead of parading history with his peers. He fails with a completeness which no artist and no lover can experience, because with them the process of creation is itself an achievement, whereas with him the only possible achievement is success.

I believe in aristocracy, though—if that is the right word, and if a democrat may use it. Not an aristocracy of power, based upon rank and influence, but an aristocracy of the sensitive, the considerate and the plucky. Its members are to be found in all nations and classes, and all through the ages, and there is a secret understanding between them when they meet. They represent the true human tradition, the one permanent victory of our queer race over cruelty and chaos. Thousands of them perish in obscurity, a few are great names. They are sensitive for others as well as for themselves, they are considerate without being fussy, their pluck is not swankiness but the power to endure, and they can take a joke. I give no examples—

it is risky to do that—but the reader may as well consider whether this is the type of person he would like to meet and to be, and whether (going farther with me) he would prefer that this type should *not* be an ascetic one. I am against asceticism myself. I am with the old Scotsman who wanted less chastity and more delicacy. I do not feel that my aristocrats are a real aristocracy if they thwart their bodies, since bodies are the instruments through which we register and enjoy the world. Still, I do not insist. This is not a major point. It is clearly possible to be sensitive, considerate and plucky and yet be an ascetic too, if anyone possesses the first three qualities, I will let him in! On they go—an invincible army, yet not a victorious one. The aristocrats, the elect, the chosen, the Best People—all the words that describe them are false, and all attempts to organize them fail. Again and again Authority, seeing their value, has tried to net them and to utilize them as the Egyptian Priesthood or the Christian Church or the Chinese Civil Service or the Group Movement, or some other worthy stunt. But they slip through the net and are gone; when the door is shut, they are no longer in the room; their temple, as one of them remarked, is the Holiness of the Heart's Affection, and their kingdom, though they never possess it, is the wide-open world.

With this type of person knocking about, and constantly crossing one's path if one has eyes to see or hands to feel, the experiment of earthly life cannot be dismissed as a failure. But it may well be hailed as a tragedy, the tragedy being that no device has been found by which these private decencies can be transmitted to public affairs. As soon as people have power they go crooked and sometimes dotty as well, because the possession of power lifts them into a region where normal honesty never pays. For instance, the man who is selling newspapers outside the Houses of Parliament can safely leave his papers to go for a drink and his cap beside them: anyone who takes a paper is sure to drop a copper into the cap. But the men who are inside the Houses of Parliament—they cannot trust one another like that, still less can the Government they compose trust other governments. No caps upon the pavement here, but suspicion, treachery and armaments. The more highly public life is organized the lower does its morality sink; the nations of today behave to each other worse than they ever did in the past, they cheat, rob, bully and bluff, make war without notice, and kill as many women and children as possible; whereas primitive tribes were at all events restrained by taboos. It is a humiliating outlook—though the greater the darkness, the brighter shine the little lights, reassuring one another, signalling: "Well, at all events, I'm still here. I don't like it very much, but how are you?" Unquenchable lights of my aristocracy! Signals of the invincible army! "Come along—anyway, let's have a good time while we can." I think they signal that too.

The Saviour of the future—if ever he comes—will not preach a new Gospel. He will merely utilize my aristocracy, he will make effective the good will and the good temper which are already existing. In other words, he will introduce a new technique. In economics, we are told that if there was a new technique of distribution, there need be no poverty, and people would not starve in one place while crops were being ploughed under in another. A similar change is needed in the sphere of morals and politics. The desire for it is by no means new; it was expressed, for example, in theological terms by Jacopone da Todi over six hundred years ago. "Ordina questo amore, O tu che m'ami," he said; "O thou who lovest me—set this love in order." His prayer was not granted, and I do not myself believe that it ever will be, but here, and not through a change of heart, is our probable route. Not by becoming better, but by ordering and distributing his native goodness, will Man shut up Force into its box, and so gain time to explore the universe and to set his mark upon it worthily. At present he only explores it at odd moments, when Force is looking the other way, and his divine creativeness appears as a trivial by-product, to be scrapped as soon as the drums beat and the bombers hum.

Such a change, claim the orthodox, can only be made by Christianity, and will be made by it in God's good time: man always has failed and always will fail to organize his own goodness, and it is presumptuous of him to try. This claim—solemn as it is—leaves me cold. I cannot believe that Christianity will ever cope with the present worldwide mess, and I think that such influence as it retains in modern society is due to the money behind it, rather than to its spiritual appeal. It was a spiritual force once, but the indwelling spirit will have to be restated if it is to calm the waters again, and probably restated in a non-Christian form. Naturally a lot of people, and people who are not only good but able and intelligent, will disagree here; they will vehemently deny that Christianity has failed, or they will argue that its failure proceeds from the wickedness of men, and really proves its ultimate success. They have Faith, with a large F. My faith has a very small one, and I only intrude it because these are strenuous and serious days, and one likes to say what one thinks while speech is comparatively free: it may not be free much longer.

The above are the reflections of an individualist and a liberal who has found liberalism crumbling beneath him and at first felt ashamed. Then, looking around, he decided there was no special reason for shame, since other people, whatever they felt, were equally insecure. And as for individualism—there seems no way of getting off this, even if one wanted to. The dictator-hero can grind down his citizens till they are all alike, but he cannot melt them into a single man. That is beyond his power. He can order them to merge, he can incite them to mass-antics, but they are obliged to be born separately, and to die separately, and, owing to these unavoidable termini, will always be running off the totalitarian rails. The memory of birth and the expectation of death always lurk within the human being, making him separate from his fellows and consequently capable of intercourse with them. Naked I came into the world, naked I shall go out of it! And a very good thing too, for it reminds me that I am naked under my shirt, whatever its color.

VIRGINIA WOOLF

PERHAPS NO English writer ever grew up as surrounded by books, writers, and the affluence that makes culture possible as Virginia Woolf. At the time of her birth (in London in 1882) her father, Leslie Stephen, was already distinguished as a philosopher, critic, and editor of the *Cornhill Magazine*. His first wife had been Thackeray's youngest daughter; his second, Virginia's mother, was descended from French nobility. Meredith, Hardy, and Henry James were his close friends, as was James Russell Lowell, who accepted the invitation to be Virginia's godfather by sending along some verses that expressed the wish that "the child would be/ A sample of heredity." Later that same year Leslie Stephen was named editor of the *Dictionary of National Biography*, and it was in the presence of that enormous undertaking that Virginia was educated. Instead of being sent to school, she was simply turned loose in her father's library, and the breadth of the knowledge she gained therein reveals itself in nearly all her essays.

Books, though, were not the whole of her education, and for the rest one must look to St. Ives in Cornwall, where the Stephen family went for its summer holidays. There, close by the sea, Virginia and the other Stephen children, Thoby, Vanessa, and Adrian—along with the children from their mother's first marriage—spent many happy days picnicking, boating, and playing games. In *To the Lighthouse* (1927) Virginia Woolf describes their summers in Cornwall with great fidelity.

When Sir Leslie died in 1904, the four Stephen children gave up the house at Hyde Park Gate and moved to 46 Gordon Square, Bloomsbury. Soon Thoby's friends, Lytton Strachey and Clive Bell, started coming around to carry on the discussions they had begun at Cambridge under the name of the "Midnight Society." And thus began what has since been known as the "Bloomsbury Group," by no means a formal organization, but merely a gathering of friends who believed (as their Cambridge mentor, G. E. Moore, had declared in his *Principia Ethica*) that the appreciation of beauty and the need for personal relationships were man's supreme endeavors.

After Thoby died of typhoid in Greece in 1906 and Vanessa married Clive Bell a year later, Virginia and Adrian moved to Fitzroy Square, a short distance away, and the Thursday night meetings followed them. New friends began coming—among them the art critic Roger Fry, the economist John Maynard Keynes, and E. M. Forster—until, by the late nineteen-twenties, the group was so famous that the word Bloomsbury had become synonymous with highbrow. Nor was it always used as a compliment; D. H. Lawrence called the "Bloomsberries" gilded youth, beetles that stung like scorpions.

In 1912 Virginia Stephen married Leonard Woolf, a socialist and political writer who had been one of Thoby's friends at Cambridge, and three years later she published her first novel, *The Voyage Out*. Then, in 1917, with no other intention than that of printing a few short works by themselves and their friends, purely for the fun of it, the Woolfs bought a hand printing press and set it up in the dining room of their house in Richmond. The first book they produced contained two stories, one by Virginia and the other by Leonard; a little later they published *Prelude* by Katherine Mansfield and *Poems 1919* by T.S. Eliot. What had started out as a lark suddenly became a successful business, and over the years that followed The Hogarth Press became famous as a publisher of new writers. Undoubtedly, the Woolfs made their greatest mistake as editors when they refused to publish Joyce's *Ulysses*.

In 1919 they bought the cottage Monks House in the village of Rodmell, near the River Ouse, in Sussex, and there they spent their weekends and holidays for the next twenty-two years. In March 1941, in a state of depression brought on both by the war and the fear that she might lose her mind and be a burden on her husband, Virginia Woolf committed suicide by drowning herself in the Ouse. Later, her husband revealed that she had suffered several nervous breakdowns earlier in her life, going back as far as her mother's death in 1895.

Along with Joyce and Proust, Virginia Woolf is one of the great innovators of the modern novel, directing the reader's attention away from a sequence of outward actions and toward the complex inner lives of her characters. In her most successful novels—*Jacob's Room* (1922), Mrs. *Dalloway* (1925), *To the Lighthouse* (1927), *The Waves* (1931), and *Between the Acts* (published posthumously in 1941)—almost nothing happens on the surface of her characters' lives. Instead, the action all takes place in their heads, in their responses both to each other and the objects they are surrounded by. Time, also, changes: the chronological time of outward actions—in which morning is separated from night by a sequence of events or "actions"—is replaced by the *real* time of an alert consciousness; morning to night becomes a sequence of impressions, intuitions, memories, anticipations. In short, the conflicts between the characters all take place within their sensibilities, and because of that, the novels make large demands on the reader's perceptions.

However difficult and annoying her novels may be, as an essayist Virginia Woolf is always perfectly lucid. Seldom does she abandon her father's advice "to write in the fewest possible words, as clearly as possible, exactly what one meant." Moreover, she obviously benefited from the more than two hundred book reviews she wrote for the *Times Literary Supplement* from 1905 until a few years before her death. And yet she was never a formal, systematic critic, but rather a common reader, personal and subjective, who read "for his own pleasure rather than to impart knowledge or correct the opinions of others." And one notices that the books she loved the best and wrote the most engagingly about were not especially the classics, but all those memoirs, letters, biographies, and autobiographies of the obscure, all those "rubbish-heaps," as she put it, of "vanished moments and forgotten lives told in faltering and feeble accents . . . ." For Virginia Woolf was a novelist even when she was writing essays, and it made little difference to her if her characters came from real life or the pages of a book. All she wanted was to illuminate those lives, make them stand before us in all their vitality and confusion. Nothing else really mattered to her. "If one wishes to better the world," she once wrote, "one must, paradoxically enough, withdraw and spend more and more time fashioning one's sentences to perfection in solitude."

[1929]

THE SHADOW ACROSS
THE PAGE*

NEXT DAY the light of the October morning was falling in dusty shafts through the uncurtained windows, and the hum of traffic rose from the street. London then was winding itself up again; the factory was astir; the machines were beginning. It was tempting, after all this reading, to look out of the window and see what London was doing on the morning of the twenty-sixth of October 1928. And what was London doing? Nobody, it seemed, was reading *Antony and Cleopatra*. London was wholly indifferent, it appeared, to Shakespeare's plays. Nobody cared a straw—and I do not blame them—for the future of fiction, the death of poetry or the development by the average woman of a prose style completely expressive of her mind. If opinions upon any of these matters had been chalked on the pavement, nobody would have stooped to read them. The nonchalance of the hurrying feet would have rubbed them out in half an hour. Here came an errand-boy; here a woman with a dog on a lead. The fascination of the London street is that no two people are ever alike; each seems bound on some private affair of his own. There were the business-like, with their little bags; there were the drifters rattling sticks upon area railings; there were affable characters to whom the streets serve for clubroom, hailing men in carts and giving information without being asked for it. Also there were funerals to which men, thus suddenly reminded of the passing of their own bodies, lifted their hats. And then a very distinguished gentleman came slowly down a doorstep and paused to avoid collision with a bustling lady who had, by some means or other, acquired a splendid fur coat and a bunch of Parma violets. They all seemed separate, self-absorbed, on business of their own.

* From Chapter Six of *A Room of One's Own*.

At this moment, as so often happens in London, there was a complete lull and suspension of traffic. Nothing came down the street; nobody passed. A single leaf detached itself from the plane tree at the end of the street, and in that pause and suspension fell. Somehow it was like a signal falling, a signal pointing to a force in things which one had overlooked. It seemed to point to a river, which flowed past, invisibly, round the corner, down the street, and took people and eddied them along, as the stream at Oxbridge had taken the undergraduate in his boat and the dead leaves. Now it was bringing from one side of the street to the other diagonally a girl in patent leather boots, and then a young man in a maroon over-coat; it was also bringing a taxi-cab; and it brought all three together at a point directly beneath my window; where the taxi stopped; and the girl and the young man stopped; and they got into the taxi; and then the cab glided off as if it were swept on by the current elsewhere.

The sight was ordinary enough; what was strange was the rhythmical order with which my imagination had invested it; and the fact that the ordinary sight of two people getting into a cab had the power to communicate something of their own seeming satisfaction. The sight of two people coming down the street and meeting at the corner seems to ease the mind of some strain, I thought, watching the taxi turn and make off. Perhaps to think, as I had been thinking these two days, of one sex as distinct from the other is an effort. It interferes with the unity of the mind. Now that effort had ceased and that unity had been restored by seeing two people come together and get into a taxi-cab. The mind is certainly a very mysterious organ, I reflected, drawing my head in from the window, about which nothing whatever is known, though we depend upon it so completely. Why do I feel that there are severances and op-positions in the mind, as there are strains from obvious causes on the body? What does one mean by "the unity of the mind," I pondered, for clearly the mind has so great a power of concentrating at any point at any moment that it seems to have no single state of being. It can separate itself from the people in the street, for ex-ample, and think of itself as apart from them, at an upper window looking down on them. Or it can think with other people spontaneously, as, for instance, in a crowd waiting to hear some piece of news read out. It can think back through its fathers or through its mothers, as I have said that a woman writing thinks back through her mothers. Again if one is a woman one is often surprised by a sudden splitting off of consciousness, say in walking down White-hall, when from being the natural inheritor of that civilisation, she becomes, on the contrary, outside of it, alien and critical. Clearly the mind is always altering its focus, and bringing the world into different perspectives. But some of these states of mind seem, even if adopted spontaneously, to be less comfortable than others. In order to keep oneself continuing in them one is unconsciously holding something back, and gradually the repression becomes an effort. But there may be some state of mind in which one could continue without effort because nothing is required to be held back. And this perhaps, I thought, coming in from the window, is one of them. For certainly when I saw the couple get into the taxi-cab the mind felt as if, after being divided, it had come together again in a natural fusion. The obvious reason would be that it is natural for the sexes to co-operate. One has a profound, if irrational, instinct in favour of the theory that the union of man and woman makes for the greatest satisfaction, the most complete happiness. But the sight of the two people getting into the taxi and the satisfaction it gave me made me also ask whether there are two sexes in the mind corresponding to the two sexes in the body, and whether they also require to be united in order to get complete satisfaction and happiness? And I went on amateurishly to sketch a plan of the soul so that in each of us two powers preside, one male, one female; and in the man's brain the man predominates over the woman, and in the woman's brain the woman predominates over the man. The normal and comfortable state of being is that when the two live in harmony together, spiritually co-operating. If one is a man, still the woman part of the brain must have effect; and a woman also must have intercourse with the man in her. Coleridge perhaps meant this when he said that a great mind is androgynous. It is when this fusion takes place that the mind is fully fertilised and uses all its faculties. Perhaps a mind that is purely masculine cannot create, any more than a mind that is purely feminine, I thought. But

it would be well to test what one meant by man-womanly, and con-
versely by woman-manly, by pausing and looking at a book or two.

Coleridge certainly did not mean, when he said that a great mind
is androgynous, that it is a mind that has any special sympathy with
women; a mind that takes up their cause or devotes itself to their
interpretation. Perhaps the androgynous mind is less apt to make
these distinctions than the single-sexed mind. He meant, perhaps,
that the androgynous mind is resonant and porous; that it transmits
emotion without impediment; that it is naturally creative, incandescent
and undivided. In fact one goes back to Shakespeare's mind as the
type of the androgynous, of the man-womanly mind, though it would
be impossible to say what Shakespeare thought of women. And if it
be true that it is one of the tokens of the fully developed mind that
it does not think specially or separately of sex, how much harder it
is to attain that condition now than ever before. Here I came to the
books by living writers, and there paused and wondered if this
fact were not at the root of something that had long puzzled me. No
age can ever have been as stridently sex-conscious as our own; those
innumerable books by men about women in the British Museum are
a proof of it. The Suffrage campaign was no doubt to blame. It must
have roused in men an extraordinary desire for self-assertion; it must
have made them lay an emphasis upon their own sex and its characteristics which they would not have troubled to think about had they
not been challenged. And when one is challenged, even by a few
women in black bonnets, one retaliates, if one has never been
challenged before, rather excessively. That perhaps accounts for
some of the characteristics that I remember to have found here, I
thought, taking down a new novel by Mr. A, who is in the prime of
life and very well thought of, apparently, by the reviewers. I opened
it. Indeed, it was delightful to read a man's writing again. It was so
direct, so straightforward after the writing of women. It indicated
such freedom of mind, such liberty of person, such confidence in
himself. One had a sense of physical well-being in the presence of
this well-nourished, well-educated, free mind, which had never
been thwarted or opposed, but had had full liberty from birth to
stretch itself in whatever way it liked. All this was admirable. But

after reading a chapter or two a shadow seemed to lie across the page. It was a straight dark bar, a shadow shaped something like the letter "I." One began dodging this way and that to catch a glimpse of the landscape behind it. Whether that was indeed a tree or a woman walking I was not quite sure. Back one was always hailed to the letter "I." One began to be tired of "I." Not but what this "I" was a most respectable "I"; honest and logical; as hard as a nut, and polished for centuries by good teaching and good feeding. I respect and admire that "I" from the bottom of my heart. But—here I turned a page or two, looking for something or other—the worst of it is that in the shadow of the letter "I" all is shapeless as mist. Is that a tree? No, it is a woman. But . . . she has not a bone in her body, I thought, watching Phoebe, for that was her name, coming across the beach. Then Alan got up and the shadow of Alan at once obliterated Phoebe. For Alan had views and Phoebe was quenched in the flood of his views. And then Alan, I thought, has passions; and here I turned page after page very fast, feeling that the crisis was approaching, and so it was. It took place on the beach under the sun. It was done very openly. It was done very vigorously. Nothing could have been more indecent. But . . . I had said "but" too often. One cannot go on saying "but." One must finish the sentence some-how, I rebuked myself. Shall I finish it, "But—I am bored!" But why was I bored? Partly because of the dominance of the letter "I" and the aridity, which, like the giant beech tree, it casts within its shade. Nothing will grow there. And partly for some more obscure reason. There seemed to be some obstacle, some impediment in Mr. A's mind which blocked the fountain of creative energy and shored it within narrow limits. And remembering the lunch party at Ox-bridge, and the cigarette ash and the Manx cat and Tennyson and Christina Rossetti all in a bunch, it seemed possible that the im-pediment lay there. As he no longer hums under his breath, "There has fallen a splendid tear from the passion-flower at the gate," when Phoebe crosses the beach, and she no longer replies, "My heart is like a singing bird whose nest is in a water'd shoot," when Alan ap-proaches what can he do? Being honest as the day and logical as the sun, there is only one thing he can do. And that he does, to

do him justice, over and over (I said turning the pages) and over
again. And that, I added, aware of the awful nature of the confession, seems somehow dull. Shakespeare's indecency uproots a
thousand other things in one's mind, and is far from being dull. But
Shakespeare does it for pleasure; Mr. A, as the nurses say, does it on
purpose. He does it in protest. He is protesting against the equality
of the other sex by asserting his own superiority. He is therefore
impeded and inhibited and self-conscious as Shakespeare might have
been if he too had known Miss Clough and Miss Davies. Doubt-
less Elizabethan literature would have been very different from
what it is if the woman's movement had begun in the sixteenth
century and not in the nineteenth.

What, then, it amounts to, if this theory of the two sides of the
mind holds good, is that virility has now become self-conscious—men,
that is to say, are now writing only with the male side of their
brains. It is a mistake for a woman to read them, for she will inevitably look for something that she will not find. It is the power of
suggestion that one most misses, I thought, taking Mr. B the critic
in my hand and reading, very carefully and very dutifully, his
remarks upon the art of poetry. Very able they were, acute and full
of learning; but the trouble was that his feelings no longer communicated; his mind seemed separated into different chambers; not
a sound carried from one to the other. Thus, when one takes a
sentence of Mr. B into the mind it falls plump to the ground—
dead; but when one takes a sentence of Coleridge into the mind,
it explodes and gives birth to all kinds of other ideas, and that is the
only sort of writing of which one can say that it has the secret of
perpetual life.

But whatever the reason may be, it is a fact that one must deplore.
For it means—here I had come to rows of books by Mr. Galsworthy
and Mr. Kipling—that some of the finest works of our greatest living
writers fall upon deaf ears. Do what she will a woman cannot find
in them that fountain of perpetual life which the critics assure her
is there. It is not only that they celebrate male virtues, enforce male
values and describe the world of men; it is that the emotion with
which these books are permeated is to a woman incomprehensible.

It is coming, it is gathering, it is about to burst on one's head, one begins saying long before the end. That picture will fall on old Jolyon's head; he will die of the shock; the old clerk will speak over him two or three obituary words; and all the swans on the Thames will simultaneously burst out singing. But one will rush away before that happens and hide in the gooseberry bushes, for the emotion which is so deep, so subtle, so symbolical to a man moves a woman to wonder. So with Mr. Kipling's officers who turn their backs; and his Sowers who sow the Seed; and his Men who are alone with their Work; and the Flag—one blushes at all these capital letters as if one had been caught eavesdropping at some purely masculine orgy. The fact is that neither Mr. Galsworthy nor Mr. Kipling has a spark of the woman in him. Thus all their qualities seem to a woman, if one may generalise, crude and immature. They lack suggestive power. And when a book lacks suggestive power, however hard it hits the surface of the mind it cannot penetrate within.

And in that restless mood in which one takes books out and puts them back again without looking at them I began to envisage an age to come of pure, of self-assertive virility, such as the letters of professors (take Sir Walter Raleigh's letters, for instance) seem to forebode, and the rulers of Italy have already brought into being. For one can hardly fail to be impressed in Rome by the sense of unmitigated masculinity; and whatever the value of unmitigated masculinity upon the state, one may question the effect of it upon the art of poetry. At any rate, according to the newspapers, there is a certain anxiety about fiction in Italy. There has been a meeting of academicians whose object it is "to develop the Italian novel." "Men famous by birth, or in finance, industry or the Fascist corporations" came together the other day and discussed the matter, and a telegram was sent to the Duce expressing the hope "that the Fascist era would soon give birth to a poet worthy of it." We may all join in that pious hope, but it is doubtful whether poetry can come out of an incubator. Poetry ought to have a mother as well as a father. The Fascist poem, one may fear, will be a horrid little abortion such as one sees in a glass jar in the museum of some country town. Such monsters never live long, it is said; one has never seen a prodigy of that sort cropping grass in a field. Two heads on one body do not make for length of life.

However, the blame for all this, if one is anxious to lay blame, rests no more upon one sex than upon the other. All seducers and reformers are responsible: Lady Bessborough when she lied to Lord Granville; Miss Davies when she told the truth to Mr. Greg. All who have brought about a state of sex-consciousness are to blame, and it is they who drive me, when I want to stretch my faculties on a book, to seek it in that happy age, before Miss Davies and Miss Clough were born, when the writer used both sides of his mind equally. One must turn back to Shakespeare then, for Shakespeare was androgynous; and so were Keats and Sterne and Cowper and Lamb and Coleridge. Shelley perhaps was sexless. Milton and Ben Jonson had a dash too much of the male in them. So had Wordsworth and Tolstoi. In our time Proust was wholly androgynous, if not perhaps a little too much of a woman. But that failing is too rare for one to complain of it, since without some mixture of the kind the intellect seems to predominate and the other faculties of the mind harden and become barren. However, I consoled myself with the reflection that this is perhaps a passing phase; much of what I have said in obedience to my promise to give you the course of my thoughts will seem out of date; much of what flames in my eyes will seem dubious to you who have not yet come of age.

Even so, the very first sentence that I would write here, I said, crossing over to the writing-table and taking up the page headed Women and Fiction, is that it is fatal for anyone who writes to think of their sex. It is fatal to be a man or woman pure and simple; one must be woman-manly or man-womanly. It is fatal for a woman to lay the least stress on any grievance; to plead even with justice any cause; in any way to speak consciously as a woman. And fatal is no figure of speech; for anything written with that conscious bias is doomed to death. It ceases to be fertilised. Brilliant and effective, powerful and masterly, as it may appear for a day or two, it must wither at nightfall; it cannot grow in the minds of others. Some collaboration has to take place in the mind between the woman and the man before the act of creation can be accomplished. Some marriage of opposites has to be consummated. The whole of the mind must lie wide open if we are to get the sense that the writer is communicating his experience with perfect fullness. There must be freedom and there must be peace. Not a wheel must grate, not a light glimmer. The curtains must be close drawn. The writer, I thought, once his experience is over, must lie back and let his mind celebrate its nuptials in darkness. He must not look or question what is being done. Rather, he must pluck the petals from a rose or watch the swans float calmly down the river. And I saw again the current which took the boat and the undergraduate and the dead leaves; and the taxi took the man and the woman, I thought, seeing them come together across the street, and the current swept them away, I thought, hearing far off the roar of London's traffic, into that tremendous stream.

LORD CHESTERFIELD'S LETTERS TO HIS SON

WHEN LORD MAHON edited the letters of Lord Chesterfield he thought it necessary to warn the intending reader that they are "by no means fitted for early or indiscriminate perusal." Only "those people whose understandings are fixed and whose principles are matured" can, so his Lordship said, read them with impunity. But that was in 1845. And 1845 looks a little distant now. It seems to us now the age of enormous houses without any bathrooms. Men smoke in the kitchen after the cook has gone to bed. Albums lie upon drawing-room tables. The curtains are very thick and the women are very pure. But the eighteenth century also has undergone a change. To us in 1930 it looks less strange, less remote than those early Victorian years. Its civilization seems more rational and more complete than the civilization of Lord Mahon and his contemporaries. Then at any rate a small group of highly educated people lived up to their ideals. If the world was smaller it was also more compact; it knew its own mind; it had its own standards. Its poetry is affected by the same security. When we read the *Rape of the Lock* we seem to find ourselves in an age so settled and so circumscribed that masterpieces were possible. Then, we say to ourselves, a poet could address himself wholeheartedly to his task and keep his mind upon it, so that the little boxes on a lady's dressing table are fixed among the solid possessions of our imaginations. A game at cards or a summer's boating party upon the Thames has power to suggest the same beauty and the same sense of things vanishing that we receive from poems aimed directly at our deepest emotions. And just as the poet could spend all his powers upon a pair of scissors and a lock of hair, so too, secure in his world and its values, the aristocrat could lay down precise laws for the education of his son. In that world also there was a certainty, a security that we are now without. What with one thing and another times have changed. We can now read Lord Chesterfield's letters without blushing, or, if we do blush, we blush in the twentieth century at passages that caused Lord Mahon no discomfort whatever. When the letters begin, Philip Stanhope, Lord Chesterfield's natural son by a Dutch governess, was a little boy of seven. And if we are to make any complaint against the father's moral teaching, it is that the standard is too high for such tender years. "Let us return to oratory, or the art of speaking well; which should never be entirely out of our thoughts," he writes to the boy of seven. "A man can make no figure without it in Parliament, or the Church, or in the law," he continues, as if the little boy were already considering his career. It seems, indeed, that the father's fault, if fault it be, is one common to distinguished men who have not themselves succeeded as they should have done and are determined to give their children—and Philip was an only child—the chances that they have lacked. Indeed, as the letters go on one may suppose that Lord Chesterfield wrote as much to amuse himself by turning over the stories of his experience, his reading, his knowledge of the world, as to instruct his son. The letters show an eagerness, an animation which prove that to write to Philip was not a task, but a delight. Tired, perhaps, with the duties of office and disillusioned with its disappointments, he takes up his pen and, in the relief of free communication at last, forgets that his correspondent is, after all, only a schoolboy who cannot understand half the things that his father says to him. But, even so, there is nothing to repel us in Lord Chesterfield's preliminary sketch of the unknown world. He is all on the side of moderation, toleration, ratiocination. Never abuse whole bodies of people, he counsels; frequent all churches, laugh at none; inform yourself about all things. Devote your mornings to study, your evenings to good society. Dress as the best people dress, behave as they behave, never be eccentric, egotistical, or absent-minded. Observe the laws of proportion, and live every moment to the full.

So, step by step, he builds up the figure of the perfect man— the man that Philip may become, he is persuaded, if he will only—

and here Lord Chesterfield lets fall the words which are to color his teaching through and through—cultivate the Graces. These ladies are, at first, kept discreetly in the background. It is well that the boy should be indulged in fine sentiments about women and poets to begin with. Lord Chesterfield adjures him to respect them both. "For my own part, I used to think myself in company as much above me when I was with Mr. Addison and Mr. Pope, as if I had been with all the Princes in Europe," he writes. But as time goes on the Virtues are more and more taken for granted. They can be left to take care of themselves. But the Graces assume tremendous proportions. The Graces dominate the life of man in this world. Their service cannot for an instant be neglected. And the service is certainly exacting. For consider what it implies, this art of pleasing. To begin with, one must know how to come into a room and then how to go out again. As human arms and legs are notoriously perverse, this by itself is a matter needing considerable dexterity. Then one must be dressed so that one's clothes seem perfectly fashionable without being new or striking; one's teeth must be perfect; one's wig beyond reproach; one's finger-nails cut in the segment of a circle; one must be able to carve, able to dance, and, what is almost as great an art, able to sit gracefully in a chair. These things are the alphabet of the art of pleasing. We now come to speech. It is necessary to speak at least three languages to perfection. But before we open our lips we must take a further precaution—we must be on our guard never to laugh. Lord Chesterfield himself never laughed. He always smiled. When at length the young man is pronounced capable of speech he must avoid all proverbs and vulgar expressions; he must enunciate clearly and use perfect grammar; he must not argue; he must not tell stories; he must not talk about himself. Then, at last, the young man may begin to practice the finest of the arts of pleasing—the art of flattery. For every man and every woman has some prevailing vanity. Watch, wait, pry, seek out their weakness "and you will then know what to bait your hook with to catch them." For that is the secret of success in the world.

It is at this point, such is the idiosyncrasy of our age, that we begin to feel uneasy. Lord Chesterfield's views upon success are far more questionable than his views upon love. For what is to be the prize of this endless effort and self-abnegation? What do we gain when we have learnt to come into rooms and to go out again; to pry into people's secrets; to hold our tongues and to flatter, to forsake the society of low-born people which corrupts and the society of clever people which perverts? What is the prize which is to reward us? It is simply that we shall rise in the world. Press for a further definition, and it amounts perhaps to this: one will be popular with the best people. But if we are so exacting as to demand who the best people are we become involved in a labyrinth from which there is no returning. Nothing exists in itself. What is good society? It is the society that the best people believe to be good. What is wit? It is what the best people think to be witty. All value depends upon somebody else's opinion. For it is the essence of this philosophy that things have no independent existence, but live only in the eyes of other people. It is a looking-glass world, this, to which we climb so slowly; and its prizes are all reflections. That may account for our baffled feeling as we shuffle, and shuffle vainly, among these urbane pages for something hard to lay our hands upon. Hardness is the last thing we shall find. But, granted the deficiency, how much that is ignored by sterner moralists is here seized upon, and who shall deny, at least while Lord Chesterfield's enchantment is upon him, that these imponderable qualities have their value and these shining Graces have their radiance? Consider for a moment what the Graces have done for their devoted servant, the Earl.

Here is a disillusioned politician, who is prematurely aged, who has lost his office, who is losing his teeth, who, worst fate of all, is growing deafer day by day. Yet, he never allows a groan to escape him. He is never dull; he is never boring; he is never slovenly. His mind is as well groomed as his body. Never for a second does he "welter in an easy-chair." Private though these letters are, and apparently spontaneous, they play with such ease in and about the single subject which absorbs them that it never becomes tedious or, what is still more remarkable, never becomes ridiculous. It may be that the art of pleasing has some connection with the art of writing. To be polite, considerate, controlled, to sink one's egotism,

to conceal rather than to obtrude one's personality may profit the
writer even as they profit the man of fashion.

Certainly there is much to be said in favor of the training, however we define it, which helped Lord Chesterfield to write his
Characters. The little papers have the precision and formality of
some old-fashioned minuet. Yet the symmetry is so natural to the
artist that he can break it where he likes; it never becomes pinched
and formal, as it would in the hands of an imitator. He can be sly;
he can be witty; he can be sententious, but never for an instant
does he lose his sense of time, and when the tune is over he calls
a halt. "Some succeeded, and others burst" he says of George the
First's mistresses: the King liked them fat. Again, "He was fixed in
the house of lords, that hospital of incurables." He smiles: he does
not laugh. Here the eighteenth century, of course, came to his help.
Lord Chesterfield, though he was polite to everything, even to the
stars and Bishop Berkeley's philosophy, firmly refused, as became a
son of his age, to dally with infinity or to suppose that things are
not quite as solid as they seem. The world was good enough and
the world was big enough as it was. This prosaic temper, while it
keeps him within the bounds of impeccable common sense, limits
his outlook. No single phrase of his reverberates or penetrates as so
many of La Bruyère's do. But he would have been the first to
deprecate any comparison with that great writer; besides, to write
as La Bruyère wrote, one must perhaps believe in something, and
then how difficult to observe the Graces! One might perhaps laugh;
one might perhaps cry. Both are equally deplorable.

But while we amuse ourselves with this brilliant nobleman and
his views on life we are aware, and the letters owe much of their
fascination to this consciousness, of a dumb yet substantial figure
on the farther side of the page. Philip Stanhope is always there. It
is true that he says nothing, but we feel his presence in Dresden, in
Berlin, in Paris, opening the letters and poring over them and looking dolefully at the thick packets which have been accumulating
year after year since he was a child of seven. He had grown into a
rather serious, rather stout, rather short young man. He had a taste
for foreign politics. A little serious reading was rather to his liking.

And by every post the letters came—urbane, polished, brilliant, imploring and commanding him to learn to dance, to learn to carve, to consider the management of his legs, and to seduce a lady of fashion. He did his best. He worked very hard in the school of the Graces, but their service was too exacting. He sat down half-way up the steep stairs which lead to the glittering hall with all the mirrors. He could not do it. He failed in the House of Commons; he subsided into some small post in Ratisbon; he died untimely. He left it to his widow to break the news which he had lacked the heart or the courage to tell his father—that he had been married all these years to a lady of low birth, who had borne him children. The Earl took the blow like a gentleman. His letter to his daughter-in-law is a model of urbanity. He began the education of his grandsons. But he seems to have become a little indifferent to what happened to himself after that. He did not care greatly if he lived or died. But still to the very end he cared for the Graces. His last words were a tribute of respect to those goddesses. Some one came into the room when he was dying; he roused himself: "Give Dayrolles a chair," he said, and said no more.

[1932]

HOW SHOULD ONE READ A BOOK?

*In the first place, I want to emphasize the note of interrogation at the end of my title. Even if I could answer the question for myself, the answer would apply only to me and not to you. The only advice, indeed, that one person can give another about reading is to take no advice, to follow your own instincts, to use your own reason, to come to your own conclusions. If this is agreed between us, then I feel at liberty to put forward a few ideas and suggestions because you will not allow them to fetter that inde-

* A paper read at a school.

pendence which is the most important quality that a reader can possess. After all, what laws can be laid down about books? The battle of Waterloo was certainly fought on a certain day; but is *Hamlet* a better play than *Lear?* Nobody can say. Each must decide that question of himself. To admit authorities, however heavily furred and gowned, into our libraries and let them tell us how to read, what to read, what value to place upon what we read, is to destroy the spirit of freedom which is the breath of those sanctuaries. Everywhere else we may be bound by laws and conventions—there we have none.

But to enjoy freedom, if the platitude is pardonable, we have of course to control ourselves. We must not squander our powers, helplessly and ignorantly, squirting half the house in order to water a single rose-bush; we must train them, exactly and powerfully, here on the very spot. This, it may be, is one of the first difficulties that faces us in a library. What is "the very spot"? There may well seem to be nothing but a conglomeration and huddle of confusion. Poems and novels, histories and memoirs, dictionaries and blue-books; books written in all languages by men and women of all tempers, races, and ages jostle each other on the shelf. And outside the donkey brays, the women gossip at the pump, the colts gallop across the fields. Where are we to begin? How are we to bring order into this multitudinous chaos and so get the deepest and widest pleasure from what we read?

It is simple enough to say that since books have classes—fiction, biography, poetry—we should separate them and take from each what it is right that each should give us. Yet few people ask from books what books can give us. Most commonly we come to books with blurred and divided minds, asking of fiction that it shall be true, of poetry that it shall be false, of biography that it shall be flattering, of history that it shall enforce our own prejudices. If we could banish all such preconceptions when we read, that would be an admirable beginning. Do not dictate to your author; try to become him. Be his fellow-worker and accomplice. If you hang back, and reserve and criticize at first, you are preventing yourself from getting the fullest possible value from what you read. But if

you open your mind as widely as possible, then signs and hints
of almost imperceptible fineness, from the twist and turn of the
first sentences, will bring you into the presence of a human being
unlike any other. Steep yourself in this, acquaint yourself with this,
and soon you will find that your author is giving you, or attempting
to give you, something far more definite. The thirty-two chapters
of a novel—if we consider how to read a novel first—are an attempt
to make something as formed and controlled as a building: but
words are more impalpable than bricks; reading is a longer and more
complicated process than seeing. Perhaps the quickest way to understand the elements of what a novelist is doing is not to read, but
to write; to make your own experiment with the dangers and difficulties of words. Recall, then, some event that has left a distinct
impression on you—how at the corner of the street, perhaps, you
passed two people talking. A tree shook; an electric light danced;
the tone of the talk was comic, but also tragic; a whole vision, an
entire conception, seemed contained in that moment.

But when you attempt to reconstruct it in words, you will find
that it breaks into a thousand conflicting impressions. Some must
be subdued; others emphasized; in the process you will lose, probably, all grasp upon the emotion itself. Then turn from your blurred
and littered pages to the opening pages of some great novelist—
Defoe, Jane Austen, Hardy. Now you will be better able to appre-
ciate their mastery. It is not merely that we are in the presence of a
different person—Defoe, Jane Austen, or Thomas Hardy—but that
we are living in a different world. Here, in *Robinson Crusoe*, we
are trudging a plain highroad; one thing happens after another;
the fact and the order of the fact is enough. But if the open air
and adventure mean everything to Defoe they mean nothing to
Jane Austen. Hers is the drawing-room, and people talking, and
by the many mirrors of their talk revealing their characters. And
if, when we have accustomed ourselves to the drawing-room and its
reflections, we turn to Hardy, we are once more spun round. The
moors are round us and the stars are above our heads. The other
side of the mind is now exposed—the dark side that comes upper-
most in solitude, not the light side that shows in company. Our

relations are not towards people, but towards Nature and destiny.
Yet different as these worlds are, each is consistent with itself. The
maker of each is careful to observe the laws of his own perspective,
and however great a strain they may put upon us they will never
confuse us, as lesser writers so frequently do, by introducing two
different kinds of reality into the same book. Thus to go from
one great novelist to another—from Jane Austen to Hardy, from
Peacock to Trollope, from Scott to Meredith—is to be wrenched
and uprooted; to be thrown this way and then that. To read a novel
is a difficult and complex art. You must be capable not only of
great fineness of perception, but of great boldness of imagination
if you are going to make use of all that the novelist—the great
artist—gives you.

But a glance at the heterogeneous company on the shelf will
show you that writers are very seldom "great artists"; far more often
a book makes no claim to be a work of art at all. These biographies
and autobiographies, for example, lives of great men, of men long
dead and forgotten, that stand cheek by jowl with the novels and
poems, are we to refuse to read them because they are not "art"? Or
shall we read them, but read them in a different way, with a different aim? Shall we read them in the first place to satisfy that curiosity which possesses us sometimes when in the evening we linger
in front of a house where the lights are lit and the blinds not yet
drawn, and each floor of the house shows us a different section of
human life in being? Then we are consumed with curiosity about
the lives of these people—the servants gossiping, the gentlemen
dining, the girl dressing for a party, the old woman at the window
with her knitting. Who are they, what are they, what are their
names, their occupations, their thoughts, and adventures?

Biographies and memoirs answer such questions, light up innumerable such houses; they show us people going about their daily
affairs, toiling, failing, succeeding, eating, hating, loving, until they
die. And sometimes as we watch, the house fades and the iron
railings vanish and we are out at sea; we are hunting, sailing,
fighting; we are among savages and soldiers; we are taking part in
great campaigns. Or if we like to stay here in England, in London,

still the scene changes; the street narrows; the house becomes small, cramped, diamond-paned, and malodorous. We see a poet, Donne, driven from such a house because the walls were so thin that when the children cried their voices cut through them. We can follow him, through the paths that lie in the pages of books, to Twicken-ham; to Lady Bedford's Park, a famous meeting-ground for nobles and poets; and then turn our steps to Wilton, the great house under the downs, and hear Sidney read the *Arcadia* to his sister; and ramble among the very marshes and see the very herons that figure in that famous romance; and then again travel north with that other Lady Pembroke, Anne Clifford, to her wild moors, or plunge into the city and control our merriment at the sight of Gabriel Harvey in his black velvet suit arguing about poetry with Spenser. Nothing is more fascinating than to grope and stumble in the alternate dark-ness and splendor of Elizabethan London. But there is no staying there. The Temples and the Swifts, the Harleys and the St. Johns beckon us on; hour upon hour can be spent disentangling their quarrels and deciphering their characters; and when we tire of them we can stroll on, past a lady in black wearing diamonds, to Samuel Johnson and Goldsmith and Garrick; or cross the channel, if we like, and meet Voltaire and Diderot, Madame du Deffand; and so back to England and Twickenham—how certain places repeat themselves and certain names!—where Lady Bedford had her Park once and Pope lived later, to Walpole's home at Strawberry Hill. But Walpole introduces us to such a swarm of new acquaintances, there are so many houses to visit and bells to ring that we may well hesitate for a moment, on the Miss Berrys' doorstep, for example, when behold, up comes Thackeray; he is the friend of the woman whom Walpole loved; so that merely by going from friend to friend, from garden to garden, from house to house, we have passed from one end of Eng-lish literature to another and wake to find ourselves here again in the present, if we can so differentiate this moment from all that have gone before. This, then, is one of the ways in which we can read these lives and letters; we can make them light up the many windows of the past; we can watch the famous dead in their familiar habits and fancy sometimes that we are very close and can surprise their secrets, and sometimes we may pull out a play or a poem that they have written and see whether it reads differently in the presence of the author. But this again rouses other questions. How far, we must ask ourselves, is a book influenced by its writer's life—how far is it safe to let the man interpret the writer? How far shall we resist or give way to the sympathies and antipathies that the man himself rouses in us—so sensitive are words, so receptive of the character of the author? These are questions that press upon us when we read lives and letters, and we must answer them for ourselves, for nothing can be more fatal than to be guided by the preferences of others in a matter so personal.

But also we can read such books with another aim, not to throw light on literature, not to become familiar with famous people, but to refresh and exercise our own creative powers. Is there not an open window on the right hand of the bookcase? How delightful to stop reading and look out! How stimulating the scene is, in its unconsciousness, its irrelevance, its perpetual movement—the colts galloping round the field, the woman filling her pail at the well, the donkey throwing back his head and emitting his long, acrid moan. The greater part of any library is nothing but the record of such fleeting moments in the lives of men, women, and donkeys. Every literature, as it grows old, has its rubbish-heap, its record of vanished moments and forgotten lives told in faltering and feeble accents that have perished. But if you give yourself up to the delight of rubbish-reading you will be surprised, indeed you will be overcome, by the relics of human life that have been cast out to molder. It may be one letter—but what a vision it gives! It may be a few sentences—but what vistas they suggest! Sometimes a whole story will come together with such beautiful humor and pathos and completeness that it seems as if a great novelist had been at work, yet it is only an old actor, Tate Wilkinson, remembering the strange story of Captain Jones; it is only a young subaltern serving under Arthur Wellesley and falling in love with a pretty girl at Lisbon; it is only Maria Allen letting fall her sewing in the empty drawing-room and sighing how she wishes she had taken Dr. Burney's good advice and had never eloped with her Rishy. None of this has any value; it is negligible in the extreme; yet how absorbing it is now and again to go through the rubbish-heaps and find rings and scissors and broken noses buried in the huge past and try to piece them together while the colt gallops round the field, the woman fills her pail at the well, and the donkey brays.

But we tire of rubbish-reading in the long run. We tire of searching for what is needed to complete the half-truth which is all that the Wilkinsons, the Bunburys, and the Maria Allens are able to offer us. They had not the artist's power of mastering and eliminating; they could not tell the whole truth even about their own lives; they have disfigured the story that might have been so shapely. Facts are all that they can offer us, and facts are a very inferior form of fiction. Thus the desire grows upon us to have done with half-statements and approximations; to cease from searching out the minute shades of human character, to enjoy the greater abstractness, the purer truth of fiction. Thus we create the mood, intense and generalized, unaware of detail, but stressed by some regular, recurrent beat, whose natural expression is poetry; and that is the time to read poetry when we are almost able to write it.

> Western wind, when wilt thou blow?
> The small rain down can rain.
> Christ, if my love were in my arms,
> And I in my bed again!

The impact of poetry is so hard and direct that for the moment there is no other sensation except that of the poem itself. What profound depths we visit then—how sudden and complete is our immersion! There is nothing here to catch hold of; nothing to stay us in our flight. The illusion of fiction is gradual; its effects are prepared; but who when they read these four lines stops to ask who wrote them, or conjures up the thought of Donne's house or Sidney's secretary; or enmeshes them in the intricacy of the past and the succession of generations? The poet is always our contemporary. Our being for the moment is centered and constricted, as in any violent shock of personal emotion. Afterwards, it is true, the sensation begins to spread in wider rings through our minds; remoter

senses are reached; these begin to sound and to comment and we
are aware of echoes and reflections. The intensity of poetry covers
an immense range of emotion. We have only to compare the force
and directness of

>   I shall fall like a tree, and find my grave,
>   Only remembering that I grieve,

with the wavering modulation of

>   Minutes are numbered by the fall of sands,
>   As by an hour glass; the span of time
>   Doth waste us to our graves, and we look on it;
>   An age of pleasure, revelled out, comes home
>   At last, and ends in sorrow; but the life,
>   Weary of riot, numbers every sand,
>   Wailing in sighs, until the last drop down,
>   So to conclude calamity in rest,

or place the meditative calm of

>   whether we be young or old,
>   Our destiny, our being's heart and home,
>   Is with infinitude, and only there;
>   With hope it is, hope that can never die,
>   Effort, and expectation, and desire,
>   And something evermore about to be,

beside the complete and inexhaustible loveliness of

>   The moving Moon went up the sky,
>   And no where did abide:
>   Softly she was going up,
>   And a star or two beside—

or the splendid fantasy of

>   And the woodland haunter
>   Shall not cease to saunter

When, far down some glade,
Of the great world's burning,
One soft flame upturning
Seems, to his discerning,
Crocus in the shade.

to bethink us of the varied art of the poet; his power to make us at
once actors and spectators; his power to run his hand into character
as if it were a glove, and be Falstaff or Lear; his power to condense,
to widen, to state, once and for ever.

"We have only to compare"—with those words the cat is out of
the bag, and the true complexity of reading is admitted. The first
process, to receive impressions with the utmost understanding, is
only half the process of reading; it must be completed, if we are to
get the whole pleasure from a book, by another. We must pass
judgment upon these multitudinous impressions; we must make of
these fleeting shapes one that is hard and lasting. But not directly.
Wait for the dust of reading to settle; for the conflict and the questioning to die down; walk, talk, pull the dead petals from a rose,
or fall asleep. Then suddenly without our willing it, for it is thus
that Nature undertakes these transitions, the book will return, but
differently. It will float to the top of the mind as a whole. And the
book as a whole is different from the book received currently in
separate phrases. Details now fit themselves into their places. We
see the shape from start to finish; it is a barn, a pig-sty, or a cathedral. Now then we can compare book with book as we compare
building with building. But this act of comparison means that our
attitude has changed; we are no longer the friends of the writer,
but his judges; and just as we cannot be too sympathetic as friends,
so as judges we cannot be too severe. Are they not criminals, books
that have wasted our time and sympathy; are they not the most
insidious enemies of society, corrupters, defilers, the writers of false
books, faked books, books that fill the air with decay and disease?
Let us then be severe in our judgments; let us compare each book
with the greatest of its kind. There they hang in the mind the
shapes of the books we have read solidified by the judgments we

have passed on them—*Robinson Crusoe, Emma, The Return of the Native*. Compare the novels with these—even the latest and least of novels has a right to be judged with the best. And so with poetry—when the intoxication of rhythm has died down and the splendor of words has faded a visionary shape will return to us and this must be compared with *Lear*, with *Phèdre*, with *The Prelude*; or if not with these, with whatever is the best or seems to us to be the best in its own kind. And we may be sure that the newness of new poetry and fiction is its most superficial quality and that we have only to alter slightly, not to recast, the standards by which we have judged the old.

It would be foolish, then, to pretend that the second part of reading, to judge, to compare, is as simple as the first—to open the mind wide to the fast flocking of innumerable impressions. To continue reading without the book before you, to hold one shadow-shape against another, to have read widely enough and with enough understanding to make such comparisons alive and illuminating—that is difficult; it is still more difficult to press further and to say, "Not only is the book of this sort, but it is of this value; here it fails; here it succeeds; this is bad; that is good." To carry out this part of a reader's duty needs such imagination, insight, and learning that it is hard to conceive any one mind sufficiently endowed; impossible for the most self-confident to find more than the seeds of such powers in himself. Would it not be wiser, then, to remit this part of reading and to allow the critics, the gowned and furred authorities of the library, to decide the question of the book's absolute value for us? Yet how impossible! We may stress the value of sympathy; we may try to sink our own identity as we read. But we know that we cannot sympathize wholly or immerse ourselves wholly; there is always a demon in us who whispers, "I hate, I love," and we cannot silence him. Indeed, it is precisely because we hate and we love that our relation with the poets and novelists is so intimate that we find the presence of another person intolerable. And even if the results are abhorrent and our judgments are wrong, still our taste, the nerve of sensation that sends shocks through us, is our chief illuminant; we learn through feeling; we cannot suppress our own idiosyncrasy without impoverishing it. But as time goes on perhaps we can train our taste; perhaps we can make it submit to some control. When it has fed greedily and lavishly upon books of all sorts—poetry, fiction, history, biography—and has stopped reading and looked for long spaces upon the variety, the incongruity of the living world, we shall find that it is changing a little; it is not so greedy, it is more reflective. It will begin to bring us not merely judgments on particular books, but it will tell us that there is a quality common to certain books. Listen, it will say, what shall we call *this*? And it will read us perhaps *Lear* and then perhaps the *Agamemnon* in order to bring out that common quality. Thus, with our taste to guide us, we shall venture beyond the particular book in search of qualities that group books together; we shall give them names and thus frame a rule that brings order into our perceptions. We shall gain a further and a rarer pleasure from that discrimination. But as a rule only lives when it is perpetually broken by contact with the books themselves—nothing is easier and more stultifying than to make rules which exist out of touch with facts, in a vacuum—now at last, in order to steady ourselves in this difficult attempt, it may be well to turn to the very rare writers who are able to enlighten us upon literature as an art. Coleridge and Dryden and Johnson, in their considered criticism, the poets and novelists themselves in their unconsidered sayings, are often surprisingly relevant; they light up and solidify the vague ideas that have been tumbling in the misty depths of our minds. But they are only able to help us if we come to them laden with questions and suggestions won honestly in the course of our own reading. They can do nothing for us if we herd ourselves under their authority and lie down like sheep in the shade of a hedge. We can only understand their ruling when it comes in conflict with our own and vanquishes it.

If this is so, if to read a book as it should be read calls for the rarest qualities of imagination, insight, and judgment, you may perhaps conclude that literature is a very complex art and that it is unlikely that we shall be able, even after a lifetime of reading, to make any valuable contribution to its criticism. We must remain

readers; we shall not put on the further glory that belongs to those
rare beings who are also critics. But still we have our responsibilities
as readers and even our importance. The standards we raise and
the judgments we pass steal into the air and become part of the
atmosphere which writers breathe as they work. An influence is
created which tells upon them even if it never finds its way into
print. And that influence, if it were well instructed, vigorous and
individual and sincere, might be of great value now when criticism
is necessarily in abeyance; when books pass in review like the
procession of animals in a shooting-gallery, and the critic has only
one second in which to load and aim and shoot and may well be
pardoned if he mistakes rabbits for tigers, eagles for barndoor fowls,
or misses altogether and wastes his shot upon some peaceful cow
grazing in a further field. If behind the erratic gunfire of the press
the author felt that there was another kind of criticism, the opinion
of people reading for the love of reading, slowly and unprofes-
sionally, and judging with great sympathy and yet with great
severity, might this not improve the quality of his work? And if by
our means books were to become stronger, richer, and more varied,
that would be an end worth reaching.

Yet who reads to bring about an end however desirable? Are
there not some pursuits that we practice because they are good in
themselves, and some pleasures that are final? And is not this among
them? I have sometimes dreamt, at least, that when the Day of
Judgment dawns and the great conquerors and lawyers and statesmen come to receive their rewards—their crowns, their laurels, their
names carved indelibly upon imperishable marble—the Almighty
will turn to Peter and will say, not without a certain envy when
He sees us coming with our books under our arms, "Look, these
need no reward. We have nothing to give them here. They have
loved reading."

THE STRANGE ELIZABETHANS

THERE ARE few greater delights than to go back three or four hundred years and become in fancy at least an Elizabethan. That such fancies are only fancies, that this "becoming an Elizabethan," this reading sixteenth-century writing as currently and certainly as we read our own is an illusion, is no doubt true. Very likely the Elizabethans would find our pronunciation of their language unintelligible; our fancy picture of what it pleases us to call Elizabethan life would rouse their ribald merriment. Still, the instinct that drives us to them is so strong and the freshness and vigor that blow through their pages are so sweet that we willingly run the risk of being laughed at, of being ridiculous.

And if we ask why we go further astray in this particular region of English literature than in any other, the answer is no doubt that Elizabethan prose, for all its beauty and bounty, was a very imperfect medium. It was almost incapable of fulfilling one of the offices of prose which is to make people talk, simply and naturally, about ordinary things. In an age of utilitarian prose like our own, we know exactly how people spend the hours between breakfast and bed, how they behave when they are neither one thing nor the other, neither angry nor loving, neither happy nor miserable. Poetry ignores these slighter shades; the social student can pick up hardly any facts about daily life from Shakespeare's plays; and if prose refuses to enlighten us, then one avenue of approach to the men and women of another age is blocked. Elizabethan prose, still scarcely separated off from the body of its poetry, could speak magnificently, of course, about the great themes—how life is short, and death certain; how spring is lovely, and winter horrid—perhaps, indeed, the lavish and towering periods that it raises above these simple platitudes are due to the fact that it has not cheapened itself

upon trifles. But the price it pays for this soaring splendor is to be
found in its awkwardness when it comes to earth—when Lady
Sidney, for example, finding herself cold at nights, has to solicit
the Lord Chamberlain for a better bedroom at Court. Then any
housemaid of her own age could put her case more simply and with
greater force. Thus, if we go to the Elizabethan prosewriters to
solidify the splendid world of Elizabethan poetry as we should go
now to our biographers, novelists, and journalists to solidify the
world of Pope, of Tennyson, of Conrad, we are perpetually baffled
and driven from our quest. What, we ask, was the life of an ordinary
man or woman in the time of Shakespeare? Even the familiar letters
of the time give us little help. Sir Henry Wotton is pompous and
ornate and keeps us stiffly at arm's length. Their histories resound
with drums and trumpets. Their broadsheets reverberate with medi-
tations upon death and reflections upon the immortality of the soul.
Our best chance of finding them off their guard and so becoming
at ease with them is to seek one of those unambitious men who
haunt the outskirts of famous gatherings, listening, observing,
sometimes taking a note in a book. But they are difficult to find.
Gabriel Harvey perhaps, the friend of Spenser and of Sidney, might
have fulfilled that function. Unfortunately the values of the time
persuaded him that to write about rhetoric, to write about Thomas
Smith, to write about Queen Elizabeth in Latin, was better worth
doing than to record the table talk of Spenser and Sir Philip Sidney.
But he possessed to some extent the modern instinct for preserving
trifles, for keeping copies of letters, and for making notes of ideas
that struck him in the margins of books. If we rummage among
these fragments we shall, at any rate, leave the highroad and perhaps hear some roar of laughter from a tavern door, where poets
are drinking; or meet humble people going about their milking and
their love-making without a thought that this is the great Elizabethan age, or that Shakespeare is at this moment strolling down
the Strand and might tell one, if one plucked him by the sleeve,
to whom he wrote the sonnets, and what he meant by Hamlet.

The first person whom we meet is indeed a milkmaid—Gabriel
Harvey's sister Mercy. In the winter of 1574 she was milking in

the fields near Saffron Walden accompanied by an old woman,
when a man approached her and offered her cakes and malmsey
wine. When they had eaten and drunk in a wood and the old
woman had wandered off to pick up sticks, the man proceeded to
explain his business. He came from Lord Surrey, a youth of about
Mercy's own age—seventeen or eighteen that is—and a married man.
He had been bowling one day and had seen the milkmaid; her hat
had blown off and "she had somewhat changed her color." In short,
Lord Surrey had fallen passionately in love with her; and sent her
by the same man gloves, a silk girdle, and an enamel posy ring
which he had torn from his own hat though his Aunt, Lady W——,
had given it him for a very different purpose. Mercy at first stood
her ground. She was a poor milkmaid, and he was a noble gentleman. But at last she agreed to meet him at her house in the village.
Thus, one very misty, foggy night just before Christmas, Lord
Surrey and his servant came to Saffron Walden. They peered in at
the malthouse, but saw only her mother and sisters; they peeped
in at the parlor, but only her brothers were there. Mercy herself was
not to be seen; and "well mired and wearied for their labor," there
was nothing for it but to ride back home again. Finally, after
further parleys, Mercy agreed to meet Lord Surrey in a neighbor's
house alone at midnight. She found him in the little parlor "in his
doublet and hose, his points untrust, and his shirt lying round
about him." He tried to force her on to the bed; but she cried out,
and the good wife, as had been agreed between them, rapped on
the door and said she was sent for. Thwarted, enraged, Lord Surrey
cursed and swore, "God confound me, God confound me," and by
way of lure emptied his pockets of all the money in them—thirteen
shillings in shillings and testers it came to—and made her finger it.
Still, however, Mercy made off, untouched, on condition that she
would come again on Christmas Eve. But when Christmas Eve
dawned she was up betimes and had put seven miles between her
and Saffron Walden by six in the morning, though it snowed and
rained so that the floods were out, and P., the servant, coming later
to the place of assignation, had to pick his way through the water
in patterns. So Christmas passed. And a week later, in the very nick

of time to save her honor, the whole story very strangely was discovered and brought to an end. On New Year's Eve her brother
Gabriel, the young fellow of Pembroke Hall, was riding back to
Cambridge when he came up with a simple countryman whom
he had met at his father's house. They rode on together, and after
some country gossip, the man said that he had a letter for Gabriel
in his pocket. Indeed, it was addressed "To my loving brother
Mr. G. H.," but when Gabriel opened it there on the road, he
found that the· address was a lie. It was not from his sister Mercy,
but to his sister Mercy. "Mine Own Sweet Mercy," it began; and
it was signed "Thine more than ever his own Phil." Gabriel could
hardly control himself—"could scarcely dissemble my sudden fancies
and comprimitt my inward passions"—as he read. For it was not
merely a love letter; it was more; it talked about possessing Mercy
according to promise. There was also a fair English noble wrapped
up in the paper. So Gabriel, doing his best to control himself before
the countryman, gave him back the letter and the coin and told him
to deliver them both to his sister at Saffron Walden with this
message: "To look ere she leap. She may pick out the English of it
herself." He rode on to Cambridge; he wrote a long letter to the
young lord, informing him with ambiguous courtesy that the game
was up. The sister of Gabriel Harvey was not to be the mistress of
a married nobleman. Rather she was to be a maid, "diligent, and
trusty and tractable," in the house of Lady Smith at Audley End.
Thus Mercy's romance breaks off; the clouds descend again; and
we no longer see the milkmaid, the old woman, the treacherous
serving man who came with malmsey and cakes and rings and
ribbons to tempt a poor girl's honor while she milked her cows.
    This is probably no uncommon story; there must have been many
milkmaids whose hats blew off as they milked their cows, and
many lords whose hearts leapt at the sight so that they plucked the
jewels from their hats and sent their servants to make treaty for
them. But it is rare for the girl's own letters to be preserved or to
read her own account of the story as she was made to deliver it at
her brother's inquisition. Yet when we try to use her words to light
up the Elizabethan field, the Elizabethan house and living room,

we are met by the usual perplexities. It is easy enough, in spite of the rain and the fog and the floods, to make a fancy piece out of the milkmaid and the meadows and the old woman wandering off to pick up sticks. Elizabethan song writers have taught us too well the habit of that particular trick. But if we resist the impulse to make museum pieces out of our reading, Mercy herself gives us little help. She was a milkmaid, scribbling love letters by the light of a farthing dip in an attic. Nevertheless, the sway of the Elizabethan convention was so strong, the accent of their speech was so masterful, that she bears herself with a grace and expresses herself with a resonance that would have done credit to a woman of birth and literary training. When Lord Surrey pressed her to yield she replied:

The thing you wot of, Milord, were a great trespass towards God, a great offence to the world, a great grief to my friends, a great shame to myself, and, as I think, a great dishonour to your lordship. I have heard my father say, Virginity is ye fairest flower in a maid's garden, and chastity ye richest dowry a poor wench can have. . . . Chastity, they say, is like unto time, which, being once lost, can no more be recovered.

Words chime and ring in her ears, as if she positively enjoyed the act of writing. When she wishes him to know that she is only a poor country girl and no fine lady like his wife, she exclaims, "Good Lord, that you should seek after so bare and country stuff abroad, that have so costly and courtly wares at home!" She even breaks into a jog-trot of jingling rhyme, far less sonorous than her prose, but proof that to write was an art, not merely a means of conveying facts. And if she wants to be direct and forcible, the proverbs she has heard in her father's house come to her pen, the Biblical imagery runs in her ears: "And then were I, poor wench, cast up for hawk's meat, to mine utter undoing, and my friends' exceeding grief." In short, Mercy the milkmaid writes a natural and noble style, which is incapable of vulgarity, and equally incapable of intimacy. Nothing, one feels, would have been easier for Mercy than to read her lover a fine discourse upon the vanity of grandeur, the loveliness of chastity, the vicissitudes of fortune. But of emotion

as between one particular Mercy and one particular Phillip, there
is no trace. And when it comes to dealing exactly in a few words
with some mean object—when, for example, the wife of Sir
Henry Sidney, the daughter of the Duke of Northumberland, has to
state her claim to a better room to sleep in, she writes for all the
world like an illiterate servant girl who can neither form her letters
nor spell her words nor make one sentence follow smoothly after
another. She haggles, she niggles, she wears our patience down with
her repetitions and her prolixities. Hence it comes about that we
know very little about Mercy Harvey, the milkmaid, who wrote
so well, or Mary Sidney, daughter to the Duke of Northumberland,
who wrote so badly. The background of Elizabethan life eludes us.

But let us follow Gabriel Harvey to Cambridge, in case we can
there pick up something humble and colloquial that will make these
strange Elizabethans more familiar to us. Gabriel, having discharged
his duty as a brother, seems to have given himself up to the life
of an intellectual young man with his way to make in the world.
He worked so hard and he played so little that he made himself
unpopular with his fellows. For it was obviously difficult to combine
an intense interest in the future of English poetry and the capacity
of the English language with card-playing, bear-baiting, and such
diversions. Nor could he apparently accept everything that Aristotle
said as gospel truth. But with congenial spirits he argued, it is clear,
hour by hour, night after night, about poetry, and meter, and the
raising of the despised English speech and the meager English
literature to a station among the great tongues and literatures of the
world. We are sometimes made to think, as we listen, of such
arguments as might now be going forward in the new Universities
of America. The young English poets speak with a bold yet uneasy
arrogance—"England, since it was England, never bred more honor-
able minds, more adventurous hearts, more valorous hands, or more
excellent wits, than of late." Yet, to be English is accounted a kind
of crime—"nothing is reputed so contemptible and so basely and so
vilely accounted of as whatsoever is taken for English." And if, in
their hopes for the future and their sensitiveness to the opinion
of older civilizations, the Elizabethans show much the same suscepti-

bility that sometimes puzzles us among the younger countries today, the sense that broods over them of what is about to happen, of an undiscovered land on which they are about to set foot, is much like the excitement that science stirs in the minds of imaginative English writers of our own time. Yet however stimulating it is to think that we hear the stir and strife of tongues in Cambridge rooms about the year 1570, it has to be admitted that to read Harvey's pages methodically is almost beyond the limits of human patience. The words seem to run redhot, molten, hither and thither, until we cry out in anguish for the boon of some meaning to set its stamp on them. He takes the same idea and repeats it over and over again:

In the sovereign workmanship of Nature herself, what garden of flowers without weeds? what orchard of trees without worms? what field of corn without cockle? what pond of fishes without frogs? what sky of light without darkness? what mirror of knowledge without ignorance? what man of earth without frailty? what commodity of the world without discommodity?

It is interminable. As we go round and round like a horse in a mill, we perceive that we are thus clogged with sound because we are reading what we should be hearing. The amplifications and the repetitions, the emphasis like that of a fist pounding the edge of a pulpit, are for the benefit of the slow and sensual ear which loves to dally over sense and luxuriate in sound—the ear which brings in, along with the spoken word, the look of the speaker and his gestures, which gives a dramatic value to what he says and adds to the crest of an extravagance some modulation which makes the word wing its way to the precise spot aimed at in the hearer's heart. Hence, when we lay Harvey's diatribes against Nash or his letters to Spenser upon poetry under the light of the eye alone, we can hardly make headway and lose our sense of any definite direction. We grasp any simple fact that floats to the surface as a drowning man grasps a plank—that the carrier was called Mrs. Kerke, that Perne kept a cub for his pleasure in his rooms at Peterhouse; that "Your last letter . . . was delivered me at mine hostesses by the

fireside, being fast hedged in round about on every side with a
company of honest, good fellows, and at that time reasonable, honest
quaffers"; that Greene died begging Mistress Isam "for a penny pot
of Malmsey," had borrowed her husband's shirt when his own was
awashing, and was buried yesterday in the new churchyard near
Bedlam at a cost of six shillings and fourpence. Light seems to dawn
upon the darkness. But no; just as we think to lay hands on Shakespeare's coat-tails, to hear the very words rapped out as Spenser
spoke them, up rise the fumes of Harvey's eloquence and we are
floated off again into disputation and eloquence, windy, wordy,
voluminous, and obsolete. How, we ask, as we slither over the
pages, can we ever hope to come to grips with these Elizabethans?
And then, turning, skipping and glancing, something fitfully and
doubtfully emerges from the violent pages, the voluminous arguments—the figure of a man, the outlines of a face, somebody who
is not "an Elizabethan" but an interesting, complex, and individual
human being.

We know him, to begin with, from his dealings with his sister.
We see him riding to Cambridge, a fellow of his college, when she
was milking with poor old women in the fields. We observe with
amusement his sense of the conduct that befits the sister of Gabriel
Harvey, the Cambridge scholar. Education had put a great gulf
between him and his family. He rode to Cambridge from a house
in a village street where his father made ropes and his mother
worked in the malthouse. Yet though his lowly birth and the consciousness that he had his way to make in the world made him
severe with his sister, fawning to the great, uneasy and self-centered
and ostentatious, it never made him ashamed of his family. The
father who could send three sons to Cambridge and was so little
ashamed of his craft that he had himself carved making ropes at his
work and the carving let in above his fireplace, was no ordinary
man. The brothers who followed Gabriel to Cambridge and were
his best allies there, were brothers to be proud of. He could be
proud of Mercy even, whose beauty could make a great nobleman
pluck the jewel from his hat. He was undoubtedly proud of himself.
It was the pride of a self-made man who must read when other

people are playing cards, who owns no undue allegiance to authority and will contradict Aristotle himself, that made him unpopular at Cambridge and almost cost him his degree. But it was an unfortunate chance that led him thus early in life to defend his rights and insist upon his merits. Moreover, since it was true—since he was abler, quicker, and more learned than other people, handsome in person too, as ever, his enemies could not deny ("a smudge piece of a handsome fellow it hath been in his days," Nash admitted) he had reason to think that he deserved success and was denied it only by the jealousies and conspiracies of his colleagues. For a time, by dint of much cabaling and much dwelling upon his own deserts, he triumphed over his enemies in the matter of the degree. He delivered lectures. He was asked to dispute before the Court when Queen Elizabeth came to Audley End. He even drew her favorable attention. "He lookt something like an Italian," she said when he was brought to her notice. But the seeds of his downfall were visible even in his moment of triumph. He had no self-respect, no self-control. He made himself ridiculous and his friends uneasy. When we read how he dressed himself up and "came ruffling it out huffty tuffty in his suit of velvet," how uneasy he was, at one moment cringing, at another "making no bones to take the wall of Sir Philip Sidney," now flirting with the ladies, now "putting bawdy riddles to them," how when the Queen praised him he was beside himself with joy and talked the English of Saffron Walden with an Italian accent, we can imagine how his enemies jeered and his friends blushed. And so, for all his merits, his decline began. He was not taken into Lord Leicester's service; he was not made Public Orator; he was not given the Mastership of Trinity Hall. But there was one society in which he succeeded. In the small, smoky rooms where Spenser and other young men discussed poetry and language and the future of English literature, Harvey was not laughed at. Harvey, on the contrary, was taken very seriously. To friends like these he seemed as capable of greatness as any of them. He too might be one of those destined to make English literature illustrious. His passion for poetry was disinterested. His learning was profound. When he held forth upon quantity and meter, upon what the Greeks had written and the Italians, and what the English might write, no doubt he created for Spenser that atmosphere of hope and ardent curiosity spiced with sound learning that serves to spur the imagination of a young writer and to make each fresh poem as it is written seem the common property of a little band of adventurers set upon the same quest. It was thus that Spenser saw him:

> Harvey, the happy above happiest men,
> I read: that, sitting like a looker-on
> Of this world's stage, doest note, with critic pen,
> The sharp dislikes of each condition.

Poets need such "lookers-on"; some one who discriminates from a watch tower above the battle; who warns; who foresees. It must have been pleasant for Spenser to listen as Harvey talked; and then to cease to listen, to let the vehement, truculent voice run on, while he slipped from theory to practice and made up a few lines of his own poetry in his head. But the looker-on may sit too long and hold forth too curiously and domineeringly for his own health. He may make his theories fit too tight to accommodate the formlessness of life. Thus when Harvey ceased to theorize and tried to practice there issued nothing but a thin dribble of arid and unappetizing verse or a copious flow of unctuous and servile eulogy. He failed to be a poet as he failed to be a statesman, as he failed to be a professor, as he failed to be a Master, as he failed, it might seem, in everything that he undertook, save that he had won the friendship of Spenser and Sir Philip Sidney.

But happily Harvey left behind him a commonplace book; he had the habit of making notes in the margins of books as he read. Looking from one to the other, from his public self to his private, we see his face lit from both sides, and the expression changes as it changes so seldom upon the face of the Elizabethans. We detect another Harvey lurking behind the superficial Harvey, shading him with doubt and effort and despondency. For, luckily, the commonplace book was small; the margins even of an Elizabethan folio narrow; Harvey was forced to be brief, and because he wrote only

for his own eye at the command of some sharp memory or experience he seems to write as if he were talking to himself. That is
true, he seems to say; or that reminds me, or again: If only I had
done this— We thus become aware of a conflict between the Harvey
who blundered among men and the Harvey who sat wisely at home
among his books. The one who acts and suffers brings his case to
the one who reads and thinks for advice and consolation.

Indeed, he had need of both. From the first his life was full of
conflict and difficulty. Harvey the rope-maker's son might put a
brave face on it, but still in the society of gentlemen the lowness
of his birth galled him. Think, then, the sedentary Harvey counseled him, of all those unknown people who have nevertheless
triumphed. Think of "Alexander, an Unexpert Youth"; think of
David, "a forward stripling, but vanquished a huge Giant"; think
of Judith and of Pope Joan and their exploits; think above all of
that "gallant virago . . . Joan of Arc, a most worthy, valiant young
wench . . . what may not an industrious and politic man do . . .
when a lusty adventurous wench might thus prevail?" And then
it seems as if the smart young men at Cambridge twitted the rope-
maker's son for his lack of skill in the gentlemanly arts. "Leave
writing," Gabriel counseled him, "which consumeth unreasonable
much time. . . . You have already plagued yourself this way."
Make yourself master of the arts of eloquence and persuasion. Go
into the world. Learn swordsmanship, riding, and shooting. All
three may be learnt in a week. And then the ambitious but uneasy
youth began to find the other sex attractive and asked advice of his
wise and sedentary brother in the conduct of his love affairs.
Manners, the other Harvey was of opinion, are of the utmost importance in dealing with women; one must be discreet, self-controlled.
A gentleman, this counselor continued, is known by his "Good
entertainment of Ladies and gentlewomen. No salutation, without
much respect and ceremony"—a reflection inspired no doubt by the
memory of some snub received at Audley End. Health and the care
of the body are of the utmost importance. "We scholars make an Ass
of our body and wit." One must "leap out of bed lustily, every
morning in ye whole year." One must be sparing in one's diet, and

active, and take regular exercise, like brother H., "who never failed
to breathe his hound once a day at least." There must be no
"buzzing or musing." A learned man must also be a man of the
world. Make it your "daily charge" "to exercise, to laugh; to proceed
boldly." And if your tormentors brawl and rail and scoff and mock
at you, the best answer is "a witty and pleasant Ironie." In any case,
do not complain, "It is gross folly, and a vile Sign of a wayward and
forward disposition, to be eftsoons complaining of this, or that, to
small purpose." And if as time goes on without preferment, one
cannot pay one's bills, one is thrust into prison, one has to bear the
taunts and insults of landladies, still remember "Glad poverty is no
poverty"; and if, as time passes and the struggle increases, it seems
as if "Life is warfare," if sometimes the beaten man has to own,
"But for hope ye Hart would burst," still his sage counselor in the
study will not let him throw up the sponge. "He beareth his misery
best, that hideth it most," he told himself.

So runs the dialogue that we invent between the two Harveys—
Harvey the active and Harvey the passive, Harvey the foolish and
Harvey the wise. And it seems on the surface that the two halves,
for all their counseling together, made but a sorry business of the
whole. For the young man who had ridden off to Cambridge full of
conceit and hope and good advice to his sister returned empty-
handed to his native village in the end. He dwindled out his last
long years in complete obscurity at Saffron Walden. He occupied
himself superficially by practicing his skill as a doctor among the
poor of the neighborhood. He lived in the utmost poverty of
buttered roots and sheep's trotters. But even so he had his consola-
tions, he cherished his dreams. As he pottered about his garden in
the old black velvet suit, purloined, Nash says, from a saddle for
which he had not paid, his thoughts were all of power and glory;
of Stukeley and Drake; of "the winners of gold and the wearers of
gold." Memories he had in abundance—"The remembrance of best
things will soon pass out of memory; if it be not often renewed
and revived," he wrote. But there was some eager stir in him, some
lust for action and glory and life and adventure that forbade him
to dwell in the past. "The present tense only to be regarded" is

one of his notes. Nor did he drug himself with the dust of scholarship. Books he loved as a true reader loves them, not as trophies to
be hung up for display, but as living beings that "must be medi-
tated, practiced and incorporated into my body and soul." A singu-
larly humane view of learning survived in the breast of the old and
disappointed scholar. "The only brave way to learn all things with
no study and much pleasure," he remarked. Dreams of the winners
of gold and the wearers of gold, dreams of action and power, fantastic though they were in an old beggar who could not pay his
reckoning, who pressed simples and lived off buttered roots in a
cottage, kept life in him when his flesh had withered and his skin
was "riddled and crumpled like a piece of burnt parchment." He
had his triumph in the end. He survived both his friends and his
enemies—Spenser and Sidney, Nash and Perne. He lived to a very
great age for an Elizabethan, to eighty-one or eighty-two; and when
we say that Harvey lived we mean that he quarreled and was tiresome and ridiculous and struggled and failed and had a face like
ours—a changing, a variable, a human face.

D. H. LAWRENCE

DAVID HERBERT Lawrence was born in the village of Eastwood in Nottinghamshire on September 11, 1885. His father was an uneducated miner with strong, uninhibited instincts, and his mother, who had been a schoolteacher before her marriage, came from a respectable, middle-class Nottingham family. Unhappy in her marriage to a man who lacked refinement and gentility, Lawrence's mother focused all her love and attention on her children, determined that they should rise in the world. Her favorite was Bertie, as she called the youngest and most delicate of her three sons, and in him she nurtured all the qualities opposite those of her husband. She taught him to sew and to cook, to detest the coarse vitality of his father, and finally, when he began to develop relationships with girls, to feel guilty about his infidelity to his mother.

From 1898 to 1901 Lawrence attended the Nottingham High School on scholarship, then went to work for a surgical goods manufacturer in Nottingham. But that winter he fell ill with pneumonia—the beginning of lung ailments that would last for the rest of his life—and had to come home, where his mother nursed him back to health. The following fall he began teaching at a school in Eastwood and continued to do so until 1906 when he became a student in the Teacher's Training Department of University College, Nottingham (having received the highest grade in all of England and Scotland in the King's Scholarship Examination). Upon receiving his teacher's certificate in 1908 Lawrence went to Croydon, outside London, where he taught school until 1911 and wrote his first two novels, *The White Peacock* and *The Trespasser*.

Up until this point in his life Lawrence was a rather unexceptional young writer—sensitive and "literary," but not particularly original or forceful. But then a series of events occurred from which he emerged drastically changed. In the winter of 1910 his mother died and Lawrence sank into a great depression. Not long afterwards he had another attack of pneumonia and had to give up teaching. Then he began to write the highly autobiographical novel, *Sons and Lovers*. And finally, in the spring of 1912, he fell in love with Frieda von Richthofen, the wife of one of his former teachers at Nottingham, and six weeks later she left her husband and three children to go with Lawrence to the continent.

For the next two years he and Frieda traveled about Austria and Italy, rarely staying in one place for more than a few months, and Lawrence began the enormous outpouring of novels, short stories, and poems that would continue—as would the incessant traveling— for the rest of his life. In 1914 Frieda's husband granted her a divorce and they returned to England and were married. Because of the outbreak of World War I, they had to remain in England for the next five years, and it became a period of mounting unhappiness for Lawrence: the war itself depressed him extremely; in 1915 his novel, *The Rainbow*, was suppressed for being obscene; and in 1917 they were ordered to move out of Cornwall because—Frieda being German—they were suspected of being German spies. Growing more and more disillusioned with the moral hypocrisy of England, Lawrence began formulating ideas for a Utopian community in which he and his friends could live in harmony and love. Nevertheless, despite the justifications he had for being depressed and unproductive, Lawrence wrote during this period a book of travel sketches, *Twilight in Italy*, a collection of poems entitled *Look! We Have Come Through!*, and one of his finest novels, *Women in Love*.

As soon as the war was over and they could get passports, the Lawrences left for Italy, and thereafter returned to England only for brief visits. For the next eleven years Lawrence wandered the globe looking for a place where he felt comfortable, but never finding it. He went to Ceylon, Australia, a ranch in New Mexico, Mexico, and then back to England; he repeated most of this cycle and returned, ultimately, to an Italian village outside Florence, where he wrote his final novel, the misunderstood and long-censored *Lady Chatterley's Lover*. In the spring of 1930, at the age of 44, D. H. Lawrence died of tuberculosis at Vence, France; five years later his body was exhumed and cremated, and Frieda took his ashes back to their ranch in the Sangre de Cristo mountains above Taos, New Mexico, where she placed them in a small chapel.

Though his career as a writer spanned only twenty years, Lawrence published nearly fifty books; and though the quality is uneven, it is remarkable that he produced as much exceptionally good writing in as many different genres as he actually did. His excellence as a novelist and short story writer often obscures the fact that he was also a fine poet and essayist and that he wrote some of the best descriptions of places ("travel books") there are, and that he was one of the most perceptive—and exciting—critics of literature in the twentieth century. He also wrote extensively on psychology, religion, and a variety of moral and philosophical issues.

Many readers find Lawrence a very disturbing writer. A demonic quality keeps emerging from his work that makes them uneasy. He's too passionate, too intense, too Pan-like. At times, reading Lawrence, it is almost like being in a forest at night, feeling the eyes of animals watching you in the dark. Lawrence believed in the power of the unconscious—one's darkest, most passionate feelings—and wanted to give them at least equal importance with the daytime qualities of the rational mind. As he once wrote, "My great religion is a belief in the blood, the flesh, as being wiser than the intellect. We can go wrong in our minds. But what our blood feels and believes and says, is always true."

F. R. Leavis called Lawrence "the great creative genius of our age, and one of the greatest figures in English literature." Whether or not one agrees with that, there is little questioning the fact that he introduced into English literature a new level of appreciation of the emotional side of life. It wasn't until after his mother was dead and he was free of her genteel aspirations for middle-class respectability that Lawrence came to see that she had been wrong, that the true flame, the vital fire, had not been in her but in his father—that tender, instinctual man who seldom thought, but who had virtually a tactile relationship with nature, darkness, and the living blood. For Lawrence, such pure physicality became the necessary antidote to the industrialism, intellectual sterility, and emotional deadness of life in the twentieth century.

ADOLF

WHEN WE were children our father often worked on the night-shift. Once it was spring-time, and he used to arrive home, black and tired, just as we were downstairs in our nightdresses. Then night met morning face to face, and the contact was not always happy. Perhaps it was painful to my father to see us gaily entering upon the day into which he dragged himself soiled and weary. He didn't like going to bed in the spring morning sunshine.

But sometimes he was happy, because of his long walk through the dewy fields in the first daybreak. He loved the open morning, the crystal and the space, after a night down pit. He watched every bird, every stir in the trembling grass, answered the whinnying of the pewits and tweeted to the wrens. If he could, he also would have whinnied and tweeted and whistled in a native language that was not human. He liked non-human things best.

One sunny morning we were all sitting at table when we heard his heavy slurring walk up the entry. We became uneasy. His was always a disturbing presence, trammelling. He passed the window darkly, and we heard him go into the scullery and put down his tin bottle. But directly he came into the kitchen. We felt at once that he had something to communicate. No one spoke. We watched his black face for a second.

"Give me a drink," he said.

My mother hastily poured out his tea. He went to pour it out into his saucer. But instead of drinking he suddenly put something on the table among the teacups. A tiny brown rabbit! A small rabbit, a mere morsel, sitting against the bread as still as if it were a made thing.

"A rabbit! A young one! Who gave it you, father?"

But he laughed enigmatically, with a sliding motion of his yellow-grey eyes, and went to take off his coat. We pounced on the rabbit.

"Is it alive? Can you feel its heart beat?"

My father came back and sat down heavily in his armchair. He dragged his saucer to him, and blew his tea, pushing out his red lips under his black moustache.

"Where did you get it, father?"

"I picked it up," he said, wiping his naked forearm over his mouth and beard.

"Where?"

"It is a wild one!" came my mother's quick voice.

"Yes, it is."

"Then why did you bring it?" cried my mother.

"Oh, we wanted it," came our cry.

"Yes, I've no doubt you did—" retorted my mother. But she was drowned in our clamour of questions.

On the field path my father had found a dead mother rabbit and three dead little ones—this one alive, but unmoving.

"But what had killed them, daddy?"

"I couldn't say, my child. I s'd think she'd aten something."

"Why did you bring it!" again my mother's voice of condemnation. "You know what it will be."

My father made no answer, but we were loud in protest.

"He must bring it. It's not big enough to live by itself. It would die," we shouted.

"Yes, and it will die now. And then there'll be *another* outcry."

My mother set her face against the tragedy of dead pets. Our hearts sank.

"It won't die, father, will it? Why will it? It won't."

"I s'd think not," said my father.

"You know well enough it will. Haven't we had it all before!" said my mother.

"They dunna always pine," replied my father testily.

But my mother reminded him of other little wild animals he had brought, which had sulked and refused to live, and brought storms of tears and trouble in our house of lunatics.

Trouble fell on us. The little rabbit sat on our lap, unmoving,

its eye wide and dark. We brought it milk, warm milk, and held
it to its nose. It sat as still as if it was far away, retreated down
some deep burrow, hidden, oblivious. We wetted its mouth and
whiskers with drops of milk. It gave no sign, did not even shake off
the wet white drops. Somebody began to shed a few secret tears.

"What did I say?" cried my mother. "Take it and put it down in
the field."

Her command was in vain. We were driven to get dressed for
school. There sat the rabbit. It was like a tiny obscure cloud. Watching it, the emotions died out of our breast. Useless to love it, to
yearn over it. Its little feelings were all ambushed. They must be
circumvented. Love and affection were a trespass upon it. A little
wild thing, it became more mute and asphyxiated still in its own
arrest, when we approached with love. We must not love it. We
must circumvent it, for its own existence.

So I passed the order to my sister and my mother. The rabbit
was not to be spoken to, nor even looked at. Wrapping it in a piece
of flannel I put it in an obscure corner of the cold parlour, and
put a saucer of milk before its nose. My mother was forbidden to
enter the parlour whilst we were at school.

"As if I should take any notice of your nonsense," she cried af-
fronted. Yet I doubt if she ventured into the parlour.

At midday, after school, creeping into the front room, there we
saw the rabbit still and unmoving in the piece of flannel. Strange
grey-brown neutralization of life, still living! It was a sore problem
to us.

"Why won't it drink its milk, mother?" we whispered. Our father
was asleep.

"It prefers to sulk its life away, silly little thing." A profound
problem. Prefers to sulk its life away! We put young dandelion
leaves to its nose. The sphinx was not more oblivious. Yet its eye was
bright.

At tea-time, however, it had hopped a few inches, out of its flannel,
and there it sat again, uncovered, a little solid cloud of muteness,
brown, with unmoving whiskers. Only its side palpitated slightly
with life.

Darkness came; my father set off to work. The rabbit was still unmoving. Dumb despair was coming over the sisters, a threat of tears before bedtime. Clouds of my mother's anger gathered as she muttered against my father's wantonness.

Once more the rabbit was wrapped in the old pit-singlet. But now it was carried into the scullery and put under the copper fireplace, that it might imagine itself inside a burrow. The saucers were placed about, four or five, here and there on the floor, so that if the little creature *should* chance to hop abroad, it could not fail to come upon some food. After this my mother was allowed to take from the scullery what she wanted and then she was forbidden to open the door.

When morning came and it was light, I went downstairs. Opening the scullery door, I heard a slight scuffle. Then I saw dabbles of milk all over the floor and tiny rabbit-droppings in the saucers. And there the miscreant, the tips of his ears showing behind a pair of boots. I peeped at him. He sat bright-eyed and askance, twitching his nose and looking at me while not looking at me.

He was alive—very much alive. But still we were afraid to trespass much on his confidence.

"Father!" My father was arrested at the door. "Father, the rabbit's alive."

"Back your life it is," said my father.

"Mind how you go in."

By evening, however, the little creature was tame, quite tame. He was christened Adolf. We were enchanted by him. We couldn't really love him, because he was wild and loveless to the end. But he was an unmixed delight.

We decided he was too small to live in a hutch—he must live at large in the house. My mother protested, but in vain. He was so tiny. So we had him upstairs, and he dropped his tiny pills on the bed and we were enchanted.

Adolf made himself instantly at home. He had the run of the house, and was perfectly happy, with his tunnels and his holes behind the furniture.

We loved him to take meals with us. He would sit on the table humping his back, sipping his milk, shaking his whiskers and his tender ears, hopping off and hobbling back to his saucer, with an air of supreme unconcern. Suddenly he was alert. He hobbled a few tiny paces, and reared himself up inquisitively at the sugar basin. He fluttered his tiny fore-paws, and then reached and laid them on the edge of the basin, whilst he craned his thin neck and peeped in. He trembled his whiskers at the sugar, then did his best to lift down a lump.

"*Do* you think I will have it! Animals in the sugar pot!" cried my mother, with a rap of her hand on the table.

Which so delighted the electric Adolf that he flung his hind-quarters and knocked over a cup.

"It's your own fault, mother. If you left him alone—"

He continued to take tea with us. He rather liked warm tea. And he loved sugar. Having nibbled a lump, he would turn to the butter. There he was shooed off by our parent. He soon learned to treat her shooing with indifference. Still, she hated him to put his nose in the food. And he loved to do it. And one day between them they overturned the cream-jug. Adolf deluged his little chest, bounced back in terror, was seized by his little ears by my mother and bounced down on the hearth-rug. There he shivered in momentary discomfort, and suddenly set off in a wild flight to the parlour.

This last was his happy hunting ground. He had cultivated the bad habit of pensively nibbling certain bits of cloth in the hearth-rug. When chased from this pasture he would retreat under the sofa. There he would twinkle in Buddhist meditation until suddenly, no one knew why, he would go off like an alarm clock. With a sudden bumping scuffle he would whirl out of the room, going through the doorway with his little ears flying. Then we would hear his thunderbolt hurtling in the parlour, but before we could follow, the wild streak of Adolf would flash past us, on an electric wind that swept him round the scullery and carried him back, a little mad thing, flying possessed like a ball round the parlour. After which ebullition he would sit in a corner composed and distant, twitching his whiskers in abstract meditation. And it was in vain we questioned him about his outbursts. He just went off like a gun, and was as calm after it as a gun that smokes placidly.

Alas, he grew up rapidly. It was almost impossible to keep him from the outer door.

One day, as we were playing by the stile, I saw his brown shadow loiter across the road and pass into the field that faced the houses. Instantly a cry of "Adolf!"—a cry he knew full well. And instantly a wind swept him away down the sloping meadow, his tail twinkling and zigzagging through the grass. After him we pelted. It was a strange sight to see him, ears back, his little loins so powerful, flinging the world behind him. We ran ourselves out of breath, but could not catch him. Then somebody headed him off, and he sat with sudden unconcern, twitching his nose under a bunch of nettles.

His wanderings cost him a shock. One Sunday morning my father had just been quarrelling with a pedlar, and we were hearing the aftermath indoors, when there came a sudden unearthly scream from the yard. We flew out. There sat Adolf cowering under a bench, whilst a great black and white cat glowered intently at him, a few yards away. Sight not to be forgotten. Adolf rolling back his eyes and parting his strange muzzle in another scream, the cat stretching forward in a slow elongation.

Ha, how we hated that cat! How we pursued him over the chapel wall and across the neighbours' gardens.

Adolf was still only half grown.

"Cats!" said my mother. "Hideous detestable animals, why do people harbour them?"

But Adolf was becoming too much for her. He dropped too many pills. And suddenly to hear him clumping downstairs when she was alone in the house was startling. And to keep him from the door was impossible. Cats prowled outside. It was worse than having a child to look after.

Yet we would not have him shut up. He became more lusty, more callous than ever. He was a strong kicker, and many a scratch on face and arms did we owe to him. But he brought his own doom on himself. The lace curtains in the parlour—my mother was rather proud of them—fell on the floor very full. One of Adolf's joys was to scuffle wildly through them as though through some foamy undergrowth. He had already torn rents in them.

One day he entangled himself altogether. He kicked, he whirled round in a mad nebulous inferno. He screamed—and brought down the curtain-rod with a smash, right on the best beloved pelargonium, just as my mother rushed in. She extricated him, but she never forgave him. And he never forgave either. A heartless wildness had come over him.

Even we understood that he must go. It was decided, after a long deliberation, that my father should carry him back to the wild-woods. Once again he was stowed into the great pocket of the pit-jacket.

"Best pop him i' th' pot," said my father, who enjoyed raising the wind of indignation.

And so, next day, our father said that Adolf, set down on the edge of the coppice, had hopped away with utmost indifference, neither elated nor moved. We heard it and believed. But many, many were the heartsearchings. How would the other rabbits receive him? Would they smell his tameness, his humanized degradation, and rend him? My mother pooh-poohed the extravagant idea.

However, he was gone, and we were rather relieved. My father kept an eye open for him. He declared that several times passing the coppice in the early morning, he had seen Adolf peeping through the nettle-stalks. He had called him, in an odd, high-voiced, cajoling fashion. But Adolf had not responded. Wildness gains so soon upon its creatures. And they become so contemptuous then of our tame presence. So it seemed to me. I myself would go to the edge of the coppice, and call softly. I myself would imagine bright eyes between the nettle-stalks, flash of a white, scornful tail past the bracken. That insolent white tail, as Adolf turned his flank on us! It reminded me always of a certain rude gesture, and a certain unprintable phrase, which may not even be suggested.

But when naturalists discuss the meaning of the rabbit's white tail, that rude gesture and still ruder phrase always come to my mind. Naturalists say that the rabbit shows his white tail in order to guide his young safely after him, as a nursemaid's flying strings are the signal to her toddling charges to follow on. How nice and naïve! I only know that my Adolf wasn't naïve. He used to whisk his flank at me, push his white feather in my eye, and say *"Merde!"* It's a rude word—but one which Adolf was always semaphoring at me, flag-wagging it with all the derision of his narrow haunches.

That's a rabbit all over—insolence, and the white flag of spiteful derision. Yes, and he keeps his flag flying to the bitter end, sporting, insolent little devil that he is. See him running for his life. Oh, how his soul is fanned to an ecstasy of fright, a fugitive whirlwind of panic. Gone mad, he throws the world behind him, with astonishing hind legs. He puts back his head and lays his ears on his sides and rolls the white of his eyes in sheer ecstatic agony of speed. He knows the awful approach behind him; bullet or stoat. He knows! He knows, his eyes are turned back almost into his head. It is agony. But it is also ecstasy. Ecstasy! See the insolent white flag bobbing. He whirls on the magic wind of terror. All his pent-up soul rushes into agonized electric emotion of fear. He flings himself on, like a falling star swooping into extinction. White heat of the agony of fear. And at the same time, bob! bob! bob! goes the white tail, *merde! merde! merde!* it says to the pursuer. The rabbit can't help it. In his utmost extremity he still flings the insult at the pursuer. He is the inconquerable fugitive, the indomitable meek. No wonder the stoat becomes vindictive.

And if he escapes, this precious rabbit! Don't you see him sitting there, in his earthly nook, a little ball of silence and rabbit triumph? Don't you see the glint on his black eye? Don't you see, in his very immobility, how the whole world is *merde* to him? No conceit like the conceit of the meek. And if the avenging angel in the shape of the ghostly ferret steals down on him, there comes a shriek of terror out of that little hump of self-satisfaction sitting motionless in a corner. Falls the fugitive. But even fallen, his white feather floats. Even in death it seems to say: "I am the meek, I am the righteous, I am the rabbit. All you rest, you are evil doers, and you shall be *bien emmerdés!"*

NOTTINGHAM AND THE
MINING COUNTRYSIDE

I WAS born nearly forty-four years ago, in Eastwood, a mining village of some three thousand souls, about eight miles from Nottingham, and one mile from the small stream, the Erewash, which divides Nottinghamshire from Derbyshire. It is hilly country, looking west to Crich and towards Matlock, sixteen miles away, and east and north-east towards Mansfield and the Sherwood Forest district. To me it seemed, and still seems, an extremely beautiful countryside, just between the red sandstone and the oak-trees of Nottingham, and the cold limestone, the ash-trees, the stone fences of Derbyshire. To me, as a child and a young man, it was still the old England of the forest and agricultural past; there were no motor-cars, the mines were, in a sense, an accident in the landscape, and Robin Hood and his merry men were not very far away.

The string of coal-mines of B.W. & Co. had been opened some sixty years before I was born, and Eastwood had come into being as a consequence. It must have been a tiny village at the beginning of the nineteenth century, a small place of cottages and fragmentary rows of little four-roomed miners' dwellings, the homes of the old colliers of the eighteenth century, who worked in the bits of mines, foot-rill mines with an opening in the hillside into which the miners walked, or windlass mines, where the men were wound up one at a time, in a bucket, by a donkey. The windlass mines were still working when my father was a boy—and the shafts of some were still there, when I was a boy.

But somewhere about 1820 the company must have sunk the first big shaft—not very deep—and installed the first machinery of the real industrial colliery. Then came my grandfather, a young man trained to be a tailor, drifting from the south of England, and got the job of company tailor for the Brinsley mine. In those days the company supplied the men with the thick flannel vests, or singlets, and the moleskin trousers lined at the top with flannel, in which the colliers worked. I remember the great rolls of coarse flannel and pit-cloth which stood in the corner of my grandfather's shop when I was a small boy, and the big, strange old sewing-machine, like nothing else on earth, which sewed the massive pit-trousers. But when I was only a child the company discontinued supplying the men with pit-clothes.

My grandfather settled in an old cottage down in a quarry-bed, by the brook at Old Brinsley, near the pit. A mile away, up at East-wood, the company built the first miners' dwellings—it must be nearly a hundred years ago. Now Eastwood occupies a lovely posi-tion on a hilltop, with the steep slope towards Derbyshire and the long slope towards Nottingham. They put up a new church, which stands fine and commanding, even if it has no real form, looking across the awful Erewash Valley at the church of Heanor, similarly commanding, away on a hill beyond. What opportunities, what op-portunities! These mining villages *might* have been like the lovely hill-towns of Italy, shapely and fascinating. And what happened?

Most of the little rows of dwellings of the old-style miners were pulled down, and dull little shops began to rise along the Notting-ham Road, while on the down-slope of the north side the company erected what is still known as the New Buildings, or the Square. These New Buildings consist of two great hollow squares of dwell-ings planked down on the rough slope of the hill, little four-room houses with the "front" looking outward into the grim, blank street, and the "back," with a tiny square brick yard, a low wall, and a w.c. and ash-pit, looking into the desert of the square, hard, uneven, jolting black earth tilting rather steeply down, with these little back yards all round, and openings at the corners. The squares were quite big, and absolutely desert, save for the posts for clothes lines, and people passing, children playing on the hard earth. And they were shut in like a barracks enclosure, very strange.

Even fifty years ago the squares were unpopular. It was "common" to live in the Square. It was a little less common to live in the Breach, which consisted of six blocks of rather more pretentious dwellings erected by the company in the valley below, two rows of three blocks, with an alley between. And it was most "common," most degraded of all to live in Dakins Row, two rows of the old dwellings, very old, black, four-roomed little places, that stood on the hill again, not far from the Square.

So the place started. Down the steep street between the squares, Scargill Street, the Wesleyans' chapel was put up, and I was born in the little corner shop just above. Across the other side the Square the miners themselves built the big, barn-like Primitive Methodist chapel. Along the hill-top ran the Nottingham Road, with its scrappy, ugly mid-Victorian shops. The little market-place, with a superb outlook, ended the village on the Derbyshire side, and was just left bare, with the Sun Inn on one side, the chemist across, with the gilt pestle-and-mortar, and a shop at the other corner, the corner of Alfreton Road and Nottingham Road.

In this queer jumble of the old England and the new, I came into consciousness. As I remember, little local speculators already began to straggle dwellings in rows, always in rows, across the fields: nasty red-brick, flat-faced dwellings with dark slate roofs. The bay-window period only began when I was a child. But most of the country was untouched.

There must be three or four hundred company houses in the squares and the streets that surround the squares, like a great bar-racks wall. There must be sixty or eighty company houses in the Breach. The old Dakins Row will have thirty to forty little holes. Then counting the old cottages and rows left with their old gardens down the lanes and along the twitchells, and even in the midst of Nottingham Road itself, there were houses enough for the popula-tion, there was no need for much building. And not much building went on when I was small.

We lived in the Breach, in a corner house. A field-path came down under a great hawthorn hedge. On the other side was the brook, with the old sheep-bridge going over into the meadows. The hawthorn hedge by the brook had grown tall as tall trees, and we used to bathe from there in the dipping-hole, where the sheep were dipped, just near the fall from the old mill-dam, where the water rushed. The mill only ceased grinding the local corn when I was a child. And my father, who always worked in Brinsley pit, and who always got up at five o'clock, if not at four, would set off in the dawn across the fields at Coney Grey, and hunt for mushrooms in the long grass, or perhaps pick up a skulking rabbit, which he would bring home at evening inside the lining of his pit-coat.

So that the life was a curious cross between industrialism and the old agricultural England of Shakespeare and Milton and Fielding and George Eliot. The dialect was broad Derbyshire, and always "thee" and "thou." The people lived almost entirely by instinct, men of my father's age could not really read. And the pit did not mechanize men. On the contrary. Under the butty system, the miners worked underground as a sort of intimate community, they knew each other practically naked, and with curious close intimacy, and the darkness and the underground remoteness of the pit "stall," and the continual presence of danger, made the physical, instinctive, and intuitional contact between men very highly developed, a contact almost as close as touch, very real and very powerful. This physical awareness and intimate *togetherness* was at its strongest down pit. When the men came up into the light, they blinked. They had, in a measure, to change their flow. Nevertheless, they brought with them above ground the curious dark intimacy of the mine, the naked sort of contact, and if I think of my childhood, it is always as if there was a lustrous sort of inner darkness, like the gloss of coal, in which we moved and had our real being. My father loved the pit. He was hurt badly, more than once, but he would never stay away. He loved the contact, the intimacy, as men in the war loved the intense male comradeship of the dark days. They did not know what they had lost till they lost it. And I think it is the same with the young colliers of today.

Now the colliers had also an instinct of beauty. The colliers' wives had not. The colliers were deeply alive, instinctively. But they had no daytime ambition, and no daytime intellect. They avoided, really, the rational aspect of life. They preferred to take life instinctively and intuitively. They didn't even care very profoundly about wages. It was the women, naturally, who nagged on this score. There was a big discrepancy, when I was a boy, between the collier who saw, at the best, only a brief few hours of daylight—often no daylight at all during the winter weeks—and the collier's wife, who had all the day to herself when the man was down pit.

The great fallacy is, to pity the man. He didn't dream of pitying himself, till agitators and sentimentalists taught him to. He was happy: or more than happy, he was fulfilled. Or he was fulfilled on the receptive side, not on the expressive. The collier went to the pub and drank in order to continue his intimacy with his mates. They talked endlessly, but it was rather of wonders and marvels, even in politics, than of facts. It was hard facts, in the shape of wife, money, and nagging home necessities, which they fled away from, out of the house to the pub, and out of the house to the pit.

The collier fled out of the house as soon as he could, away from the nagging materialism of the woman. With the women it was always: This is broken, now you've got to mend it! or else: We want this, that and the other, and where is the money coming from? The collier didn't know and didn't care very deeply—his life was otherwise. So he escaped. He roved the countryside with his dog, prowling for a rabbit, for nests, for mushrooms, anything. He loved the countryside, just the indiscriminating feel of it. Or he loved just to sit on his heels and watch—anything or nothing. He was not intellectually interested. Life for him did not consist in facts, but in a flow. Very often, he loved his garden. And very often he had a genuine love of the beauty of flowers. I have known it often and often, in colliers.

Now the love of flowers is a very misleading thing. Most women love flowers as possessions, and as trimmings. They can't look at a flower, and wonder a moment, and pass on. If they see a flower that arrests their attention, they must at once pick it, pluck it. Possession! A possession! Something added on to *me*! And most of the

so-called love of flowers today is merely this reaching out of possession and egoism: something I've *got*: something that embellishes
me. Yet I've seen many a collier stand in his back garden looking
down at a flower with that odd, remote sort of contemplation which
shows a *real* awareness of the presence of beauty. It would not even
be admiration, or joy, or delight, or any of those things which so
often have a root in the possessive instinct. It would be a sort of
contemplation: which shows the incipient artist.

The real tragedy of England, as I see it, is the tragedy of ugliness.
The country is so lovely: the man-made England is so vile. I know
that the ordinary collier, when I was a boy, had a peculiar sense
of beauty, coming from his intuitive and instinctive consciousness,
which was awakened down pit. And the fact that he met with just
cold ugliness and raw materialism when he came up into daylight,
and particularly when he came to the Square or the Breach, and to
his own table, killed something in him, and in a sense spoiled him
as a man. The woman almost invariably nagged about material things.
She was taught to do it; she was encouraged to do it. It was a
mother's business to see that her sons "got on," and it was the man's
business to provide the money. In my father's generation, with the
old wild England behind them, and the lack of education, the man
was not beaten down. But in my generation, the boys I went to
school with, colliers now, have all been beaten down, what with
the din-din-dinning of Board Schools, books, cinemas, clergymen,
the whole national and human consciousness hammering on the
fact of material prosperity above all things.

The men are beaten down, there is prosperity for a time, in their
defeat—and then disaster looms ahead. The root of all disaster is
disheartenment. And men are disheartened. The men of England,
the colliers in particular, are disheartened. They have been betrayed and beaten.

Now though perhaps nobody knew it, it was ugliness which really
betrayed the spirit of man, in the nineteenth century. The great
crime which the moneyed classes and promoters of industry committed in the palmy Victorian days was the condemning of the
workers to ugliness, ugliness, ugliness: meanness and formless and

ugly surroundings, ugly ideals, ugly religion, ugly hope, ugly love, ugly clothes, ugly furniture, ugly houses, ugly relationship between workers and employers. The human soul needs actual beauty even more than bread. The middle classes jeer at the colliers for buying pianos—but what is the piano, often as not, but a blind reaching out for beauty. To the woman it is a possession and a piece of furniture and something to feel superior about. But see the elderly colliers trying to learn to play, see them listening with queer alert faces to their daughter's execution of *The Maiden's Prayer*, and you will see a blind, unsatisfied craving for beauty. It is far more deep in the men than the women. The women want show. The men want beauty, and still want it.

If the company, instead of building those sordid and hideous Squares, then, when they had that lovely site to play with, there on the hill top: if they had put a tall column in the middle of the small market-place, and run three parts of a circle of arcade round the pleasant space, where people could stroll or sit, and with handsome houses behind! If they had made big, substantial houses, in apartments of five or six rooms, and with handsome entrances. If above all, they had encouraged song and dancing—for the miners still sang and danced—and provided handsome space for these. If only they had encouraged some form of beauty in dress, some form of beauty in interior life—furniture, decoration. If they had given prizes for the handsomest chair or table, the loveliest scarf, the most charming room that the men or women could make! If only they had done this, there would never have been an industrial problem. The industrial problem arises from the base forcing of all human energy into a competition of mere acquisition.

You may say the working man would not have accepted such a form of life: the Englishman's home is his castle, etc., etc.—"my own little home." But if you can hear every word the next-door people say, there's not much castle. And if you can see everybody in the square if they go to the w.c.! And if your one desire is to get out of your "castle" and your "own little home"!—well, there's not much to be said for it. Anyhow, it's only the woman who idolizes "her own little home"—and it's always the woman at her worst, her most greedy, most possessive, most mean. There's nothing to be said for the "little home" any more: a great scrabble of ugly pettiness over the face of the land.

As a matter of fact, till 1800 the English people were strictly a rural people—very rural. England has had towns for centuries, but they have never been real towns, only clusters of village streets. Never the real *urbs*. The English character has failed to develop the real *urban* side of a man, the civic side. Siena is a bit of a place, but it is a real city, with citizens intimately connected with the city. Nottingham is a vast place sprawling towards a million, and it is nothing more than an amorphous agglomeration. There *is* no Nottingham, in the sense that there is Siena. The Englishman is stupidly undeveloped, as a citizen. And it is partly due to his "little home" stunt, and partly to his acceptance of hopeless paltriness in his surrounding. The new cities of America are much more genuine cities, in the Roman sense, than is London or Manchester. Even Edinburgh used to be more of a true city than any town England ever produced.

That silly little individualism of "the Englishman's home is his castle" and "my own little home" is out of date. It would work almost up to 1800, when every Englishman was still a villager, and a cottager. But the industrial system has brought a great change. The Englishman still likes to think of himself as a "cottager"—"my home, my garden." But it is puerile. Even the farm-labourer today is psychologically a town-bird. The English are town-birds through and through, today, as the inevitable result of their complete industrialization. Yet they don't know how to build a city, how to think of one, or how to live in one. They are all suburban, pseudo-cottagy, and not one of them knows how to be truly urban—the citizen as the Romans were citizens—or the Athenians—or even the Parisians, till the war came.

And this is because we have frustrated that instinct of community which would make us unite in pride and dignity in the bigger gesture of the citizen, not the cottager. The great city means beauty, dignity, and a certain splendour. This is the side of the Englishman that has been thwarted and shockingly betrayed. England is a mean and petty scrabble of paltry dwellings called "homes." I believe in their heart of hearts all Englishmen loathe their little homes—but not the women. What we want is a bigger gesture, a greater scope, a certain splendour, a certain grandeur, and beauty, big beauty. The American does far better than we, in this.

And the promoter of industry, a hundred years ago, dared to perpetrate the ugliness of my native village. And still more monstrous, promoters of industry today are scrabbling over the face of England with miles and square miles of red-brick "homes," like horrible scabs. And the men inside these little red rat-traps get more and more helpless, being more and more humiliated, more and more dissatisfied, like trapped rats. Only the meaner sort of women go on loving the little home which is no more than a rat-trap to her man.

Do away with it all, then. At no matter what cost, start in to alter it. Never mind about wages and industrial squabbling. Turn the attention elsewhere. Pull down my native village to the last brick. Plan a nucleus. Fix the focus. Make a handsome gesture of radiation from the focus. And then put up big buildings, handsome, that sweep to a civic centre. And furnish them with beauty. And make an absolute clean start. Do it place by place. Make a new England. Away with little homes! Away with scrabbling pettiness and paltriness. Look at the contours of the land, and build up from these, with a sufficient nobility. The English may be mentally or spiritually developed. But as citizens of splendid cities they are more ignominious than rabbits. And they nag, nag, nag all the time about politics and wages and all that, like mean narrow housewives.

[1936]

PAN IN AMERICA

AT THE beginning of the Christian era, voices were heard off the coasts of Greece, out to sea, on the Mediterranean, wailing: "Pan is dead! Great Pan is dead!"

The father of fauns and nymphs, satyrs and dryads and naiads was dead, with only the voices in the air to lament him. Humanity hardly noticed.

But who was he, really? Down the long lanes and overgrown ridings of history we catch odd glimpses of a lurking rustic god with a goat's white lightning in his eyes. A sort of fugitive, hidden among leaves, and laughing with the uncanny derision of one who feels himself defeated by something lesser than himself.

An outlaw, even in the early days of the gods. A sort of Ishmael among the bushes.

Yet always his lingering title: The Great God Pan. As if he was, or had been, the greatest.

Lurking among the leafy recesses, he was almost more demon than god. To be feared, not loved or approached. A man who should see Pan by daylight fell dead, as if blasted by lightning.

Yet you might dimly see him in the night, a dark body within the darkness. And then, it was a vision filling the limbs and the trunk of a man with power, as with new, strong-mounting sap. The Pan-power! You went on your way in the darkness secretly and subtly elated with blind energy, and you could cast a spell, by your mere presence, on women and on men. But particularly on women.

In the woods and the remote places ran the children of Pan, all the nymphs and fauns of the forest and the spring and the river and the rocks. These, too, it was dangerous to see by day. The man who looked up to see the white arms of a nymph flash as she darted behind the thick wild laurels away from him followed helplessly. He was a nympholept. Fascinated by the swift limbs and the wild, fresh sides of the nymph, he followed for ever, for ever, in the endless monotony of his desire. Unless came some wise being who could absolve him from the spell.

But the nymphs, running among the trees and curling to sleep under the bushes, made the myrtles blossom more gaily, and the spring bubble up with greater urge, and the birds splash with a strength of life. And the lithe flanks of the faun gave life to the oakgroves, the vast trees hummed with energy. And the wheat sprouted like green rain returning out of the ground, in the little fields, and the vine hung its black drops in abundance, urging a secret.

Gradually men moved into cities. And they loved the display of people better than the display of a tree. They liked the glory they got of overpowering one another in war. And, above all, they loved the vainglory of their own words, the pomp of argument and the vanity of ideas.

So Pan became old and grey-bearded and goat-legged, and his passion was degraded with the lust of senility. His power to blast and to brighten dwindled. His nymphs became coarse and vulgar.

Till at last the old Pan died, and was turned into the devil of the Christians. The old god Pan became the Christian devil, with the cloven hoofs and the horns, the tail, and the laugh of derision. Old Nick, the Old Gentleman who is responsible for all our wickednesses, but especially our sensual excesses—this is all that is left of the Great God Pan.

It is strange. It is a most strange ending for a god with such a name. Pan! All! That which is everything has goat's feet and a tail! With a black face!

This really is curious.

Yet this was all that remained of Pan, except that he acquired brimstone and hell-fire, for many, many centuries. The nymphs turned into the nasty-smelling witches of a Walpurgis night, and the fauns that danced became sorcerers riding the air, or fairies no bigger than your thumb.

But Pan keeps on being reborn, in all kinds of strange shapes. There he was, at the Renaissance. And in the eighteenth century he had quite a vogue. He gave rise to an "ism," and there were many pantheists, Wordsworth one of the first. They worshipped Nature in her sweet-and-pure aspect, her Lucy Gray aspect.

"Oft have I heard of Lucy Gray," the school-child began to recite, on examination-day.

"So have I," interrupted the bored inspector.

Lucy Gray, alas, was the form that William Wordsworth thought fit to give to the Great God Pan.

And then he crossed over to the young United States: I mean Pan did. Suddenly he gets a new name. He becomes the Oversoul, the Allness of everything. To this new Lucifer Gray of a Pan Whitman sings the famous *Song of Myself*: "I am All, and All is Me." That is: "I am Pan, and Pan is me."

The old goat-legged gentleman from Greece thoughtfully strokes his beard, and answers: "All A is B, but all B is not A." Aristotle did not live for nothing. All Walt is Pan, but all Pan is not Walt.

This, even to Whitman, is incontrovertible. So the new American pantheism collapses.

Then the poets dress up a few fauns and nymphs, to let them run riskily—oh, would there were any risk!—in their private "grounds." But, alas, these tame guinea-pigs soon became boring. Change the game.

We still *pretend* to believe that there is One mysterious Something-or-other back of Everything, ordaining all things for the ultimate good of humanity. It wasn't back of the Germans in 1914, of course, and whether it's back of the bolshevist is still a grave question. But still, it's back of *us*, so that's all right.

Alas, poor Pan! Is this what you've come to? Legless, hornless, faceless, even smileless, you are less than everything or anything, except a lie.

And yet here, in America, the oldest of all, old Pan is still alive. When Pan was greatest, he was not even Pan. He was nameless and unconceived, mentally. Just as a small baby new from the womb may say Mama! Dada! whereas in the womb it said nothing; so humanity, in the womb of Pan, said nought. But when humanity was born into a separate idea of itself, it said *Pan*.

In the days before man got too much separated off from the universe, he *was* Pan, along with all the rest.

As a tree still is. A strong-willed, powerful thing-in-itself, reaching up and reaching down. With a powerful will of its own it thrusts green hands and huge limbs at the light above, and sends huge legs and gripping toes down, down between the earth and rocks, to the earth's middle.

Here, on this little ranch under the Rocky Mountains, a big pine

tree rises like a guardian spirit in front of the cabin where we live.
Long, long ago the Indians blazed it. And the lightning, or the
storm, has cut off its crest. Yet its column is always there, alive and
changeless, alive and changing. The tree has its own aura of life.
And in winter the snow slips off it, and in June it sprinkles down
its little catkin-like pollen-tips, and it hisses in the wind, and it
makes a silence within a silence. It is a great tree, under which the
house is built. And the tree is still within the allness of Pan. At
night, when the lamplight shines out of the window, the great
trunk dimly shows, in the near darkness, like an Egyptian column,
supporting some powerful mystery in the over-branching darkness.
By day, it is just a tree.

It is just a tree. The chipmunks skelter a little way up it, the
little black-and-white birds, tree-creepers, walk quick as mice on its
rough perpendicular, tapping; the bluejays throng on its branches,
high up, at dawn, and in the afternoon you hear the faintest rustle
of many little wild doves alighting in its upper remoteness. It is a
tree, which is still Pan.

And we live beneath it, without noticing. Yet sometimes, when
one suddenly looks far up and sees those wild doves there, or when
one glances quickly at the inhuman-human hammering of a wood-
pecker, one realizes that the tree is asserting itself as much as I am.
It gives out life, as I give out life. Our two lives meet and cross
one another, unknowingly: the tree's life penetrates my life, and
my life the tree's. We cannot live near one another, as we do,
without affecting one another.

The tree gathers up earth-power from the dark bowels of the
earth, and a roaming sky-glitter from above. And all unto itself,
which is a tree, woody, enormous, slow but unyielding with life,
bristling with acquisitive energy, obscurely radiating some of its
great strength.

It vibrates its presence into my soul, and I am with Pan. I think
no man could live near a pine tree and remain quite suave and
supple and compliant. Something fierce and bristling is communicated. The piny sweetness is rousing and defiant, like turpentine,
the noise of the needles is keen with aeons of sharpness. In the

volleys of wind from the western desert, the tree hisses and resists. It does not lean eastward at all. It resists with a vast force of resistance, from within itself, and its column is a ribbed, magnificent assertion.

I have become conscious of the tree, and of its interpenetration into my life. Long ago, the Indians must have been even more acutely conscious of it, when they blazed it to leave their mark on it.

I am conscious that it helps to change me, vitally. I am even conscious that shivers of energy cross my living plasm, from the tree, and I become a degree more like unto the tree, more bristling and turpentiney, in Pan. And the tree gets a certain shade and alertness of my life, within itself.

Of course, if I like to cut myself off, and say it is all bunk, a tree is merely so much lumber not yet sawn, then in a great measure I shall *be* cut off. So much depends on one's attitude. One can shut many, many doors of receptivity in oneself; or one can open many doors that are shut.

I prefer to open my doors to the coming of the tree. Its raw earth-power and its raw sky-power, its resinous erectness and resistance, its sharpness of hissing needles and relentlessness of roots, all that goes to the primitive savageness of a pine tree, goes also to the strength of man.

Give me of your power, then, oh tree! And I will give you of mine.

And this is what men must have said, more naïvely, less sophisticatedly, in the days when all was Pan. It is what, in a way, the aboriginal Indians still say, and still *mean*, intensely: especially when they dance the sacred dance, with the tree; or with the spruce twigs tied above their elbows.

Give me your power, oh tree, to help me in my life. And I will give you my power: even symbolized in a rag torn from my clothing.

This is the oldest Pan.

Or again, I say: "Oh you, you big tree, standing so strong and swallowing juice from the earth's inner body, warmth from the sky, beware of me. Beware of me, because I am strongest. I am going to

cut you down and take your life and make you into beams for my
house, and into a fire. Prepare to deliver up your life to me."

Is this any less true than when the lumberman glances at a pine
tree, sees if it will cut good lumber, dabs a mark or a number upon
it, and goes his way absolutely without further thought or feeling?
Is he truer to life? Is it truer to life to insulate oneself entirely from
the influence of the tree's life, and to walk about in an inanimate
forest of standing lumber, marketable in St. Louis, Mo.? Or is it
truer to life to know, with a pantheistic sensuality, that the tree
has its own life, its own assertive existence, its own living relatedness to me: that my life is added to, or militated against, by the
tree's life?

Which is really truer?

Which is truer, to live among the living, or to run on wheels?

And who can sit with the Indians around a big camp-fire of logs,
in the mountains at night, when a man rises and turns his breast
and his curiously-smiling bronze face away from the blaze, and
stands voluptuously warming his thighs and buttocks and loins, his
back to the fire, faintly smiling the inscrutable Pan-smile into the
dark trees surrounding, without hearing him say, in the Pan-voice:
"Aha! Tree! Aha! Tree! Who has triumphed now? I drank the heat
of your blood into my face and breast, and now I am drinking it
into my loins and buttocks and legs, oh tree! I am drinking your
heat right through me, oh tree! Fire is life, and I take your life for
mine. I am drinking it up, oh tree, even into my buttocks. Aha!
Tree! I am warm! I am strong! I am happy, tree, in this cold night
in the mountains!"

And the old man, glancing up and seeing the flames flapping
in flamy rags at the dark smoke, in the upper fire-hurry towards
the stars and the dark spaces between the stars, sits stonily and
inscrutably: yet one knows that he is saying: "Go back, oh fire! Go
back like honey! Go back, honey of life, to where you came from,
before you were hidden in the tree. The trees climb into the sky
and steal the honey of the sun, like bears stealing from a hollow
tree-trunk. But when the tree falls and is put on to the fire, the
honey flames and goes straight back to where it came from. And

the smell of burning pine is as the smell of honey."

So the old man says, with his lightless Indian eyes. But he is careful never to utter one word of the mystery. Speech is the death of Pan, who can but laugh and sound the reed-flute.

Is it better, I ask you, to cross the room and turn on the heat at the radiator, glancing at the thermometer and saying: "We're just a bit below the level, in here"? Then to go back to the newspaper!

What can a man do with his life but live it? And what does life consist in, save a vivid relatedness between the man and the living universe that surrounds him? Yet man insulates himself more and more into mechanism, and repudiates everything but the machine and the contrivance of which he himself is master, god in the machine.

Morning comes, and white ash lies in the fire-hollow, and the old man looks at it broodingly.

"The fire is gone," he says in the Pan silence, that is so full of unutterable things. "Look! there is no more tree. We drank his warmth, and he is gone. He is way, way off in the sky, his smoke is in the blueness, with the sweet smell of a pine-wood fire, and his yellow flame is in the sun. It is morning, with the ashes of night. There is no more tree. Tree is gone. But perhaps there is fire among the ashes. I shall blow it, and it will be alive. There is always fire, between the tree that goes and the tree that stays. One day I shall go—"

So they cook their meat, and rise, and go in silence.

There is a big rock towering up above the trees, a cliff. And silently a man glances at it. You hear him say, without speech:

"Oh, you big rock! If a man fall down from you, he dies. Don't let me fall down from you. Oh, you big pale rock, you are so still, you know lots of things. You know a lot. Help me, then, with your stillness. I go to find deer. Help me find deer."

And the man slips aside, and secretly lays a twig, or a pebble, some little object in a niche of the rock, as a pact between him and the rock. The rock will give him some of its radiant-cold stillness and enduring presence, and he makes a symbolic return, of gratitude.

Is it foolish? Would it have been better to invent a gun, to shoot his game from a great distance, so that he need not approach it with any of that living stealth and preparedness with which one live thing approaches another? Is it better to have a machine in one's hands, and so avoid the life-contact: the trouble! the pains! Is it better to see the rock as a mere nothing, not worth noticing because it has no value, and you can't eat it as you can a deer?

But the old hunter steals on, in the stillness of the eternal Pan, which is so full of soundless sounds. And in his soul he is saying: "Deer! Oh, you thin-legged deer! I am coming! Where are you, with your feet like little stones bounding down a hill? I know you. Yes, I know you. But you don't know me. You don't know where I am, and you don't know me, anyhow. But I know you. I am thinking of you. I shall get you. I've got to get you. I got to; so it will be.—I shall get you, and shoot an arrow right in you."

In this state of abstraction, and subtle, hunter's communion with the quarry—a weird psychic connexion between hunter and hunted —the man creeps into the mountains.

And even a white man who is a born hunter must fall into this state. Gun or no gun! He projects his deepest, most primitive hunter's consciousness abroad, and finds his game, not by accident, nor even chiefly by looking for signs, but primarily by a psychic attraction, a sort of telepathy: the hunter's telepathy. Then when he finds his quarry, he aims with a pure, spellbound volition. If there is no flaw in his abstracted huntsman's *will*, he cannot miss. Arrow or bullet, it flies like a movement of pure will, straight to the spot. And the deer, once she has let her quivering alertness be overmastered or stilled by the hunter's subtle, hypnotic, *following* spell, she cannot escape.

This is Pan, the Pan-mystery, the Pan-power. What can men who sit at home in their studies, and drink hot milk and have lamb's-wool slippers on their feet, and write anthropology, what *can* they possibly know about men, the men of Pan?

Among the creatures of Pan there is an eternal struggle for life, between lives. Man, defenceless, rapacious man, has needed the qualities of every living thing, at one time or other. The hard, silent abidingness of rock, the surging resistance of a tree, the still evasion of a puma, the dogged earth-knowledge of the bear, the light alert-ness of the deer, the sky-prowling vision of the eagle: turn by turn man has needed the power of every living thing. Tree, stone, or hill, river, or little stream, or waterfall, or salmon in the fall—man can be master and complete in himself, only by assuming the living powers of each of them, as the occasion requires.

He used to make himself master by a great effort of will, and sensitive, intuitive cunning, and immense labour of body.

Then he discovered the "idea." He found that all things were related by certain *laws*. The moment man learned to abstract, he began to make engines that would do the work of his body. So, instead of concentrating upon his quarry, or upon the living things which made his universe, he concentrated upon the engines or instruments which should intervene between him and the living universe, and give him mastery.

This was the death of the great Pan. The idea and the engine came between man and all things, like a death. The old connexion, the old Allness, was severed, and can never be ideally restored. Great Pan is dead.

Yet what do we live for, except to live? Man has lived to conquer the phenomenal universe. To a great extent he has succeeded. With all the mechanism of the human world, man is to a great extent master of all life, and of most phenomena.

And what then? Once you have conquered a thing, you have lost it. Its real relation to you collapses.

A conquered world is no good to man. He sits stupefied with boredom upon his conquest.

We need the universe to live again, so that we can live with it. A conquered universe, a dead Pan, leaves us nothing to live with.

You have to abandon the conquest, before Pan will live again. You have to live to live, not to conquer. What's the good of con-quering even the North Pole, if after the conquest you've nothing left but an inert fact? Better leave it a mystery.

It was better to be a hunter in the woods of Pan, than it is to be a clerk in a city store. The hunter hungered, laboured, suffered

tortures of fatigue. But at least he lived in a ceaseless living relation
to his surrounding universe.

At evening, when the deer was killed, he went home to the tents,
and threw down the deer-meat on the swept place before the tent
of his women. And the women came out to greet him softly, with
a sort of reverence, as he stood before the meat, the life-stuff. He
came back spent, yet full of power, bringing the life-stuff. And the
children looked with black eyes at the meat, and at that wonder-
being, the man, the bringer of meat.

Perhaps the children of the store-clerk look at their father with
a *tiny* bit of the same mystery. And perhaps the clerk feels a fragment of the old glorification, when he hands his wife the paper dollars.

But about the tents the women move silently. Then when the
cooking-fire dies low, the man crouches in silence and toasts meat
on a stick, while the dogs lurk round like shadows and the children
watch avidly. The man eats as the sun goes down. And as the
glitter departs, he says: "Lo, the sun is going, and I stay. All goes,
but still I stay. Power of deer-meat is in my belly, power of sun
is in my body. I am tired, but it is with power. There the small
moon gives her first sharp sign. So! So! I watch her. I will give her
something; she is very sharp and bright, and I do not know her
power. Lo! I will give the woman something for this moon, which
troubles me above the sunset, and has power. Lo! how very curved
and sharp she is! Lo! how she troubles me!"

Thus, always aware, always watchful, subtly poising himself in
the world of Pan, among the powers of the living universe, he sus-
stains his life and is sustained. There is no boredom, because *everything* is alive and active, and danger is inherent in all movement.
The contact between all things is keen and wary: for wariness is
also a sort of reverence, or respect. And nothing, in the world of
Pan, may be taken for granted.

So when the fire is extinguished, and the moon sinks, the man
says to the woman: "Oh, woman, be very soft, be very soft and
deep towards me, with the deep silence. Oh, woman, do not speak
and stir and wound me with the sharp horns of yourself. Let me

come into the deep, soft places, the dark, soft places deep as between the stars. Oh, let me lose there the weariness of the day:
let me come in the power of the night. Oh, do not speak to me, nor
break the deep night of my silence and my power. Be softer than
dust, and darker than any flower. Oh, woman, wonderful is the
craft of your softness, the distance of your dark depths. Oh, open
silently the deep that has no end, and do not turn the horns of the
moon against me."

This is the might of Pan, and the power of Pan.

And still, in America, among the Indians, the oldest Pan is alive.
But here, also, dying fast.

It is useless to glorify the savage. For he will kill Pan with his
own hands, for the sake of a motor-car. And a bored savage, for
whom Pan is dead, is the stupefied image of all boredom.

And we cannot return to the primitive life, to live in tepees and
hunt with bows and arrows.

Yet live we must. And once life has been conquered, it is pretty
difficult to live. What are we going to do, with a conquered universe? The Pan relationship, which the world of man once had
with all the world, was better than anything man has now. The
savage, today, if you give him the chance, will become more mechanical and unliving than any civilized man. But civilized man, having
conquered the universe, may as well leave off bossing it. Because,
when all is said and done, life itself consists in a live relatedness
between man and his universe: sun, moon, stars, earth, trees,
flowers, birds, animals, men, everything—and not in a "conquest"
of anything by anything. Even the conquest of the air makes the
world smaller, tighter, and more airless.

And whether we are a store-clerk or a bus-conductor, we can
still choose between the living universe of Pan, and the mechanical
conquered universe of modern humanity. The machine has no
windows. But even the most mechanized human being has only got
his windows nailed up, or bricked in.

WHY THE NOVEL MATTERS

WE HAVE curious ideas of ourselves. We think of ourselves as a body with a spirit in it, or a body with a soul in it, or a body with a mind in it. *Mens sana in corpore sano*. The years drink up the wine, and at last throw the bottle away, the body, of course, being the bottle.

It is a funny sort of superstition. Why should I look at my hand, as it so cleverly writes these words, and decide that it is a mere nothing compared to the mind that directs it? Is there really any huge difference between my hand and my brain? Or my mind? My hand is alive, it flickers with a life of its own. It meets all the strange universe in touch, and learns a vast number of things, and knows a vast number of things. My hand, as it writes these words, slips gaily along, jumps like a grasshopper to dot an *i*, feels the table rather cold, gets a little bored if I write too long, has its own rudiments of thought, and is just as much *me* as is my brain, my mind, or my soul. Why should I imagine that there is a *me* which is more *me* than my hand is? Since my hand is absolutely alive, me alive.

Whereas, of course, as far as I am concerned, my pen isn't alive at all. My pen *isn't* me alive. Me alive ends at my finger-tips.

Whatever is me alive is me. Every tiny bit of my hands is alive, every little freckle and hair and fold of skin. And whatever is me alive is me. Only my finger-nails, those ten little weapons between me and an inanimate universe, they cross the mysterious Rubicon between me alive and things like my pen, which are not alive, in my own sense.

So, seeing my hand is all alive, and me alive, wherein is it just a bottle, or a jug, or a tin can, or a vessel of clay, or any of the rest of that nonsense? True, if I cut it it will bleed, like a can of cherries. But then the skin that is cut, and the veins that bleed, and the bones that should never be seen, they are all just as alive as the blood that flows. So the tin can business, or vessel of clay, is just bunk.

And that's what you learn, when you're a novelist. And that's what you are very liable *not* to know, if you're a parson, or a philosopher, or a scientist, or a stupid person. If you're a parson, you talk about souls in heaven. If you're a novelist, you know that paradise is in the palm of your hand, and on the end of your nose, because both are alive; and alive, and man alive, which is more than you can say, for certain, of paradise. Paradise is after life, and I for one am not keen on anything that is *after* life. If you are a philosopher, you talk about infinity, and the pure spirit which knows all things. But if you pick up a novel, you realize immediately that infinity is just a handle to this self-same jug of a body of mine; while as for knowing, if I find my finger in the fire, I know that fire burns, with a knowledge so emphatic and vital, it leaves Nirvana merely a conjecture. Oh, yes, my body, me alive, *knows*, and knows intensely. And as for the sum of all knowledge, it can't be anything more than an accumulation of all the things I know in the body, and you, dear reader, know in the body.

These damned philosophers, they talk as if they suddenly went off in steam, and were then much more important than they are when they're in their shirts. It is nonsense. Every man, philosopher included, ends in his own finger-tips. That's the end of his man alive. As for the words and thoughts and sighs and aspirations that fly from him, they are so many tremulations in the ether, and not alive at all. But if the tremulations reach another man alive, he may receive them into his life, and his life may take on a new colour, like a chameleon creeping from a brown rock on to a green leaf. All very well and good. It still doesn't alter the fact that the so-called spirit, the message or teaching of the philosopher or the saint, isn't alive at all, but just a tremulation upon the ether, like a radio message. All this spirit stuff is just tremulations upon the ether. If you, as man alive, quiver from the tremulation of the ether into new life, that is because you are man alive, and you take sustenance and stimulation into your alive man in a myriad ways. But to say that the message, or the spirit which is communicated to you, is more important than your living body, is nonsense. You might as well say that the potato at dinner was more important.

Nothing is important but life. And for myself, I can absolutely see life nowhere but in the living. Life with a capital L is only man alive. Even a cabbage in the rain is cabbage alive. All things that are alive are amazing. And all things that are dead are subsidiary to the living. Better a live dog than a dead lion. But better a live lion than a live dog. *C'est la vie!*

It seems impossible to get a saint, or a philosopher, or a scientist, to stick to this simple truth. They are all, in a sense, renegades. The saint wishes to offer himself up as spiritual food for the multitude. Even Francis of Assisi turns himself into a sort of angel-cake, of which anyone may take a slice. But an angel-cake is rather less than man alive. And poor St. Francis might well apologize to his body, when he is dying: "Oh, pardon me, my body, the wrong I did you through the years!" It was no wafer, for others to eat.

The philosopher, on the other hand, because he can think, decides that nothing but thoughts matter. It is as if a rabbit, because he can make little pills, should decide that nothing but little pills matter. As for the scientist, he has absolutely no use for me so long as I am man alive. To the scientist, I am dead. He puts under the microscope a bit of dead me, and calls it me. He takes me to pieces, and says first one piece, and then another piece, is me. My heart, my liver, my stomach have all been scientifically me, according to the scientist; and nowadays I am either a brain, or nerves, or glands, or something more up-to-date in the tissue line.

Now I absolutely flatly deny that I am a soul, or a body, or a mind, or an intelligence, or a brain, or a nervous system, or a bunch of glands, or any of the rest of these bits of me. The whole is greater than the part. And therefore, I, who am man alive, am greater than my soul, or spirit, or body, or mind, or consciousness, or anything else that is merely a part of me. I am a man, and alive. I am man alive, and as long as I can, I intend to go on being man alive.

For this reason I am a novelist. And being a novelist, I consider myself superior to the saint, the scientist, the philosopher, and the poet, who are all great masters of different bits of man alive, but never get the whole hog.

The novel is the one bright book of life. Books are not life. They are only tremulations on the ether. But the novel as a tremulation can make the whole man alive tremble. Which is more than poetry, philosophy, science, or any other book-tremulation can do.

The novel is the book of life. In this sense, the Bible is a great confused novel. You may say, it is about God. But it is really about man alive. Adam, Eve, Sarai, Abraham, Isaac, Jacob, Samuel, David, Bath-Sheba, Ruth, Esther, Solomon, Job, Isaiah, Jesus, Mark, Judas, Paul, Peter: what is it but man alive, from start to finish? Man alive, not mere bits. Even the Lord is another man alive, in a burning bush, throwing the tablets of stone at Moses's head.

I do hope you begin to get my idea, why the novel is supremely important, as a tremulation on the ether. Plato makes the perfect ideal being tremble in me. But that's only a bit of me. Perfection is only a bit, in the strange make-up of man alive. The Sermon on the Mount makes the selfless spirit of me quiver. But that, too, is only a bit of me. The Ten Commandments set the old Adam shivering in me, warning me that I am a thief and a murderer, unless I watch it. But even the old Adam is only a bit of me.

I very much like all these bits of me to be set trembling with life and the wisdom of life. But I do ask that the whole of me shall tremble in its wholeness, some time or other.

And this, of course, must happen in me, living.

But as far as it can happen from a communication, it can only happen when a whole novel communicates itself to me. The Bible— but *all* the Bible—and Homer, and Shakespeare: these are the supreme old novels. These are all things to all men. Which means that in their wholeness they affect the whole man alive, which is the man himself, beyond any part of him. They set the whole tree trembling with a new access of life, they do not just stimulate growth in one direction.

I don't want to grow in any one direction any more. And, if I can help it, I don't want to stimulate anybody else into some particular direction. A particular direction ends in a *cul-de-sac*. We're in a *cul-de-sac* at present.

I don't believe in any dazzling revelation, or in any supreme Word. "The grass withereth, the flower fadeth, but the Word of the Lord shall stand for ever." That's the kind of stuff we've drugged ourselves with. As a matter of fact, the grass withereth, but comes up all the greener for that reason, after the rains. The flower fadeth, and therefore the bud opens. But the Word of the Lord, being man-uttered and a mere vibration on the ether, becomes staler and staler, more and more boring, till at last we turn a deaf ear and it ceases to exist, far more finally than any withered grass. It is grass that renews its youth like the eagle, not any Word.

We should ask for no absolutes, or absolute. Once and for all and for ever, let us have done with the ugly imperialism of any absolute. There is no absolute good, there is nothing absolutely right. All things flow and change, and even change is not absolute. The whole is a strange assembly of apparently incongruous parts, slipping past one another.

Me, man alive, I am a very curious assembly of incongruous parts. My yea! of today is oddly different from my yea! of yesterday. My tears of tomorrow will have nothing to do with my tears of a year ago. If the one I love remains unchanged and unchanging, I shall cease to love her. It is only because she changes and startles me into change and defies my inertia, and is herself staggered in her inertia by my changing, that I can continue to love her. If she stayed put, I might as well love the pepper-pot.

In all this change, I maintain a certain integrity. But woe betide me if I try to put my finger on it. If I say of myself, I am this, I am that!—then, if I stick to it, I turn into a stupid fixed thing like a lamp-post. I shall never know wherein lies my integrity, my individuality, my me. I *can* never know it. It is useless to talk about my ego. That only means that I have made up an *idea* of myself, and that I am trying to cut myself out to pattern. Which is no good. You can cut your cloth to fit your coat, but you can't clip bits off your living body, to trim it down to your idea. True, you can put yourself into ideal corsets. But even in ideal corsets, fashions change.

Let us learn from the novel. In the novel, the characters can do nothing but *live*. If they keep on being good, according to pattern, or bad, according to pattern, or even volatile, according to pattern, they cease to live, and the novel falls dead. A character in a novel has got to live, or it is nothing.

We, likewise, in life have got to live, or we are nothing.

What we mean by living is, of course, just as indescribable as what we mean by *being*. Men get ideas into their heads, of what they mean by Life, and they proceed to cut life out to pattern. Sometimes they go into the desert to seek God, sometimes they go into the desert to seek cash, sometimes it is wine, woman, and song, and again it is water, political reform, and votes. You never know what it will be next: from killing your neighbour with hideous bombs and gas that tears the lungs, to supporting a Foundlings Home and preaching infinite Love, and being co-respondent in a divorce.

In all this wild welter, we need some sort of guide. It's no good inventing Thou Shalt Nots!

What then? Turn truly, honourably to the novel, and see wherein you are man alive, and wherein you are dead man in life. You may love a woman as man alive, and you may be making love to a woman as sheer dead man in life. You may eat your dinner as man alive, or as a mere masticating corpse. As man alive you may have a shot at your enemy. But as a ghastly simulacrum of life you may be firing bombs into men who are neither your enemies nor your friends, but just things you are dead to. Which is criminal, when the things happen to be alive.

To be alive, to be man alive, to be whole man alive: that is the point. And at its best, the novel, and the novel supremely, can help you. It can help you not to be dead man in life. So much of a man walks about dead and a carcass in the street and house, today: so much of women is merely dead. Like a pianoforte with half the notes mute.

But in the novel you can see, plainly, when the man goes dead, the woman goes inert. You can develop an instinct for life, if you will, instead of a theory of right and wrong, good and bad.

In life, there is right and wrong, good and bad, all the time. But what is right in one case is wrong in another. And in the novel you see one man becoming a corpse, because of his so-called goodness, another going dead because of his so-called wickedness. Right and wrong is an instinct: but an instinct of the whole consciousness in a man, bodily, mental, spiritual at once. And only in the novel are *all* things given full play, or at least, they may be given full play, when we realize that life itself, and not inert safety, is the reason for living. For out of the full play of all things emerges the only thing that is anything, the wholeness of a man, the wholeness of a woman, man alive, and live woman.

EDMUND WILSON

Photo: Sylvia Salmi

Edmund Wilson was born on May 8, 1895, in Red Bank, New Jersey. For several generations his forebears had been moderately prosperous as doctors, lawyers, and ministers, and there was a tradition in the family of high ideals and dedicated public service that stretched back to the eighteenth century. By the 1870's, however, such idealism only served to alienate them from the channels in which they might have been able to operate effectively, and it was Edmund Wilson's observation of this dilemma—the failure of his father's generation to achieve the aims they had set out with—that motivated much of his thought both as a social critic and literary journalist. As a writer his role would not be primarily that of a creative artist but a critic—a kind of envoy of taste and moral freedom—in the service of social and cultural change.

That Edmund Wilson was serious-minded was evident even in his youth. According to one story, his parents once tried to lure him away from his books and toward the more normal occupations of boys by presenting him with a complete baseball outfit. However, upon arriving at the ball field, he immediately gave it away and sat down under a tree with a book. And it is this quality of his nature— the asceticism of the "grind" or "bookworm"—that characterized Wilson ever since. (He taught himself many languages in order to read the literature in those languages.) At Princeton he was "the shy little scholar of Holder Court," according to his friend F. Scott Fitzgerald. He rode an English bicycle, edited the *Nassau Literary Magazine,* and had friends among the faculty, notably Christian Gauss. But he also made lasting friendships with Fitzgerald and John Peale Bishop, and to them, as to few afterwards, he was known affectionately as "Bunny."

After his graduation in 1916, Wilson worked for a year as a reporter on the New York *Evening Sun* and shared an apartment with three other young men. But when America entered the war, he enlisted, "Not because I cared much about the war, but because— aside from social pressure—I wanted to get away from my old life." For the next eighteen months he served as a private at Base Hospital

36 and with the Intelligence Corps in France. (Wilson's journals from those years are printed in *A Prelude,* published in 1967.) Although he hated army life, he considered his relationships with other people less superficial than they had been in school, and it was during this period that he determined the direction his life was to take in the future: "One day in France, sick in bed, I swore to myself that when the war was over I should stand outside society altogether. I should do without the comforts and amenities of the conventional world altogether, and I should devote myself to the great human interests which transcend standards of living and convention: Literature, History, the Creation of Beauty, the Discovery of Truth."

Upon returning to New York, however, he temporarily put aside these noble ambitions to become managing editor of *Vanity Fair.* Although he left after a year to devote his full time to writing, nothing that Wilson did over the next eight years was to prepare one for his achievements of the 1930's and since. He published four books, including his only novel, *I Thought of Daisy* (1929), and he wrote some interesting book reviews for *The New Republic* (for which he was literary editor from 1926 to 1931). But for the most part it was rather lightweight stuff, not "the Creation of Beauty, the Discovery of Truth."

But then came the stock market crash of 1929 and the Depression, and suddenly Wilson found himself with the social conditions that his heritage, in a roundabout way, had prepared him for: at last the idealist of eighteenth-century American republicanism could settle down to serious work. As a reporter for *The New Republic* he went to observe the poor and unemployed wherever they were: in the coal fields of West Virginia and the textile mills of New England, in the Negro ghettos of Chicago, and at the construction site of the Hoover Dam in Nevada. The articles he sent back were brilliant—and remain the best reporting that we have on the Depression years (collected in *The American Earthquake*)—but the spectacle he witnessed did more than serve as a vehicle for the demonstration of his talents as a writer. The plight of the unemployed stirred him deeply. Becoming more and more disenchanted with the possibility that the capitalist system could right itself,

Wilson, along with many other idealistic intellectuals of that period, began to look in the direction of communism as the only way out. Finally, in 1935, he went to Russia to see at first hand how it was actually working. Although the book that contains the record of that trip, *Travels in Two Democracies* (1936), concludes with the assertion that the Soviet Union is the "moral top of the world," nevertheless there are signs throughout it that Utopia had not quite come up to his expectations. With the Stalinist purges of the late thirties, Wilson's flirtations with communism came to an end. He closes *To the Finland Station* (1940), his study of the growth of communism, with the declaration that in the hands of Lenin's successors the philosophic basis of Marxist socialism had become thoroughly debased.

All through this period of social-political engagement, Wilson was also writing essays on literary subjects, mainly with the aim of introducing to American readers the major European writers of the twentieth century. Collected in three volumes—*Axel's Castle* (1931), *The Triple Thinkers* (1938), and *The Wound and the Bow* (1941) —the best of these essays are outstanding illustrations of the use of biographical material and psychological insight in revealing the meanings of a writer's works. Moreover, they were written with such style and vitality that they quickly established Wilson's reputation as our most prominent nonacademic critic. Like Johnson and Hazlitt in earlier centuries, and like Virginia Woolf, E. M. Forster, and Aldous Huxley in our own, Wilson thought of himself as a literary journalist, and thus kept clear of the more pedantic exercises of the scholarly journals. From the forties on, most of his literary criticism appeared in *The New Yorker*.

Edmund Wilson wrote on a great variety of subjects, ranging from the Dead Sea Scrolls to the income tax. Indeed, he wrote on everything that interested him. He wrote a defense of the property rights of the Iroquois Indians, and a book of short stories, *Memoirs of Hecate County,* that was banned for being pornographic. He wrote plays, poems, travel books, and diaries. In 1962, at the age of 67, he published his last major work, *Patriotic Gore*, a study of American literature during the period of the Civil War. After that—except for

well-publicized literary skirmishes with Vladimir Nabokov and the
Modern Language Association—Wilson withdrew further and further
from the changes he saw occurring in the America of the mid-sixties.
In 1970 he wrote the misanthropic "Epilogue" to his final book,
Upstate, and on June 12, 1972, Edmund Wilson died in Talcottville,
New York, in the old stone house he had visited as a boy and had
finally come to look upon as his last refuge from the barbarism and
uniformity of modern culture.

BURLESQUE SHOWS

THERE IS a rumor that the National Winter Garden Burlesque has fallen a victim to the current purity wave and been obliged to abate the Aristophanic license for which it was formerly celebrated. The management of the National Winter Garden (not the Broadway Winter Garden, of course, but the one at Second Avenue and Houston Street) has been kind enough to supply the *New Republic* with a season pass, and, as the result of a recent visit, the writer of these notes is happy to announce that this report is entirely without foundation and to recommend the Minsky Brothers' Follies as still among the most satisfactory shows in town. The great thing about the National Winter Garden is that, though admittedly as vulgar as possible, it has nothing of the peculiar smartness and hardness one is accustomed to elsewhere in New York. It is refreshing because it lies quite outside the mechanical routine of Broadway. Though more ribald, it is more honest and less self-conscious than the ordinary risqué farce and, though crude, on the whole more attractive than most of the hideous comic-supplement humors of uptown revue and vaudeville. Nor is it to be confounded with the uptown burlesque show of the type of the Columbia, which is now as wholesome and as boring as any expensive musical comedy. The National Winter Garden has a tradition and a vein of its own.

For one thing, the Minsky Brothers go in for a kind of beauty which has long passed out of fashion elsewhere. The National Winter Garden has no use for the slim legs and shallow breasts the modern American taste for which has been so successfully exploited by Ziegfeld and the other uptown producers. Save for their bobbed hair and modern shoes, the chorus at the National Winter Garden might have come out of the pictures of Casino girls in old *Munsey's Magazines* of the nineties. And the humor of the National Winter

Garden differs, also, from the humor of other shows. It mainly consists of gags, to be sure, but they are not the gags you are used to.
For all their violence, the comic interludes have a certain freshness
and wit. In the current version of *Anthony and Cleopatra,* a perennial
Minsky classic, Julius Caesar, in a tin helmet and smoking a big
cigar, catches Anthony (the Jewish comic) on a divan with Cleopatra
(the principal strip-tease girl) and wallops him over the bottom with
the flat of an enormous sword. "I'm dying! I'm dying!" groans Anthony, as he staggers around in a circle; and Caesar and Cleopatra,
the Roman soldiers and the Egyptian slave-girls break into a rousing
shimmy to the refrain of "He's dying! He's dying!" "I hear de
voices of de angels!" says Anthony. "What do they say?" asks Caesar.
"I don't know: I don't speak Polish." He is groggy; he totters; he
faints. "I hear de cockroaches calling me!" he cries; and from the
orchestra sounds, acrid and sinister, the cry of the expectant roaches.
"Bring me the wassup," say Cleopatra, and her slave-girl, kneeling,
presents a box, from which Cleopatra takes a huge property phallus.
(At some point in the development of the ancient act, the word *asp*
was evidently confused with *wasp.*) It is impossible to report in these
pages all the incidents of the series that follow. Cleopatra falls prone
on her lover's body, and Caesar, with pathetic reverence, places on her
posterior a wreath, which he waters with a watering-pot. Charmian
and Britannicus, after some play of their own with the wassup,
finally fall lifeless, too, the girl as she flops on the soldier exploding a
toy balloon which he has been wearing as a false chest. This curious
piece of East Side folk-drama has been popular at Minsky's for years,
and it is always a little different. Sometimes Caesar makes his entrance on a bicycle, blowing his own bugle; sometimes his entrance
is heralded by a flourish of trumpets from the orchestra, as the company lines up and looks out the wings: Caesar enters from the other
direction and gooses the last man, so that the whole row fall down
like dominoes. There is also a remarkable gallows skit, which begins
as an affecting piece of realism and ends as a low joke.

The orchestra at the National Winter Garden is energetic even
in summer. The girls are not only robust but take a certain jolly
interest in the show and sometimes betray their roles by laughing

inappropriately at the jokes. The audience are keenly appreciative, and the house peals with easy thunder more infectious than the punctual crashes uptown. The theater, at the top of an office building, is very well ventilated; and just now you can see through an open exit the foothills of the downtown buildings against a pale lilac-gray sky. After the show, you can walk down the fire-escape.

The most celebrated performer of the National Winter Garden was a Yiddish comedian named Jack Shargel, who has now retired from the stage. To these raw buffooneries he is said to have brought a touch of the wistfulness of a Lew Fields or a Charlie Chaplin. A connoisseur of the theater in its best days has described to me a scene in which Jack Shargel received a rose from a beautiful lady just going off the stage. He kissed it, he smelt it in ecstasy, then, with a graceful and infinitely tender gesture, he stretched out his hand and tossed it away: it fell with a crash of glass.

COMMUNISTS AND COPS

THE COMMUNISTS have announced their intention of leading a "hunger march" on January 20. The city administration has agreed to receive a delegation at City Hall, but has not unreasonably refused a request to allow the Communists to make speeches from the steps.

In consequence, from ten o'clock on, a cordon of two hundred policemen are on guard around City Hall and the little park in front of it. You cannot get anywhere near the building without running the gauntlet of the cops and presenting unimpeachable credentials. It is like some scene on an old-fashioned German parade ground. The only human figures in the park are the immobile policemen, equestrian and on foot, with their blue coats and flat blue military caps, and the great snow-white booby Civic Virtue, with his thick trunk and sulky Irish face, trampling on confused female bodies.

At one o'clock promptly, the Communists arrive to the number of about 2,000, and the demonstration begins. The demonstrators deliver speeches and march around City Hall Park. A good many of them are Jews and some are Negroes—mostly small scrubby zealous people wearing red neckties, red hats or red dresses. A good many of the women have glasses. They have also succeeded in recruiting from the breadlines and employment agencies a considerable number of seedy men, to whom they have held out the hope that the authorities may be induced to provide unemployment insurance. They carry placards: "We Want No Charity," "No Evictions for the Unemployed," "We Demand Armories and Public Buildings for the Unemployed." They concentrate at the foot of the park opposite the Federal Building, and speakers get up on the iron dustbins. A crowd gathers—the newspaper photographers climb onto the roofs of the Coca-Cola and orange-drink stands and dominate the scene with their cameras.

The first speaker is a young Negro named Newton, the editor of the Communist Negro paper and secretary of the League of Struggle for Negro Rights, who was one of the Communists arrested last May in Atlanta for circulating radical leaflets. He was threatened with the death penalty under an ancient law which was originally intended as a weapon for dealing with rebellious slaves. Newton had never been in the South before: he is an educated Negro from Boston. Some years ago, while working in a hotel, he got a two-week vacation and arranged to go to a Y.M.C.A. camp; but when he arrived there, they wouldn't have him and gave him his money back. Later on, he met a Negro Communist, who told him that the Communists were working to abolish race discrimination, and he joined the Communist party. He is a good-looking fellow, with large sensitive dark eyes, skin closer to coffee than to mahogany and a thick but straight and rather unnegroid nose. He is joined almost immediately by other speakers, among them a Negro of a quite different type, blacker, with a round face and an old soft hat, whose voice sounds falsetto above the rest. Speaker after speaker leaps onto the dustbin till there is only a babel of yelling—then speechmaking is given up. The group on the dustbin begins rousing the crowd with methods like those of a college cheerleader—"We—want—*work-or wages!* We—want—*work-or wages!*" The harsh fanatical rhythm goes on and on—the people in the crowd get caught up into it and begin to shout with the leaders.

The street has become packed and impassable, and now the crowd is jamming the road. The taxis and the mail trucks cannot get by, and the police decide to break things up. Coming behind the speakers' stand, they push the people along the sidewalk. "Oh-oh!" exclaims a gaping bystander. "He's hittin' 'em on the head." From the road a mounted policeman starts out to ride into the crowd. As he does so, he screws up one side of his mouth: he is a clean-cut young fellow with his mind on holding in his horse. He scarcely does more than turn its head in the direction of the overthronged sidewalk and make a pretense of riding into it. "That's right!—go after 'em!" a young man among the bystanders eggs him on.

The crowd becomes liquefied and begins to move. A nice-looking boy about ten in an old red-plaid Mackinaw—Comrade Charley, a Young Pioneer, who lives in Brighton Beach—shouts from above people's heads with a voice that sounds strangely fresh and live amid the systematic yelling of the grown-ups. He is carried aloft on the shoulders of an exceedingly tall Negro, another worker in the League of Struggle for Negro Rights, who has recently served a sentence of three months for breaking up an anti-lynching meeting of the Pullman porters' association. The Pullman porters' association are Socialists, but, according to the Negro Communists, keep on the right side of white respectability and have been guilty of suppressing the evidence in connection with the lynching of a porter in Georgia.

The demonstration pushes slowly around the park. "Aw that's a lotta crap!" yells one of the spectators. "Oh, yeah?" retorts a fierce little Communist. "What the hell do you know about it?" "We want bread!" another shouts. "Try and get it!" somebody answers. A shabby elderly Jew, who speaks English very thickly, is handing out leaflets on unemployment insurance and repeating conscientiously again and again: "Dis has got to become a law vedder de bosses like it or not!"

The police watch behind iron posts that protect City Hall from the traffic. Some are Negroes brought down from Harlem, who have almost the same Prussian stature, the same square faces and mail-slot mouths as their white fellow officers. The policemen seem to fall into two classes: the husky good-natured kind who accomplish their disciplinary duties with conviction but without ferocity, and the stupid staring-eyed type frankly hired as mobilizable brutes. Some of these are evidently Jews, especially provided like the Negroes to deal with agitators of their own race. In any case, the police offer a curious contrast to everybody else present: if the Communists mostly look stunted, the office workers out for lunch are hardly more prepossessing; and the policemen seem the only healthy full-sized people and the only people decently dressed in these choked-up streets of milling human beings, bewildered or determined or half-scared or angry at being delayed, but all alike looking undersized, undernourished, dingy-featured, drearily dressed.

Only when the Communists sing one of their songs—*Solidarity*

Forever or *The International*—does any note arise from among them of enthusiasm or human warmth.

> *It's the final conflict!*
> *Let each stand in his place!*
> *The International Soviet*
> *Shall be the human race!*

The bald words, the banal tune, by reason of all they have been coming to mean, do lift up the heart for a moment as the Communists raise their arms and wave them in time to the refrain.

All around them under the gray winter sky rise the high ugly walls of downtown New York, keeping the marchers, the crowd and the traffic crammed into the tight little space still left between the impregnably guarded park and the dense concentration of buildings: the men's wear shops, Schrafft's soda fountains, Liggett's drug-stores and cafeterias of Nassau Street and Broadway; the World Building with its rusty green dome, the red brick with green trimmings of the Sun Building, standing narrow and perpendicular like the fragments of some incomplete structure; a corner with cheap chop-suey signs over cheap investment-loan signs, a brick office building from whose flat cold red every suggestion of genuine color seems to have faded out past hope of revival by the sun; the somewhat handsomer high gray cliff of the Woolworth Building, eroded and lined like a giant butte and diminishing in tiers toward the top; the lower Federal Building, with its squashed-down, square-sided dome and its spotting of portholes like moles above a bulk of gray machine-made public dignity.

In this cramped and inhospitable area, the Communists produce simply confusion—a confusion which gets worse and worse. From the other side of the park, a woman's dreadful scream is heard.

In the meantime, at City Hall, to which it has been escorted by cops, a delegation is presenting demands. Mayor Walker is said to be ill—according to the Communists, afraid to face them—and they are received by the affable Mr. Kerrigan.

F. G. Biedenkapp, who acts as the spokesman, demands unemployment insurance; free gas, electricity and coal, no evictions for the unemployed, and free clothing and food for their children; reduced rents; the throwing open of vacant apartments and public buildings, and the use of schools and public halls for meeting places; the distribution of unemployment relief through a board composed entirely of workers and Communists, which shall also take over all the employment-agency work now being done by the State Labor Department, the Y.M.C.A. and all other organizations; no discrimination among workers on account of race, color, nationality or sex; and the immediate release of comrades who have been jailed in connection with previous demonstrations.

To this Mr. Kerrigan replies that "the city is constituted according to law, and a number of your demands would be illegal if carried out," that "if the city officials tried to carry them out they would be immediately removed," that the city officials are contributing out of their salaries for unemployment relief, that the city employment fund is to be increased, that the city is going to try to bring pressure to bear at Albany to amend the law in such a way as to make it possible to stop evictions, that the city has set up a free employment agency which will have the effect of suppressing private agencies and eliminating "the deception and dishonesty practised by some of them," that the Board of Education is already doing what it can to feed the children of the unemployed.

"I don't want to say," he concludes, "that if you don't like it here, you can go back to Russia, because many of you were born here—but I will say that I will pay the full fare, one way, of any ten of you who want to go there. That is about all we can do under the present system." F. G. Biedenkapp, in reply to this, declares the committee "entirely dissatisfied" with Mr. Kerrigan's "explanations and excuses"—and the Communists, under escort, withdraw.

Once outside, they make haste to climb onto the statue of Benjamin Franklin in front of the Sun Building. They shout that their demands have been refused: "We saw the acting mayor and told him our demands and he said that it was against the law to grant them. The unemployed workers must change the laws!"

This is a signal for the demonstration to swarm. They hang their placards all over the statue. Franklin stands with a discolored green bronze crown, one hand stretched out to the world as if in patriarchal blessing and at his feet some large funeral wreaths, presented by the Sons of the American Revolution. Comrade Charley, full of pep in his red Mackinaw, climbs up on the great bourgeois's shoulders and displays a placard: "Free Food for Our Children!" A crowd gathers on the opposite curbs. The statue is situated on a little lozenge of pavement between Nassau Street and Park Row, in such a way that any disturbance around it will cause a maximum jam of the traffic to and from Brooklyn Bridge: the Communists have picked a strategic point for obstructing the downtown life of the city. Taxis bawl and streetcars clang—curious office workers overflow the sidewalks, asking one another what is going on. Somebody in the Sun Building, from a high-up floor, drops a paper-bag full of water over the massed swarm around the statue. The bag comes apart in the air, and people watch the falling whirl of water.

The police decide at last to put an end to the demonstration. They force their way into the crowd and start pulling down the placards and speakers. An unintelligible mêlée ensues. The Communists flee before the police, and the by-standers get mixed up with them. One has a glimpse of a last indomitable speaker with a wild livid crazy face still vituperating alone on the statue—he has vanished a second later. People suddenly yell: "Look out!" Mounted cops begin galloping along the sidewalks, and everybody runs before them, demonstrators and innocent pedestrians alike. A Communist, grabbing apples from an unemployed apple-vendor, bombards the policemen with them and then crowns one of the horses with the crate. Another seizes a horse by the tail—a detective clutches him by the collar and beats him—two women rush to his rescue and almost pull the policeman off his horse. The traffic is impatient; the spectators dismayed; the unemployed have scattered like leaves.

The Communists rally, shouting "Close up ranks!", and rush up the entrance of the flat raised tunnel which leads to the Brooklyn Bridge subway, completely taking possession of the wide flight of steps and booing and hooting the police as if from baseball bleachers.

The police stretch a rope along the back of the park and excitedly patrol the paths. At one stop, quite remote from the disturbance, there is a shoe-shining stand with a row of men peacefully sitting in the chairs and reading the tabloids as they have their shoes shined—but at the sudden appearance of the charging police, they all spring out of their seats simultaneously and leap over the iron fence. A gray flight of pigeons rises from the park, the only free living things in sight.

Now the Communists are routed from the bridge entrance. Some are chased under the monumental, the more than Roman, arches of the Municipal Building—they lurk there awhile and then return. Others, retreating down Center Street, return to the battle through Elm.

A patrol wagon and an ambulance arrive, a stretcher is carried out of City Hall. You read the next morning in the papers that the demonstrators have had their arms broken, their skulls fractured, their teeth knocked out; an auditor from the Comptroller's office has had his head cut open against the Municipal Building; a policeman, who fell into the hands of the demonstrators and got kicked in the stomach by them, is in the hospital with internal injuries.

The Communists are shouting, "We want bread, not horses' hoofs!" and trying to rally around speakers on the curbs. But the speakers get dislodged, the groups dwindle. Among the passers-by behind the park, a small plump sharp-beaked Jewish woman in red— great wrath in a tiny body, like one of Virgil's bees—is wandering by herself and screaming, "Down with the police!"

At the corner of Centre Street, a dingy little man who is walking by, pauses as a spattering on the sidewalk turns out to be too thick, too red and too profuse for spit. He says in a foolish way to nobody in particular, with a mixture of surprise and awe: "Blood!"

Now the streets are completely cleared—the great suction pumps of downtown New York have pulled up their populations again. The people are coming out of the subway unimpeded, going up the steps to Brooklyn Bridge—the taxis are on their way down to Wall Street, the trucks on their way to the docks. The pretzel man with his basket and the roast-chestnut man have come out again. The battle has been obliterated. No one passing has ever heard of it. Many of the people who witnessed it or in some way became involved in it never even knew what it was about. They are neither sympathetic with the Communists nor particularly indignant with them—they are not even particularly angry at having been chased by the police. They feel no real stake in the city in the sense of its being their community, and they consequently take very little interest in abuses of administration which do not vitally affect themselves. If they have jobs in these hard times, they are glad enough to hang on to them, without worrying about the unemployed. And they have all long ago gone about their business.

[1933]

THE OLD STONE HOUSE

As I go north for the first time in years, in the slow, the constantly stopping, milk train—which carries passengers only in the back part of the hind car and has an old stove to heat it in winter—I look out through the dirt-yellowed double pane and remember how once, as a child, I used to feel thwarted in summer till I had got the windows open and there was nothing between me and the widening pastures, the great boulders, the black and white cattle, the rivers, stony and thin, the lone elms like feather-dusters, the high air which sharpens all outlines, makes all colors so breathtakingly vivid, in the clear light of late afternoon.

The little stations again: Barnevald, Stittville, Steuben—a tribute to the Prussian general who helped drill our troops for the Revolution. The woman behind me in the train talks to the conductor with a German accent. They came over here for land and freedom.

Boonville: that pale boxlike building, smooth gray, with three floors of slots that look in on darkness and a roof like a flat overlapping lid—cold dark clear air, fresh water. Like nothing else but upstate New York. Rivers that run quick among stones, or, deeper, stained dark with dead leaves. I used to love to follow them—should still. A fresh breath of water off the Black River, where the blue closed gentians grow. Those forests, those boulder-strewn pastures, those fabulous distant falls!

There was never any train to Talcottville. Our house was the center of the town. It is strange to get back to this now: it seems not quite like anything else that I have ever known. But is this merely the apparent uniqueness of places associated with childhood?

The settlers of this part of New York were a first westward migration from New England. At the end of the eighteenth century, they drove ox-teams from Connecticut and Massachusetts over into the wild northern country below Lake Ontario and the St. Lawrence River, and they established here an extension of New England.

Yet an extension that was already something new. I happened last week to be in Ipswich, Mass., the town from which one branch of my family came; and, for all the New England pride of white houses and green blinds, I was oppressed by the ancient crampedness. Even the House of the Seven Gables, which stimulated the imagination of Hawthorne, though it is grim perhaps, is not romantic. It, too, has the tightness and the self-sufficiency of that little provincial merchant society, which at its best produced an intense little culture, quite English in its concreteness and practicality—as the block letters of the signs along the docks made Boston look like Liverpool. But life must have hit its head on those close and low-ceilinged coops. That narrowness, that meagerness, that stinginess, still grips New England today: the drab summer cottages along the shore seem almost as slit-windowed and pinched as the gray twin-houses of a mill town like Lawrence or Fall River. I can feel the relief myself of coming away from Boston to these first uplands of the Adirondacks, where, discarding the New England religion but still speaking the language of New England, the settlers found limitless space. They were a part of the new America, now forever for a century on the move; and they were to move on themselves before they would be able to build here anything comparable to the New England civilization. The country, magnificent and vast, has never really been humanized as New England has: the landscape still overwhelms the people. But this house, one of the few of its kind among later wooden houses and towns, was an attempt to found a civilization. It blends in a peculiar fashion the amenities of the eastern seaboard with the rudeness and toughness of the new frontier.

It was built at the end of the eighteenth century: the first event recorded in connection with it is a memorial service for General Washington. It took four or five years in the building. The stone had to be quarried and brought out of the river. The walls are a foot and a half thick, and the plaster was applied to the stone without any intervening lattice. The beams were secured by enormous nails, made by hand and some of them eighteen inches long. Solid and simple as a fortress, the place has also the charm of something which has been made to order. There is a front porch with white wooden columns which support a white wooden balcony that runs along the second floor. The roof comes down close over the balcony, and the balcony and the porch are draped with vines. Large ferns grow along the porch, and there are stone hitching-posts and curious stone ornaments, cut out of the quarry like the house: on one side, a round bottomed bowl in which red geraniums bloom, and on the other, an unnamable object, crudely sculptured and vaguely pagoda-like. The front door is especially handsome: the door itself is dark green and equipped with a brass knocker, and the woodwork which frames it is white; it is crowned with a wide fanlight and flanked by two narrow panes of glass, in which a white filigree of ironwork makes a webbing like ice over winter ponds. On one of the broad sides of the building, where the mortar has come off the stone, there is a dappling of dark gray under pale gray like the dappling of light in shallow water, and the feathers of the elms make dapplings of sun among their shadows of large lace on the grass.

The lawn is ungraded and uneven like the pastures, and it merges eventually with the fields. Behind, there are great clotted masses of myrtle-beds, lilac-bushes, clumps of pink phlox and other things I cannot identify; pink and white hollyhocks, some of them leaning, fine blue and purple dye of larkspur; a considerable vegetable garden, with long rows of ripe gooseberries and currants, a patch of yellow pumpkin flowers, and bushes of raspberries, both white and red—among which are sprinkled like confetti the little flimsy California poppies, pink, orange, white and red. In an old dark red barn behind, where the hayloft is almost collapsing, I find spinning-wheels, a carder, candle-molds, a patent bootjack, obsolete implements of carpentry, little clusters of baskets for berry-picking and a gigantic pair of scales such as is nowadays only seen in the hands of allegorical figures.

The house was built by the Talcotts, after whom the town was named. They owned the large farm in front of the house, which stretches down to the river and beyond. They also had a profitable grist mill, but—I learn from the county history—were thought to have "adopted a policy adverse to the building up of the village at the point where natural advantages greatly favored," since they "refused to sell village lots to mechanics, and retained the water power on Sugar River, although parties offered to invest liberally in manufactures." In time, there were only two Talcotts left, an old maid and her widowed sister. My great-grandfather, Thomas Baker, who lived across the street and had been left by the death of his wife with a son and eight daughters, paid court to Miss Talcott and married her. She was kind to the children, and they remembered her with affection. My great-grandfather acquired in this way the house, the farm and the quarry.

All but two of my great-grandfather's daughters, of whom my grandmother was one—"six of them beauties," I understand—got married and went away. Only one of them was left in the house at the time when I first remember Talcottville: my great-aunt Rosalind, a more or less professional invalid and a figure of romantic melancholy, whose fiancé had been lost at sea. When I knew her, she was very old. It was impressive and rather frightening to call on her— you did it only by special arrangement, since she had to prepare herself to be seen. She would be beautifully dressed in a lace cap, a lavender dress and a white crocheted shawl, but she had become so bloodless and shrunken as dreadfully to resemble a mummy and reminded one uncomfortably of Miss Haversham in Dickens' *Great Expectations*. She had a certain high and formal coquetry and was the only person I ever knew who really talked like the characters in old novels. When she had been able to get about, she had habitually treated the townspeople with a condescension almost baronial. According to the family legend, the great-grandmother of great-grandmother Baker had been a daughter of one of the Earls of Essex, who had eloped with a gardener to America.

Another of my Baker great-aunts, who was one of my favorite relatives, had married and lived in the town and had suffered tragic disappointments. Only her strong intellectual interests and a mind capable of philosophic pessimism had maintained her through the wreck of her domestic life. She used to tell me how, a young married woman, she had taught herself French by the dictionary and grammar, sitting up at night alone by the stove through one of their cold and dark winters. She had read a great deal of French, subscribed to French magazines, without ever having learned to pronounce it. She had rejected revealed religion and did not believe in immortality; and when she felt that she had been relieved of the last of her family obligations—though her hair was now turning gray—she came on to New York City and lived there alone for years, occupying herself with the theater, reading, visits to her nephews and nieces—with whom she was extremely popular—and all the spectacle and news of the larger world which she had always loved so much but from which she had spent most of her life removed.

When she died, only the youngest of the family was left, the sole brother, my great-uncle Tom. His mother must have been worn out with childbearing—she died after the birth of this ninth child— and he had not turned out so well as the others. He had been born with no roof to his mouth and was obliged to wear a false gold palate, and it was difficult to understand him. He was not really simple-minded—he had held a small political job under Cleveland,

and he usually beat me at checkers—but he was childlike and ill-equipped to deal with life in any very effective way. He sold the farm to a German and the quarry to the town. Then he died, and the house was empty, except when my mother and father would come here to open it up for two or three months in the summer.

I have not been back here in years, and I have never before examined the place carefully. It has become for me something like a remembered dream—unearthly with the powerful impressions of childhood. Even now that I am here again, I find I have to shake off the dream. I keep walking from room to room, inside and outside, upstairs and down, with uneasy sensations of complacency that are always falling through to depression.

These rooms are very well proportioned; the white mantelpieces are elegant and chaste, and the carving on each one is different. The larger of the two living rooms now seems a little bare because the various members of the family have claimed and taken away so many things; and there are some disagreeable curtains and carpets, for which the wife of my great-uncle Tom is to blame. But here are all the things, I take note, that are nowadays sold in antique stores: red Bohemian-glass decanters; a rusty silver snuff-box; a mirror with the American eagle painted at the top of the glass. Little mahogany tables with slim legs; a set of curly-maple furniture, deep seasoned yellow like satin; a yellow comb-backed rocker, with a design of green conch-shells that look like snails. A small bust of Dante with the nose chipped, left behind as defective by one of my cousins when its companion piece, Beethoven, was taken away; a little mahogany melodeon on which my Aunt "Lin" once played. Large engravings of the family of Washington and of the "Reformers Presenting Their Famous Protest before the Diet of Spires"; a later engraving of Dickens. Old tongs and poker, impossibly heavy. A brown mahogany desk inlaid with yellow birdwood, which contains a pair of steel-rimmed spectacles and a thing for shaking sand on wet ink. Daguerrotypes in fancy cases: they seem to last much better than photographs—my grandmother looks fresh and cunning— I remember that I used to hear that the first time my grandfather saw her, she was riding on a load of hay—he came back up here to marry her as soon as he had got out of medical school. An old wooden flute—originally brought over from New England, I remember my great-uncle's telling me, at the time when they traveled by ox-team—he used to get a lonely piping out of it—I try it but cannot make a sound. Two big oval paintings, in tarnished gilt frames, of landscapes romantic and mountainous: they came from the Utica house of my great-grandfather Baker's brother—he married a rich wife and invented excelsior—made out of the northern lumber—and was presented with a solid-silver table service by the grateful city of Utica.

Wallpaper molded by the damp from the stone; uninviting old black haircloth furniture. A bowl of those enormous up-country sweet peas, incredibly fragrant and bright—they used to awe and trouble me—why?

In the dining room, a mahogany china closet, which originally—in the days when letters were few and great-grandfather Baker was postmaster—was the whole of the village post office. My grandmother's pewter tea-service, with its design of oak-leaves and acorns, which I remember from her house in New Jersey. Black iron cranes, pipkins and kettles for cooking in the fireplace; a kind of flat iron pitchfork for lifting the bread in and out, when they baked at the back of the hearth. On the sideboard, a glass decanter with a gilt black-letter label: "J. Rum." If there were only some rum in the decanter!—if the life of the house were not now all past!—the kitchens that trail out behind are almost too old-smelling, too long deserted, to make them agreeable to visit—in spite of the delightful brown crocks with long-tailed blue birds painted on them, a different kind of bird on each crock.

In the ample hall with its staircase, two large colored pictures of trout, one rising to bait, one leaping. Upstairs, a wooden pestle and mortar; a perforated tin box for hot coals to keep the feet warm in church or on sleigh-rides; a stuffed heron; a horrible bust of my cousin Dorothy Read in her girlhood, which her mother had done of her in Germany. The hair-ribbon and the ruffles are faithfully reproduced in marble, and the eyes have engraved pupils. It stands on a high pedestal, and it used to be possible, by pressing a button, to make it turn around. My Cousin Grace, Dorothy's mother, used to show it off and invite comparison with the original, especially calling attention to the nose; but what her mother had never known was that Dorothy had injured her nose in some rather disgraceful row with her sister. One day when the family were making an excursion, Dorothy pleaded indisposition and bribed a man with a truck to take the bust away and drop it into a pond. But Uncle Tom got this out of the man, dredged the statue up and replaced it on its pedestal. An ugly chair with a round rag back; an ugly bed with the head of Columbus sticking out above the pillows like a figurehead. Charming old bedquilts, with patterns of rhomboids in softened browns, greens and pinks, or of blue polka-dotted hearts that ray out on stiff phallic stalks. A footstool covered in white, which, however, when you step on a tab at the side, opens up into a cuspidor—some relic, no doubt, of the times when the house was used for local meetings. (There used to be a musical chair, also brought back from Germany, but it seems to have disappeared.) A jar of hardly odorous dried rose-leaves, and a jar of little pebbles and shells that keep their bright colors in alcohol.

The original old panes up here have wavy lines in the glass. There are cobweb-filthy books, which I try to examine: many religious works, the annals of the state legislature, a book called *The Young Wife, or Duties of Women in the Marriage Relation*, published in Boston in 1838 and containing a warning against tea and coffee, which "loosen the tongue, fire the eye, produce mirth and wit, excite the animal passions, and lead to remarks about ourselves and others, that we should not have made in other circumstances, and which it were better for us and the world, never to have made." But there is also, I noticed downstairs, Grant Allan's *The Woman Who Did* from 1893.

I come upon the *History of Lewis County* and read it with a certain pride. I am glad to say to myself that it is a creditable piece of work—admirably full in its information on geology, flora and fauna, on history and local politics; diversified with anecdotes and biographies never overflattering and often pungent; and written in a sound English style. Could anyone in the country today, I wonder, command such a sound English style? I note with gratification that the bone of a prehistoric cuttlefish, discovered in one of the limestone caves, is the largest of its kind on record, and that a flock of wild swans was seen here in 1821. In the eighties, there were still wolves and panthers. There are still bears and deer today.

I also look into the proceedings of the New York State Assembly. My great-grandfather Thomas Baker was primarily a politician and at that time a member of the Assembly. I have heard that he was a Jacksonian Democrat, and that he made a furious scene when my grandmother came back from New Jersey and announced that she had become a Republican: it "spoiled her whole visit." There is a photograph of great-grandfather Baker in an oval gilt frame, with his hair sticking out in three spikes and a wide and declamatory mouth. I look through the Assembly record to see what sort of role he played. It is the forties; the Democrats are still angry over the Bank of United States. But when I look up Thomas Baker in the index, it turns out that he figures solely as either not being present or as requesting leave of absence. They tell me he used to go West to buy cattle.

That sealed-up space on the second floor which my father had knocked out—who did they tell me was hidden in it? I have just learned from one of the new road-signs which explain historical associations that there are caves somewhere here in which slaves were hidden. Could this have been a part of the underground route for smuggling Negroes over the border into Canada? Is the attic, the "kitchen chamber," which is always so suffocating in summer, still full of those carpetbags and crinolines and bonnets and beaver-hats that we used to get out of the old cowhide trunks and use to dress up for charades?

It was the custom for the married Baker daughters to bring their children back in the summer; and their children in time brought their children. In those days, how I loved coming up here! It was a reunion with cousins from Boston and New York, Ohio and Wisconsin, as well as with the Talcottville and Utica ones: we fished and swam in the rivers, had all sorts of excursions and games.

Later on, I got to dislike it: the older generation died, the younger did not much come. I wanted to be elsewhere, too. The very fullness with life of the past, the memory of those many families of cousins and uncles and aunts, made the emptiness of the present more oppressive. Isn't it still?—didn't my gloom come from that, the night of my first arrival? Wasn't it the dread of that that kept me away? I am aware, as I walk through the rooms, of the amplitude and completeness of the place—the home of a big old-fashioned family that had to be a city in itself. And not merely did it house a clan: the whole life of the community passed through it. And now for five sixths of the year it is nothing but an unheated shell, a storehouse of unused antiques, with no intimate relation to the county.

The community itself today is somewhat smaller than the community of those days, and its condition has very much changed. It must seem to the summer traveler merely one of the clusters of houses that he shoots through along the state highway; and there may presently be little left save our house confronting, across the road, the hot-dog stand and the gasoline station.*

For years I have had a recurrent dream. I take a road that runs toward the west. It is summer; I pass by a strange summer forest, in which there are mysterious beings, though I know that, on the whole, they are shy and benign. If I am fortunate and find the way, I arrive at a wonderful river, which runs among boulders, with rapids, between alders and high weedy trees, through a countryside fresh, green and wide. We go in swimming; it is miles away from anywhere. We plunge in the smooth flowing pools. We make our way to the middle of the stream and climb up on the pale round gray stones and sit naked in the sun and the air, while the river glides away below us. And I know that it is the place for which I have always longed, the place of wildness and freedom, to find

* This description may seem inconsistent with my account of our Talcott-ville location in another book, A Piece of My Mind, but the main highway was later shifted, put through along another road, and my mother had succeeded, in the meantime, in getting rid of the hot-dog stand by buying back the lot across the street.

which is the height of what one may hope for—the place of unalloyed delight.

As I walk about Talcottville now, I discover that the being-haunted forest is a big grove which even in daytime used to be lonely and dark and where great white Canadian violets used to grow out of the deep black leaf-mold. Today it is no longer dark, because half the trees have been cut down. The river of my dream, I see, is simply an idealized version of the farther and less frequented and more adventurous bank of Sugar River, which had to be reached by wading. Both river and forest are west of the road that runs through the village, which accounts for my always taking that direction in my dream. I remember how Sugar River—out of the stone of which our house is built—used, in my boyhood, so to fascinate me that I had an enlargement made of one of the photographs I had taken of it—a view of "the Big Falls"—and kept it in my room all winter. Today the nearer bank has been largely blasted away to get stone for the new state highway, and what we used to call "the Little Falls" is gone.

I visit the house of my favorite great-aunt, and my gloom returns and overwhelms me. The huge root of an elm has split the thick slabs of the pavement so that you have to walk over a hump; and one of the big square stone fence-posts is toppling. Her flowers, with no one to tend them, go on raggedly blooming in their seasons. There has been nobody in her house since she died. It is all too appropriate to her pessimism—that dead end she always foresaw. As I walk around the house, I remember how, once on the back porch there, she sang me old English ballads, including that gruesome one, "Oh, where have you been, Randall, my son?"—about the man who had gone to Pretty Peggy's house and been given snakes to eat:

> "What had you for supper, Randall, my son?"
> "Fresh fish fried in butter. Oh, make my bed soon!
> For I'm sick at my heart and I fain would lie down!"

She was old then—round-shouldered and dumpy—after the years when she had looked so handsome, straight-backed and with the fashionable aigrette in her hair. And the song she sang seemed to have been drawn out of such barbarous reaches of the past, out of something so surprisingly different from the college-women's hotels in New York in which I had always known her as living: that England to which, far though she had come from it, she was yet so much nearer than I—that queer troubling world of legend which I knew from Percy's *Reliques* but with which she had maintained a real contact through centuries of women's voices—for she sang it without a smile, completely possessed by its spirit—that it made my flesh creep, disconcerted me.

My great-aunt is dead, and all her generation are dead—and the new generations of the family have long ago left Talcottville behind and have turned into something quite different. They were already headed for the cities by the middle of the last century, as can be seen by the rapid dispersal of great grandfather Baker's daughters. Yet there were still, in my childhood, a few who stayed on in this country as farmers. They were very impressive people, the survivors of a sovereign race who had owned their own pastures and fields and governed their own community. Today the descendants of these are performing mainly minor functions in a machine which they do not control. They have most of them become thoroughly urbanized, and they are farther from great-grandfather Baker than my grandmother, his daughter, was when she came back from New Jersey a Republican. One of her children, a retired importer in New York, was complaining to me the other day that the outrageous demands of the farmers were making business recovery impossible, and protesting that if the advocates of the income tax had their way, the best people would no longer be able to live up to their social positions. A cousin, who bears the name of one of his Ipswich ancestors, a mining engineer on the Coast and a classmate and admirer of Hoover, invested and has lost heavily in Mexican real estate and the industrial speculations of the boom. Another, with another of the old local names, is now at the head of an organization whose frankly avowed purpose is to rescue the New York manufacturers from taxation and social legislation. He has seen his native city of

Utica decline as a textile center through the removal of its mills to the South, where taxes are lighter and labor is cheaper; and he is honestly convinced that his efforts are directed toward civic betterment.

Thus the family has come imperceptibly to identify its interests with those of what my great-grandfather Baker would have called the "money power." They work for it and acquiesce in it—they are no longer the sovereign race of the first settlers of Lewis County, and in the cities they have achieved no sovereignty. They are much too scrupulous and decent, and their tastes are too comparatively simple for them ever to have rolled up great fortunes during the years of expansion and plunder. They have still the frank accent and the friendly eye of the older American world, and they seem rather taken aback by the turn that things have been taking.

And what about me? As I come back in the train, I find that— other causes contributing—my depression of Talcottville deepens. I did not find the river and the forest of my dream—I did not find the magic of the past. I have been too close to the past: there in that house, in that remote little town which has never known industrial progress since the Talcotts first obstructed the development of the water power of Sugar River, you can see exactly how rural Americans were living a century and a half ago. And who would go back to it? Not I. Let people who have never known country life complain that the farmer has been spoiled by his radio and his Ford. Along with the memory of exaltation at the immensity and freedom of that countryside, I have memories of horror at its loneliness: houses burning down at night, sometimes with people in them, where there was no fire department to save them, and husbands or wives left alone by death—the dark nights and the prisoning winters. I do not grudge the sacrifice of the Sugar River falls for the building of the new state highway, and I do not resent the hot-dog stand. I am at first a little shocked at the sight of a transformer on the road between Talcottville and Boonville, but when I get to the Talcottville house, I am obliged to be thankful for it— no more oil-lamps in the evenings! And I would not go back to that old life if I could: that civilization of northern New York—why should I idealize it?—was too lonely, too poor, too provincial.

I look out across the Hudson and see Newburgh: with the neat-windowed cubes of its dwellings and docks, distinct as if cut by a burin, built so densely up the slope of the bank and pierced by an occasional steeple, undwarfed by tall modern buildings and with only the little old-fashioned ferry to connect it with the opposite bank, it might still be an eighteenth-century city. My father's mother came from there. She was the granddaughter of a carpet-importer from Rotterdam. From him came the thick Spanish coins which the children of my father's family were supposed to cut their teeth on. The business, which had been a considerable one, declined as the sea trade of the Hudson became concentrated in New York. My father and mother went once—a good many years ago—to visit the old store by the docks, and were amazed to find a solitary old clerk still scratching up orders and sales on a slate that hung behind the counter.

And the slate and the Spanish coins, though they symbolize a kind of life somewhat different from that evoked by Talcottville, associate themselves in my mind with such things as the old post office turned china closet. And as I happen to be reading Herndon's *Life of Lincoln*, that, too, goes to flood out the vision with its extension still further west, still further from the civilized seaboard, of the life of the early frontier. Through Herndon's extraordinary memoir, one of the few really great American books of its kind, which America has never accepted, preferring to it the sentimentalities of Sandburg and the ladies who write Christmas stories—the past confronts me even more plainly than through the bootjacks and daguerreotypes of Talcottville, and makes me even more uneasy. Here you are back again amid the crudeness and the poverty of the American frontier, and here is a man of genius coming out of it and perfecting himself. The story is not merely moving, it becomes almost agonizing. The ungainly boorish boy from the settler's clearing, with nobody and nothing behind him, hoping that his grandfather had been a planter as my great-aunt Rosalind hoped that she was a descendant of the Earls of Essex, the morbid young man

looking passionately toward the refinement and the training of the
East but unable to bring himself to marry the women who represented it for him—rejoining across days in country stores, nights in
godforsaken hotels, rejoining by heroic self-discipline the creative
intelligence of the race, to find himself the conscious focus of its
terrible unconscious parturition—his miseries burden his grandeur.
At least they do for me at this moment.

> *Old Abe Lincoln came out of the wilderness,*
> *Out of the wilderness, out of the wilderness—*

The echo of the song in my mind inspires me with a kind of awe—
I can hardly bear the thought of Lincoln.

Great-grandfather Baker's politics and the Talcottville general
store, in which people sat around and talked before the new chain
store took its place—Lincoln's school was not so very much different.
And I would not go back to that.

Yet as I walk up the steps of my house in New York, I am
forced to recognize, with a sinking, that I have never been able to
leave it. This old wooden booth I have taken between First and
Second Avenues—what is it but the same old provincial America?
And as I open the door with its loose knob and breathe in the
musty smell of the stair-carpet, it seems to me that I have not
merely stuck in the world where my fathers lived but have actually,
in some ways, lost ground in it. This gray paintless clapboarded
front, these lumpy and rubbed yellow walls—they were probably
once respectable, but they must always have been commonplace.
They have never had even the dignity of the house in Lewis
County. But I have rented them because, in my youth, I had been
used to living in houses and have grown to loathe city apartments.

So here, it seems, is where I must live: in an old cramped and
sour frame-house—having failed even worse than my relatives at
getting out of the American big-business era the luxuries and the
prestige that I unquestionably should very much have enjoyed. Here
is where I end by living—among the worst instead of the best of
this city that took the trade away from Newburgh—the sordid and
unhealthy children of my sordid and unhealthy neighbors, who howl

outside my windows night and day. It is this, in the last analysis—
there is no doubt about it now!—which has been rankling and causing my gloom: to have left that early world behind yet never to
have really succeeded in what was till yesterday the new.

[1 9 4 9]

MIAMI

COTTON BLOSSOM EXPRESS: I went to sleep in the winter
darkness, and wake up to a dazzle of golden light on green palms
and low-growing pines that drip with Florida moss. An extraordinary pageant of bird-life presents itself outside the window: snowy
egrets, several kinds of heron—some bluish, some beige—and other
darker long-winged birds that I take to be buzzards—all looking
as if they had flown right out of Audubon: how excited he must
have been when he came here. There are also some smaller birds
that fly in flocks with quick twinkling wing-beats, and one experiences a pleasure that has something in common with the pleasure
derived from music in following the contrasts of tempo between
these and the slower rhythms of the larger birds that hover. They
all fly quite close to the train and not far from the endless pale
swamps and plains. It is wonderful to watch an egret alighting and
folding its wings, deliberately, with dignity and grace.

Miami: I have never been here before and am astounded and
appalled by this place. It is not that it is particularly different from
other American seaside resorts, from Asbury Park to Coronado
Beach, but that here both the cheap and the expensive aspects have

been developed on a scale that I have never elsewhere seen equalled. You have acres of nougat-like shops, mountain-ranges of vanilla ice-cream hotels. Miami Beach goes on for miles, with its monotonous lines of palms, its thousands of hotels and houses which seem to have had imposed on them, by the exigency of a city-planning board, a blanched and insipid uniformity. It even makes one feel more kindly toward Southern California, with its elements of lunatic fantasy. What draws people down to this vacuum? How do they amuse themselves here?

These vacationists look soft and vapid. You rarely see a really pretty girl, and the men do not give the impression of doing much fishing or swimming. You find them at the movies in the evening. The American ideal of luxury is in Miami carried to lengths that I have never encountered before. At my hotel, I had the annoyance of removing encasements of cellophane from the toilet-seat and the drinking tumbler. In the movie-house, the seats are the kind that swing noiselessly back and forth to let people get in and out, and their cushions melt beneath one like a featherbed. A subdued indirect lighting, like the sweet creamy liquid of an ice-cream soda, bathes a dove-gray and shrimp-pink interior, the walls of which are ornamented with large cameo-like white seashells framing naked mythological figures that seem to have been badly imitated from the bas-reliefs of Paul Manship in Rockefeller Center, and with branching white plaster exfoliations that remind one of the legs and defensive antennae of the crawfish in the Miami aquarium. The film—*Oh, You Beautiful Doll*—was a technicolor that covered the whole surface of a high and overpowering screen with a routine sentimental romance, trumped up to manufacture glamor from the career of an American song-writer whose songs were widely sung in my college days. They were commonplace enough then, and today they are simply sickly. These attempts on the part of Hollywood to exploit the immediate past—in which the fashions of the eighties and nineties are sometimes confused with those of the twenties—show the precipitous decline of the movies as purveyors of entertainment, since the producers, after wrecking such contemporary talent as their salaries have tempted to Hollywood, have now been obliged to fall back on the favorites, first, second or third rate, of the day before yesterday and yesterday, when it was possible for a producer or an actor, a composer or a dancer, to perfect an art of his own and create for himself a reputation. Yet this product has its steady customers: one finds oneself among them here. Comfortably padded in the muffled atmosphere that seems to smell of scented face-powder—one cannot tell whether the theater has been perfumed or the women are all using the same cosmetics—this inert and featureless drove that have been drifting through the bleached sunny streets now sit watching stereotyped characters that are made to appear impressive by being photographed in very bright colors and gigantically magnified. The three shorts that follow the first showing of the film all happen to deal with animals: a hunting number, an animated cartoon that gets some not ill-deserved laughs, and a picture about racing whippets. The commentator seems slightly embarrassed at the spectacle of the uniformed attendants who have a full-time job grooming the whippets. "You may think they work as hard as the dogs," he propounds, with his microphone emphasis that gropes through time and space and can never drive any nails. "Well, they work a lot *harder!*" The truth is that so many Americans, specialized in operating machines or in transacting long-distance business, have deteriorated as animal organisms, that we now have a special pleasure in watching almost any agile animal. What the audience gets out of these animal shorts is the same thing that I have been getting out of looking out the window at the birds and contrasting them with the Miami vacationers.

This is all the kind of thing, I realize, that strikes foreigners who visit this country, but that I have long ago arranged my life in such a way as to avoid or ignore, so that I am likely to be shocked by and to discount the uncomplimentary reports of visitors. Miami is a rude revelation: I had not really known this was going on. I read uneasily of President Truman's recent arrival in Florida for one of a long series of sunlit holidays. This is the place where he seems most at home. It is only when I get to the airfield that my national self-respect picks up. It is a feat to have conceived, to have built and to navigate these passenger planes. We humans have con-

trived our wings by deliberate calculations, out of inorganic materials, instead of growing them out of our bodies, and this does leave
us less hardy than the buzzard, less graceful than the white egret;
but we have, after all, by our planes, in other ways surpassed the
birds, and there had been moments in Miami when I was doubtful
of that before I took off for Haiti. And those disparate rhythms of
flight that I found so delightful to watch, Walt Disney, in his film
Snow White, where deer and rabbits and other animals are shown
running together at different speeds and gaits, has rendered them
for the first time in plastic art. The multiplied drawings of the
studio that turns out the Disney cartoons are as anonymous as the
hundreds of parts that go to make up a plane. I couldn't myself have
invented the simplest of these mechanisms or processes; but the
current prestige of the United States is partly derived from these,
and I cannot help feeling a pride in them.

[1 9 7 1]

UPSTATE: EPILOGUE, 1970

WHAT I have written above shows the gradual but steady
expiration of the world of New York State as I knew it in my
childhood and the modifications that its life has undergone. It is
true that Lowville and Boonville have changed less—unless perhaps
Charlottesville, Virginia—than any other part of this country that I
knew when I was a child. But, as has been seen, it has reflected all
the changes that, to a greater degree, have been taking place in the
life of the country as a whole. I do not mean to deplore all these
changes. Anyone who still takes seriously the American democratic
ideal of opportunity for everyone to prosper according to his best
abilities and to enjoy such advantages as he can understand ought
not to complain of the many cars, the "mobile homes," of the movies

and television sets, of the grills for outdoor cooking. None of these things seems to me attractive, but I probably have no right to be contemptuous about them or to blame them entirely on the people who manufacture and advertize them. If people want them, why should they not have them? Don't young people live better in trailers than they did in old-fashioned frame houses, which were often so ill-built and dreary. I remember that in Red Bank, New Jersey, a typical bourgeois suburb, the general possession of motor cars and of comfortable modern houses immensely cheered and brightened that suburban life. We were only four miles from the ocean, but nobody could get there to swim unless the family had a carriage or, later, an automobile, which at that time was expensive and required a driver. Few people habitually rode bicycles. But presently a trolley was installed, which ran between Red Bank and Seabright. And now everybody owns a car, and in summer one can go to the beach every day. Our old house in Red Bank stood not far from a kind of suburban slum, unsightly and supposed to be something of a den of immorality. My mother's new house that she bought after my father's death, more convenient and much lighter than our gloomy old place, stood in a new street called Buena Vista, and all along it were a class of people that in the past could never have lived so well. On the opposite side of the street from us was the family of a bank clerk, whose wife was pretty and well dressed and whose equally attractive daughter was a great friend of my daughter's. It is true that, when I walked along this street, the radio could be heard from every house and all were playing the same program, so that, no matter how far one walked, the continuity was never interrupted. The implications of this uniformity did not at that time escape me; but I generally approved of what was going on. This, for the people of the United States, was an improvement in their condition. Today in upstate Lewis County there is a whole community of trailers among the trees of a little woodland behind and across the road from the great mansion and mowed grounds of Constable Hall. Constable Hall is now a museum, and the big houses of the well-to-do professional men and dairy owners and merchants have now either been turned into funeral homes or are inhabited by several families. To what other uses could these places be put? And the people who ride in cars, though they are frequently killed or injured in accidents, have no longer such constricted lives. The old way of living up here threw them back on their own capacity for instructing and amusing themselves: reading, playing the piano, sentimental songs, charades, as well as making pies, jams and bread-stuffs and quilting and embroidery and the other household arts. But they often, even in the bigger towns, did not see very much of the world. Our old trips in carriages to Carthage and Rome now seem so slow as almost to be comic. I am able to go to Rome now as often as I like to have dinner and see a movie. I have described the quality of the dinners—though Rome has still, dating from 1908, an excellent Italian restaurant; but at worst they are better than the savorless meat and the vegetables in what we called "birds' bathtubs" of the local hotels where we used to have to eat in the course of our longer journeys. And even the worst of the movies are better than the rare melodramas that occasionally made us laugh in Boonville.

Of course there used to be a much greater difference between the "educated" and the "uneducated." Lowville Academy was once a great local center of schooling to which students came from miles around. The "Ivy League" colleges were places of training for what were called "the learned professions": law, medicine, the pulpit, certain kinds of science and the academic career. Today every young American enjoys the inalienable right to enroll at a state university and, as soon as he pleases, drop out. Negro and white children both may go all the way through primary school without ever learning to read. An "education guidance" man I know, who can certainly not in his work or his life be accused of being undemocratic, has told me that he has come to the conclusion that it is useless to try to educate a good many of the children beyond a necessary minimum. The problem of preventing the abler and more brilliant students from being retarded by the incapacity of the duller ones has some-times been dealt with in the colleges by having special courses and classes for the former. I do not know enough about the present system to offer predictions or suggestions. I suppose that such voca-tional schools as the one I have described above must represent a new attempt to deal with the partially educable. It is a kind of successor to and substitute for the old apprentice system. There are in any case now relatively few examples of young people ambitious of meeting, outside the fields of technology, the higher standards of competence and culture.

My reaction to all the things that I disapprove and dislike is that of a member of a once privileged class which is being eliminated all over the world and has very little means any longer of asserting its superior "values." In this, the situation in the United States is not now very different from that in many other parts of the world—including the Soviet Union, except that in the latter the old educated and travelled and comfortable groups were less numerous and more quickly and completely suppressed. But our groups of well-to-do landowners and merchants and able professional men who made the American Revolution have now largely been reduced to the Nixons and Agnews of the present administration, who are hardly superior to the mediocrities that preside over the Soviet Union. It was thought by Veblen and others, that the technocrats would take over as a ruling class, and this to some extent has taken place. I cannot foresee the future, but can only go on with my old occupations.

The fading-out in New York within such a brief period of the ideal of feudal grandeur is of course only a special case of the swift transience of everything in the United States. These mansions mostly date from the early years of the nineteenth century, and the family estates were acquired in the later years of the eighteenth. Their ideal was represented at its most pretentious by the great building called Hyde-Clarke Hall, which stands at the northeast of Otsego Lake, on the waters of which it looks out. This imposing "pile," as the old writers would have called it, was first built in 1817—the facade was added in 1834. The first of the family in this country was an Englishman, George W. Clarke, who came over in 1703 and was Lieutenant-Governor of the Province of New York. He had been at Eton with Wellington, after whom he named a hill on Otsego Lake, now usually known, however, as the Sleeping Lion. He married the daughter of Edward Hyde, the royal governor of North Carolina, and became, by the law of coverture, the owner of the Hyde estate in England. His great-grandson, who had inherited the Clarke estate in America, came over here after the Revolution and built for himself Hyde-Clarke Hall out of the limestone available in this region. The architect was also an Englishman, and he seems to have aimed to reproduce the design of Elizabethan houses—the house is built around a court—though it is masked by the neo-classic portico which was eventually added. The Hyde-Clarkes lived with great magnificence; and they kept up the feudal tradition by resisting the demands of their many tenants at the time that the "rent war" was causing trouble. But the son of the Clarke who built the house had a mania for buying land—it was as if he wanted to own the old province. He would buy and then mortgage, and went bankrupt, leaving nothing, as he said, but his clothes. The family sold the land in 1888. But in the meantime, in vying with the English great houses, they had succeeded in creating a legend. They were even supposed to have a ghost, and there was a saying that no woman could be happy there: all the ladies suffered from afflictions and disasters.

The state bought the house in 1964 for $500,000; it was then in such bad condition that it was proposed to demolish it and make tennis-courts for the state park in which it is now enclosed. But a Friends of Hyde Hall was organized in order to rescue and restore it. It was estimated that this could be done for a minimum of half a million, but it looks as if a million would be nearer the mark. The plan has been to bring back the original furniture, now in storage, and to turn it into a museum.

The old place is still a dominating presence. It is much larger than either Henderson House or Constable Hall—190 by 90 feet—but less attractive than either. Four high pillars, composed of round segments of stone, which would hardly seem out of place in Karnac, support an ironwork balcony, rather fancy but of the utmost dignity, and an entablature with a classical pediment. An oval window under the peak of the triangle and four square windows below. The walls are built of two kinds of stonework, both smoother and more tightly fitted than ours. There are palatial reception and living rooms, all with big marble mantels, mottled in white and black; a library and a chapel. But inside it is now all a dark desolation. The wallpaper is peeling in sheets, and the plaster is falling from the ceilings, leaving naked the narrow slats. The shuttered light is too dim to make out the ornamental cornices. On certain rooms are placards: UNSAFE. The floors have become rather flimsy, and one hesitates to climb the stairway—which, like ours, has brown banisters and a curlicue fringe along the steps. Old mattresses lying in piles. Even the rooms to which the family resorted when the place became otherwise uninhabitable could never be lived in now. Here there are a few old photographs lying on floors and tables; a copy of the Tauchnitz edition of *Lord Ormont and His Aminta,* which was considered very naughty in its day. The Clarkes seem to have been strangely careless of their property, as the Clarke who bought land was reckless. The "office" of one of the masters of the house who died in 1835 was locked up after his death and never opened till 1890, by which time the floor had collapsed and the furniture had fallen into the basement. In a barn that is going to pieces, there are the gruesome remains of a grand piano, which was never unpacked from its case but left out on a porch to rot. The story is that it had been ordered from London to be played on some special occasion but, when it came too late, was simply scrapped. In one of the downstairs rooms, there are toilet seats and other bathroom fixtures of comparatively recent date, which do not ever seem to have been installed. In proportion as the family abandoned the house, the wild life about invaded it, and when people slept there they took care to stop up the cracks under the doors in order to keep out the snakes. Hyde Hall, with its grand view, set among its ancient trees, is now a boarded-up slab of masonry, with a ragged screen of brush behind it, above which is vulgarly flourishing the pink wild flower called Bouncing Bet. When I last saw the house, there were boys on the balcony investigating the bats in the attic. They were going to get an exterminator.

But this passing of such splendors as New York State could pretend to has made me feel not only the transcience of all forms of life in America, but at my age the constant flow and perishable character, rather than the constant renewal and hope, of everything on the earth. Greece and Rome and classical France left behind them much more durable monuments than our old mansions gone to ruin and our broken-off fragments of old canals; but the aeons of time required for the mammalian plantigrades of the human race to achieve what we can now see to be a very moderate and partial degree of civilization has been coming to discourage and bore me. I look at the creatures on the street and I think, well, we have begun to walk upright and our toes, now more or less impractical, are shrinking like the toes of elephants' feet. We have now arrived at a skill of uttering and writing sounds that can convey rather special meanings. But our problems of future development are still absolutely appalling. I do not have any chance, and feel that I should not have the patience, to wait through the countless millennia that would get us past our ages of blind quarreling and of our blindness in sexual selection that makes so much trouble for the children we breed. How much longer must it be before the inhabitants of Russia, ignorant and easily led, spread over such enormous spaces and with so little hunger for information that at the time of the last war there were people to be found in Siberia who not only did not know that there was a war or even that there had been a revolution—how long will it be before such people can organize a modern democracy and cease to attempt to exterminate their original and creative countrymen? I speak of a modern democracy, but how long will it be, for that matter, before the United States can organize a livable society which is free from the even more modern tyranny of bureaucracy? Democracy is actually one of those vague words which are supposed to command approval without giving us a chance to take stock of what our "democracy" consists of. Can I even be sure that, in the language I use, I am formulating these issues correctly? Will these terms not seem very crude to a remotely distant future?—that future I cannot wait for. And where do we get the standards by which we judge our earthly conditions and which are bound to be subject to continual change? When I think of these struggles and transformations to come, I am almost ready to call it a day, at this time of my waning powers, for my own more or less well-meaning efforts. After all, are not my literary activities, like new roads and vocational schools, clumsy gestures in the interest of ends that can only be reached—and what then?—in the course of innumerable centuries that are now entirely unimaginable? As one grows weaker, one becomes more helpless, more lazy, and also more indifferent. Will the Soviet Union last? a Soviet citizen has just demanded. Will General Electric and General Motors—are they "Capitalism," "Democracy?"—last longer than Hyde Hall, which, even in Republican America, was supposed to be still representing Feudalism? We have spent no one knows how many million years, as have the black widow spider, the hammerhead shark, the deadly amanita and the leaf-nosed bat, building up or assembling or creating—we do not even know how to put it—what we call our bodies and brains, our consciousness. Only now are we beginning a little to understand how these organs and members work. The process of finding out more is going to be very tedious. At least, that is how I feel toward the end of a fairly long life that has left me with the feeling—illusion?—that I have seen or sampled many kinds of experience, that I know what this planet is, what its climates in different places and at different seasons are, what its flora and fauna are, what both its more primitive men and more mechanized men are like—so that, not expecting any real novelty, I have no longer any curiosity beyond such as the satisfaction of which will keep me mildly amused while my faculties are gradually decaying. My young vision of New York State now hardly exists, though I do not think, as I did last year, that I shall sell my old place here. In spite of the encroachments of the highways and the element of impoverished ambitionless inhabitants, I have still, I think, just enough money to keep the old place going, and I am still as comfortable here as I can hope to be anywhere. That the old life is passing away, that all around me are anarchy and what seems to me stupidity, does not move me much any more. I have learned to read the papers calmly and not to hate the fools I read about. As long as my health holds out, I shall have to go on living, and I am glad to have had some share in some of the better aspects of the life of this planet and of northern New York.

E. B. WHITE

THE YOUNGEST of six children, E. B. White was born in Mt. Vernon, New York, on July 11, 1899. At the time, Mt. Vernon was still a small town—certainly not the beginning of suburbia that it is today—and White's father, who was prospering as a piano manufacturer, had moved his family up from Brooklyn because he thought Mt. Vernon would be a better place to raise children. As it turned out, it was almost perfect. Their house was large, the streets were shady, and the town was as peaceful as an upper-middle-class suburb could be at the turn of the century. "There was," White has written, describing their house, "an iron vase on the lawn and a copy of *Wet Days at Edgewood* on the library table." Years later, he recalled the things he did: "I rode my bicycle sitting backward on the handle bars, I made up poems, I played selections from 'Aida' on the piano. In winter, I tended goal in the hockey games on the frozen pond in the Dell." To such idyllic pastimes was added, in 1905, a camp on one of the Belgrade lakes in Maine, and each August for many years thereafter the family went there for its summer vacation. Indeed, one gathers from his writings that there were few catastrophes in White's childhood more serious than hay fever, and from that he is still a sufferer. In 1917 he graduated from Mt. Vernon High School, and the following fall he entered Cornell University.

Unlike their cousins, the novelists, the American humorists of this century seem more or less to have taken to college, and White was no exception. He joined a fraternity, got gentlemanly marks in his courses, rode a motorcycle, and spent two months during his sophomore year as a private in the U.S. Army. (Enlisting only a few weeks before the Armistice, he got no farther than the campus drill field and faced no enemy worse than a flu epidemic, "which I met stoically with a bag of licorice drops.") His real interest, however, was writing, and in his senior year he was editor-in-chief of the *Cornell Daily Sun*.

After his graduation in 1921, White tried his hand for a while at various jobs in New York City, but was dissatisfied and restless.

Then, in March of 1922, he and a friend decided to head West in White's Model T Ford. It was a leisurely trip, and when they arrived in Seattle six months later, White took a job as a reporter with the Seattle *Times*. But poetry, not journalism, was the thing he had his eye on in those days, and when the job fell through the following summer, it was with relief that he began looking around for something to do. What turned up was a steamer on its way to Alaska and Siberia, and White determined to go with it. With the last of his money he bought a one-way ticket as far as Skagway, and trusted that once on board he could get a job that would take him the full round trip. Luckily, he did, and that fall he returned to New York City.

For the next two years he worked in an advertising agency and tried to write poetry, but without much success. Then, in 1925, *The New Yorker* was founded, and very soon White was submitting poems and sketches. Harold Ross, the editor, was so impressed that he asked White to come to work, which he did, and for the next eleven years his wit and good sense did much to make the magazine the success that it was. He not only wrote many of the "Notes and Comments" that appeared in the "Talk of the Town," but also thought up the witty captions and taglines that turned normal space-fillers into capsule editorials on the absurdities of both man and the press. Even though most of his work during those years was unsigned, the recurrent style was unmistakable to anyone who read *The New Yorker* regularly. In 1929 White published his first two books: *The Lady Is Cold*, a collection of light verse, and *Is Sex Necessary?*, a spoof on scientific sex literature written in collaboration with his office mate, James Thurber.

In 1937, "desiring," he said, "to simplify my life," E.B. White left New York and moved his family to a salt water farm in North Brooklin, Maine. The following summer he began a regular monthly column for *Harper's Magazine* entitled "One Man's Meat," and it was soon apparent that an aspect of his character that had hitherto remained largely hidden was beginning to emerge. The essays that he sent down from Maine revealed a depth one wouldn't have expected from his earlier *New Yorker* pieces. The wit and clear sight into the nature of things were still there, but with a difference. No longer were they being exercised for the sake of cleverness alone—the thing one regrets about much of the work of Benchley, Sullivan, and even Thurber at times—but more seriously, as a means of revealing not merely man's absurdities, but his virtues as well. White, it turned out, could be as serious as he could be clever. Although *Quo Vadimus?* or *The Case for the Bicycle*, a collection of sketches that had appeared in *The New Yorker*, was published in 1939, the sort of humor that it contained was already a thing of the past. In 1943 he wrote the last of his columns for *Harper's* and returned to New York City, where he resumed the writing of *The New Yorker's* editorial page. The magazine's staff had been depleted by the war, and Ross had asked him to help. A few years later he moved back to Maine and began writing his "Letters from the East" (and other points of the compass) for *The New Yorker*; and Maine is where he still lives.

Altogether White has written eleven books and either edited or collaborated on four others. Two of the most charming are children's stories that take their place alongside such modern classics as *The Wind in the Willows* and the Pooh books: *Stuart Little* (1945) and *Charlotte's Web* (1952). In 1941 he and his wife, Katharine S. White, edited *A Subtreasury of American Humor*, and in 1959 he revised, introduced, and wrote a chapter on style for a grammar handbook he had used as a student at Cornell. To everyone's surprise, *The Elements of Style*, by William Strunk, Jr., and E. B. White, became a national best-seller. White's best essays appear in three collections: *One Man's Meat* (1944), *The Second Tree from the Corner* (1954), and *The Points of My Compass* (1962).

The themes that White comes back to in essay after essay are, first, that the natural is preferable to the artificial or mechanical, and, secondly, that even though time moves on apace and things constantly change, the larger patterns of Nature are recurrent. The first idea is generally presented as a lament for the past, and thus the imperceptive reader often comes away with the impression that White is a nostalgic reactionary. Read closely, however, the essays are quite clear in their scorn for sentimentality, and whatever homage is paid the past proves to be not a love for the simple and uncomplicated, but just the opposite, a love of the excitement and adventure that is inseparable from physical hardships. As our material goods and comforts increase, White would say, we lose touch with reality; we are dehumanized; we become no better than the machine we created; indeed, worse (see "The Hour of Letdown" in *The Second Tree from the Corner*). Fortunately, however, there is always Nature, and no matter how furiously we hack away at her, in the end she is victorious. These beliefs, and the proof of his life, place White directly in the tradition of his fellow New Englanders, Thoreau and Frost.

"With some writers," White wrote in *The Elements of Style*, "style not only reveals the spirit of the man, it reveals his identity, as surely as would his fingerprints." Then he added, a little later, "The approach to style is by way of plainness, simplicity, orderliness, sincerity." Taken together, the two statements—however simple they appear on the surface—imply an extremely subtle attitude toward style. "How," one might ask, "am I to do both at the same time—be plain, simple, orderly, and sincere, and yet reveal the complexities of my identity?" No easy, practicable answer is given, for White knows that it is a problem that can be solved only by each solitary writer in his own unending struggle to make the words he sets down on paper approach the temper of his thought. But he does tell us two important things. The first is a belief: "The whole duty of a writer is to please and satisfy himself, and the true writer always plays to an audience of one." And the second is a method: "I write by ear, always with difficulty and seldom with any exact notion of what is taking place under the hood." In short, style, E. B. White would say, is a matter of character, intuition, faith, mystery . . . and hard work.

THE WORLD OF TOMORROW

I wasn't really prepared for the World's Fair last week, and it certainly wasn't prepared for me. Between the two of us there was considerable of a mixup.

The truth is that my ethmoid sinuses broke down on the eve of Fair Day, and this meant I had to visit the Fair carrying a box of Kleenex concealed in a copy of the *Herald Tribune*. When you can't breathe through your nose, Tomorrow seems strangely like the day before yesterday. The Fair, on its part, was having trouble too. It couldn't find its collar button. Our mutual discomfort established a rich bond of friendship between us, and I realize that the World's Fair and myself actually both need the same thing—a nice warm day.

The road to Tomorrow leads through the chimney pots of Queens. It is a long, familiar journey, through Mulsified Shampoo and Mobilgas, through Bliss Street, Kix, Astring-O-Sol, and the Majestic Auto Seat Covers. It winds through Textene, Blue Jay Corn Plasters; through Musterole and the delicate pink blossoms on the fruit trees in the ever-hopeful back yards of a populous borough, past Zemo, Alka-Seltzer, Baby Ruth, past Iodent and the Fidelity National Bank, by trusses, belts, and the clothes that fly bravely on the line under the trees with the new little green leaves in Queens' incomparable springtime. Suddenly you see the first intimation of the future, of man's dream—the white ball and spire—and there is the ramp and the banners flying from the pavilions and the brave hope of a glimpsed destination. Except for the Kleenex, I might have been approaching the lists at Camelot, for I felt that perhaps here would be the tournament all men wait for, the field of honor, the knights and the ladies under these bright banners, beyond these great walls. A closer inspection, however, on the other side of the turnstile, revealed that it was merely Heinz jousting with Beech-

Nut—the same old contest on a somewhat larger field, with accommodations for more spectators, and rather better facilities all round.

The place is honeycombed with streets—broad, gusty streets, with tulips bending to the gale and in the air the sound of distant choirs. There are benches all along for the weary and the halt, but though science's failure to cope with the common cold had embittered my heart and slowed my step, the ball and spire still beckoned me on. It was not particularly surprising, somehow, when at last after so many months of anticipation and after so much of actual travail and suffering, when at last I arrived, paper handkerchiefs in hand, at the very threshold of Tomorrow, when I finally presented myself there at the base of the white phallus, face to face with the girl in the booth behind the little bars behind the glass window with the small round hole, expectant, ready to see at last what none had ever seen, Tomorrow—it was not, somehow, particularly surprising to see the window close in my face and hear a bald contemporary voice say, "There will be a short wait of a few minutes, please."

That's the way it is with the future. Even after Grover Whalen has touched it with his peculiar magic, there is still a short wait.

The lady behind me was not surprised either, but she seemed apprehensive.

"Anything wrong in there?" she asked testily.

"No, Madam," said the guard. "Just some minor difficulty in the Perisphere."

The lady was not satisfied. "Is there anything in there to scare you?" she asked, looking at the Perisphere rolling motionless in the gray vapors that have hung for centuries above the Flushing Meadows.

"No, Madam," he replied. "The longest escalator in the world moves very slowly."

I clocked the wait. It was twenty minutes. Not bad, for a man who's waited all his life.

Much depends, when you ascend into the interior of the Perisphere, on the moment at which you happen to arrive at the top of the escalator and teeter off in a sidewise direction onto one of the two great moving rings that turn endlessly above the City of Man. If you arrive just as day has faded into night, and without any advance information about being shunted from an upward moving stairway onto a sidewise moving balcony, the experience is something that stays with you. I was lucky. The City of Man, when it first broke on my expectant sight, was as dark as a hall bedroom, and for a second or two I didn't catch on that I myself was in motion—except celestially. If I hadn't recognized Mr. Kaltenborn's electric voice, I would have felt lonelier than perhaps the situation warranted.

"As day fades into night," he said, with the majestic huskiness which science has given speech, "each man seeks home, for here are children, comfort, neighbors, recreation—the good life of the well-planned city."

Trembling in violet light beneath me, there it was—the towers, now to the adjusted eye dimly visible—"a brave new world [such a big voice you have, Grandpa!] built by united hands and hearts. Here brain and brawn, faith and courage, are linked in high endeavor as men march on toward unity and peace. Listen! From office, farm, and factory they come with joyous song."

I don't know how long it takes in there. Ten minutes, maybe. But when I emerged from the great ball, to begin the descent of the Helicline, it had come on to rain.

To be informative about the Fair is a task for someone with a steadier nose than mine. I saw all as in a dream, and I cherish the dream and have put it away in lavender. The great size of the place has been a temporary disadvantage these first few days, when the draftiness, the chill, the disorder, the murky bath of canned reverence in which many of the commercial exhibits are steeped have conspired to give the place the clammy quality of a seaside resort in mid-November. But this same great size, come the first warm, expansive days, will suddenly become the most valuable asset of the Fair. The refurbished ash heap, rising from its own smolder, is by far the biggest show that has ever been assembled on God's earth, and it is going to be a great place to go on a fine summer night, a great place to go on a sunny spring morning. After all, nobody can embrace Culture in a topcoat.

The architecture is amusing enough, the buildings are big enough, to give the visitor that temporary and exalted feeling of being in the presence of something pretty special, something full of aspiration, something which at times is even exciting. And the exhibition is cock-eyed enough to fall, as it naturally does, in line with all carnivals, circuses, and wonderlands. The buildings (there are two hundred of them) have color and a certain dash, here and there a certain beauty. They are of the type that shows up best in strong light. Like any Miami Beach cottage, they look incredibly lovely in sunlight, adorned with a necklace of vine shadow against a clear white skin, incredibly banal and gloom-infested on cloudy days, when every pimple of plaster shows up in all its ugly pretension. The designers of this twentieth-century bazaar have been resourceful and have kept the comfort of the people in mind. Experience has taught them much. The modern technique of sight-seeing is this: you sit in a chair (wired for sound) or stand on a platform (movable, glass-embowered) and while sitting, standing, you are brought mysteriously and reverently into easy view of what you want to see. There is no shoving in the exhibit hall of Tomorrow. There is no loitering and there is usually no smoking. Even in the girl show in the amusement area, the sailor is placed in a rather astringent attitude, behind glass, for the adoration of the female form. It is all rather serious-minded, this World of Tomorrow, and extremely impersonal. A ride on the Futurama of General Motors induces approximately the same emotional response as a trip through the Cathedral of St. John the Divine. The countryside unfolds before you in five-million-dollar micro-loveliness, conceived in motion and executed by Norman Bel Geddes. The voice is a voice of utmost respect, of complete religious faith in the eternal benefaction of faster travel. The highways unroll in ribbons of perfection through the fertile and rejuvenated America of 1960—a vision of the day to come, the unobstructed left turn, the vanished grade crossing, the town which beckons but does not impede, the millennium of passionless motion. When night falls in the General

Motors exhibit and you lean back in the cushioned chair (yourself in motion and the world so still) and hear (from the depths of the chair) the soft electric assurance of a better life—the life which rests on wheels alone—there is a strong, sweet poison which infects the blood. I didn't want to wake up. I liked 1960 in purple light, going a hundred miles an hour around impossible turns ever onward toward the certified cities of the flawless future. It wasn't till I passed an apple orchard and saw the trees, each blooming under its own canopy of glass, that I perceived that even the General Motors dream, as dreams so often do, left some questions unanswered about the future. The apple tree of Tomorrow, abloom under its inviolate hood, makes you stop and wonder. How will the little boy climb it? Where will the little bird build its nest?

I made a few notes at the Fair, a few hints of what you may expect of Tomorrow, its appointments, its characteristics.

In Tomorrow, people and objects are lit not from above but from below. Trees are lit from below. Even the cow on the rotolactor appears to be lit from below—the buried flood lamp illuminates the distended udder.

In Tomorrow one voice does for all. But it is a little unsure of itself; it keeps testing itself; it says, "Hello! One, two, three, four. Hello! One, two, three, four."

Rugs do not slip in Tomorrow, and the bassinets of newborn infants are wired against kidnappers.

There is no talking back in Tomorrow. You are expected to take it or leave it alone. There are sailors there (which makes you feel less lonely) and the sound of music.

The living room of Tomorrow contains the following objects: a broadloom carpet, artificial carnations, a television radio victrola incessantly producing an image of someone or something which is somewhere else, a glass bird, a chrome steel lamp, a terra-cotta zebra, some veneered book cabinets containing no visible books, another cabinet out of which a small newspaper slowly pours in a never-ending ribbon, and a small plush love seat in the shape of a new moon.

In Tomorrow, most sounds are not the sounds themselves but a memory of sounds, or an electrification. In the case of a cow, the moo will come to you not from the cow but from a small aperture above your head.

Tomorrow is a little on the expensive side. I checked this with my cabdriver in Manhattan to make sure. He was full of praise about the Fair, but said he hadn't seen it and might, in fact, never see it. "I hack out there, but I got it figured that for me and the wife to go all through and do it right—no cheapskate stuff—it would break the hell out of a five-dollar bill. In my racket, I can't afford it."

Tomorrow does not smell. The World's Fair of 1939 has taken the body odor out of man, among other things. It is all rather impersonal, this dream. The country fair manages better, where you can hang over the rail at the ox-pulling and smell the ox. It's not only that the sailors can't get at the girls through the glass, but even so wholesome an exhibit as Swift's Premium Bacon produces twenty lovesick maidens in a glass pit hermetically sealed from the ultimate consumer.

The voice of Mr. Kaltenborn in the City of Man says, "They come with joyous song," but the truth is there is very little joyous song in the Fair grounds. There is a great deal of electrically transmitted joy, but very little spontaneous joy. Tomorrow's music, I noticed, came mostly from Yesterday's singer. In fact, if Mr. Whalen wants a suggestion from me as to how to improve his show (and I am reasonably confident he doesn't), it would be to snip a few wires, hire a couple of bands, and hand out ticklers. Gaiety is not the keynote in Tomorrow. I finally found it at the tag end of a chilly evening, far along in the Amusement Area, in a tent with some colored folks. There was laughing and shouting there, and a beautiful brown belly-dancer.

Another gay spot, to my surprise, was the American Telephone & Telegraph Exhibit. It took the old Telephone Company to put on the best show of all. To anyone who draws a lucky number, the company grants the privilege of making a long-distance call. This

call can be to any point in the United States, and the bystanders
have the exquisite privilege of listening in through earphones and
of laughing unashamed. To understand the full wonder of this, you
must reflect that there are millions of people who have never either
made or received a long-distance call, and that when Eddie Pancha,
a waiter in a restaurant in El Paso, Texas, hears the magic words
"New York is calling . . . Go ahead, please," he is transfixed in holy
dread and excitement. I listened for two hours and ten minutes to
this show, and I'd be there this minute if I were capable of standing
up. I had the good luck to be listening at the earphone when a little
boy named David Wagstaff won the toss and put in a call to tell his
father in Springfield, Mass., what a good time he was having at
the World's Fair. David walked resolutely to the glass booth before
the assembled kibitzers and in a tiny, timid voice gave the operator
his call, his little new cloth hat set all nicely on his head. But his
father wasn't there, and David was suddenly confronted with the
necessity of telling his story to a man named Mr. Henry, who
happened to answer the phone and who, on hearing little David
Wagstaff's voice calling from New York, must surely have thought
that David's mother had been run down in the B.-M. T. and that
David was doing the manly thing.

"Yes, David," he said, tensely.

"Tell my father this," began David, slowly, carefully, determined
to go through with the halcyon experience of winning a lucky call
at the largest Fair the world had yet produced.

"Yes, David."

"We got on the train, and . . . and . . . had a nice trip, and at
New Haven, when they were taking off the car and putting
another car on, it was *awfully* funny because the car gave a great—
big—BUMP!"

Then followed David's three-minute appreciation of the World
of Tomorrow and the Citadel of Light, phrased in the crumbling
remnants of speech that little boys are left with when a lot of
people are watching, and when their thoughts begin to run down,
and when Perispheres begin to swim mistily in time. Mr. Henry—
the invisible and infinitely surprised Mr. Henry—maintained a
respectful and indulgent silence. I don't know what he was think-

ing, but I would swap the Helicline for a copy of his attempted transcription of David's message to his father.

My own memory of the Fair, like David's, has begun to dim. From so much culture, from so much concentrated beauty and progress, one can retain only a fragment. I remember the trees at night, shivering in their burlap undershirts, the eerie shadows clinging to the wrong side of their branches. I remember the fountains playing in the light, I remember the girl who sat so still, so clean, so tangible, producing with the tips of her fingers the synthetic speech—but the words were not the words she wanted to say, they were not the words that were in her mind. I remember the little old Stourbridge Lion, puffing in under its own steam to start the railroads bursting across America. But mostly the Fair has vanished, leaving only the voice of little David Wagstaff and the rambling ecstasy of his first big trip away from home; so many million dollars spent on the idea that our trains and our motorcars should go fast and smoothly, and the child remembering, not the smoothness, but the great—big—BUMP.

So (as the voice says) man dreams on. And the dream is still a contradiction and an enigma—the biologist peeping at bacteria through his microscope, the sailor peeping at the strip queen through binoculars, the eyes so watchful, and the hopes so high. Out in the honky-tonk section, in front of the Amazon show, where the ladies exposed one breast in deference to the fleet, kept one concealed in deference to Mr. Whalen, there was an automaton—a giant man in white tie and tails, with enormous rubber hands. At the start of each show, while the barker was drumming up trade, a couple of the girls would come outside and sit in the robot's lap. The effect was peculiarly lascivious—the extra-size man, exploring with his gigantic rubber hands the breasts of the little girls, the girls with their own small hands (by comparison so small, by comparison so terribly real) restrainingly on his, to check the unthinkable impact of his mechanical passion. Here was the Fair, all fairs, in pantomime; and here the strange mixed dream that made the Fair: the heroic man, bloodless and perfect and enormous, created in his own image, and in his hand (rubber, aseptic) the literal desire, the warm and living breast.

WALDEN

Miss NIMS, take a letter to Henry David Thoreau. Dear Henry: I thought of you the other afternoon as I was approaching Concord doing fifty on Route 62. That is a high speed at which to hold a philosopher in one's mind, but in this century we are a nimble bunch.

On one of the lawns in the outskirts of the village a woman was cutting the grass with a motorized lawn mower. What made me think of you was that the machine had rather got away from her, although she was game enough, and in the brief glimpse I had of the scene it appeared to me that the lawn was mowing the lady. She kept a tight grip on the handles, which throbbed violently with every explosion of the one-cylinder motor, and as she sheered around bushes and lurched along at a reluctant trot behind her impetuous servant, she looked like a puppy who had grabbed something that was too much for him. Concord hasn't changed much, Henry; the farm implements and the animals still have the upper hand.

I may as well admit that I was journeying to Concord with the deliberate intention of visiting your woods; for although I have never knelt at the grave of a philosopher nor placed wreaths on moldy poets, and have often gone a mile out of my way to avoid some place of historical interest, I have always wanted to see Walden Pond. The account which you left of your sojourn there is, you will be amused to learn, a document of increasing pertinence; each year it seems to gain a little headway, as the world loses ground. We may all be transcendental yet, whether we like it or not. As our common complexities increase, any tale of individual simplicity (and yours is the best written and the cockiest) acquires a new fascination; as our goods accumulate, but not our well-being, your report of an existence without material adornment takes on a certain awkward credibility.

My purpose in going to Walden Pond, like yours, was not to live cheaply or to live dearly there, but to transact some private business with the fewest obstacles. Approaching Concord, doing forty, doing forty-five, doing fifty, the steering wheel held snug in my palms, the highway held grimly in my vision, the crown of the road now serving me (on the righthand curves), now defeating me (on the lefthand curves), I began to rouse myself from the stupefaction which a day's motor journey induces. It was a delicious evening, Henry, when the whole body is one sense, and imbibes delight through every pore, if I may coin a phrase. Fields were richly brown where the harrow, drawn by the stripped Ford, had lately sunk its teeth; pastures were green; and overhead the sky had that same everlasting great look which you will find on Page 144 of the Oxford pocket edition. I could feel the road entering me, through tire, wheel, spring, and cushion; shall I not have intelligence with earth too? Am I not partly leaves and vegetable mold myself?—a man of infinite horsepower, yet partly leaves.

Stay with me on 62 and it will take you into Concord. As I say, it was a delicious evening. The snake had come forth to die in a bloody S on the highway, the wheel upon its head, its bowels flat now and exposed. The turtle had come up too to cross the road and die in the attempt, its hard shell smashed under the rubber blow, its intestinal yearning (for the other side of the road) forever squashed. There was a sign by the wayside which announced that the road had a "cotton surface." You wouldn't know what that is, but neither, for that matter, did I. There is a cryptic ingredient in many of our modern improvements—we are awed and pleased without knowing quite what we are enjoying. It is something to be traveling on a road with a cotton surface.

The civilization round Concord today is an odd distillation of city, village, farm, and manor. The houses, yards, fields look not quite suburban, not quite rural. Under the bronze beech and the blue spruce of the departed baron grazes the milch goat of the heirs. Under the porte-cochère stands the reconditioned station wagon; under the grape arbor sit the puppies for sale. (But why do men degenerate ever? What makes families run out?)

It was June and everywhere June was publishing her immemorial

stanza; in the lilacs, in the syringa, in the freshly edged paths and
the sweetness of moist beloved gardens, and the little wire wickets
that preserve the tulips' front. Farmers were already moving the
fruits of their toil into their yards, arranging the rhubarb, the asparagus, the strictly fresh eggs on the painted stands under the little
shed roofs with the patent shingles. And though it was almost a
hundred years since you had taken your ax and started cutting out
your home on Walden Pond, I was interested to observe that the
philosophical spirit was still alive in Massachusetts: in the center
of a vacant lot some boys were assembling the framework of the
rude shelter, their whole mind and skill concentrated in the rather
inauspicious helter-skeleton of studs and rafters. They too were
escaping from town, to live naturally, in a rich blend of savagery
and philosophy.

That evening, after supper at the inn, I strolled out into the
twilight to dream my shapeless transcendental dreams and see that
the car was locked up for the night (first open the right front door,
then reach over, straining, and pull up the handles of the left rear
and the left front till you hear the click, then the handle of the
right rear, then shut the right front but open it again remembering
that the key is still in the ignition switch, remove the key, shut the
right front again with a bang, push the tiny keyhole cover to one
side, insert key, turn, and withdraw). It is what we all do, Henry.
It is called locking the car. It is said to confuse thieves and keep
them from making off with the laprobe. Four doors to lock behind
one robe. The driver himself never uses a laprobe, the free movement of his legs being vital to the operation of the vehicle; so that
when he locks the car it is a pure and unselfish act. I have in my life
gained very little essential heat from laprobes, yet I have ever been
at pains to lock them up.

The evening was full of sounds, some of which would have
stirred your memory. The robins still love the elms of New England
villages at sundown. There is enough of the thrush in them to make
song inevitable at the end of day, and enough of the tramp to
make them hang round the dwellings of men. A robin, like many
another American, dearly loves a white house with green blinds.
Concord is still full of them.

Your fellow-townsmen were stirring abroad—not many afoot, most of them in their cars; and the sound which they made in Concord at evening was a rustling and a whispering. The sound lacks steadfastness and is wholly unlike that of a train. A train, as you know who lived so near the Fitchburg line, whistles once or twice sadly and is gone, trailing a memory in smoke, soothing to ear and mind. Automobiles, skirting a village green, are like flies that have gained the inner ear—they buzz, cease, pause, start, shift, stop, halt, brake, and the whole effect is a nervous polytone curiously disturbing.

As I wandered along, the toc toc of ping pong balls drifted from an attic window. In front of the Reuben Brown house a Buick was drawn up. At the wheel, motionless, his hat upon his head, a man sat, listening to Amos and Andy on the radio (it is a drama of many scenes and without an end). The deep voice of Andrew Brown, emerging from the car, although it originated more than two hundred miles away, was unstrained by distance. When you used to sit on the shore of your pond on Sunday morning, listening to the church bells of Acton and Concord, you were aware of the excellent filter of the intervening atmosphere. Science has attended to that, and sound now maintains its intensity without regard for distance. Properly sponsored, it goes on forever.

A fire engine, out for a trial spin, roared past Emerson's house, hot with readiness for public duty. Over the barn roofs the martins dipped and chittered. A swarthy daughter of an asparagus grower, in culottes, shirt, and bandanna, pedalled past on her bicycle. It was indeed a delicious evening, and I returned to the inn (I believe it was your house once) to rock with the old ladies on the concrete veranda.

Next morning early I started afoot for Walden, out Main Street and down Thoreau, past the depot and the Minuteman Chevrolet Company. The morning was fresh, and in a bean field along the way I flushed an agriculturalist, quietly studying his beans. Thoreau Street soon joined Number 126, an artery of the State. We number our highways nowadays, our speed being so great we can remember little of their quality or character and are lucky to remember their number. (Men have an indistinct notion that if they keep up this activity long enough all will at length ride somewhere, in next to no time.) Your pond is on 126.

I knew I must be nearing your woodland retreat when the Golden Pheasant lunchroom came into view—Sealtest ice cream, toasted sandwiches, hot frankfurters, waffles, tonics, and lunches. Were I the proprietor, I should add rice, Indian meal, and molasses —just for old time's sake. The Pheasant, incidentally, is for sale: a chance for some nature lover who wishes to set himself up beside a pond in the Concord atmosphere and live deliberately, fronting only the essential facts of life on Number 126. Beyond the Pheasant was a place called Walden Breezes, an oasis whose porch pillars were made of old green shutters sawed into lengths. On the porch was a distorting mirror, to give the traveler a comical image of himself, who had miraculously learned to gaze in an ordinary glass without smiling. Behind the Breezes, in a sun-parched clearing, dwelt your philosophical descendants in their trailers, each trailer the size of your hut, but all grouped together for the sake of congeniality. Trailer people leave the city, as you did, to discover solitude and in any weather, at any hour of the day or night, to improve the nick of time; but they soon collect in villages and get bogged deeper in the mud than ever. The camp behind Walden Breezes was just rousing itself to the morning. The ground was packed hard under the heel, and the sun came through the clearing to bake the soil and enlarge the wry smell of cramped housekeeping. Cushman's bakery truck had stopped to deliver an early basket of rolls. A camp dog, seeing me in the road, barked petulantly. A man emerged from one of the trailers and set forth with a bucket to draw water from some forest tap.

Leaving the highway I turned off into the woods toward the pond, which was apparent through the foliage. The floor of the forest was strewn with dried old oak leaves and *Transcripts*. From beneath the flattened popcorn wrapper (*granum explosum*) peeped the frail violet. I followed a footpath and descended to the water's edge. The pond lay clear and blue in the morning light, as you have seen it so many times. In the shallows a man's waterlogged shirt undulated gently. A few flies came out to greet me and convoy me to your cove, past the No Bathing signs on which the fellows and the girls had scrawled their names. I felt strangely excited suddenly to be snooping around your premises, tiptoeing along watchfully, as though not to tread by mistake upon the intervening century. Before I got to the cove I heard something which seemed to me quite wonderful: I heard your frog, a full, clear *troonk*, guiding me, still hoarse and solemn, bridging the years as the robins had bridged them in the sweetness of the village evening. But he soon quit, and I came on a couple of young boys throwing stones at him.

Your front yard is marked by a bronze tablet set in a stone. Four small granite posts, a few feet away, show where the house was. On top of the tablet was a pair of faded blue bathing trunks with a white stripe. Back of it is a pile of stones, a sort of cairn, left by your visitors as a tribute I suppose. It is a rather ugly little heap of stones, Henry. In fact the hillside itself seems faded, browbeaten; a few tall skinny pines, bare of lower limbs, a smattering of young maples in suitable green, some birches and oaks, and a number of trees felled by the last big wind. It was from the bole of one of these fallen pines, torn up by the roots, that I extracted the stone which I added to the cairn—a sentimental act in which I was interrupted by a small terrier from a nearby picnic group, who confronted me and wanted to know about the stone.

I sat down for a while on one of the posts of your house to listen to the bluebottles and the dragonflies. The invaded glade sprawled shabby and mean at my feet, but the flies were tuned to the old vibration. There were the remains of a fire in your ruins, but I doubt that it was yours; also two beer bottles trodden into the soil and become part of earth. A young oak had taken root in your house, and two or three ferns, unrolling like the ticklers at a banquet. The only other furnishings were a DuBarry pattern sheet, a page torn from a picture magazine, and some crusts in wax paper.

Before I quit I walked clear round the pond and found the place where you used to sit on the northeast side to get the sun in the fall, and the beach where you got sand for scrubbing your floor. On the eastern side of the pond, where the highway borders it, the

State has built dressing rooms for swimmers, a float with diving towers, drinking fountains of porcelain, and rowboats for hire. The pond is in fact a State Preserve, and carries a twenty-dollar fine for picking wild flowers, a decree signed in all solemnity by your fellow-citizens Walter C. Wardwell, Erson B. Barlow, and Nathaniel I. Bowditch. There was a smell of creosote where they had been building a wide wooden stairway to the road and the parking area. Swimmers and boaters were arriving; bodies plunged vigorously into the water and emerged wet and beautiful in the bright air. As I left, a boatload of town boys were splashing about in mid-pond, kidding and fooling, the young fellows singing at the tops of their lungs in a wild chorus:

> Amer-ica, Amer-ica, God shed his grace on thee,
> And crown thy good with brotherhood
> From sea to shi-ning sea!

I walked back to town along the railroad, following your custom. The rails were expanding noisily in the hot sun, and on the slope of the roadbed the wild grape and the blackberry sent up their creepers to the track.

The expense of my brief sojourn in Concord was:

Canvas shoes	$1.95
Baseball bat	.25 } gifts to take back
Left-handed fielder's glove	1.25 } to a boy
Hotel and meals	4.25
In all	$7.70

As you see, this amount was almost what you spent for food for eight months. I cannot defend the shoes or the expenditure for shelter and food: they reveal a meanness and grossness in my nature which you would find contemptible. The baseball equipment, however, is the kind of impediment with which you were never on even terms. You must remember that the house where you practiced the sort of economy which I respect was haunted only by mice and squirrels. You never had to cope with a shortstop.

ONCE MORE TO THE LAKE

ONE SUMMER, along about 1904, my father rented a camp on a lake in Maine and took us all there for the month of August. We all got ringworm from some kittens and had to rub Pond's Extract on our arms and legs night and morning, and my father rolled over in a canoe with all his clothes on; but outside of that the vacation was a success and from then on none of us ever thought there was any place in the world like that lake in Maine. We returned summer after summer—always on August 1st for one month. I have since become a salt-water man, but sometimes in summer there are days when the restlessness of the tides and the fearful cold of the sea water and the incessant wind which blows across the afternoon and into the evening make me wish for the placidity of a lake in the woods. A few weeks ago this feeling got so strong I bought myself a couple of bass hooks and a spinner and returned to the lake where we used to go, for a week's fishing and to revisit old haunts.

I took along my son, who had never had any fresh water up his nose and who had seen lily pads only from train windows. On the journey over to the lake I began to wonder what it would be like. I wondered how time would have marred this unique, this holy spot—the coves and streams, the hills that the sun set behind, the camps and the paths behind the camps. I was sure that the tarred road would have found it out and I wondered in what other ways it would be desolated. It is strange how much you can remember about places like that once you allow your mind to return into the grooves which lead back. You remember one thing, and that suddenly reminds you of another thing. I guess I remembered clearest of all the early mornings, when the lake was cool and motionless, remembered how the bedroom smelled of the lumber it was made of and of the wet woods whose scent entered through the screen. The partitions in the camp were thin and did not extend clear to the top of the rooms, and as I was always the first up I would dress softly so as not to wake the others, and sneak out into the sweet out-doors and start out in the canoe, keeping close along the shore in the long shadows of the pines. I remembered being very careful never to rub my paddle against the gunwale for fear of disturbing the stillness of the cathedral.

The lake had never been what you would call a wild lake. There were cottages sprinkled around the shores, and it was in farming country although the shores of the lake were quite heavily wooded. Some of the cottages were owned by nearby farmers, and you would live at the shore and eat your meals at the farmhouse. That's what our family did. But although it wasn't wild, it was a fairly large and undisturbed lake and there were places in it which, to a child at least, seemed infinitely remote and primeval.

I was right about the tar: it led to within half a mile of the shore. But when I got back there, with my boy, and we settled into a camp near a farmhouse and into the kind of summertime I had known, I could tell that it was going to be pretty much the same as it had been before—I knew it, lying in bed the first morning, smelling the bedroom, and hearing the boy sneak quietly out and go off along the shore in a boat. I began to sustain the illusion that he was I, and therefore, by simple transposition, that I was my father. This sensa-tion persisted, kept cropping up all the time we were there. It was not an entirely new feeling, but in this setting it grew much stronger. I seemed to be living a dual existence. I would be in the middle of some simple act, I would be picking up a bait box or laying down a table fork, or I would be saying something, and suddenly it would be not I but my father who was saying the words or making the gesture. It gave me a creepy sensation.

We went fishing the first morning. I felt the same damp moss covering the worms in the bait can, and saw the dragonfly alight on the tip of my rod as it hovered a few inches from the surface of the water. It was the arrival of this fly that convinced me beyond any doubt that everything was as it always had been, that the years

were a mirage and there had been no years. The small waves were
the same, chucking the rowboat under the chin as we fished at
anchor, and the boat was the same boat, the same color green and
the ribs broken in the same places, and under the floor-boards the
same fresh-water leavings and débris—the dead helgramite, the wisps
of moss, the rusty discarded fishhook, the dried blood from yesterday's catch. We stared silently at the tips of our rods, at the dragonflies that came and went. I lowered the tip of mine into the water,
tentatively, pensively dislodging the fly, which darted two feet away,
poised, darted two feet back, and came to rest again a little farther
up the rod. There had been no years between the ducking of this
dragonfly and the other one—the one that was part of memory. I
looked at the boy, who was silently watching his fly, and it was
my hands that held his rod, my eyes watching. I felt dizzy and
didn't know which rod I was at the end of.

We caught two bass, hauling them in briskly as though they
were mackerel, pulling them over the side of the boat in a business-
like manner without any landing net, and stunning them with a
blow on the back of the head. When we got back for a swim before
lunch, the lake was exactly where we had left it, the same number
of inches from the dock, and there was only the merest suggestion of
a breeze. This seemed an utterly enchanted sea, this lake you could
leave to its own devices for a few hours and come back to, and find
that it had not stirred, this constant and trustworthy body of water.
In the shallows, the dark, water-soaked sticks and twigs, smooth and
old, were undulating in clusters on the bottom against the clean
ribbed sand, and the track of the mussel was plain. A school of
minnows swam by, each minnow with its small individual shadow,
doubling the attendance, so clear and sharp in the sunlight. Some
of the other campers were in swimming, along the shore, one of
them with a cake of soap, and the water felt thin and clear and
unsubstantial. Over the years there had been this person with the
cake of soap, this cultist, and here he was. There had been no years.

Up to the farmhouse to dinner through the teeming, dusty field,
the road under our sneakers was only a two-track road. The middle
track was missing, the one with the marks of the hooves and the

splotches of dried, flaky manure. There had always been three tracks to choose from in choosing which track to walk in; now the choice was narrowed down to two. For a moment I missed terribly the middle alternative. But the way led past the tennis court, and something about the way it lay there in the sun reassured me; the tape had loosened along the backline, the alleys were green with plantains and other weeds, and the net (installed in June and removed in September) sagged in the dry noon, and the whole place steamed with midday heat and hunger and emptiness. There was a choice of pie for dessert, and one was blueberry and one was apple, and the waitresses were the same country girls, there having been no passage of time, only the illusion of it as in a dropped curtain—the waitresses were still fifteen; their hair had been washed, that was the only difference—they had been to the movies and seen the pretty girls with the clean hair.

Summertime, oh summertime, pattern of life indelible, the fade-proof lake, the woods unshatterable, the pasture with the sweetfern and the juniper forever and ever, summer without end; this was the background, and the life along the shore was the design, the cottagers with their innocent and tranquil design, their tiny docks with the flagpole and the American flag floating against the white clouds in the blue sky, the little paths over the roots of the trees leading from camp to camp and the paths leading back to the out-houses and the can of lime for sprinkling, and at the souvenir counters at the store the miniature birch-bark canoes and the post cards that showed things looking a little better than they looked. This was the American family at play, escaping the city heat, wondering whether the newcomers in the camp at the head of the cove were "common" or "nice," wondering whether it was true that the people who drove up for Sunday dinner at the farmhouse were turned away because there wasn't enough chicken.

It seemed to me, as I kept remembering all this, that those times and those summers had been infinitely precious and worth saving. There had been jollity and peace and goodness. The arriving (at the beginning of August) had been so big a business in itself, at the railway station the farm wagon drawn up, the first smell of the pine-laden air, the first glimpse of the smiling farmer, and the great importance of the trunks and your father's enormous authority in such matters, and the feel of the wagon under you for the long ten-mile haul, and at the top of the last long hill catching the first view of the lake after eleven months of not seeing this cherished body of water. The shouts and cries of the other campers when they saw you, and the trunks to be unpacked, to give up their rich burden. (Arriving was less exciting nowadays, when you sneaked up in your car and parked it under a tree near the camp and took out the bags and in five minutes it was all over, no fuss, no loud wonderful fuss about trunks.)

Peace and goodness and jollity. The only thing that was wrong now, really, was the sound of the place, an unfamiliar nervous sound of the outboard motors. This was the note that jarred, the one thing that would sometimes break the illusion and set the years moving. In those other summertimes all motors were inboard; and when they were at a little distance, the noise they made was a sedative, an ingredient of summer sleep. They were one-cylinder and two-cylinder engines, and some were make-and-break and some were jump-spark, but they all made a sleepy sound across the lake. The one-lungers throbbed and fluttered, and the twin-cylinder ones purred and purred, and that was a quiet sound too. But now the campers all had outboards. In the daytime, in the hot mornings, these motors made a petulant, irritable sound; at night, in the still evening when the afterglow lit the water, they whined about one's ears like mosquitoes. My boy loved our rented outboard, and his great desire was to achieve singlehanded mastery over it, and authority, and he soon learned the trick of choking it a little (but not too much), and the adjustment of the needle valve. Watching him I would remember the things you could do with the old one-cylinder engine with the heavy flywheel, how you could have it eating out of your hand if you got really close to it spiritually. Motor boats in those days didn't have clutches, and you would make a landing by shutting off the motor at the proper time and coasting in with a dead rudder. But there was a way of reversing them, if you learned the trick, by cutting the switch and putting it on again exactly on the final dying revolution of the flywheel, so that it would kick back against compression and begin reversing. Approaching a dock in a strong following breeze, it was difficult to slow up sufficiently by the ordinary coasting method, and if a boy felt he had complete mastery over his motor, he was tempted to keep it running beyond its time and then reverse it a few feet from the dock. It took a cool nerve, because if you threw the switch a twentieth of a second too soon you would catch the flywheel when it still had speed enough to go up past center, and the boat would leap ahead, charging bull-fashion at the dock.

We had a good week at the camp. The bass were biting well and the sun shone endlessly, day after day. We would be tired at night and lie down in the accumulated heat of the little bedrooms after the long hot day and the breeze would stir almost imperceptibly outside and the smell of the swamp drift in through the rusty screens. Sleep would come easily and in the morning the red squirrel would be on the roof, tapping out his gay routine. I kept remembering everything, lying in bed in the mornings—the small steamboat that had a long rounded stern like the lip of a Ubangi, and how quietly she ran on the moonlight sails, when the older boys played their mandolins and the girls sang and we ate doughnuts dipped in sugar, and how sweet the music was on the water in the shining night, and what it had felt like to think about girls then. After breakfast we would go up to the store and the things were in the same place—the minnows in a bottle, the plugs and spinners disarranged and pawed over by the youngsters from the boys' camp, the fig newtons and the Beeman's gum. Outside, the road was tarred and cars stood in front of the store. Inside, all was just as it had always been, except there was more Coca-Cola and not so much Moxie and root beer and birch beer and sarsaparilla. We would walk out with a bottle of pop apiece and sometimes the pop would backfire up our noses and hurt. We explored the streams, quietly, where the turtles slid off the sunny logs and dug their way into the soft bottom; and we lay on the town wharf and fed worms to the tame bass. Everywhere we went I had trouble making out which was I, the one walking at my side, the one walking in my pants.

One afternoon while we were there at that lake a thunderstorm came up. It was like the revival of an old melodrama that I had seen long ago with childish awe. The second-act climax of the drama of the electrical disturbance over a lake in America had not changed in any important respect. This was the big scene, still the big scene. The whole thing was so familiar, the first feeling of oppression and heat and a general air around camp of not wanting to go very far away. In midafternoon (it was all the same) a curious darkening of the sky, and a lull in everything that had made life tick; and then the way the boats suddenly swung the other way at their moorings with the coming of a breeze out of the new quarter, and the premonitory rumble. Then the kettle drum, then the snare, then the bass drum and cymbals, then crackling light against the dark, and the gods grinning and licking their chops in the hills. Afterward the calm, the rain steadily rustling in the calm lake, the return of light and hope and spirits, and the campers running out in joy and relief to go swimming in the rain, their bright cries perpetuating the deathless joke about how they were getting simply drenched, and the children screaming with delight at the new sensation of bathing in the rain, and the joke about getting drenched linking the generations in a strong indestructible chain. And the comedian who waded in carrying an umbrella.

When the others went swimming my son said he was going in too. He pulled his dripping trunks from the line where they had hung all through the shower, and wrung them out. Languidly, and with no thought of going in, I watched him, his hard little body, skinny and bare, saw him wince slightly as he pulled up around his vitals the small, soggy, icy garment. As he buckled the swollen belt suddenly my groin felt the chill of death.

[1948]

DEATH OF A PIG

I SPENT SEVERAL day and nights in mid-September with an ailing pig and I feel driven to account for this stretch of time, more particularly since the pig died at last, and I lived, and things might easily have gone the other way round and none left to do the accounting. Even now, so close to the event, I cannot recall the hours sharply and am not ready to say whether death came on the third night or the fourth night. This uncertainty afflicts me with a sense of personal deterioration; if I were in decent health I would know how many nights I had sat up with a pig.

The scheme of buying a spring pig in blossomtime, feeding it through summer and fall, and butchering it when the solid cold weather arrives, is a familiar scheme to me and follows an antique pattern. It is a tragedy enacted on most farms with perfect fidelity to the original script. The murder, being premeditated, is the first degree but is quick and skillful, and the smoked bacon and ham provide a ceremonial ending whose fitness is seldom questioned.

Once in a while something slips—one of the actors goes up in his lines and the whole performance stumbles and halts. My pig simply failed to show up for a meal. The alarm spread rapidly. The classic outline of the tragedy was lost. I found myself cast suddenly in the role of pig's friend and physician—a farcical character with an enema bag for a prop. I had a presentiment, the very first afternoon, that the play would never regain its balance and that my sympathies were now wholly with the pig. This was slapstick—the sort of dramatic treatment that instantly appealed to my old dachshund, Fred, who joined the vigil, held the bag, and, when all was over, presided at the interment. When we slid the body into the grave, we both were shaken to the core. The loss we felt was not the loss of ham but the loss of pig. He had evidently become precious to me, not that he represented a distant nourishment in a hungry time, but that he had suffered in a suffering world. But I'm running ahead of my story and shall have to go back.

My pigpen is at the bottom of an old orchard below the house. The pigs I have raised have lived in a faded building that once was an icehouse. There is a pleasant yard to move about in, shaded by an apple tree that overhangs the low rail fence. A pig couldn't ask for anything better—or none has, at any rate. The sawdust in the icehouse makes a comfortable bottom in which to root, and a warm bed. This sawdust, however, came under suspicion when the pig took sick. One of my neighbors said he thought the pig would have done better on new ground—the same principle that applies in planting potatoes. He said there might be something unhealthy about that sawdust, that he never thought well of sawdust.

It was about four o'clock in the afternoon when I first noticed that there was something wrong with the pig. He failed to appear at the trough for his supper, and when a pig (or a child) refuses supper a chill wave of fear runs through any household, or ice-household. After examining my pig, who was stretched out in the sawdust inside the building, I went to the phone and cranked it four times. Mr. Dameron answered. "What's good for a sick pig?" I asked. (There is never any identification needed on a country phone; the person on the other end knows who is talking by the sound of the voice and by the character of the question.)

"I don't know, I never had a sick pig," said Mr. Dameron, "but I can find out quick enough. You hang up and I'll call Henry."

Mr. Dameron was back on the line again in five minutes. "Henry says roll him over on his back and give him two ounces of castor oil or sweet oil, and if that doesn't do the trick give him an injection of soapy water. He says he's almost sure the pig's plugged up, and even if he's wrong, it can't do any harm."

I thanked Mr. Dameron. I didn't go right down to the pig, though. I sank into a chair and sat still for a few minutes to think about my troubles, and then I got up and went to the barn, catching up on some odds and ends that needed tending to. Unconsciously I held off, for an hour, the deed by which I would officially recognize

the collapse of the performance of raising a pig; I wanted no interruption in the regularity of feeding, the steadiness of growth, the
even succession of days. I wanted no interruption, wanted no oil,
no deviation. I just wanted to keep on raising a pig, full meal after
full meal, spring into summer into fall. I didn't even know whether
there were two ounces of castor oil on the place.

Shortly after five o'clock I remembered that we had been invited
out to dinner that night and realized that if I were to dose a pig
there was no time to lose. The dinner date seemed a familiar conflict: I move in a desultory society and often a week or two will
roll by without my going to anybody's house to dinner or anyone's
coming to mine, but when an occasion does arise, and I am sum-
moned, something usually turns up (an hour or two in advance) to
make all human intercourse seem vastly inappropriate. I have come
to believe that there is in hostesses a special power of divination,
and that they deliberately arrange dinners to coincide with pig
failure or some other sort of failure. At any rate, it was after five
o'clock and I knew I could put off no longer the evil hour.

When my son and I arrived at the pigyard, armed with a small
bottle of castor oil and a length of clothesline, the pig had emerged
from his house and was standing in the middle of his yard, list-
lessly. He gave us a slim greeting. I could see that he felt uncom-
fortable and uncertain. I had brought the clothesline thinking I'd
have to tie him (the pig weighed more than a hundred pounds) but
we never used it. My son reached down, grabbed both front legs,
upset him quickly, and when he opened his mouth to scream I
turned the oil into his throat—a pink, corrugated area I had never
seen before. I had just time to read the label while the neck of the
bottle was in his mouth. It said Puretest. The screams, slightly
muffled by oil, were pitched in the hysterically high range of
pigsound, as though torture were being carried out, but they didn't
last long: it was all over rather suddenly, and, his legs released, the
pig righted himself.

In the upset position the corners of his mouth had been turned
down, giving him a frowning expression. Back on his feet again,
he regained the set smile that a pig wears even in sickness. He

stood his ground, sucking slightly at the residue of oil; a few drops leaked out of his lips while his wicked eyes, shaded by their coy little lashes, turned on me in disgust and hatred. I scratched him gently with oily fingers and he remained quiet, as though trying to recall the satisfaction of being scratched when in health, and seeming to rehearse in his mind the indignity to which he had just been subjected. I noticed, as I stood there, four or five small dark spots on his back near the tail end, reddish brown in color, each about the size of a housefly. I could not make out what they were. They did not look troublesome but at the same time they did not look like mere surface bruises or chafe marks. Rather they seemed blemishes of internal origin. His stiff white bristles almost completely hid them and I had to part the bristles with my fingers to get a good look.

Several hours later, a few minutes before midnight, having dined well and at someone else's expense, I returned to the pighouse with a flashlight. The patient was asleep. Kneeling, I felt his ears (as you might put your hand on the forehead of a child) and they seemed cool, and then with the light made a careful examination of the yard and the house for sign that the oil had worked. I found none and went to bed.

We had been having an unseasonable spell of weather—hot, close days, with the fog shutting in every night, scaling for a few hours in midday, then creeping back again at dark, drifting in first over the trees on the point, then suddenly blowing across the fields, blotting out the world and taking possession of houses, men, and animals. Everyone kept hoping for a break, but the break failed to come. Next day was another hot one. I visited the pig before breakfast and tried to tempt him with a little milk in his trough. He just stared at it, while I made a sucking sound through my teeth to remind him of past pleasures of the feast. With very small, timid pigs, weanlings, this ruse is often quite successful and will encourage them to eat; but with a large, sick pig the ruse is senseless and the sound I made must have made him feel, if anything, more miserable. He not only did not crave food, he felt a positive revulsion to it. I found a place under the apple tree where he had vomited in the night.

At this point, although a depression had settled over me, I didn't suppose that I was going to lose my pig. From the lustiness of a healthy pig a man derives a feeling of personal lustiness; the stuff that goes into the trough and is received with such enthusiasm is an earnest of some later feast of his own, and when this suddenly comes to an end and the food lies stale and untouched, souring in the sun, the pig's imbalance becomes the man's vicariously, and life seems insecure, displaced, transitory.

As my own spirits declined, along with the pig's, the spirits of my vile old dachshund rose. The frequency of our trips down the footpath through the orchard to the pigyard delighted him, although he suffers greatly from arthritis, moves with difficulty, and would be bedridden if he could find anyone willing to serve him meals on a tray.

He never missed a chance to visit the pig with me, and he made many professional calls on his own. You could see him down there at all hours, his white face parting the grass along the fence as he wobbled and stumbled about, his stethoscope dangling—a happy quack, writing his villainous prescriptions and grinning his corrosive grin. When the enema bag appeared, and the bucket of warm suds, his happiness was complete, and he managed to squeeze his enormous body between the two lowest rails of the yard and then assumed full charge of the irrigation. Once, when I lowered the bag to check the flow, he reached in and hurriedly drank a few mouthfuls of the suds to test their potency. I have noticed that Fred will feverishly consume any substance that is associated with trouble—the bitter flavor is to his liking. When the bag was above reach, he concentrated on the pig and was everywhere at once, a tower of strength and inconvenience. The pig, curiously enough, stood rather quietly through this colonic carnival, and the enema, though ineffective, was not as difficult as I had anticipated.

I discovered, though, that once having given a pig an enema there is no turning back, no chance of resuming one of life's more stereotyped roles. The pig's lot and mine were inextricably bound now, as though the rubber tube were the silver cord. From then until the time of his death I held the pig steadily in the bowl of my mind; the task of trying to deliver him from his misery became a strong obsession. His suffering soon became the embodiment of all earthly wretchedness. Along toward the end of the afternoon, defeated in physicking, I phoned the veterinary twenty miles away and placed the case formally in his hands. He was full of questions, and when I casually mentioned the dark spots on the pig's back, his voice changed its tone.

"I don't want to scare you," he said, "but when there are spots, erysipelas has to be considered."

Together we considered erysipelas, with frequent interruptions from the telephone operator, who wasn't sure the connection had been established.

"If a pig has erysipelas can he give it to a person?" I asked.

"Yes, he can," replied the vet.

"Have they answered?" asked the operator.

"Yes, they have," I said. Then I addressed the vet again. "You better come over here and examine this pig right away."

"I can't come myself," said the vet, "but McFarland can come this evening if that's all right. Mac knows more about pigs than I do anyway. You needn't worry too much about the spots. To indicate erysipelas they would have to be deep hemorrhagic infarcts."

"Deep hemorrhagic what?" I asked.

"Infarcts," said the vet.

"Have they answered?" asked the operator.

"Well," I said, "I don't know what you'd call these spots, except they're about the size of a housefly. If the pig has erysipelas I guess I have it, too, by this time, because we've been very close lately."

"McFarland will be over," said the vet.

I hung up. My throat felt dry and I went to the cupboard and got a bottle of whiskey. Deep hemorrhagic infarcts—the phrase began fastening its hooks in my head. I had assumed that there could be nothing much wrong with a pig during the months it was being groomed for murder; my confidence in the essential health and endurance of pigs had been strong and deep, particularly in the health of pigs that belonged to me and that were part of my proud

scheme. The awakening had been violent and I minded it all the
more because I knew that what could be true of my pig could be
true also of the rest of my tidy world. I tried to put this distasteful
idea from me, but it kept recurring. I took a short drink of the
whiskey and then, although I wanted to go down to the yard and
look for fresh signs, I was scared to. I was certain I had erysipelas.

It was long after dark and the supper dishes had been put away
when a car drove in and McFarland got out. He had a girl with
him. I could just make her out in the darkness—she seemed young
and pretty. "This is Miss Owen," he said. "We've been having a
picnic supper on the shore, that's why I'm late."

McFarland stood in the driveway and stripped off his jacket,
then his shirt. His stocky arms and capable hands showed up in my
flashlight's gleam as I helped him find his coverall and get zipped
up. The rear seat of his car contained an astonishing amount of
paraphernalia, which he soon overhauled, selecting a chain, a
syringe, a bottle of oil, a rubber tube, and some other things
I couldn't identify. Miss Owen said she'd go along with us and see
the pig. I led the way down the warm slope of the orchard, my light
picking out the path for them, and we all three climbed the fence,
entered the pighouse, and squatted by the pig while McFarland
took a rectal reading. My flashlight picked up the glitter of an
engagement ring on the girl's hand.

"No elevation," said McFarland, twisting the thermometer in the
light. "You needn't worry about erysipelas." He ran his hand slowly
over the pig's stomach and at one point the pig cried out in pain.

"Poor piggledy-wiggledy!" said Miss Owen.

The treatment I had been giving the pig for two days was then
repeated, somewhat more expertly, by the doctor, Miss Owen and I
handing him things as he needed them—holding the chain that he
had looped around the pig's upper jaw, holding the syringe, holding
the bottle stopper, the end of the tube, all of us working in darkness
and in comfort, working with the instinctive teamwork induced by
emergency conditions, the pig unprotesting, the house shadowy, protecting, intimate. I went to bed tired but with a feeling of relief
that I had turned over part of the responsibility of the case to a

licensed doctor. I was beginning to think, though, that the pig was not going to live.

He died twenty-four hours later, or it might have been forty-eight—there is a blur in time here, and I may have lost or picked up a day in the telling and the pig one in the dying. At intervals during the last day I took cool fresh water down to him and at such times as he found the strength to get to his feet he would stand with head in the pail and snuffle his snout around. He drank a few sips but no more; yet it seemed to comfort him to dip his nose in water and bobble it about, sucking in and blowing out through his teeth. Much of the time, now, he lay indoors half buried in sawdust. Once, near the last, while I was attending him I saw him try to make a bed for himself but he lacked the strength, and when he set his snout into the dust he was unable to plow even the little furrow he needed to lie down in.

He came out of the house to die. When I went down, before going to bed, he lay stretched in the yard a few feet from the door. I knelt, saw that he was dead, and left him there: his face had a mild look, expressive neither of deep peace nor of deep suffering, although I think he had suffered a good deal. I went back up to the house and to bed, and cried internally—deep hemorrhagic intears. I didn't wake till nearly eight the next morning, and when I looked out the open window the grave was already being dug, down beyond the dump under a wild apple. I could hear the spade strike against the small rocks that blocked the way. Never send to know for whom the grave is dug, I said to myself, it's dug for thee. Fred, I well knew, was supervising the work of digging, so I ate breakfast slowly.

It was a Saturday morning. The thicket in which I found the gravediggers at work was dark and warm, the sky overcast. Here, among alders and young hackmatacks, at the foot of the apple tree, Lennie had dug a beautiful hole, five feet long, three feet wide, three feet deep. He was standing in it, removing the last spadefuls of earth while Fred patrolled the brink in simple but impressive circles. disturbing the loose earth of the mound so that it trickled back in. There had been no rain in weeks and the soil, even three feet down, was dry and powdery. As I stood and stared, an enormous earthworm which had been partially exposed by the spade at the bottom dug itself deeper and made a slow withdrawal, seeking even remoter moistures at even lonelier depths. And just as Lennie stepped out and rested his spade against the tree and lit a cigarette, a small green apple separated itself from a branch overhead and fell into the hole. Everything about this last scene seemed over-written—the dismal sky, the shabby woods, the imminence of rain, the worm (legendary bedfellow of the dead), the apple (conventional garnish of a pig).

But even so, there was a directness and dispatch about animal burial, I thought, that made it a more decent affair than human burial: there was no stopover in the undertaker's foul parlor, no wreath nor spray; and when we hitched a line to the pig's hind legs and dragged him swiftly from his yard, throwing our weight into the harness and leaving a wake of crushed grass and smoothed rubble over the dump, ours was a businesslike procession, with Fred, the dishonorable pallbearer, staggering along in the rear, his perverse bereavement showing in every seam in his face; and the post mortem performed handily and swiftly right at the edge of the grave, so that the inwards that had caused the pig's death preceded him into the ground and he lay at last resting squarely on the cause of his own undoing.

I threw in the first shovelful, and then we worked rapidly and without talk, until the job was complete. I picked up the rope, made it fast to Fred's collar (he is a notorious ghoul), and we all three filed back up the path to the house, Fred bringing up the rear and holding back every inch of the way, feigning unusual stiffness. I noticed that although he weighed far less than the pig, he was harder to drag, being possessed of the vital spark.

The news of the death of my pig traveled fast and far, and I received many expressions of sympathy from friends and neighbors, for no one took the event lightly and the premature expiration of a pig is, I soon discovered, a departure which the community marks solemnly on its calendar, a sorrow in which it feels fully involved.

I have written this account in penitence and in grief, as a man who failed to raise his pig, and to explain my deviation from the classic course of so many raised pigs. The grave in the woods is unmarked, but Fred can direct the mourner to it unerringly and with immense good will, and I know he and I shall often revisit it, singly and together, in seasons of reflection and despair, on flagless memorial days of our own choosing.

[1956]

THE RING OF TIME

AFTER THE lions had returned to their cages, creeping angrily through the chutes, a little bunch of us drifted away and into an open doorway nearby, where we stood for a while in semidarkness, watching a big brown circus horse go harumphing around the practice ring. His trainer was a woman of about forty, and the two of them, horse and woman, seemed caught up in one of those desultory treadmills of afternoon from which there is no apparent escape. The day was hot, and we kibitzers were grateful to be briefly out of the sun's glare. The long rein, or tape, by which the woman guided her charge counterclockwise in his dull career formed the radius of their private circle, of which she was the revolving center; and she, too, stepped a tiny circumference of her own, in order to accommodate the horse and allow him his maximum scope. She had on a short-skirted costume and a conical straw hat. Her legs were bare and she wore high heels, which probed deep into the loose tanbark and kept her ankles in a state of constant turmoil. The great size and meekness of the horse, the repetitious exercise, the heat of the afternoon, all exerted a hypnotic charm that invited boredom; we spectators were experiencing a languor—we neither expected relief nor felt entitled to any. We had paid a dollar to get into the grounds, to be sure, but we had got our dollar's worth a few minutes before, when the lion trainer's whiplash had got caught around a toe of one of the lions. What more did we want for a dollar?

Behind me I heard someone say, "Excuse me, please," in a low voice. She was halfway into the building when I turned and saw her—a girl of sixteen or seventeen, politely threading her way through us onlookers who blocked the entrance. As she emerged in front of us, I saw that she was barefoot, her dirty little feet fighting the uneven ground. In most respects she was like any of two or three dozen showgirls you encounter if you wander about the winter quarters of Mr. John Ringling North's circus, in Sarasota—cleverly proportioned, deeply browned by the sun, dusty, eager, and almost naked. But her grave face and the naturalness of her manner gave her a sort of quick distinction and brought a new note into the gloomy octagonal building where we had all cast our lot for a few moments. As soon as she had squeezed through the crowd, she spoke a word or two to the older woman, whom I took to be her mother, stepped to the ring, and waited while the horse coasted to a stop in front of her. She gave the animal a couple of affectionate swipes on his enormous neck and then swung herself aboard. The horse immediately resumed his rocking canter, the woman goading him on, chanting something that sounded like "Hop! Hop!"

In attempting to recapture this mild spectacle, I am merely acting as recording secretary for one of the oldest of societies—the society of those who, at one time or another, have surrendered, without even a show of resistance, to the bedazzlement of a circus rider. As a writing man, or secretary, I have always felt charged with the safe-keeping of all unexpected items of worldly or unworldly enchant-ment, as though I might be held personally responsible if even a small one were to be lost. But it is not easy to communicate anything of this nature. The circus comes as close to being the world in microcosm as anything I know; in a way, it puts all the rest of show business in the shade. Its magic is universal and complex. Out of its wild disorder comes order; from its rank smell rises the good aroma of courage and daring; out of its preliminary shabbiness comes the final splendor. And buried in the familiar boasts of its advance agents lies the modesty of most of its people. For me the circus is at its best before it has been put together. It is at its best at certain moments when it comes to a point, as through a burning glass, in the activity and destiny of a single performer out of so many. One ring is always bigger than three. One rider, one aerialist, is always greater than six. In short, a man has to catch the circus unawares to experience its full impact and share its gaudy dream.

The ten-minute ride the girl took achieved—as far as I was concerned, who wasn't looking for it, and quite unbeknownst to her, who wasn't even striving for it—the thing that is sought by performers everywhere, on whatever stage, whether struggling in the tidal currents of Shakespeare or bucking the difficult motion of a horse. I somehow got the idea she was just cadging a ride, improving a shining ten minutes in the diligent way all serious artists seize free moments to hone the blade of their talent and keep themselves in trim. Her brief tour included only elementary postures and tricks, perhaps because her warmup at this hour was unscheduled and the ring was not rigged for a real practice session. She swung herself off and on the horse several times, gripping his mane. She did a few knee-stands—or whatever they are called—dropping to her knees and quickly bouncing back up on her feet again. Most of the time she simply rode in a standing position, well aft on the beast, her hands hanging easily at her sides, her head erect, her straw-colored ponytail lightly brushing her shoulders, the blood of exertion showing faintly through the tan of her skin. Twice she managed a one-foot stance—a sort of ballet pose, with arms outstretched. At one point the neck strap of her bathing suit broke and she went twice around the ring in the classic attitude of a woman making minor repairs to a garment. The fact that she was standing on the back of a moving horse while doing this invested the matter with a clownish significance that perfectly fitted the spirit of the circus—jocund, yet charming. She just rolled the strap into a neat ball and stowed it inside her bodice while the horse rocked and rolled beneath her in dutiful innocence. The bathing suit proved as self-reliant as its owner and stood up well enough without benefit of strap.

The richness of the scene was in its plainness, its natural condition—of horse, of ring, of girl, even to the girl's bare feet that gripped the bare back of her proud and ridiculous mount. The enchantment grew not out of anything that happened or was performed but out of something that seemed to go round and around and around with the girl, attending her, a steady gleam in the shape of a cricle—a ring of ambition, of happiness, of youth. (And the positive pleasures of equilibrium under difficulties.) In a week or two, all would be changed, all (or almost all) lost: the girl would wear makeup, the horse would wear gold, the ring would be painted, the bark would be clean for the feet of the horse, the girl's feet would be clean for the slippers that she'd wear. All, all would be lost.

As I watched with the others, our jaws adroop, our eyes alight, I became painfully conscious of the element of time. Everything in the hideous old building seemed to take the shape of a circle, conforming to the course of the horse. The rider's gaze, as she peered straight ahead, seemed to be circular, as though bent by force of circumstance; then time itself began running in circles, and so the beginning was where the end was, and the two were the same, and one thing ran into the next and time went round and around and got nowhere. The girl wasn't so young that she did not know the delicious satisfaction of having a perfectly behaved body and the fun of using it to do a trick most people can't do, but she was too young to know that time does not really move in a circle at all. I thought: "She will never be as beautiful as this again"—a thought that made me acutely unhappy—and in a flash my mind (which is too much of a busybody to suit me) had projected her twenty-five years ahead, and she was now in the center of the ring, on foot, wearing a conical hat and high-heeled shoes, the image of the older woman, holding the long rein, caught in the treadmill of an afternoon long in the future. "She is at that enviable moment in life [I thought] when she believes she can go once around the ring, make one complete circuit, and at the end be exactly the same age as at the start." Everything in her movements, her expression, told you that for her the ring of time was perfectly formed, changeless, predictable, without beginning or end, like the ring in which she was travelling at this moment with the horse that wallowed under her. And then I slipped back into my trance, and time was circular again—time, pausing quietly with the rest of us, so as not to disturb the balance of a performer.

Her ride ended as casually as it had begun. The older woman stopped the horse, and the girl slid to the ground. As she walked toward us to leave, there was a quick, small burst of applause. She smiled broadly, in surprise and pleasure; then her face suddenly regained its gravity and she disappeared through the door.

It has been ambitious and plucky of me to attempt to describe what is indescribable, and I have failed, as I knew I would. But I have discharged my duty to my society; and besides, a writer, like an acrobat, must occasionally try a stunt that is too much for him. At any rate, it is worth reporting that long before the circus comes to town, its most notable performances have already been given. Under the bright lights of the finished show, a performer need only reflect the electric candle power that is directed upon him; but in the dark and dirty old training rings and in the makeshift cages, whatever light is generated, whatever excitement, whatever beauty, must come from original sources—from internal fires of professional hunger and delight, from the exuberance and gravity of youth. It is the difference between planetary light and the combustion of stars.

GEORGE ORWELL

BORN AT Motihari, Bengal, in 1903, the son of a minor official in the Bengal Civil Service, George Orwell attended private schools in England on scholarships from the age of eight until he was graduated from Eton in 1921. But then, instead of going on to one of the universities as might have been expected, Orwell took the advice of a tutor who suggested that he "see something of the world" and joined the Indian Imperial Police. For five years he was a police officer in Burma, then resigned, as he said, "mainly because I could not go on any longer serving an imperialism which I had come to regard as very largely a racket."

For the next year and a half he lived in Paris on his savings and tried to write, but with little success. When his money ran out in the summer of 1929, he got his first taste of poverty as a *plongeur* (dishwasher) in a Paris restaurant, then as a tramp and day-laborer in London and the south of England. Indeed, being a tramp, sleeping in doss-houses, and eating hand-me-out meals so stimulated Orwell's imagination (and perhaps the psychic needs of an acute class-consciousness from having been a scholarship boy in exclusive schools) that even after he became a schoolteacher, and later a clerk in a London book shop, he continued to dress up in old clothes and go "on the bum" on weekends. In 1933 he published his first book, *Down and Out in Paris and London*, a vivid account of his experiences during the summer of 1929, and for the first time used the pseudonym "George Orwell." As with most other writers who have taken pen-names, the purpose was to keep a secret —in this case from his former Eton schoolmates: that he had once been "down and out." Though he published poetry and many book reviews during the next three years under his real name, Eric Blair, he continued to use the name "Orwell" for his books (the novels *Burmese Days*, *A Clergyman's Daughter*, and *Keep the Aspidistra Flying*).

Between the summer of 1936 and the spring of 1937 Orwell underwent a great metamorphosis. Until then he had been a rather shabby, "serious"—but conventional—young poet on the fringes of the London literati, a very Gissing-like, unsuccessful writer, not at all interested in politics. But then a number of things happened. First, Victor Gollancz commissioned him to go to the north of England and observe the lives of the unemployed coal miners and to write a book about it, which the Left Book Club, a socialist organization, would publish (*The Road to Wigan Pier*). Next, he got married, which meant he had to start earning a bit more money. Then John Lehmann invited him to submit something for a new magazine he was editing, and Orwell wrote his first real *essay* (as opposed to book review or reportage): he called it "Shooting an Elephant." And finally, in December, 1936, he left for the Spanish Civil War.

At the time that he arrived in Barcelona, Orwell was so naive about politics that he had only the vaguest notion which faction of the Left (the Republican, or Socialist, side) he wished to join. He was interested in the war mainly as a *war*, not as a battle of political ideologies. But his experiences over the next four months changed everything. To put it very simply, what Orwell discovered was that politics was all lies: that the Tory-dominated British press was distorting the truth about what was happening in Spain; and that the Soviets, who were presumably on the side of the workers, were in fact maneuvering to bring about a socialist defeat. As Orwell wrote many years later, "The Spanish war and other events in 1936-37 turned the scale and thereafter I knew where I stood. Every line of serious work that I have written since 1936 has been written, directly or indirectly, *against* totalitarianism and *for* democratic socialism, as I understand it." In April, 1937, Orwell was severely wounded while fighting on the Aragon front and was lucky to get out of Spain alive. When he got back to England he wrote the first of his important books, *Homage to Catalonia* (1938).

If the political events he observed in Spain were the turning point of Orwell's intellectual life, his near death might be called its psychological equivalent, for after 1936 Eric Blair vanished: no more poetry, no more *belles lettres* book reviews, and only one more conventional novel, *Coming Up for Air* (1939). "George Orwell" became George Orwell, a fiercely dedicated political journalist. But even that doesn't describe the writer who emerged from Spain, for Orwell was more than a mere journalist; he became a devil's advocate of twentieth-century liberalism, an iconoclast in the temples of socialism and communism. His last two books, *Animal Farm* (1945) and *1984* (1949), must be read not as novels nor even strictly as satires—though of course *Animal Farm is* a satire—but as Arguments in the service of truth and human freedom.

Orwell died of tuberculosis in 1950, a few months after finishing *1984*. Looking back over his work, the critic V. S. Pritchett declared that Orwell had been "the conscience of his generation," a claim one might examine by reading Orwell's *Collected Essays, Journalism and Letters,* published in 1968 in four volumes.

Orwell was never a member of any political organization. Though he approved of many aspects of socialism, he was never a socialist. Though he defended the rights of the poor and oppressed, and occasionally (as in *1984*) sentimentalized their virtues, he never thought that their limited consciousness was the desired goal of man. Orwell believed in only one thing: honesty—or as he said in one of his essays, the "power of facing unpleasant facts." What he had discovered in Spain in 1937 was that objective truth could cease to exist, that the people who controlled the means of communication could—and *did*—alter at will, and therefore, as his friend Arthur Koestler has said, history was dead. This, then, was Orwell's great perception, and it was his fear that this sort of "thought-control" was happening not only in the "totalitarian" countries but the "democracies" as well that underlay everything he wrote during the last thirteen years of his life.

As a writer, Orwell's rules were very simple: be clear, be concrete, and avoid all frills and mannerisms. But even these rules, as fine as they are, go only part way in explaining the particular forcefulness of his writing. To understand the rest, one must recall Joseph Conrad's credo: "My task, which I am trying to achieve is, by the power of the written word, to make you hear, to make you feel— it is, above all, to make you *see*." Hearing, feeling, seeing—that is precisely what we are doing when we read George Orwell, and because of it we shall go on reading him for a long time to come.

[1936]

SHOOTING AN ELEPHANT

In MOULMEIN, in lower Burma, I was hated by large numbers of people—the only time in my life that I have been important enough for this to happen to me. I was sub-divisional police officer of the town, and in an aimless, petty kind of way anti-European feeling was very bitter. No one had the guts to raise a riot, but if a European woman went through the bazaars alone somebody would probably spit betel juice over her dress. As a police officer I was an obvious target and was baited whenever it seemed safe to do so. When a nimble Burman tripped me up on the football field and the referee (another Burman) looked the other way, the crowd yelled with hideous laughter. This happened more than once. In the end the sneering yellow faces of young men that met me everywhere, the insults hooted after me when I was at a safe distance, got badly on my nerves. The young Buddhist priests were the worst of all. There were several thousands of them in the town and none of them seemed to have anything to do except stand on street corners and jeer at Europeans.

All this was perplexing and upsetting. For at that time I had already made up my mind that imperialism was an evil thing and the sooner I chucked up my job and got out of it the better. Theoretically—and secretly, of course—I was all for the Burmese and all against their oppressors, the British. As for the job I was doing, I hated it more bitterly than I can perhaps make clear. In a job like that you see the dirty work of Empire at close quarters. The wretched prisoners huddling in the stinking cages of the lock-ups, the gray, cowed faces of the long-term convicts, the scarred buttocks of the men who had been flogged with bamboos—all these oppressed me with an intolerable sense of guilt. But I could get nothing into perspective. I was young and ill educated and I had had to think

out my problems in the utter silence that is imposed on every Englishman in the East. I did not even know that the British Empire
is dying, still less did I know that it is a great deal better than the
younger empires that are going to supplant it. All I knew was that
I was stuck between my hatred of the empire I served and my rage
against the evil-spirited little beasts who tried to make my job impossible. With one part of my mind I thought of the British Raj
as an unbreakable tyranny, as something clamped down, in *saecula
saeculorum*, upon the will of prostrate peoples; with another part
I thought that the greatest joy in the world would be to drive a
bayonet into a Buddhist priest's guts. Feelings like these are the
normal by-products of imperialism; ask any Anglo-Indian official, if
you can catch him off duty.

One day something happened which in a roundabout way was
enlightening. It was a tiny incident in itself, but it gave me a better
glimpse than I had had before of the real nature of imperialism—
the real motives for which despotic governments act. Early one
morning the sub-inspector at a police station the other end of the
town rang me up on the 'phone and said that an elephant was
ravaging the bazaar. Would I please come and do something about
it? I did not know what I could do, but I wanted to see what was
happening and I got on to a pony and started out. I took my rifle,
an old .44 Winchester and much too small to kill an elephant, but
I thought the noise might be useful *in terrorem*. Various Burmans
stopped me on the way and told me about the elephant's doings.
It was not, of course, a wild elephant, but a tame one which had
gone "must." It had been chained up, as tame elephants always are
when their attack of "must" is due, but on the previous night it had
broken its chain and escaped. Its mahout, the only person who
could manage it when it was in that state, had set out in pursuit,
but had taken the wrong direction and was now twelve hours'
journey away, and in the morning the elephant had suddenly re-
appeared in the town. The Burmese population had no weapons
and were quite helpless against it. It had already destroyed somebody's bamboo hut, killed a cow and raided some fruit-stalls and
devoured the stock; also it had met the municipal rubbish van and,

when the driver jumped out and took to his heels, had turned the van over and inflicted violences upon it.

The Burmese sub-inspector and some Indian constables were waiting for me in the quarter where the elephant had been seen. It was a very poor quarter, a labyrinth of squalid bamboo huts, thatched with palm-leaf, winding all over a steep hillside. I remember that it was a cloudy, stuffy morning at the beginning of the rains. We began questioning the people as to where the elephant had gone and, as usual, failed to get any definite information. That is invariably the case in the East; a story always sounds clear enough at a distance, but the nearer you get to the scene of events the vaguer it becomes. Some of the people said that the elephant had gone in one direction, some said that he had gone in another, some professed not even to have heard of any elephant. I had almost made up my mind that the whole story was a pack of lies, when we heard yells a little distance away. There was a loud, scandalized cry of "Go away, child! Go away this instant!" and an old woman with a switch in her hand came round the corner of a hut, violently shooing away a crowd of naked children. Some more women followed, clicking their tongues and exclaiming; evidently there was something that the children ought not to have seen. I rounded the hut and saw a man's dead body sprawling in the mud. He was an Indian, a black Dravidian coolie, almost naked, and he could not have been dead many minutes. The people said that the elephant had come suddenly upon him round the corner of the hut, caught him with its trunk, put its foot on his back and ground him into the earth. This was the rainy season and the ground was soft, and his face had scored a trench a foot deep and a couple of yards long. He was lying on his belly with arms crucified and head sharply twisted to one side. His face was coated with mud, the eyes wide open, the teeth bared and grinning with an expression of unendurable agony. (Never tell me, by the way, that the dead look peaceful. Most of the corpses I have seen looked devilish.) The friction of the great beast's foot had stripped the skin from his back as neatly as one skins a rabbit. As soon as I saw the dead man I sent an orderly to a friend's house nearby to borrow an elephant rifle.

I had already sent back the pony, not wanting it to go mad with fright and throw me if it smelt the elephant.

The orderly came back in a few minutes with a rifle and five cartridges, and meanwhile some Burmans had arrived and told us that the elephant was in the paddy fields below, only a few hundred yards away. As I started forward practically the whole population of the quarter flocked out of the houses and followed me. They had seen the rifle and were all shouting excitedly that I was going to shoot the elephant. They had not shown much interest in the elephant when he was merely ravaging their homes, but it was different now that he was going to be shot. It was a bit of fun to them, as it would be to an English crowd; besides they wanted the meat. It made me vaguely uneasy. I had no intention of shooting the elephant—I had merely sent for the rifle to defend myself if necessary—and it is always unnerving to have a crowd following you. I marched down the hill, looking and feeling a fool, with the rifle over my shoulder and an ever-growing army of people jostling at my heels. At the bottom, when you got away from the huts, there was a metalled road and beyond that a miry waste of paddy fields a thousand yards across, not yet ploughed but soggy from the first rains and dotted with coarse grass. The elephant was standing eight yards from the road, his left side toward us. He took not the slightest notice of the crowd's approach. He was tearing up bunches of grass, beating them against his knees to clean them, and stuffing them into his mouth.

I had halted on the road. As soon as I saw the elephant I knew with perfect certainty that I ought not to shoot him. It is a serious matter to shoot a working elephant—it is comparable to destroying a huge and costly piece of machinery—and obviously one ought not to do it if it can possibly be avoided. And at that distance, peacefully eating, the elephant looked no more dangerous than a cow. I thought then and I think now that his attack of "must" was already passing off; in which case he would merely wander harmlessly about until the mahout came back and caught him. Moreover, I did not in the least want to shoot him. I decided that I would watch him for a little while to make sure that he did not turn savage again, and then go home.

But at that moment I glanced round at the crowd that had followed me. It was an immense crowd, two thousand at the least and growing every minute. It blocked the road for a long distance on either side. I looked at the sea of yellow faces above the garish clothes—faces all happy and excited over this bit of fun, all certain that the elephant was going to be shot. They were watching me as they would watch a conjurer about to perform a trick. They did not like me, but with the magical rifle in my hands I was momentarily worth watching. And suddenly I realized that I should have to shoot the elephant after all. The people expected it of me and I had got to do it; I could feel their two thousand wills pressing me forward, irresistibly. And it was at this moment, as I stood there with the rifle in my hands, that I first grasped the hollowness, the futility of the white man's dominion in the East. Here was I, the white man with his gun, standing in front of the unarmed native crowd—seemingly the leading actor of the piece; but in reality I was only an absurd puppet pushed to and fro by the will of those yellow faces behind. I perceived in this moment that when the white man turns tyrant it is his own freedom that he destroys. He becomes a sort of hollow, posing dummy, the conventionalized figure of a sahib. For it is the condition of his rule that he shall spend his life in trying to impress the "natives," and so in every crisis he has got to do what the "natives" expect of him. He wears a mask, and his face grows to fit it. I had got to shoot the elephant. I had committed myself to doing it when I sent for the rifle. A sahib has got to act like a sahib; he has got to appear resolute, to know his own mind and do definite things. To come all that way, rifle in hand, with two thousand people marching at my heels, and then to trail feebly away, having done nothing—no, that was impossible. The crowd would laugh at me. And my whole life, every white man's life in the East, was one long struggle not to be laughed at.

But I did not want to shoot the elephant. I watched him beating his bunch of grass against his knees with that preoccupied grandmotherly air that elephants have. It seemed to me that it would be murder to shoot him. At that age I was not squeamish about killing animals, but I had never shot an elephant and never wanted to. (Somehow it always seems worse to kill a *large* animal.) Besides,

there was the beast's owner to be considered. Alive, the elephant
was worth at least a hundred pounds; dead, he would only be worth
the value of his tusks, five pounds, possibly. But I had got to act
quickly. I turned to some experienced-looking Burmans who had
been there when we arrived, and asked them how the elephant
had been behaving. They all said the same thing: he took no notice
of you if you left him alone, but he might charge if you went too
close to him.

It was perfectly clear to me what I ought to do. I ought to walk
up to within, say, twenty-five yards of the elephant and test his
behavior. If he charged, I could shoot; if he took no notice of me,
it would be safe to leave him until the mahout came back. But also
I knew that I was going to do no such thing. I was a poor shot
with a rifle and the ground was soft mud into which one would
sink at every step. If the elephant charged and I missed him, I
should have about as much chance as a toad under a steam-roller.
But even then I was not thinking particularly of my own skin, only
of the watchful yellow faces behind. For at that moment, with the
crowd watching me, I was not afraid in the ordinary sense, as I
would have been if I had been alone. A white man mustn't be
frightened in front of "natives"; and so, in general, he isn't frightened. The sole thought in my mind was that if anything went
wrong those two thousand Burmans would see me pursued, caught,
trampled on, and reduced to a grinning corpse like that Indian up
the hill. And if that happened it was quite probable that some of
them would laugh. That would never do. There was only one alternative. I shoved the cartridges into the magazine and lay down on
the road to get a better aim.

The crowd grew very still, and a deep, low, happy sigh, as of
people who see the theater curtain go up at last, breathed from
innumerable throats. They were going to have their bit of fun after
all. The rifle was a beautiful German thing with cross-hair sights.
I did not then know that in shooting an elephant one would shoot
to cut an imaginary bar running from ear-hole to ear-hole. I ought,
therefore, as the elephant was sideways on, to have aimed straight
at his ear-hole; actually I aimed several inches in front of this,
thinking the brain would be further forward.

When I pulled the trigger I did not hear the bang or feel the kick—one never does when a shot goes home—but I heard the devilish roar of glee that went up from the crowd. In that instant, in too short a time, one would have thought, even for the bullet to get there, a mysterious, terrible change had come over the elephant. He neither stirred nor fell, but every line of his body had altered. He looked suddenly stricken, shrunken, immensely old, as though the frightful impact of the bullet had paralyzed him without knocking him down. At last, after what seemed a long time—it might have been five seconds, I dare say—he sagged flabbily to his knees. His mouth slobbered. An enormous senility seemed to have settled upon him. One could have imagined him thousands of years old. I fired again into the same spot. At the second shot he did not collapse but climbed with desperate slowness to his feet and stood weakly upright, with legs sagging and head drooping. I fired a third time. That was the shot that did for him. You could see the agony of it jolt his whole body and knock the last remnant of strength from his legs. But in falling he seemed for a moment to rise, for as his hind legs collapsed beneath him he seemed to tower upward like a huge rock toppling, his trunk reaching skyward like a tree. He trumpeted, for the first and only time. And then down he came, his belly toward me, with a crash that seemed to shake the ground even where I lay.

I got up. The Burmans were already racing past me across the mud. It was obvious that the elephant would never rise again, but he was not dead. He was breathing very rhythmically with long rattling gasps, his great mound of a side painfully rising and falling. His mouth was wide open—I could see far down into caverns of pale pink throat. I waited a long time for him to die, but his breathing did not weaken. Finally I fired my two remaining shots into the spot where I thought his heart must be. The thick blood welled out of him like red velvet, but still he did not die. His body did not even jerk when the shots hit him, the tortured breathing continued without a pause. He was dying, very slowly and in great agony, but in some world remote from me where not even a bullet could damage him further. I felt that I had got to put an end to that dreadful noise. It seemed dreadful to see the great beast lying there, powerless to move and yet powerless to die, and not even to be able to finish him. I sent back for my small rifle and poured shot after shot into his heart and down his throat. They seemed to make no impression. The tortured gasps continued as steadily as the ticking of a clock.

In the end I could not stand it any longer and went away. I heard later that it took him half an hour to die. Burmans were bringing dahs and baskets even before I left, and I was told they had stripped his body almost to the bones by the afternoon.

Afterward, of course, there were endless discussions about the shooting of the elephant. The owner was furious, but he was only an Indian and could do nothing. Besides, legally I had done the right thing, for a mad elephant has to be killed, like a mad dog, if its owner fails to control it. Among the Europeans opinion was divided. The older men said I was right, the younger men said it was a damn shame to shoot an elephant for killing a coolie, because an elephant was worth more than any damn Coringhee coolie. And afterward I was very glad that the coolie had been killed; it put me legally in the right and it gave me a sufficient pretext for shooting the elephant. I often wondered whether any of the others grasped that I had done it solely to avoid looking a fool.

[1946]

POLITICS AND
THE ENGLISH LANGUAGE

Most people who bother with the matter at all would admit that the English language is in a bad way, but it is generally assumed that we cannot by conscious action do anything about it. Our civilization is decadent and our language—so the argument runs—must inevitably share in the general collapse. It follows that any struggle against the abuse of language is a sentimental archaism, like preferring candles to electric light or hansom cabs to aeroplanes. Underneath this lies the half-conscious belief that language is a natural growth and not an instrument which we shape for our own purposes.

Now, it is clear that the decline of a language must ultimately have political and economic causes: it is not due simply to the bad influence of this or that individual writer. But an effect can become a cause, reinforcing the original cause and producing the same effect in an intensified form, and so on indefinitely. A man may take to drink because he feels himself to be a failure, and then fail all the more completely because he drinks. It is rather the same thing that is happening to the English language. It becomes ugly and inaccurate because our thoughts are foolish, but the slovenliness of our language makes it easier for us to have foolish thoughts. The point is that the process is reversible. Modern English, especially written English, is full of bad habits which spread by imitation and which can be avoided if one is willing to take the necessary trouble. If one gets rid of these habits one can think more clearly, and to think clearly is a necessary first step toward political regeneration: so that the fight against bad English is not frivolous and is not the exclusive concern of professional writers. I will come back to this presently, and I hope that by that time the meaning of what I have said here will have become clearer. Meanwhile, here are five specimens of the English language as it is now habitually written.

These five passages have not been picked out because they are especially bad—I could have quoted far worse if I had chosen—but because they illustrate various of the mental vices from which we now suffer. They are a little below the average, but are fairly representative samples. I number them so that I can refer back to them when necessary:

(1) I am not, indeed, sure whether it is not true to say that the Milton who once seemed not unlike a seventeenth-century Shelley had not become, out of an experience ever more bitter in each year, more alien [sic] to the founder of that Jesuit sect which nothing could induce him to tolerate.

> Professor Harold Laski
> (Essay in *Freedom of Expression*)

(2) Above all, we cannot play ducks and drakes with a native battery
of idioms which prescribes such egregious collocations of vocables as the
Basic *put up with* for *tolerate* or *put at a loss* for *bewilder*.

Professor Lancelot Hogben (*Interglossa*)

(3) On the one side we have the free personality: by definition it is
not neurotic, for it has neither conflict nor dream. Its desires, such as
they are, are transparent, for they are just what institutional approval
keeps in the forefront of consciousness; another institutional pattern
would alter their number and intensity; there is little in them that is
natural, irreducible, or culturally dangerous. But *on the other side*, the
social bond itself is nothing but the mutual reflection of these self-secure
integrities. Recall the definition of love. Is not this the very picture of a
small academic? Where is there a place in this hall of mirrors for either
personality or fraternity?

Essay on psychology in *Politics* (New York)

(4) All the "best people" from the gentlemen's clubs, and all the
frantic fascist captains, united in common hatred of Socialism and bestial
horror of the rising tide of the mass revolutionary movement, have
turned to acts of provocation, to foul incendiarism, to medieval legends
of poisoned wells, to legalize their own destruction of proletarian organizations, and rouse the agitated petty-bourgeoisie to chauvinistic fervor
on behalf of the fight against the revolutionary way out of the crisis.

Communist pamphlet

(5) If a new spirit *is* to be infused into this old country, there is
one thorny and contentious reform which must be tackled, and that
is the humanization and galvanization of the B.B.C. Timidity here will
bespeak canker and atrophy of the soul. The heart of Britain may be
sound and of strong beat, for instance, but the British lion's roar at
present is like that of Bottom in Shakespeare's *Midsummer Night's
Dream*—as gentle as any sucking dove. A virile new Britain cannot continue indefinitely to be traduced in the eyes, or rather ears, of the world
by the effete languors of Langham Place, brazenly masquerading as
"standard English." When the Voice of Britain is heard at nine o'clock,
better far and infinitely less ludicrous to hear aitches honestly dropped
than the present priggish, inflated, inhibited, school-ma'amish arch
braying of blameless bashful mewing maidens!

Letter in *Tribune*

Each of these passages has faults of its own, but, quite apart from avoidable ugliness, two qualities are common to all of them. The first is staleness of imagery; the other is lack of precision. The writer either has a meaning and cannot express it, or he inadvertently says something else, or he is almost indifferent as to whether his words mean anything or not. This mixture of vagueness and sheer incompetence is the most marked characteristic of modern English prose, and especially of any kind of political writing. As soon as certain topics are raised, the concrete melts into the abstract and no one seems able to think of turns of speech that are not hackneyed: prose consists less and less of *words* chosen for the sake of their meaning, and more and more of *phrases* tacked together like the sections of a prefabricated henhouse. I list below, with notes and examples, various of the tricks by means of which the work of prose-construction is habitually dodged:

Dying metaphors. A newly invented metaphor assists thought by evoking a visual image, while on the other hand a metaphor which is technically "dead" (e.g. *iron resolution*) has in effect reverted to being an ordinary word and can generally be used without loss of vividness. But in between these two classes there is a huge dump of worn-out metaphors which have lost all evocative power and are merely used because they save people the trouble of inventing phrases for themselves. Examples are: *Ring the changes on, take up the cudgels for, toe the line, ride roughshod over, stand shoulder to shoulder with, play into the hands of, no axe to grind, grist to the mill, fishing in troubled waters, on the order of the day, Achilles' heel, swan song, hotbed.* Many of these are used without knowledge of their meaning (what is a "rift," for instance?), and incompatible metaphors are frequently mixed, a sure sign that the writer is not interested in what he is saying. Some metaphors now current have been twisted out of their original meaning without those who use them ever being aware of the fact. For example, *toe the line* is sometimes written *tow the line.* Another example is *the hammer and the anvil*, now always used with the implication that the anvil gets the worst of it. In real life it is always the anvil that breaks the hammer, never the other way about: a writer who stopped to think what he was saying would be aware of this, and would avoid perverting the original phrase.

Operators or *verbal false limbs*. These save the trouble of picking out appropriate verbs and nouns, and at the same time pad each sentence with extra syllables which give it an appearance of symmetry. Characteristic phrases are *render inoperative, militate against, make contact with, be subjected to, give rise to, give grounds for, have the effect of, play a leading part (role) in, make itself felt, take effect, exhibit a tendency to, serve the purpose of,* etc., etc. The keynote is the elimination of simple verbs. Instead of being a single word, such as *break, stop, spoil, mend, kill,* a verb becomes a *phrase,* made up of a noun or adjective tacked on to some general-purpose verb such as *prove, serve, form, play, render.* In addition, the passive voice is wherever possible used in preference to the active, and noun constructions are used instead of gerunds (*by examination of* instead of *by examining*). The range of verbs is further cut down by means of the *-ize* and *de-* formations, and the banal statements are given an appearance of profundity by means of the *not un-* formation. Simple conjunctions and prepositions are replaced by such phrases as *with respect to, having regard to, the fact that, by dint of, in view of, in the interests of, on the hypothesis that;* and the ends of sentences are saved from anticlimax by such resounding commonplaces as *greatly to be desired, cannot be left out of account, a development to be expected in the near future, deserving of serious consideration, brought to a satisfactory conclusion,* and so on and so forth.

Pretentious diction. Words like *phenomenon, element, individual* (as noun), *objective, categorical, effective, virtual, basic, primary, promote, constitute, exhibit, exploit, utilize, eliminate, liquidate,* are used to dress up simple statement and give an air of scientific impartiality to biased judgments. Adjectives like *epoch-making, epic, historic, unforgettable, triumphant, age-old, inevitable, inexorable, veritable,* are used to dignify the sordid processes of international politics, while writing that aims at glorifying war usually takes on an archaic color, its characteristic words being: *realm, throne,* *chariot, mailed fist, trident, sword, shield, buckler, banner, jackboot, clarion.* Foreign words and expressions such as *cul de sac, ancien régime, deus ex machina, mutatis mutandis, status quo, gleichschaltung, weltanschauung,* are used to give an air of culture and elegance. Except for the useful abbreviations *i.e., e.g.,* and *etc.,* there is no real need for any of the hundreds of foreign phrases now current in English. Bad writers, and especially scientific, political, and sociological writers, are nearly always haunted by the notion that Latin or Greek words are grander than Saxon ones, and unnecessary words like *expedite, ameliorate, predict, extraneous, deracinated, clandestine, subaqueous,* and hundreds of others constantly gain ground from their Anglo-Saxon opposite numbers.* The jargon peculiar to Marxist writing (*hyena, hangman, cannibal, petty bourgeois, these gentry, lackey, flunkey, mad dog, White Guard,* etc.) consists largely of words and phrases translated from Russian, German, or French; but the normal way of coining a new word is to use a Latin or Greek root with the appropriate affix and, where necessary, the size formation. It is often easier to make up words of this kind (*deregionalize, impermissible, extramarital, nonfragmentary* and so forth) than to think up the English words that will cover one's meaning. The result, in general, is an increase in slovenliness and vagueness.

Meaningless words. In certain kinds of writing, particularly in art criticism and literary criticism, it is normal to come across long passages which are almost completely lacking in meaning.† Words

---

* An interesting illustration of this is the way in which the English flower names which were in use till very recently are being ousted by Greek ones, *snapdragon* becoming *antirrhinum, forget-me-not* becoming *myosotis,* etc. It is hard to see any practical reason for this change of fashion: it is probably due to an instinctive turning away from the more homely word and a vague feeling that the Greek word is scientific.

† Example: "Comfort's catholicity of perception and image, strangely Whitmanesque in range, almost the exact opposite in aesthetic compulsion, continues to evoke that trembling atmospheric accumulative hinting at a cruel, an inexorably serene timelessness. . . . Wrey Gardiner scores by aiming at simple bull's-eyes with precision. Only they are not so simple, and through this contented sadness runs more than the surface bittersweet of resignation." (*Poetry Quarterly.*)

like *romantic, plastic, values, human, dead, sentimental, natural, vitality*, as used in art criticism, are strictly meaningless, in the sense that they not only do not point to any discoverable object, but are hardly ever expected to do so by the reader. When one critic writes, "The outstanding feature of Mr. X's work is its living quality," while another writes, "The immediately striking thing about Mr. X's work is its peculiar deadness," the reader accepts this as a simple difference of opinion. If words like *black* and *white* were involved, instead of the jargon words *dead* and *living*, he would see at once that language was being used in an improper way. Many political words are similarly abused. The word *Fascism* has now no meaning except in so far as it signifies "something not desirable." The words *democracy, socialism, freedom, patriotic, realistic, justice*, have each of them several different meanings which cannot be reconciled with one another. In the case of a word like *democracy*, not only is there no agreed definition, but the attempt to make one is resisted from all sides. It is almost universally felt that when we call a country democratic we are praising it: consequently the defenders of every kind of régime claim that it is a democracy, and fear that they might have to stop using the word if it were tied down to any one meaning. Words of this kind are often used in a consciously dishonest way. That is, the person who uses them has his own private definition, but allows his hearer to think he means something quite different. Statements like *Marshal Pétain was a true patriot, The Soviet press is the freest in the world, The Catholic Church is opposed to persecution*, are almost always made with intent to deceive. Other words used in variable meanings, in most cases more or less dishonestly, are: *class, totalitarian, science, progressive, reactionary, bourgeois, equality.*

Now that I have made this catalogue of swindles and perversions, let me give another example of the kind of writing that they lead to. This time it must of its nature be an imaginary one. I am going to translate a passage of good English into modern English of the worst sort. Here is a well-known verse from *Ecclesiastes*:

I returned and saw under the sun, that the race is not to the swift, nor the battle to the strong, neither yet bread to the wise, nor yet riches to men of understanding, nor yet favor to men of skill; but time and chance happeneth to them all.

Here it is in modern English:

Objective consideration of contemporary phenomena compels the conclusion that success or failure in competitive activities exhibits no tendency to be commensurate with innate capacity, but that a considerable element of the unpredictable must invariably be taken into account.

This is a parody, but not a very gross one. Exhibit (3), above, for instance, contains several patches of the same kind of English. It will be seen that I have not made a full translation. The beginning and ending of the sentence follow the original meaning fairly closely, but in the middle the concrete illustrations—race, battle, bread—dissolve into the vague phrase "success or failure in competitive activities." This had to be so, because no modern writer of the kind I am discussing—no one capable of using phrases like "objective consideration of contemporary phenomena"—would ever tabulate his thoughts in that precise and detailed way. The whole tendency of modern prose is away from concreteness. Now analyze these two sentences a little more closely. The first contains forty-nine words but only sixty syllables, and all its words are those of everyday life. The second contains thirty-eight words of ninety syllables: eighteen of its words are from Latin roots, and one from Greek. The first sentence contains six vivid images, and only one phrase ("time and chance") that could be called vague. The second contains not a single fresh, arresting phrase, and in spite of its ninety syllables it gives only a shortened version of the meaning contained in the first. Yet without a doubt it is the second kind of sentence that is gaining ground in modern English. I do not want to exaggerate. This kind of writing is not yet universal, and outcrops of simplicity will occur here and there in the worst-written page. Still, if you or I were told to write a few lines on the uncertainty of human fortunes, we should probably come much nearer to my imaginary sentence than to the one from *Ecclesiastes*.

As I have tried to show, modern writing at its worst does not consist in picking out words for the sake of their meaning and inventing images in order to make the meaning clearer. It consists in gumming

together long strips of words which have already been set in order
by someone else, and making the results presentable by sheer humbug. The attraction of this way of writing is that it is easy. It is
easier—even quicker, once you have the habit—to say *In my opinion
it is not an unjustifiable assumption that* than to say *I think.* If
you use ready-made phrases, you not only don't have to hunt about
for words; you also don't have to bother with the rhythms of your
sentences, since these phrases are generally so arranged as to be more
or less euphonious. When you are composing in a hurry—when you
are dictating to a stenographer, for instance, or making a public
speech—it is natural to fall into a pretentious, Latinized style. Tags
like *a consideration which we should do well to bear in mind* or *a
conclusion to which all of us would readily assent* will save many
a sentence from coming down with a bump. By using stale metaphors, similes, and idioms, you save much mental effort, at the cost
of leaving your meaning vague, not only for your reader but for
yourself. This is the significance of mixed metaphors. The sole aim
of a metaphor is to call up a visual image. When these images
clash—as in *The Fascist octopus has sung its swan song, the jackboot
is thrown into the melting pot*—it can be taken as certain that the
writer is not seeing a mental image of the objects he is naming; in
other words he is not really thinking. Look again at the examples
I gave at the beginning of this essay. Professor Laski (1) uses five
negatives in fifty-three words. One of these is superfluous, making
nonsense of the whole passage, and in addition there is the slip—
alien for akin—making further nonsense, and several avoidable
pieces of clumsiness which increase the general vagueness. Professor
Hogben (2) plays ducks and drakes with a battery which is able to
write prescriptions, and, while disapproving of the everyday phrase
put up with, is unwilling to look *egregious* up in the dictionary and
see what it means; (3), if one takes an uncharitable attitude towards
it, is simply meaningless: probably one could work out its intended
meaning by reading the whole of the article in which it occurs. In
(4), the writer knows more or less what he wants to say, but an
accumulation of stale phrases chokes him like tea leaves blocking
a sink. In (5), words and meaning have almost parted company.

People who write in this manner usually have a general emotional meaning—they dislike one thing and want to express solidarity with another—but they are not interested in the detail of what they are saying. A scrupulous writer, in every sentence that he writes, will ask himself at least four questions, thus: What am I trying to say? What words will express it? What image or idiom will make it clearer? Is this image fresh enough to have an effect? And he will probably ask himself two more: Could I put it more shortly? Have I said anything that is avoidably ugly? But you are not obliged to go to all this trouble. You can shirk it by simply throwing your mind open and letting the ready-made phrases come crowding in. They will construct your sentences for you—even think your thoughts for you, to a certain extent—and at need they will perform the important service of partially concealing your meaning even from yourself. It is at this point that the special connection between politics and the debasement of language becomes clear.

In our time it is broadly true that political writing is bad writing. Where it is not true, it will generally be found that the writer is some kind of rebel, expressing his private opinions and not a "party line." Orthodoxy, of whatever color, seems to demand a lifeless, imitative style. The political dialects to be found in pamphlets, leading articles, manifestoes, White Papers and the speeches of undersecretaries do, of course, vary from party to party, but they are all alike in that one almost never finds in them a fresh, vivid, home-made turn of speech. When one watches some tired hack on the platform mechanically repeating the familiar phrases—*bestial atrocities, iron heel, bloodstained tyranny, free peoples of the world, stand shoulder to shoulder*—one often has a curious feeling that one is not watching a live human being but some kind of dummy: a feeling which suddenly becomes stronger at moments when the light catches the speaker's spectacles and turns them into blank discs which seem to have no eyes behind them. And this is not altogether fanciful. A speaker who uses that kind of phraseology has gone some distance towards turning himself into a machine. The appropriate noises are coming out of his larynx, but his brain is not involved as it would be if he were choosing his words for himself. If the speech he is making is one that he is accustomed to make over and over again, he may be almost unconscious of what he is saying, as one is when one utters the responses in church. And this reduced state of consciousness, if not indispensable, is at any rate favorable to political conformity.

In our time, political speech and writing are largely the defense of the indefensible. Things like the continuance of British rule in India, the Russian purges and deportations, the dropping of the atom bombs on Japan, can indeed be defended, but only by arguments which are too brutal for most people to face, and which do not square with the professed aims of political parties. Thus political language has to consist largely of euphemism, question-begging and sheer cloudy vagueness. Defenseless villages are bombarded from the air, the inhabitants driven out into the countryside, the cattle machine-gunned, the huts set on fire with incendiary bullets: this is called *pacification*. Millions of peasants are robbed of their farms and sent trudging along the roads with no more than they can carry: this is called *transfer of population* or *rectification of frontiers*. People are imprisoned for years without trial, or shot in the back of the neck or sent to die of scurvy in Arctic lumber camps: this is called *elimination of unreliable elements*. Such phraseology is needed if one wants to name things without calling up mental pictures of them. Consider for instance some comfortable English professor defending Russian totalitarianism. He cannot say outright, "I believe in killing off your opponents when you can get good results by doing so." Probably, therefore, he will say something like this:

"While freely conceding that the Soviet régime exhibits certain features which the humanitarian may be inclined to deplore, we must, I think, agree that a certain curtailment of the right to political opposition is an unavoidable concomitant of transitional periods, and that the rigors which the Russian people have been called upon to undergo have been amply justified in the sphere of concrete achievement."

The inflated style is itself a kind of euphemism. A mass of Latin words falls upon the facts like soft snow, blurring the outlines and covering up all the details. The great enemy of clear language is insincerity. When there is a gap between one's real and one's declared aims, one turns as it were instinctively to long words and exhausted idioms, like a cuttlefish squirting out ink. In our age there is no such thing as "keeping out of politics." All issues are political issues, and politics itself is a mass of lies, evasions, folly, hatred and schizophrenia. When the general atmosphere is bad, language must suffer. I should expect to find—this is a guess which I have not sufficient knowledge to verify—that the German, Russian and Italian languages have all deteriorated in the last ten or fifteen years, as a result of dictatorship.

But if thought corrupts language, language can also corrupt thought. A bad usage can spread by tradition and imitation, even among people who should and do know better. The debased language that I have been discussing is in some ways very convenient. Phrases like *a not unjustifiable assumption, leaves much to be desired, would serve no good purpose, a consideration which we should do well to bear in mind,* are a continuous temptation, a packet of aspirins always at one's elbow. Look back through this essay, and for certain you will find that I have again and again committed the very faults I am protesting against. By this morning's post I have received a pamphlet dealing with conditions in Germany. The author tells me that he "felt impelled" to write it. I open it at random, and here is almost the first sentence that I see: "[The Allies] have an opportunity not only of achieving a radical transformation of Germany's social and political structure in such a way as to avoid a nationalistic reaction in Germany itself, but at the same time of laying the foundations of a co-operative and unified Europe." You see, he "feels impelled" to write—feels, presumably, that he has something new to say—and yet his words, like cavalry horses answering the bugle, group themselves automatically into the familiar dreary pattern. This invasion of one's mind by ready-made phrases (*lay the foundations, achieve a radical transformation*) can only be prevented if one is constantly on guard against them, and every such phrase anaesthetizes a portion of one's brain.

I said earlier that the decadence of our language is probably curable. Those who deny this would argue, if they produced an argument at all, that language merely reflects existing social conditions, and that we cannot influence its development by any direct tinkering with words and constructions. So far as the general tone or spirit of a language goes, this may be true, but it is not true in detail. Silly words and expressions have often disappeared, not through any evolutionary process but owing to the conscious action of a minority. Two recent examples were *explore every avenue* and *leave no stone unturned*, which were killed by the jeers of a few journalists. There is a long list of flyblown metaphors which could similarly be got rid of if enough people would interest themselves in the job; and it should also be possible to laugh the *not un-* formation out of existence,* to reduce the amount of Latin and Greek in the average sentence, to drive out foreign phrases and strayed scientific words, and, in general, to make pretentiousness unfashionable. But all these are minor points. The defense of the English language implies more than this, and perhaps it is best to start by saying what it does *not* imply.

To begin with it has nothing to do with archaism, with the salvaging of obsolete words and turns of speech, or with the setting up of a "standard English" which must never be departed from. On the contrary, it is especially concerned with the scrapping of every word or idiom which has outworn its usefulness. It has nothing to do with correct grammar and syntax, which are of no importance so long as one makes one's meaning clear, or with the avoidance of Americanisms, or with having what is called a "good prose style." On the other hand it is not concerned with fake simplicity and the attempt to make written English colloquial. Nor does it even imply in every case preferring the Saxon word to the Latin one, though it does imply using the fewest and shortest words that will cover one's meaning. What is above all needed is to let the meaning choose the word, and not the other way about. In prose, the worst thing one can do with words is to surrender to them. When you

* One can cure oneself of the *not un-* formation by memorizing this sentence: *A not unblack dog was chasing a not unsmall rabbit across a not ungreen field.*

think of a concrete object, you think wordlessly, and then, if you want to describe the thing you have been visualizing you probably hunt about till you find the exact words that seem to fit it. When you think of something abstract you are more inclined to use words from the start, and unless you make a conscious effort to prevent it, the existing dialect will come rushing in and do the job for you, at the expense of blurring or even changing your meaning. Probably it is better to put off using words as long as possible and get one's meaning as clear as one can through pictures or sensations. Afterward one can choose—not simply *accept*—the phrases that will best cover the meaning, and then switch round and decide what impression one's words are likely to make on another person. This last effort of the mind cuts out all stale or mixed images, all prefabricated phrases, needless repetitions, and humbug and vagueness generally. But one can often be in doubt about the effect of a word or a phrase, and one needs rules that one can rely on when instinct fails. I think the following rules will cover most cases:

(i) Never use a metaphor, simile, or other figure of speech which you are used to seeing in print.

(ii) Never use a long word where a short one will do.

(iii) If it is possible to cut a word out, always cut it out.

(iv) Never use the passive where you can use the active.

(v) Never use a foreign phrase, a scientific word, or a jargon word if you can think of an everyday English equivalent.

(vi) Break any of these rules sooner than say anything outright barbarous.

These rules sound elementary, and so they are, but they demand a deep change of attitude in anyone who has grown used to writing in the style now fashionable. One could keep all of them and still write bad English, but one could not write the kind of stuff that I quoted in those five specimens at the beginning of this article.

I have not here been considering the literary use of language, but merely language as an instrument for expressing and not for concealing or preventing thought. Stuart Chase and others have come near to claiming that all abstract words are meaningless, and have used this as a pretext for advocating a kind of political quietism. Since you don't know what Fascism is, how can you struggle against Fascism? One need not swallow such absurdities as this, but one ought to recognize that the present political chaos is connected with the decay of language, and that one can probably bring about some improvement by starting at the verbal end. If you simplify your English, you are freed from the worst follies of orthodoxy. You cannot speak any of the necessary dialects, and when you make a stupid remark its stupidity will be obvious, even to yourself. Political language—and with variations this is true of all political parties, from Conservatives to Anarchists—is designed to make lies sound truthful and murder respectable, and to give an appearance of solidity to pure wind. One cannot change this all in a moment, but one can at least change one's own habits, and from time to time one can even, if one jeers loudly enough, send some worn-out and useless phrase—some *jackboot, Achilles' heel, hotbed, melting pot, acid test, veritable inferno,* or other lump of verbal refuse—into the dustbin where it belongs.

[1946]

SOME THOUGHTS
ON THE COMMON TOAD

Before the swallow, before the daffodil, and not much later than the snowdrop, the common toad salutes the coming of spring after his own fashion, which is to emerge from a hole in the ground, where he has lain buried since the previous autumn, and crawl as rapidly as possible towards the nearest suitable patch of water. Something—some kind of shudder in the earth, or perhaps merely a rise of a few degrees in the temperature—has told him that it is time to wake up: though a few toads appear to sleep the clock round and miss out a year from time to time—at any rate, I have more than once dug them up, alive and apparently well, in the middle of the summer.

At this period, after his long fast, the toad has a very spiritual look, like a strict Anglo-Catholic toward the end of Lent. His movements are languid but purposeful, his body is shrunken, and by contrast his eyes look abnormally large. This allows one to notice, what one might not at another time, that a toad has about the most beautiful eye of any living creature. It is like gold, or more exactly it is like the golden-colored semi-precious stone which one sometimes sees in signet rings, and which I think is called a chrysoberyl.

For a few days after getting into the water the toad concentrates on building up his strength by eating small insects. Presently he has swollen to his normal size again, and then he goes through a phase of intense sexiness. All he knows, at least if he is a male toad, is that he wants to get his arms round something, and if you offer him a stick, or even your finger, he will cling to it with surprising strength and take a long time to discover that it is not a female toad. Frequently one comes upon shapeless masses of ten or twenty toads rolling over and over in the water, one clinging to another without distinction of sex. By degrees, however, they sort themselves out into couples, with the male duly sitting on the female's back. You can now distinguish males from females, because the male is smaller, darker and sits on top, with his arms tightly clasped round the female's neck. After a day or two the spawn is laid in long strings which wind themselves in and out of the reeds and soon become invisible. A few more weeks, and the water is alive with masses of tiny tadpoles which rapidly grow larger, sprout hind legs, then forelegs, then shed their tails: and finally, about the middle of the summer, the new generation of toads, smaller than one's thumbnail but perfect in every particular, crawl out of the water to begin the game anew.

I mention the spawning of the toads because it is one of the phenomena of spring which most deeply appeal to me, and because the toad, unlike the skylark and the primrose, has never had much of a boost from the poets. But I am aware that many people do not like reptiles or amphibians, and I am not suggesting that in order to enjoy the spring you have to take an interest in toads. There are also the crocus, the missel thrush, the cuckoo, the blackthorn, etc. The point is that the pleasures of spring are available to everybody, and cost nothing. Even in the most sordid street the coming of spring will register itself by some sign or other, if it is only a brighter blue between the chimney pots or the vivid green of an elder sprouting on a blitzed site. Indeed it is remarkable how Nature goes on existing unofficially, as it were, in the very heart of London. I have seen a kestrel flying over the Deptford gasworks, and I have heard a first-rate performance by a blackbird in the Euston Road. There must be some hundreds of thousands, if not millions, of birds living inside the four-mile radius, and it is rather a pleasing thought that none of them pays a half-penny of rent.

As for spring, not even the narrow and gloomy streets round the Bank of England are quite able to exclude it. It comes seeping in everywhere, like one of those new poison gases which pass through all filters. The spring is commonly referred to as "a miracle," and during the past five or six years this worn-out figure of speech has taken on a new lease of life. After the sort of winters we have had to endure recently, the spring does seem miraculous, because it has become gradually harder and harder to believe that it is actually going to happen. Every February since 1940 I have found myself thinking that this time winter is going to be permanent. But Persephone, like the toads, always rises from the dead at about the same moment. Suddenly, toward the end of March, the miracle happens and the decaying slum in which I live is transfigured. Down in the square the sooty privets have turned bright green, the leaves are thickening on the chestnut trees, the daffodils are out, the wallflowers are budding, the policeman's tunic looks positively a pleasant shade of blue, the fish-monger greets his customers with a smile, and even the sparrows are quite a different color, having felt the balminess of the air and nerved themselves to take a bath, their first since last September.

Is it wicked to take a pleasure in spring, and other seasonal changes? To put it more precisely, is it politically reprehensible, while we are all groaning, under the shackles of the capitalist system, to point out that life is frequently more worth living because of a blackbird's song, a yellow elm tree in October, or some other natural phenomenon which does not cost money and does not have what the editors of the left-wing newspapers call a class angle? There is no doubt that many people think so. I know by experience that a favorable reference to "Nature" in one of my articles is liable to bring me abusive letters, and though the keyword in these letters is usually "sentimental," two ideas seem to be mixed up in them. One is that any pleasure in the actual process of life encourages a sort of political quietism. People, so the thought runs, ought to be discontented, and it is our job to multiply our wants and not simply to increase our enjoyment of the things we have already. The other idea is that this is the age of machines and that to dislike the machine, or even to want to limit its domination, is backward-looking, reactionary, and slightly ridiculous. This is often backed up by the statement that a love of Nature is a foible of urbanized people who have no notion what Nature is really like. Those who really have to deal with the soil, so it is argued, do not love the soil, and do not take the faintest interest in birds or flowers, except from a strictly utilitarian point of view. To love the country one must live in the town, merely taking an occasional week-end ramble at the warmer times of year.

This last idea is demonstrably false. Medieval literature, for instance, including the popular ballads, is full of an almost Georgian enthusiasm for Nature, and the art of agricultural peoples such as the Chinese and Japanese centers always round trees, birds, flowers, rivers, mountains. The other idea seems to me to be wrong in a subtler way. Certainly we ought to be discontented, we ought not simply to find out ways of making the best of a bad job, and yet if we kill all pleasure in the actual process of life, what sort of future are we preparing for ourselves? If a man cannot enjoy the return of spring, why should he be happy in a labor-saving Utopia? What will he do with the leisure that the machine will give him?

I have always suspected that if our economic and political problems are ever really solved, life will become simpler instead of more
complex, and that the sort of pleasure one gets from finding the
first primose will loom larger than the sort of pleasure one gets
from eating an ice to the tune of a Wurlitzer. I think that by re-
taining one's childhood love of such things as trees, fishes, butterflies, and—to return to my first instance—toads, one makes a peaceful
and decent future a little more probable, and that by preaching
the doctrine that nothing is to be admired except steel and concrete,
one merely makes it a little surer that human beings will have no
outlet for their surplus energy except in hatred and leader-worship.

At any rate, spring is here, even in London, N.1, and they can't
stop you enjoying it. This is a satisfying reflection. How many a
time have I stood watching the toads mating, or a pair of hares
having a boxing match in the young corn, and thought of all the
important persons who would stop me enjoying this if they could.
But luckily they can't. So long as you are not actually ill, hungry,
frightened, or immured in a prison or a holiday camp, spring is
still spring. The atom bombs are piling up in the factories, the
police are prowling through the cities, the lies are streaming from
the loudspeakers, but the earth is still going round the sun, and
neither the dictators nor the bureaucrats, deeply as they disapprove
of the process, are able to prevent it.

[1949]

REFLECTIONS ON GANDHI

SAINTS SHOULD always be judged guilty until they are proved
innocent, but the tests that have to be applied to them are not, of
course, the same in all cases. In Gandhi's case the questions one feels
inclined to ask are: to what extent was Gandhi moved by vanity—

by the consciousness of himself as a humble, naked old man, sitting on a praying mat and shaking empires by sheer spiritual power—and to what extent did he compromise his own principles by entering politics, which of their nature are inseparable from coercion and fraud? To give a definite answer one would have to study Gandhi's acts and writings in immense detail, for his whole life was a sort of pilgrimage in which every act was significant. But this partial auto-biography,* which ends in the nineteen-twenties, is strong evidence in his favor, all the more because it covers what he would have called the unregenerate part of his life and reminds one that inside the saint, or near-saint, there was a very shrewd, able person who could, if he had chosen, have been a brilliant success as a lawyer, an administrator, or perhaps even a businessman.

At about the time when the autobiography first appeared I remember reading its opening chapters in the ill-printed pages of some Indian newspaper. They made a good impression on me, which Gandhi himself, at that time, did not. The things that one associated with him—home-spun cloth, "soul forces," and vegetarianism—were unappealing, and his medievalist program was obviously not viable in a backward, starving, overpopulated country. It was also apparent that the British were making use of him, or thought they were making use of him. Strictly speaking, as a Nationalist, he was an enemy, but since in every crisis he would exert himself to prevent violence—which, from the British point of view, meant preventing any effective action whatever—he could be regarded as "our man." In private this was sometimes cynically admitted. The attitude of the Indian millionaires was similar. Gandhi called upon them to repent, and naturally they preferred him to the Socialists and Communists who, given the chance, would actually have taken their money away. How reliable such calculations are in the long run is doubtful; as Gandhi himself says, "in the end deceivers deceive only themselves"; but at any rate the gentleness with which he was nearly always handled was due partly to the feeling that he was useful. The British Conservatives only became really angry with

* The Story of my Experiments with Truth. By M. K. Gandhi. Translated from the Gujarati by Mahadex Desai. Public Affairs Press.

him when, as in 1942, he was in effect turning his non-violence against a different conqueror.

But I could see even then that the British officials who spoke of him with a mixture of amusement and disapproval also genuinely liked and admired him, after a fashion. Nobody ever suggested that he was corrupt, or ambitious in any vulgar way, or that anything he did was actuated by fear or malice. In judging a man like Gandhi one seems instinctively to apply high standards, so that some of his virtues have passed almost unnoticed. For instance, it is clear even from the autobiography that his natural physical courage was quite outstanding: the manner of his death was a later illustration of this, for a public man who attached any value to his own skin would have been more adequately guarded. Again, he seems to have been quite free from that maniacal suspiciousness which, as E. M. Forster rightly says in *A Passage to India*, is the besetting Indian vice, as hypocrisy is the British vice. Although no doubt he was shrewd enough in detecting dishonesty, he seems wherever possible to have believed that other people were acting in good faith and had a better nature through which they could be approached. And though he came of a poor middle-class family, started life rather unfavorably, and was probably of unimpressive physical appearance, he was not afflicted by envy or by the feeling of inferiority. Color feeling, when he first met it in its worst form in South Africa, seems rather to have astonished him. Even when he was fighting what was in effect a color war, he did not think of people in terms of race or status. The governor of a province, a cotton millionaire, a half-starved Dravidian coolie, a British private soldier were all equally human beings, to be approached in much the same way. It is noticeable that even in the worst possible circumstances, as in South Africa when he was making himself unpopular as the champion of the Indian community, he did not lack European friends.

Written in short lengths for newspaper serialization, the autobiography is not a literary masterpiece, but it is the more impressive because of the commonplaceness of much of its material. It is well to be reminded that Gandhi started out with the normal ambitions of a young Indian student and only adopted his extremist opinions by degrees and, in some cases, rather unwillingly. There was a time, it is interesting to learn, when he wore a top hat, took dancing lessons, studied French and Latin, went up the Eiffel Tower, and even tried to learn the violin—all this was the idea of assimilating European civilization as thoroughly as possible. He was not one of those saints who are marked out by their phenomenal piety from childhood onward, nor one of the other kind who forsake the world after sensational debaucheries. He makes full confession of the misdeeds of his youth, but in fact there is not much to confess. As a frontispiece to the book there is a photograph of Gandhi's possessions at the time of his death. The whole outfit could be purchased for about £5, and Gandhi's sins, at least his fleshly sins, would make the same sort of appearance if placed all in one heap. A few cigarettes, a few mouthfuls of meat, a few annas pilfered in childhood from the maidservant, two visits to a brothel (on each occasion he got away without "doing anything"), one narrowly escaped lapse with his landlady in Plymouth, one outburst of temper—that is about the whole collection. Almost from childhood onward he had a deep earnestness, an attitude ethical rather than religious, but, until he was about thirty, no very definite sense of direction. His first entry into anything describable as public life was made by way of vegetarianism. Underneath his less ordinary qualities one feels all the time the solid middle-class businessmen who were his ancestors. One feels that even after he had abandoned personal ambition he must have been a resourceful, energetic lawyer and a hardheaded political organizer, careful in keeping down expenses, an adroit handler of committees and an indefatigable chaser of subscriptions. His character was an extraordinarily mixed one, but there was almost nothing in it that you can put your finger on and call bad, and I believe that even Gandhi's worst enemies would admit that he was an interesting and unusual man who enriched the world simply by being alive. Whether he was also a lovable man, and whether his teachings can have much value for those who do not accept the religious beliefs on which they are founded, I have never felt fully certain.

Of late years it has been the fashion to talk about Gandhi as

though he were not only sympathetic to the Western left-wing movement, but were integrally part of it. Anarchists and pacifists, in
particular, have claimed him for their own, noticing only that he
was opposed to centralism and State violence and ignoring the other-
worldly, anti-humanist tendency of his doctrines. But one should,
I think, realize that Gandhi's teachings cannot be squared with the
belief that Man is the measure of all things and that our job is to
make life worth living on this earth, which is the only earth we
have. They make sense only on the assumption that God exists and
that the world of solid objects is an illusion to be escaped from.
It is worth considering the disciplines which Gandhi imposed on
himself and which—though he might not insist on every one of his
followers observing every detail—he considered indispensable if one
wanted to serve either God or humanity. First of all, no meat-eating,
and if possible no animal food in any form. (Gandhi himself, for
the sake of his health, had to compromise on milk, but seems to have
felt this to be a backsliding.) No alcohol or tobacco, and no spices
or condiments even of a vegetable kind, since food should be taken
not for its own sake but solely in order to preserve one's strength.
Secondly, if possible, no sexual intercourse. If sexual intercourse
must happen, then it should be for the sole purpose of begetting
children and presumably at long intervals. Gandhi himself, in his
middle thirties, took the vow of *brahmacharya*, which means not
only complete chastity but the elimination of sexual desire. This
condition, it seems, is difficult to attain without a special diet and
frequent fasting. One of the dangers of milk-drinking is that it is
apt to arouse sexual desire. And finally—this is the cardinal point—
for the seeker after goodness there must be no close friendships and
no exclusive loves whatever.

Close friendships, Gandhi says, are dangerous, because "friends
react on one another" and through loyalty to a friend one can be
led into wrong-doing. This is unquestionably true. Moreover, if one
is to love God, or to love humanity as a whole, one cannot give
one's preference to any individual person. This again is true, and it
marks the point at which the humanistic and the religious attitude
cease to be reconcilable. To an ordinary human being, love means

nothing if it does not mean loving some people more than others. The autobiography leaves it uncertain whether Gandhi behaved in an inconsiderate way to his wife and children, but at any rate it makes clear that on three occasions he was willing to let his wife or a child die rather than administer the animal food prescribed by the doctor. It is true that the threatened death never actually occurred, and also that Gandhi—with, one gathers, a good deal of moral pressure in the opposite direction—always gave the patient the choice of staying alive at the price of committing a sin: still, if the decision had been solely his own, he would have forbidden the animal food, whatever the risks might be. There must, he says, be some limit to what we will do in order to remain alive, and the limit is well on this side of chicken broth. This attitude is perhaps a noble one, but, in the sense which—I think—most people would give to the word, it is inhuman. The essence of being human is that one does not seek perfection, that one *is* sometimes willing to commit sins for the sake of loyalty, that one does not push asceticism to the point where it makes friendly intercourse impossible, and that one is prepared in the end to be defeated and broken up by life, which is the inevitable price of fastening one's love upon other human individuals. No doubt alcohol, tobacco, and so forth, are things that a saint must avoid, but sainthood is also a thing that human beings must avoid. There is an obvious retort to this, but one should be wary about making it. In this yogi-ridden age, it is too readily assumed that "non-attachment" is not only better than a full acceptance of earthly life, but that the ordinary man only rejects it because it is too difficult: in other words, that the average human being is a failed saint. It is doubtful whether this is true. Many people genuinely do not wish to be saints, and it is probable that some who achieve or aspire to sainthood have never felt much temptation to be human beings. If one could follow it to its psychological roots, one would, I believe, find that the main motive for "non-attachment" is a desire to escape from the pain of living, and above all from love, which, sexual or non-sexual, is hard work. But it is not necessary here to argue whether the other-worldly or the humanistic ideal is "higher." The point is that they are incompatible.

One must choose between God and Man, and all "radicals" and "progressives," from the mildest liberal to the most extreme anarchist, have in effect chosen Man.

However, Gandhi's pacifism can be separated to some extent from his other teachings. Its motive was religious, but he claimed also for it that it was a definite technique, a method, capable of producing desired political results. Gandhi's attitude was not that of most Western pacifists. *Satyagraha*, first evolved in South Africa, was a sort of non-violent warfare, a way of defeating the enemy without hurting him and without feeling or arousing hatred. It entailed such things as civil disobedience, strikes, lying down in front of railway trains, enduring police charges without running away and without hitting back, and the like. Gandhi objected to "passive resistance" as a translation of *Satyagraha*: in Gujarati, it seems, the word means "firmness in the truth." In his early days Gandhi served as a stretcher-bearer on the British side in the Boer War, and he was prepared to do the same again in the war of 1914-18. Even after he had completely abjured violence he was honest enough to see that in war it is usually necessary to take sides. He did not—indeed, since his whole political life centered round a struggle for national independence, he could not—take the sterile and dishonest line of pretending that in every war both sides are exactly the same and it makes no difference who wins. Nor did he, like most Western pacifists, specialize in avoiding awkward questions. In relation to the late war, one question that every pacifist had a clear obligation to answer was: "What about the Jews? Are you prepared to see them exterminated? If not, how do you propose to save them without resorting to war?" I must say that I have never heard, from any Western pacifist, an honest answer to this question, though I have heard plenty of evasions, usually of the "you're another" type. But it so happens that Gandhi was asked a somewhat similar question in 1938 and that his answer is on record in Mr. Louis Fischer's *Gandhi and Stalin*. According to Mr. Fischer, Gandhi's view was that the German Jews ought to commit collective suicide, which "would have aroused the world and the people of Germany to Hitler's violence." After the war he justified himself:

the Jews had been killed anyway, and might as well have died significantly. One has the impression that this attitude staggered even so warm an admirer as Mr. Fischer, but Gandhi was merely being honest. If you are not prepared to take life, you must often be prepared for lives to be lost in some other way. When, in 1942, he urged non-violent resistance against a Japanese invasion, he was ready to admit that it might cost several million deaths.

At the same time there is reason to think that Gandhi, who after all was born in 1869, did not understand the nature of totalitarianism and saw everything in terms of his own struggle against the British government. The important point here is not so much that the British treated him forbearingly as that he was always able to command publicity. As can be seen from the phrase quoted above, he believed in "arousing the world," which is only possible if the world gets a chance to hear what you are doing. It is difficult to see how Gandhi's methods could be applied in a country where opponents of the régime disappear in the middle of the night and are never heard of again. Without a free press and the right of assembly, it is impossible not merely to appeal to outside opinion, but to bring a mass movement into being, or even to make your intentions known to your adversary. Is there a Gandhi in Russia at this moment? And if there is, what is he accomplishing? The Russian masses could only practice civil disobedience if the same idea happened to occur to all of them simultaneously, and even then, to judge by the history of the Ukraine famine, it would make no difference. But let it be granted that non-violent resistance can be effective against one's own government, or against an occupying power: even so, how does one put it into practice internationally? Gandhi's various conflicting statements on the late war seem to show that he felt the difficulty of this. Applied to foreign politics, pacifism either stops being pacifist or becomes appeasement. Moreover the assumption, which served Gandhi so well in dealing with individuals, that all human beings are more or less approachable and will respond to a generous gesture, needs to be seriously questioned. It is not necessarily true, for example, when you are dealing with lunatics. Then the question becomes: Who is sane? Was Hitler

sane? And is it not possible for one whole culture to be insane by
the standards of another? And, so far as one can gauge the feelings
of whole nations, is there any apparent connection between a
generous deed and a friendly response? Is gratitude a factor in
international politics?

These and kindred questions need discussion, and need it ur-
gently, in the few years left to us before somebody presses the button
and the rockets begin to fly. It seems doubtful whether civilization
can stand another major war, and it is at least thinkable that the
way out lies through non-violence. It is Gandhi's virtue that he
would have been ready to give honest consideration to the kind
of question that I have raised above; and, indeed, he probably did
discuss most of these questions somewhere or other in his innumerable newspaper articles. One feels of him that there was much that
he did not understand, but not that there was anything that he was
frightened of saying or thinking. I have never been able to feel
much liking for Gandhi, but I do not feel sure that as a political
thinker he was wrong in the main, nor do I believe that his life
was a failure. It is curious that when he was assassinated, many of
his warmest admirers exclaimed sorrowfully that he had lived just
long enough to see his life work in ruins, because India was engaged
in a civil war which had always been foreseen as one of the by-
products of the transfer of power. But it was not in trying to smooth
down Hindu-Moslem rivalry that Gandhi had spent his life. His
main political objective, the peaceful ending of British rule, had
after all been attained. As usual the relevant facts cut across one
another. On the other hand, the British did get out of India without
fighting, an event which very few observers indeed would have
predicted until about a year before it happened. On the other hand,
this was done by a Labour government, and it is certain that a Conservative government, especially a government headed by Churchill,
would have acted differently. But if, by 1945, there had grown up
in Britain a large body of opinion sympathetic to Indian independence, how far was this due to Gandhi's personal influence? And if,
as may happen, India and Britain finally settle down into a decent
and friendly relationship, will this be partly because Gandhi, by

keeping up his struggle obstinately and without hatred, disinfected the political air? That one even thinks of asking such questions indicates his stature. One may feel, as I do, a sort of aesthetic distaste for Gandhi, one may reject the claims of sainthood made on his behalf (he never made any such claim himself, by the way), one may also reject sainthood as an ideal and therefore feel that Gandhi's basic aims were anti-human and reactionary: but regarded simply as a politician, and compared with the other leading political figures of our time, how clean a smell he has managed to leave behind!

NORMAN MAILER

ON THE back cover of *St. George and the Godfather* (his book on the 1972 political conventions), underneath a picture of the author looking puckish, a bit frazzled, and yet as if he might once have been a prizefighter, there is a publisher's blurb that begins, "NORMAN MAILER—America's # 1 National Character. . . ." For many readers it is this quality of Mailer's personality—his sometimes indecent public behavior, irrepressible egomania, and the apparent clownishness of some of his involvements (running for mayor of New York, making films)—that overshadows everything else, and turns them off.

Many writers have misbehaved in public yet been forgiven—Ernest Hemingway, F. Scott Fitzgerald, and Dylan Thomas, to name a few recent examples. The problem with Mailer is that his writing is pervaded with the same qualities that many find offensive in the man. As a writer he is cocky, exhibitionistic, and egotistical. To try to defend qualities that go so much against the grain of our sense of the proper role of the author within his work (i.e., self-effacing, controlled, subtle) is probably hopeless; but unless one understands that Mailer chose this style, that he did so because he found the conventional mode inadequate for describing his vision of contemporary American life, his originality and worth as a writer cannot be appreciated.

Mailer himself describes the way he writes (and lives) as "existential." But perhaps it is easier to understand if one thinks of it merely as nakedness, then sees this nakedness as an intellectual and emotional—hence, *moral*—reaction to a world that he thinks of as having gone mad with self-deception, hypocrisy, and the put-on. In the preface to *Existential Errands* Mailer says: "For in our world of gesture, role, costume, supposition, and borrowed manner . . . there is except for attrition no way out but by way of that moment which proves deeper than any of our pretenses, that stricken existential moment in which Camp is stripped of its marks of quotation, and put-ons shrivel in the livid air." In short, if one is to see Mailer as more than an egomaniac, one must take him on the terms of his

personal vision of "our world" and thus accept the appropriateness
of his manner. And if one is able to do that, then it becomes clear
that he is one of the most obsessively moral writers that America
has ever had, a Dostoevskian "underground man" right out in the
open, taking our cat-calls—indeed, eliciting them—for how else,
he might ask, is one to save the nation from its own insanity.

Norman Mailer was born in Long Branch, New Jersey, on January 31, 1923. When he was 4 the family moved to Brooklyn, where
he grew up and attended the public schools. At the age of 16 he
entered Harvard, intending to become an aeronautical engineer (the
major in which he did receive a B.S. degree in 1943); but during
his freshman year he became interested in literature and began
writing, and in his sophomore year won *Story* magazine's annual
college fiction contest. Having determined "by December 8th or 9th
in 1941, in the forty-eight hours after Pearl Harbor" that he was
going to write "a great war novel" and therefore that a safe commis-
sion or a desk job would deprive him of the firsthand experience he
felt he needed, Mailer was inducted into the army in 1944 and
became a rifleman with the 112th Cavalry.

When he was discharged in 1946, having served for a year and a
half in the Pacific, Mailer immediately went to work on his war
novel, which he completed in fifteen months. *The Naked and the
Dead* was published in 1948 and Mailer, at the age of 25, became the
most celebrated young writer in America, both popular with the
public and praised by the critics. The glory lasted only a few years,
however, for with his second novel, *Barbary Shore* (1951), and
his third, *The Deer Park* (1955), he fell into critical disrepute.

Discouraged, having less and less success with his fiction, and
disillusioned with leftist politics, Mailer drifted into a period in
which he became obsessed with "murder, suicide, orgy, psychosis"
and got deeply involved with drugs. Though he was writing regularly for *The Village Voice* (which he had helped found in 1955),
by the late fifties Mailer seemed done for as a writer. As he has
said, "I began to live with the conviction that I had burned out
my talent." Determined to prove that he wasn't finished yet, Mailer
moved out of New York and began writing with excruciating honesty

about his state of mind during that self-destructive period. Published in *Advertisements for Myself* (1959) as a running commentary on his life and work, these autobiographical confessions seemed to many readers the most powerful writing Mailer had done up till then.

Since then, despite the notoriety of his life, Mailer has become one of the most productive writers in America. Between 1965 and 1972 he published ten books, the most notable being the novel *Why Are We in Vietnam?* (1967), and the two reports on public events: *The Armies of the Night* (1968), an account of the 1967 protest march on the Pentagon, and *Miami and the Siege of Chicago* (also 1968), which analyzes the political conventions of that year. For the latter two he won a host of honors, including a Pulitzer Prize and two National Book Awards.

In the exuberance of his style and self-assertiveness of his intelligence, Mailer most closely resembles D. H. Lawrence of the other writers in this book. Though his best work is often too long to fit our notion of an essay, he is indeed an essayist—one who has brought to the form all the dramatic qualities of the novel—and it seems likely that his innovations will be imitated for many years to come.

DEMOCRACY AND THE
SEARCH FOR STYLE

IN TWENTY years it may be taken for granted that 1964 was the year in which a major party nominated a major pretender to conservatism. It was a loss, and it was conceivably a horror, for 1964 was also a year in which a real conservative still had a great deal to say to the nation. He could have demonstrated with no vast difficulty that America was under the yoke of a monstrous building boom whose architecture gave promise of being the ugliest in the history of man, that our labor unions had watered the value of labor until physical work had become as parasitical as white-collar work, and that our medicine had been overburdened beyond repair by a proliferation of wonder drugs whose side effects (with the notable exception of thalidomide) were still largely unknown—hence a delayed mass poisoning might yet be the fruit of this research. Our fruits, our vegetables, our cattle had lost the opportunity to feed on native soil and organic food; the balance of nature, the fisheries, the economy of marine life, and the insect economies were being disrupted to the root by marinas and insecticides; our old neighborhoods and old homes were being—one could swear it—systematically demolished, and our educational system was glutted by a host of intellectual canapés: art appreciation, domestic economy, sexual efficiency, the modern novel, and so forth.

A real conservative could also have pointed out that the Civil Rights Act, no matter how imperfect and conceivably unconstitutional, was an act to be voted for, since finally there was a matter more important than the protection of property rights—it was spiritual rights: the Negro was entitled to his spiritual rights even if there were hard niggling costs to the rights of the Constitution.

Finally, a great conservative could have noted that the health of Communism was its misery, that like all top-heavy structures its greatest danger was in its growth. Prosperity was Communism's poison, but attack from capitalism was its transfusion of blood. So the time was open for a great debate. Should we go back to isolationism? Did we not already possess enough nuclear Doomsdays to protect ourselves, was it not perhaps time to recognize that the industrialization of the backward nations was a thankless venture which wise men would avoid? Might it not be best to let the Communists have Asia and Africa after all? Would they not strangle on the meal? Yes, America was perhaps ready to listen to the sophistications of a conservative, if such a man was there to appear in 1964.

But what a conservative came down the pike! Marooned in a hopeless traffic with hate groups and bigots, Southern bullies and oil pirates, offering a program of sinister hints that a Federal police force would protect the young ladies of our land on their walk through our streets at night; reasoning with all the homely assurance of a filthy sock that he would protect the past by destroying the present (as in those remarks about scorching the foliage in Vietnam in order to keep the guerrillas from concealing themselves); wasting the substance of his campaign in pointless technical arguments with the Pentagon; and boring reconciliations and new feuds with the stricken Moderates of his party—the alleged conservative candidate was perhaps no more than a demagogue of the Right with a manly Christian air, a sweet voice, eyeglasses, and total innocence of a sense of contradiction, a spirit so naturally conservative that on the grounds of his home he raised the American flag with an electronic flagpole. Up at dawn, down at dusk, commanded the photoelectric cells in the mast. Well, one couldn't vote for such a man. He pressed the wrong buttons.

The mandate would go therefore to Lyndon Johnson. So most of America had seemed to decide by the eve of election. But it was nonetheless a vote heavy with gloom, and stricken with a sense of possible bad consequence, for there was much about Johnson which appealed not at all, and some of the evidence was intimate. He had written a book. That is intimate evidence. *My Hope for*

America, he had called it. Now, of course, a book written by a high official must not be judged by average standards, or one would be forced to say, for example, that Jack Kennedy was not a very good writer and that Bobby Kennedy, at last reading, wrote a dead stick's prose—his style almost as bad as J. Edgar Hoover's. But even at its worst, the prose style of Jack Kennedy (and his ghost writers) is to the prose style of L. B. J. (and *his* ghost writers) as de Tocqueville is to Ayn Rand. It is even not impossible that *My Hope for America* is the worst book ever written by any political leader anywhere.

The private personality of L. B. J., as reported by the authority of the best gossip, is different from his public presence. He is, one is told, not too unlike Broderick Crawford in *All the King's Men,* roaring, smarting, bellowing, stabbing fingers on advisers' chests, hugging his daughters, enjoying his food, mean and unforgiving, vindictive, generous, ebullient, vain, suddenly depressed, then roguish, then overbearing, suddenly modest again only to bellow once more. It is somewhat like the description of an early Renaissance prince, and if one looks hard at the photograph of the President on the cover of *My Hope for America,* a leader of *condottieri* stands forth—hard, greedy, exceptionally intelligent eyes whose cynicism is spiked by a fierce pride, big fleshy inquisitive (and acquisitive) nose, thin curved mouth (a boss mouth) and a slab of round hard jaw, deep dimple on the upper lip, deep dimple on the chin. It is not a bad face altogether, it is sufficiently worldly to inspire a kind of confidence that while no age of high ideals is close at hand, yet no martyrs are to be tortured, for there is small profit in that.

It is a face and a concealed personality which could even, considering the Republican alternative, inspire a touch of happiness, if it were not for the public image—that bottomless sea of overweening piety which collects here in this slim volume, this cove of Presidential prose whose waters are so brackish that a spoonful is enough to sicken the mind for hours. *My Hope for America* is an abominable, damnable book, and what makes it doubly awful is that nearly all of its ideas are blessed. It is in fact difficult to disagree with almost any one of them.

Who can argue on the side of poverty, or against justice, or against the idea of a Great Society? Let Barry Goldwater argue, not I. No, the ideals in this book are double-barreled, double-ringed, a double end of the cornucopia. More for the poor, more for the rich; more for peace, more for war; dedicatedly opposed to Communism, cautiously conciliatory; out to raise the income of poor nations, out to squash the economy of Cuba; all out for the Negro, all violence to be checked in city streets; all for the Democratic party, all for a party which includes Democrats *and* Republicans. There is even, and it is the achievement of this book, a curious sense of happiness running through its paragraphs. It is that happiness which is found at the end of the vision. It is as if the dream of Rousseau and Condorcet and Bakunin and Herzen and Marx and Lenin and Trotsky and John Dewey and the Webbs and Keynes and Roosevelt, Drieser, and Darrow—name any of a hundred, any of that long stream of political engineers who dreamed of changing a material world by material means to make all men free and equal—had come down at the end to Little Ol' Lyndon, and hot damn, he had said, discovering Progressive religion in 1964, that's the ticket, that's the liver-eating ticket! And he was off to bring it off. And happy as a clam. That's the happiness which comes off this book. It is like a dream of heaven in a terminal ward.

For beneath this odd disembodied happiness is a prose more sinister than the most pious of Lyndon Johnson's misrepresentations of his own personality; it is a prose which stirs half-heard cries of the death by suffocation of Western Civilization, it is a prose almost so bad and so deadening as the Georgian catechisms Josef Stalin used to hammer out: "Why is the Communist Party the party of the Soviet people? The Communist Party is the party of the Soviet people because . . . " It was enough at the time, reading Stalin, to keep from becoming a Communist. Now, reading Lyndon!—the horror is that one must still vote for him. But what a book is *My Hope for America.*

Examine it: 127 pages, a little more than 200 words to a page, most of the pages half pages or blank pages so that in bulk there are 17,000 words collected in 13 short chapters; they have titles like this—*President of All the People, A President's Faith and Vision, Building the Atlantic Partnership, This Developing World, Creative Federalism.* Each page of each chapter is divided into paragraphs. Page 8 has 12 paragraphs; the average page has four or five with a generous space between each paragraph. This is not because the remarks have the resonant echo of Pascal's *Pensées*, rather—one idea does not lead to another. So the space must be there. It is useful for burying whichever infinitesimal part of the brain died in the gas of the preceding phrase.

Yet every altruistic idea and every well-tuned moderation which Lyndon Johnson's political experience has put together over the years is somehow worked into the organum of his credo. It is impossible to disagree with a single of its humanistic desires ("We know that we can learn from the culture, the arts, and the traditions of other countries"); it is equally impossible to feel the least pleasure at the thought these goods may yet come to be—just so bad and disheartening is the style of this book:

Reality rarely matches dream. But only dreams give nobility to purpose. This is the star I hope to follow—which I know most of you have seen, and which I first glimpsed many years ago in the Texas night.

When the helpless call for help—the hearing must hear, the seeing must see, and the able must act.

It is an America where every man has an equal chance for the well-being that is essential to the enjoyment of the freedom that we brag about.

The Gulf of Tonkin may be distant Asian waters, but none can be detached about what happened there.

High-school students will be writing essays on these paragraphs. One's stomach turns over. It is certain that if Barry Goldwater had written the same book, everyone would be agreed his style was a menace. Still, what is quoted up to here is still English, English more or less. It is in the depth of the real prose articulated by Johnson and his corps of ghost writers that the heart of the darkness resides. For Johnson is not a writer and has no wish to be. He is a communications engineer. He uses words in interlocking aggregates which fence in thoughts like cattle. At bottom, the style consists of nothing but connectives and aggregate words—that is, political phrases five words long which are one aggregate word and so should be hyphenated. Example:

And it is one-of-the-great-tasks-of-Presidential-leadership to make our people aware that they share-a-fundamental-unity-of-interest-and-purpose-and-belief.

The essence of totalitarian prose is that it does not define, it does not deliver. It oppresses. It obstructs from above. It is profoundly contemptuous of the minds who will receive the message. So it does its best to dull this consciousness with sentences which are nothing but bricked-in power structures. Or alternately a totalitarian prose slobbers upon an audience a sentimentality so debauched that admiration for shamelessness is inspired. But then, sentimentality is the emotional promiscuity of those who have no sentiment:

When I was a child, one of my first memories was hearing the powder go off on an anvil on Armistice Day. I remember the terror that flowed from the Lusitania. I remember seeing boys come marching home, and the welcome we gave them at our little schoolhouse. When Pearl Harbor was attacked . . .

There is one expanding horror in American life. It is that our long odyssey toward liberty, democracy and freedom-for-all may be achieved in such a way that utopia remains forever closed, and we live in freedom and hell, debased of style, not individual from one another, void of courage, our fear rationalized away. We will all have enough money and we will all have a vote. The money will buy appliances made of plastic, and the money will buy books just as bad as *My Hope for America* or *The Conscience of a Conservative*.

The dream of democracy—that the average man possesses riches within himself worthy of a lord—will evolve into some anomalous electronic shape of human, half genius, half lout, and the liberation of existence will not take place. Only the buildings will continue to be built—bigger housing for all, slum clearance, urban renewal, Edward Durrell Stone, until we will look as if indeed we lost a war, as if we had been bombed to the ground, and built ourselves up again just so quickly and cheaply as the barracks could be slapped together.

"In the next forty years," writes Johnson, "we must rebuild the entire urban United States." But who will do it? Whose vision will prevail? Which head of horror may condemn generations not yet born to look at faceless buildings and roofless roofs, the totalitarianism stealing in from without, from the formless forms and imprisoned air of a new society which had lost the clue that a democracy could become equable only if it became great, that finally the world would continue to exist only by an act of courage and a search for style. Democracy flowers with style; without it, there is a rot of wet weeds. Which is why we love the memory so of F. D. R. and J. F. K. For they offered high style to the poor. And that is worth more than a housing project. That is the war against poverty.

Still, Lyndon Johnson must be given a vote. Because *My Hope for America* contains one good sentence, one more than Barry Goldwater could claim. This sentence reads: " . . . the wall between rich and poor is a wall of glass through which all can see." It inspires a corollary which is almost as good—the space between hypocrisy and honest manner may not forever insulate the powerful from the poor.

CITIES HIGHER THAN

MOUNTAINS

IN LYNDON Johnson's book, *My Hope for America*, the fifth chapter is titled "Toward the Great Society." It contains this paragraph:

. . . fifty years from now, . . . there will be four hundred million Americans, four-fifths of them in urban areas. In the remainder of this century, . . . we will have to build homes, highways, and facilities equal to all those built since this country was first settled. In the next forty years we must rebuild the entire urban United States.

It is a staggering sentence. The city we inhabit at this moment is already close to a total reconstruction of the world our parents knew in their childhood. If there is no nuclear war, if we shift from cold war to some kind of peace, and there is a worldwide rise in the standard of living, then indeed we will build a huge new country. It is possible that not one in a thousand of the buildings put up by 1899 will still be standing in the year 2000.

But what will America look like? How will its architecture appear? Will it be the architecture of a Great Society, or continue to be the architecture of an empty promiscuous panorama where no one can distinguish between hospitals and housing projects, factories and colleges, concert halls, civic centers, and airport terminals? The mind recoils from the thought of an America rebuilt completely in the shape of those blank skyscrapers forty stories high, their walls dead as an empty television screen, their form as interesting as a box of cleansing tissue propped on end. They are buildings which reveal nothing so much as the deterioration in real value of the dollar bill. They are denuded of ornament (which costs money), their windows are not subtly recessed into the wall but are laid flush with the surface like a patch of collodion on the skin, there is no instant where a roof with a tower, a gable, a spire, a mansard, a ridge or even a mooring mast for a dirigible intrudes itself into the sky, reminding us that every previous culture of man attempted to engage the heavens.

No, our modern buildings go flat, flat at the top, flat as eternal monotony, flat as the last penny in a dollar. There is so much corruption in the building codes, overinflation in the value of land, featherbedding built into union rules, so much graft, so much waste, so much public relations, and so much emptiness inflated upon so much emptiness that no one tries to do more with the roof than leave it flat.

As one travels through the arbitrary new neighborhoods of the present, those high squat dormitories which imprison the rich as well as the poor, one is not surprised that the violence is greater than it used to be in the old slum, up are the statistics for juvenile delinquency and for dope addiction. To live in the old slum jungle left many half crippled, and others part savage, but it was at least an environment which asked for wit. In the prison vistas of urban renewal, the violence travels from without to within, there is no wit— one travels down a long empty corridor to reach one's door, long as the corridors in the public schools, long as the corridors in the hospitals at the end of the road; the landscape of modern man takes on a sense of endless empty communications.

Sterile as an operating table is the future vista of suburban spread, invigorating as a whiff of deodorant is the sight of new office buildings. Small elation sits upon us as we contemplate the future, for the picturesque will be uprooted with the ugly, our populations will double, and in a city like New York, the brownstone will be replaced by a cube sixteen stories high with a huge park for parking cars and a little grass. The city will go up a little and it will go out, it will spread. We will live with glass walls in a cold climate. The

entire world will come to look like Queens Boulevard. We will have
been uprooted so many times that future man will come to bear the
same relation to the past that a hydroponic plant bears to soil.

Yet some part of us is aware that to uproot the past too completely
is a danger without measure. It must at the least produce a profound
psychic discomfort. For we do not know how much our perception
of the present and our estimate of the future depend upon our
sense of what has gone before. To return to an old neighborhood
and discover it has disappeared is a minor woe for some; it is close
to a psychological catastrophe for others, an amputation where the
lost nerves still feel pain. This century must appear at times like a
great beast which has lost its tail, but who could argue that the
amputation was not self-inflicted?

There seems at loose an impulse to uproot every vestige of the past,
an urge so powerful one wonders if it is not with purpose, if it is
not in the nature of twentieth-century man to uproot himself not
only from his past, but from his planet. Perhaps we live on the
edge of a great divide in history and so are divided ourselves between
the desire for a gracious, intimate, detailed and highly particular
landscape and an urge less articulate to voyage out on explorations
not yet made. Perhaps the blank faceless abstract quality of our
modern architecture is a reflection of the anxiety we feel before the
void, a kind of visual static which emanates from the psyche of us
all, as if we do not know which way to go.

If we are to spare the countryside, if we are to protect the style
of the small town and of the exclusive suburb, keep the organic
center of the metropolis and the old neighborhoods, maintain those
few remaining streets where the tradition of the nineteenth century
and the muse of the eighteenth century still linger on the mood
in the summer cool of an evening, if we are to avoid a megalopolis
five hundred miles long, a city without shape or exit, a nightmare
of ranch houses, highways, suburbs and industrial sludge, if we are
to save the dramatic edge of a city—that precise moment when we
leave the outskirts and race into the country, the open country—if
we are to have a keen acute sense of concentration and a breath of

release, then there is only one solution: the cities must climb, they must not spread, they must build up, not by increments, but by leaps, up and up, up to the heavens.

We must be able to live in houses one hundred stories high, two hundred stories high, far above the height of buildings as we know them now. New cities with great towers must rise in the plain, cities higher than mountains, cities with room for 400,000,000 to live, or that part of 400,000,000 who wish to live high in a landscape of peaks and spires, cliffs and precipices. For the others, for those who wish to live on the ground and with the ground, there will then be new room to live—the traditional small town will be able to survive, as will the old neighborhoods in the cities. But first a way must be found to build upward, to triple and triple again the height of all buildings as we know them now.

Picture, if you please, an open space where twenty acrobats stand, each locking hands with two different partners. Conceive then of ten acrobats standing on the shoulders of these twenty, and five upon the ten acrobats, and three more in turn above them, then two, then one. We have a pyramid of figures: six thousand to eight thousand pounds is supported upon a base of twenty pairs of shoes.

It enables one to think of structures more complex, of pyramids of steel which rise to become towers. Imagine a tower half a mile high and stressed to bear a vast load. Think of six or eight such towers and of bridges built between them, even as huge vines tie the branches of one high tree to another; think of groups of apartments built above these bridges (like the shops on the Ponte Vecchio in Florence) and apartments suspended beneath each bridge, and smaller bridges running from one complex of apartments to another, and of apartments suspended from cables, apartments kept in harmonious stress to one another by cables between them.

One can now begin to conceive of a city, or a separate part of a city, which is as high as it is wide, a city which bends ever so subtly in a high wind with the most delicate flexing of its near-to-numberless parts even as the smallest strut in a great bridge reflects the passing of an automobile with some fine-tuned quiver. In the subtlety of its swayings the vertical city might seem to be ready to live itself. It might be agreeable to live there.

The real question, however, has not yet been posed. It is whether a large fraction of the population would find it reasonable to live one hundred or two hundred stories in the air. There is the dread of heights. Would that tiny pit of suicide, planted like the small seed of murder in civilized man, flower prematurely into breakdown, terror and dread? Would it demand too much of a tenant to stare down each morning on a flight of 2,000 feet? Or would it prove a deliverance for some? Would the juvenile delinquent festering in the violence of his monotonous corridors diminish in his desire for brutality if he lived high in the air and found the intensity of his inexpressible vision matched by the intensity of the space through a fall?

That question returns us to the perspective of twentieth-century man. Caught between our desire to cling to the earth and to explore the stars, it is not impossible that a new life lived half a mile in the air, with streets in the clouds and chasms beyond each railing could prove nonetheless more intimate and more personal to us than the present congestions of the housing-project city. For that future man would be returned some individuality from his habitation. His apartment in the sky would be not so very different in its internal details from the apartments of his neighbors, no more than one apartment is varied from another in Washington Square Village. But his situation would now be different from any other. His windows would look out on a view of massive constructions and airy bridges, of huge vaults and fine intricacies. The complexity of our culture could be captured again by the imagination of the architect: our buildings could begin to look a little less like armored tanks and more like clipper ships. Would we also then feel the dignity of sailors on a four-master at sea? Living so high, thrust into space, might we be returned to that mixture of awe and elation, of dignity and self-respect and a hint of dread, that sense of zest which a man must have known working his way out along a yardarm in a stiff breeze at sea? Would the fatal monotony of mass culture dissolve a hint before the quiet swaying of a great and vertical city?

GRANDMA WITH
ORANGE HAIR*

THERE WAS not much to see through the canvas arch of the vehicle. A view of a service road they passed along, a little bumping, a bit of swaying—in two minutes they arrived at the next stop. It was the southwest wall of the Pentagon, so much was obvious, for the sun shone brightly here.

Probably they were at the rear of a large mess hall or cafeteria, since a loading platform extended for a considerable distance to either side of where the truck had come in. There were MPs and Marshals on the platform, maybe twenty or thirty, as many again in the back-up area where they had come in. At a long desk at the base of the loading platform, the prisoners were being booked. Each had a Marshal beside him. It was quiet and orderly. The Nazi was standing next to Mailer, but now neither looked at the other. It was indeed all over. The Nazi looked quietly spent, almost gentle—as if the outbursts had been his duty, but duty done, he was just a man again—no need to fight.

They took Mailer's name, having trouble with the spelling again. He was now certain it was not trivial harassment but simple unfamiliarity. The clerk, a stout Marshal with the sort of face that belonged to a cigar, worked carefully at his sheets. The questions were routine—name, address, why arrested—but he entered them with a slow-moving pen which spoke of bureaucratic sacraments taken up, and records set down in perpetuity.

When this was over, Mailer was led by the Marshal who had first arrested him, over to the open door of a sort of school bus painted olive-drab. There was, however, a delay in boarding it, and the

* Chapter Three, Part IV, of *The Armies of the Night.*

Marshal said, "I'm sorry, Mr. Mailer, we have to wait here for a minute to get your number."

"I don't mind."

They were being particularly polite with each other. Mailer had a clear opportunity to look again at this Marshal's face; the *vibrations* of the arrest now utterly discharged, he had an agreeable face indeed, quiet, honest, not unintelligent, not unhumorous. And he talked with the pleasant clipped integrity of a West Virginia accent. Mailer was going to ask him if he came from West Virginia, then out of some random modesty about putting too intensive a question and being wrong, he said instead, "May I ask your name?" It was as one might have expected, a name like Tompkins or Hudkins. "May I ask which state you're from, Marshal?"

"It's West Virginia, Mr. Mailer."

"My wife and I had a young lady work for us once who came from West Virginia. Your accent is similar to hers."

"Is that a fact?"

"Yes, I was wondering if you might be related. There's a suggestion of family resemblance." He mentioned the name. No relation.

Now the necessary paper was delivered to the Marshal. He signed it, and Mailer could board the bus. He had been given the number 10. He was the tenth man arrested at the Pentagon.

"Well, goodbye, Mr. Mailer. Nice talking to you."

"Yes."

Perhaps they were troubled partisans. Or did each wish to show the other that the enemy possessed good manners?

No, thought Mailer, it was ritual. At the moment of the arrest, cop and criminal knew each other better than mates, or at least knew some special *piece* of each other better than mates, yes an arrest was carnal. Not sexual, carnal—of the meat, strangers took purchase of each other's meat. Then came the reciprocal tendency to be pleasant. Beneath all those structures advertised as majestic in law and order there was this small carnal secret which the partners of a bust could share. It was tasty to chat afterward, all sly pleasures present that the secret was concealed. Mailer thought of a paragraph he had written once about police—it had probably acted upon him

as much as anything else to first imagine his movie. Now his mind
remembered the approximate sense of the paragraph, which actually
(indulging Mailer's desire to be quoted) went exactly like this:

. . . they contain explosive contradictions within themselves. Supposed
to be law-enforcers, they tend to conceive of themselves as the law. They
are more responsible than the average man, they are more infantile. They
are attached umbilically to the concept of honesty, they are profoundly
corrupt. They possess more physical courage than the average man, they
are unconscionable bullies; they serve the truth, they are psychopathic
liars . . . their work is authoritarian, they are cynical; and finally if something in their heart is deeply idealistic, they are also bloated with greed.
There is no human creation so contradictory, so finally enigmatic, as the
character of the average cop . . .

Yes, and without an arrest, he would never have known that this
very nice Marshal from West Virginia with his good American face
and pleasant manners and agreeable accent, had also a full quiver of
sadism and a clammy sweat of possession as he put the arm on you.
But indeed, what knowledge had the Marshal of him?

Inside the bus, at the rear of the aisle, was a locked cage and three
or four protesters were enclosed there; jailed within their jailing.
They greeted him with jeers, cat-calls, hellos, requests for cigarettes,
water—after the first impact, it was not ill-spirited. "Hey, look," said
one of the kids behind the bars, "they got older people in with us
too."

"What time does this bus leave for Plainfield?" Mailer asked. The
laughter came back. It was going to be all right. He could hear them
whispering.

"You Norman Mailer?" asked one.

"Yes."

"Hey, great. Listen, man, we got to talk."

"I hope we don't have too much time." More laughter. He was
beginning to feel good for the first time since his arrest. "What did
you gentlemen do to be given such honor?" asked Mailer with a
wave at their cage.

"We're the ones who were resisting arrest."

"Did you resist it much?"

"Are you kidding?" said one dark-haired gloomy thin young pirate with a large Armenian mustache and a bloodied handkerchief on his head, "if we put our hands in front of our face to keep from being beaten to death, they said we were resisting." Hoots and jeers at the fell accuracy of this.

"Well, did you all just sit there and take it?"

"I got in a couple of good shots at my Marshal," said one of the kids. It was hard to tell if he was lying. Something about their incarceration in the cage made it difficult to separate them, or perhaps it was that they seemed part of a team, of a musical group—the Monsters, or the Freaks, or the Caged Kissers—they had not known each other an hour ago, but the cage did the work of making them an ensemble.

The rest of the bus was slowly filling. Mailer had first taken a seat next to a young minister wearing his collar, and they chatted not unhappily for a few minutes, and then both crossed the aisle to sit on the side of the bus which looked out on the loading platform and the table where they had been booked. From these seats, Mailer had a view of the Marshals and MPs outside, of new arrests arriving in trucks, and of the prisoners coming into the bus, one by one, every couple of minutes. After a while, he realized the bus would not move until it was filled, and this, short of massive new arrests, would take at least an hour.

It was not disagreeable waiting. Each new prisoner was obliged to make an entrance like an actor coming on stage for his first appearance: since prisoners in transit are an enforced audience, new entrance automatically becomes theater. Some new men sauntered on the bus, some bowed to the faces in the aisle, some grinned, some scowled and sat down immediately; one or two principled pacifists practicing total non-cooperation were dragged off the 2½-ton trucks, bumped along the ground, tugged over to the bus, and thrown in by the Marshals. Bleeding a little, looking dazed, the three or four young men who arrived by this route were applauded with something not unlike the enthusiasm a good turn gets in a music hall. Handsome young boys got on the bus, and slovenly oafs, hippies, and walking wounded. One boy had a pant leg soaked in blood. A fat sad fellow with a huge black beard now boarded; a trim and skinny kid who looked like he played minor league shortstop took a seat, a Japanese boy, androgynous in appearance, told a few prisoners around him that none of the Marshals had been able to decide if he was a boy or a girl, so they had not known—for he would not tell them—whether a Marshal or a Matron should search him. This was quickly taken up with pleasure and repeated down the bus.

Outside, a truck would arrive every five or ten minutes and some boys and girls would dismount and go to the base of the loading platform to be booked, the boys to enter the bus, the girls to go off to another bus. Still no sign of Lowell or Macdonald. Mailer kept hoping they would appear in the next haul of prisoners. After a while he began to study the Marshals.

Their faces were considerably worse than he had expected. He had had the fortune to be arrested by a man who was incontestably one of the pleasanter Marshals on duty at the Pentagon, he had next met what must be the toughest Marshal in the place—the two had given him a false spectrum. The gang of Marshals now studied outside the bus were enough to firm up any fading loyalty to his own cause: they had the kind of faces which belong to the bad guys in a Western. Some were fat, some were too thin, but nearly all seemed to have those subtle anomalies of the body which come often to men from small towns who have inherited strong features, but end up, by their own measure, in failure. Some would have powerful chests, but abrupt paunches, the skinny ones would have a knob in the shoulder, or a hitch in their gait, their foreheads would have odd cleaving wrinkles, so that one man might look as if an ax had struck him between the eyes, another paid tithe to ten parallel deep lines rising in ridges above his eye brows. The faces of all too many had a low cunning mixed with a stroke of rectitude: if the mouth was slack, the nose was straight and severe; should the lips be tight, the nostrils showed an outsize greed. Many of them looked to be ex-First Sergeants, for they liked to stand with the heels of their hands on the top of their hips, or they had that way of walking, belly forward, which a man will promote when he is in comfortable circumstances with himself and packing a revolver in a belt holster. The toes turn out; the belly struts. They were older men than he might have expected, some in their late thirties, more in their forties, a few looked to be over fifty, but then that may have been why they were here to receive prisoners rather than out on the line—in any case they emitted a collective spirit which, to his mind, spoke of little which was good, for their eyes were blank and dull, that familiar small-town cast of eye which speaks of apathy rising to fanaticism only to subside in apathy again. (Mailer had wondered more than once at that curious demand of small-town life which leaves something good and bright in the eyes of some, is so deadening for others —it was his impression that people in small towns had eyes which were generally livelier or emptier than the more concentrated look of city vision.) These Marshals had the dead eye and sour cigar, that sly shuffle of propriety and rut which so often comes out in a small-town sheriff as patriotism and the sweet stink of a crooked dollar. Small-town sheriffs sidled over to a crooked dollar like a High Episcopalian hooked on a closet queen. If one could find the irredeemable madness of America (for we are a nation where weeds will breed in the gilding tank) it was in those late afternoon race track faces coming into the neon lights of the parimutuel windows, or those early morning hollows in the eye of the soul in places like Vegas where the fevers of America go livid in the hum of the night, and Grandmother, the church-goer, orange hair burning bright now crooned over the One-Arm Bandit, pocketbook open, driving those half-dollars home, home to the slot.

"Madame, we are burning children in Vietnam."

"Boy, you just go get yourself lost. Grandma's about ready for a kiss from the jackpot."

The burned child is brought into the gaming hall on her hospital bed.

"Madame, regard our act in Vietnam."

"I hit! I hit! Hot deedy, I hit. Why, you poor burned child—you just brought me luck. Here, honey, here's a lucky half-dollar in reward. And listen sugar, tell the nurse to change your sheets. Those sheets sure do stink. I hope you ain't got gangrene. Hee hee, hee

hee. I get a supreme pleasure mixing with gooks in Vegas."

One did not have to look for who would work in the concentration camps and the liquidation centers—the garrison would be filled with applicants from the pages of a hundred American novels, from *Day of the Locust* and *Naked Lunch* and *The Magic Christian,* one could enlist half the Marshals outside this bus, simple, honest, hardworking government law-enforcement agents, yeah! There was something at loose now in American life, the poet's beast slinking to the marketplace. The country had always been wild. It had always been harsh and hard, it had always had a fever—when life in one American town grew insupportable, one could travel, the fever to travel was in the American blood, so said all, but now the fever had left the blood, it was in the cells, the cells traveled, and the cells were as insane as Grandma with orange hair. The small towns were disappearing in the bypasses and the supermarkets and the shopping centers, the small town in America was losing its sense of the knuckle, the herb, and the root, the walking sticks were no longer cut from trees, nor were they cured, the schools did not have crazy old teachers now but teaching aids, and in the libraries, *National Geographic* gave way to *TV Guide.* Enough of the old walled town had once remained in the American small town for gnomes and dwarfs and knaves and churls (yes, and owls and elves and crickets) to live in the constellated cities of the spiders below the eaves in the old leaning barn which—for all one knew—had been a secret ear to the fevers of the small town, message center for the inhuman dreams which passed through the town at night in sleep and came to tell their insane tale of the old barbarian lust to slaughter villages and drink their blood, yes who knew which ghosts, and which crickets, with which spider would commune—which prayers and whose witch's curses would travel those subterranean trails of the natural kingdom about the town, who knows which fevers were forged in such communion and returned on the blood to the seed, it was an era when the message came by the wind and not by the wire (for the town gossip began to go mad when the telephone tuned its buds to the tip of her tongue) the American small town grew out of itself, and grew out of itself again and again, harmony between communication and the wind, between lives and ghosts, insanity, the solemn reaches of nature where insanity could learn melancholy (and madness some measure of modesty) had all been lost now, lost to the American small town. It had grown out of itself again and again, its cells traveled, worked for government, found security through wars in foreign lands, and the nightmares which passed on the winds in the old small towns now traveled on the nozzle tip of the flame thrower, no dreams now of barbarian lusts, slaughtered villages, battles of blood, no, nor any need for them—technology had driven insanity out of the wind and out of the attic, and out of all the lost primitive places: one had to find it now wherever fever, force, and machines could come together, in Vegas, at the race track, in pro football, race riots for the Negro, suburban orgies—none of it was enough—one had to find it in Vietnam; that was where the small town had gone to get its kicks.

That was on the faces of the Marshals. It was a great deal to read on the limited evidence before him, but he had known these faces before—they were not so different from the cramped, mean, stern, brave, florid, bestial, brutish, narrow, calculating, incurious, hardy, wily, leathery, simple, good, stingy, small-town faces he had once been familiar with in his outfit overseas, all those Texans from all those small towns, it was if he could tell—as at a college reunion— the difference these more than twenty years had made. If it were legitimate to read the change in American character by the change in the faces of one's classmates, then he could look at these Marshals like men he had known in the Army, but now revisited, and some- thing had gone out of them, something had come in. If there was a common unattractive element to the Southern small-town face, it was in that painful pinch between their stinginess and their greed. No excess of love seemed ever to come off a poor white Southerner, no fats, no riches, no sweets, just the avidity for such wealth. But there had been sadness attached to this in the old days, a sorrow; in the pinch of their cheeks was the kind of abnegation and loneli- ness which spoke of what was tender and what was lost forever. So they had dignity. Now the hollows in their faces spoke of men who were rabid and toothless, the tenderness had turned corrosive, the abnegation had been replaced by hate, dull hate, cloud banks of hate, the hatred of failures who had not lost their greed. So he was reminded of a probability he had encountered before: that, nuclear bombs all at hand, the true war party of America was in all the small towns, even as the peace parties had to collect in the cities and the suburbs. Nuclear warfare was dividing the nation. The day of power for the small-town mind was approaching—who else would be left when atomic war was done would reason the small-town mind, and in measure to the depth of their personal failure, would love Vietnam, for Vietnam was the secret hope of a bigger war, and that bigger war might yet clear the air of races, faces, in fact—technologies—all that alienation they could not try to comprehend.

It was not a happy meditation. Among the soldiers he had known, there was the chance to talk. He did not see many faces here who would ever talk. Cheers. They were dragging a girl out of one of the trucks now. Pale-skinned, with light brown hair, no lipstick, dungarees, she had that unhappy color which came from too many trips to marijuana garden. Nonetheless, she waved to her boyfriend while being dragged along the ground. He was eventually dragged into their bus.

Mailer began to chat with the young clergyman. His name was John Boyle, and he was Presbyterian Chaplain at Yale. The number of his arrest was nine. They joked about this—he had beaten Mailer to the Bench. Actually he had seen the Protagonist get arrested, had followed to see if he were being treated properly (a sign of Mailer's age, a proper sign of status!) was turned back with assurances, wandered behind Pentagon lines, and in the course of protesting the arrest of a demonstrator, was apprehended himself (although the Marshal had wanted to release him when he saw his collar).

"Well," said Mailer, "at least we have low numbers."

"Do you think that will mean much?"

"We should be the first to get out."

From where he sat in the bus, he could see square vertical columns back of the loading platform, columns reminiscent of Egyptian architecture: Mailer now had a rumination about the nature of Egyptian architecture and its relation to the Pentagon, those ultra-excremental forms of ancient Egyptian architecture, those petrified excrements of the tomb and the underground chambers here at the Pentagon, but he was not an Egyptologist, no sir, and the connection eluded him. He must pursue it later. Something there. But the rumination running down, we may quickly leave his thoughts.

[1968]

MIAMI BEACH

THEY SNIPPED the ribbon in 1915, they popped the cork, Miami Beach was born. A modest burg they called a city, nine-tenths jungle. An island. It ran along a coastal barrier the other side of Biscayne Bay from young Miami—in 1868 when Henry Lum, a California 'forty-niner, first glimpsed the island from a schooner, you may be certain it was jungle, cocoanut palms on the sand, mangrove swamp and palmetto thicket ten feet off the beach. But by 1915, they were working the vein. John S. Collins, a New Jersey nurseryman (after whom Collins Avenue is kindly named) brought in bean fields and avocado groves; a gent named Fisher, Carl G., a Hoosier—he invented Prestolite, a millionaire—bought up acres from Collins, brought in a work-load of machinery, men, even two elephants, and jungle was cleared, swamps were filled, small residential islands were made out of baybottom mud, dredged, then relocated, somewhat larger natural islands adjacent to the barrier island found themselves improved, streets were paved, sidewalks put in with other amenities—by 1968, one hundred years after Lum first glommed the beach, large areas of the original coastal strip were covered over altogether with macadam, white condominium, white luxury hotel and white stucco flea-bag. Over hundreds, then thousands of acres, white sidewalks, streets and white buildings covered the earth where the jungle had been. Is it so dissimilar from covering your poor

pubic hair with adhesive tape for fifty years? The vegetal memories
of that excised jungle haunted Miami Beach in a steam-pot of
miasmas. Ghosts of expunged flora, the never-born groaning in
vegetative chancery beneath the asphalt came up with a tropical
curse, an equatorial leaden wet sweat of air which rose from the
earth itself, rose right up through the baked asphalt and into the
heated air which entered the lungs like a hand slipping into a
rubber glove.

The temperature was not that insane. It hung around 87° day
after day, at night it went down to 82°, back to the same 87° in the
A.M.—the claims of the News Bureau for Miami Beach promised
that in 1967 temperature exceeded 90° only four times. (Which
the Island of Manhattan could never begin to say.) But of course
Miami Beach did not have to go that high, for its humidity was up
to 87° as well—it was, on any and every day of the Republican Convention of 1968, one of the hottest cities in the world. The reporter
was no expert on tropical heats—he had had, he would admit, the
island of Luzon for a summer in World War II; and basic training
in the pine woods of Fort Bragg, North Carolina, in August; he
had put in a week at Las Vegas during July—temperatures to 110°;
he had crossed the Mojave Desert once by day; he was familiar
with the New York subway in the rush hour on the hottest day of
the year. These were awesome immersions—one did not have to
hit the Congo to know what it was like in a hothouse in hell—but
that 87° in Miami Beach day after day held up in competition
against other sulphuric encounters. Traveling for five miles up the
broken-down, forever in-a-state-of-alteration and repair of Collins
Avenue, crawling through 5 P.M. Miami Beach traffic in the pure
miserable fortune of catching an old taxi without air conditioning,
dressed in shirt and tie and jacket—formal and implicitly demanded
uniform of political journalists—the sensation of breathing, then
living, was not unlike being obliged to make love to a 300-pound
woman who has decided to get on top. Got it? You could not
dominate a thing. That uprooted jungle had to be screaming beneath.

Of course it could have been the air conditioning: natural climate
transmogrified by technological climate. They say that in Miami
Beach the air conditioning is pushed to that icy point where women

may wear fur coats over their diamonds in the tropics. For ten miles, from the Diplomat to the Di Lido, above Hallandale Beach Boulevard down to Lincoln Mall, all the white refrigerators stood, piles of white refrigerators six and eight and twelve stories high, twenty stories high, shaped like sugar cubes and ice-cube trays on edge, like mosques and palaces, shaped like matched white luggage and portable radios, stereos, plastic compacts and plastic rings, Moorish castles shaped like waffle irons, shaped like the baffle plates on white plastic electric heaters, and cylinders like Waring blenders, buildings looking like giant op art and pop art paintings, and sweet wedding cakes, cottons of kitsch and piles of dirty cotton stucco, yes, for ten miles the hotels for the delegates stood on the beach side of Collins Avenue: the Eden Roc and the Fontainebleau (Press Headquarters), the Di Lido and the De Lano, the Ivanhoe, Deauville, Sherry Frontenac and the Monte Carlo, the Cadillac, Caribbean and the Balmoral, the Lucerne, Hilton Plaza, Doral Beach, the Sorrento, Marco Polo, Casablanca, and Atlantis, the Hilyard Manor, Sans Souci, Algiers, Carillon, Seville, the Gaylord, the Shore Club, the Nautilus, Montmartre, and the Promenade, the Bal Harbour on North Bay Causeway, and the Twelve Caesars, the Regency and the Americana, the Diplomat, Versailles, Coronado, Sovereign, the Waldman (dig!), the Beau Rivage, the Crown Hotel, even Holiday Inn, all oases for technological man. Deep air conditioning down to 68°, ice-palaces to chill the fevered brain—when the air conditioning worked. And their furnishings were monumentally materialistic. Not all of them: the cheaper downtown hotels like the Di Lido and the Nautilus were bare and mean with vinyl coverings on the sofas and the glare of plastic off the rugs and tables and tiles, inexpensive hotel colors of pale brown and buff and dingy cream, sodden gray, but the diadems like the Fontainebleau and the Eden Roc, the Doral Beach, the Hilton Plaza (Headquarters for Nixon), the Deauville (Hq for Reagan) or the Americana—Rockefeller and the New York State delegation's own ground—were lavish with interlockings, curves, vaults and runs of furnishings as intertwined as serpents in the roots of a mangrove tree. All the rivers of the very worst taste twisted down to the delta of each lobby in each grand Miami Beach hotel—rare was the central room which did not look like the lobby of a movie palace, imitation of late-Renaissance imitations of Greek and Roman statues, imitations of baroque and rococo and brothel Victorian and Art Nouveau and Bauhaus with gold grapes and cornucopias welded to the modern bronze tubing of the chair, golden moldings which ran like ivy from room to room, chandeliers complex as the armature of dynamos, and curvilinear steps in the shape of amoebas and palettes, cocktail lounge bars in deep rose or maroon with spun-sugar white tubes of plaster decor to twist around the ceiling. There was every color of iridescence, rainbows of vulgarity, aureoles of gorgeous taste, opium den of a middle-class dollar, materialistic as meat, sweat, and the cigar. It is said that people born under Taurus and Capricorn are the most materialistic of us all. Take a sample of the residents in the census of Miami B.—does Taurus predominate more than one-twelfth of its share? It must, or astrology is done, for the Republicans, Grand Old Party with a philosophy rather than a program, had chosen what must certainly be the materialistic capital of the world for their convention. Las Vegas might offer competition, but Las Vegas was materialism in the service of electricity—fortunes could be lost in the spark of the dice. Miami was materialism baking in the sun, then stepping back to air-conditioned caverns where ice could nestle in the fur. It was the first of a hundred curiosities—that in a year when the Republic hovered on the edge of revolution, nihilism, and lines of police on file to the horizon, visions of future Vietnams in our own cities upon us, the party of conservatism and principle, of corporate wealth and personal frugality, the party of cleanliness, hygiene, and balanced budget, should have set itself down on a sultan's strip.

That was the first of a hundred curiosities, but there were mysteries as well. The reporter had moved through the convention quietly, as anonymously as possible, wan, depressed, troubled. Something profoundly unclassifiable was going on among the Republicans and he did not know if it was conceivably good or a concealment of something bad—which was the first time a major social phenomenon like a convention had confused him so. He had covered others. The

Democratic Convention in 1960 in Los Angeles which nominated
John F. Kennedy, and the Republican in San Francisco in 1964
which installed Barry Goldwater, had encouraged some of his very
best writing. He had felt a gift for comprehending those conventions.
But the Republican assembly in Miami Beach in 1968 was a different affair—one could not tell if nothing much was going on, or to
the contrary, nothing much was going on near the surface but
everything was shifting down below. So dialogue with other journalists merely depressed him—the complaints were unanimous that this
was the dullest convention anyone could remember. Complaints
took his mind away from the slow brooding infusion he desired in
the enigmas of conservatism and/or Republicanism, and any hope
of perspective on the problem beyond. The country was in a throe,
a species of eschatological heave. The novelist John Updike was
not necessarily one of his favorite authors, but after the assassination
of Robert F. Kennedy, it was Updike who had made the remark
that God might have withdrawn His blessing from America. It
was a thought which could not be forgotten for it gave insight to
the perspectives of the Devil and his political pincers: Left-wing
demons, white and Black, working to inflame the conservative heart
of America, while Right-wing devils exacerbated Blacks and drove
the mind of the New Left and liberal middle class into prides of
hopeless position. And the country roaring like a bull in its wounds,
coughing like a sick lung in the smog, turning over in sleep at the
sound of motorcycles, shivering at its need for new phalanxes of
order. Where were the new phalanxes one could trust? The reporter
had seen the faces of too many police to balm his dreams with the
sleep they promised. Even the drinks tasted bad in Miami in the
fever and the chill.

THE SIEGE OF CHICAGO

Chapter 16

MEANWHILE, A mass meeting was taking place about the bandshell in Grant Park, perhaps a quarter of a mile east of Michigan Avenue and the Conrad Hilton. The meeting was under the auspices of the Mobilization, and a crowd of ten or fifteen thousand appeared. The Mayor had granted a permit to assemble, but had refused to allow a march. Since the Mobilization had announced that it would attempt, no matter how, the march to the Amphitheatre that was the first purpose of their visit to Chicago, the police were out in force to surround the meeting.

An episode occurred during the speeches. Three demonstrators climbed a flag pole to cut down the American flag and put up a rebel flag. A squad of police charged to beat them up, but got into trouble themselves, for when they threw tear gas, the demonstrators lobbed the canisters back, and the police, choking on their own gas, had to fight their way clear through a barrage of rocks. Then came a much larger force of police charging the area, overturning benches, busting up members of the audience, then heading for Rennie Davis at the bullhorn. He was one of the coordinators of the Mobilization, his face was known, he had been fingered and fingered again by plainclothesmen. Now urging the crowd to sit down and be calm, he was attacked from behind by the police, his head laid open in a three-inch cut, and he was unconscious for a period. Furious at the attack, Tom Hayden, who had been in disguise these last two days to avoid any more arrests for himself, spoke to the crowd, said he was leaving to perform certain special tasks, and suggested that others break up into small groups and go out into the streets of the Loop "to do what they have to do." A few left with him; the majority remained. While it was a People's Army and therefore utterly unorganized by uniform or unity, it had a variety of special troops and regular troops; everything from a few qualified Kamikaze who were ready to charge police lines in a Japanese snake dance and dare on the consequence, some vicious beatings, to various kinds of small saboteurs, rock-throwers, gauntlet-runners—some of the speediest of the kids were adept at taunting cops while keeping barely out of range of their clubs—not altogether alien to running the bulls at Pamplona. Many of those who remained, however, were still nominally pacifists, protesters, Gandhians—they believed in non-violence, in the mystical interposition of their body to the attack, as if the violence of the enemy might be drained by the spiritual act of passive resistance over the years, over the thousands, tens of thousands, hundreds of thousands of beatings over the years. So Allen Ginsberg was speaking now to them.

The police looking through the plexiglass face shields they had flipped down from their helmets were then obliged to watch the poet with his bald head, soft eyes magnified by horn-rimmed eyeglasses, and massive dark beard, utter his words in a croaking speech. He had been gassed Monday night and Tuesday night, and had gone to the beach at dawn to read Hindu Tantras to some of the Yippies, the combination of the chants and the gassings had all but burned out his voice, his beautiful speaking voice, one of the most powerful and hypnotic instruments of the Western world was down to the scrapings of the throat now, raw as flesh after a curettage.

"The best strategy for you," said Ginsberg, "in cases of hysteria, overexcitement or fear, is still to chant 'OM' together. It helps to quell flutterings of butterflies in the belly. Join me now as I try to lead you."

The crowd chanted with Ginsberg. They were of a generation which would try every idea, every drug, every action—it was even possible a few of them had made out with freaky kicks on tear gas these last few days—so they would chant OM. There were Hindu fanatics in the crowd, children who loved India and scorned everything in the West; there were cynics who thought the best thing to be said for a country which allowed its excess population to die by the millions in famine-ridden fields was that it would not be ready soon to try to dominate the rest of the world. There were also militants who were ready to march. And the police there to prevent them, busy now in communication with other detachments of police, by way of radios whose aerials were attached to their helmets, thereby giving them the look of giant insects.

A confused hour began. Lincoln Park was irregular in shape with curving foot walks; but Grant Park was indeed not so much a park as a set of belts of greenery cut into files by major parallel avenues between Michigan Avenue and Lake Michigan half a mile away. Since there were also cross streets cutting the belts of green perpendicularly, a variety of bridges and pedestrian overpasses gave egress to the city. The park was in this sense an alternation of lawn with superhighways. So the police were able to pen the crowd. But not completely. There were too many bridges, too many choices, in effect, for the police to anticipate. To this confusion was added the fact that every confrontation of demonstrators with police, now buttressed by the National Guard, attracted hundreds of newsmen, and hence began a set of attempted negotiations between spokesmen for the demonstrators and troops; the demonstrators finally tried to force a bridge and get back to the city. Repelled by tear gas, they went to other bridges, still other bridges, finally found a bridge lightly guarded, broke through a passage and were loose in the city at six-thirty in the evening. They milled about in the Loop for a few minutes, only to encounter the mules and three wagons of the Poor People's Campaign. City officials, afraid of provoking the Negroes on the South Side, had given a permit to the Reverend Abernathy, and he was going to march the mules and wagons down Michigan Avenue and over to the convention. An impromptu march of the demonstrators formed behind the wagons immediately on encountering them and ranks of marchers, sixty, eighty, a hundred in line across the width of Michigan Avenue began to move forward in the gray early twilight of 7 P.M.; Michigan Avenue was now suddenly jammed with people in the march, perhaps so many as four or five thousand people, including onlookers on the sidewalk who jumped

in. The streets of the Loop were also reeking with tear gas—the
wind had blown some of the gas west over Michigan Avenue from
the drops on the bridges, some gas still was penetrated into the
clothing of the marchers. In broken ranks, half a march, half a
happy mob, eyes red from gas, faces excited by the tension of the
afternoon, and the excitement of the escape from Grant Park, now
pushing down Michigan Avenue toward the Hilton Hotel with
dreams of a march on to the Amphitheatre four miles beyond, and
in the full pleasure of being led by the wagons of the Poor People's
March, the demonstrators shouted to everyone on the sidewalk, "Join
us, join us, join us," and the sidewalk kept disgorging more people
ready to march.

But at Balbo Avenue, just before Michigan Avenue reached the
Hilton, the marchers were halted by the police. It was a long halt.
Perhaps thirty minutes. Time for people who had been walking on
the sidewalk to join the march, proceed for a few steps, halt with
the others, wait, get bored, and leave. It was time for someone in
command of the hundreds of police in the neighborhood to communicate with his headquarters, explain the problem, time for the dilemma
to be relayed, alternatives examined, and orders conceivably sent
back to attack and disperse the crowd. If so, a trap was first set. The
mules were allowed to cross Balbo Avenue, then were separated by
a line of police from the marchers, who now, several thousand com-
pressed in this one place, filled the intersection of Michigan Avenue
and Balbo. There, dammed by police on three sides, and cut off from
the wagons of the Poor People's March, there, right beneath the
windows of the Hilton which looked down on Grant Park and
Michigan Avenue, the stationary march was abruptly attacked. The
police attacked with tear gas, with Mace, and with clubs, they attacked like a chain saw cutting into wood, the teeth of the saw the
edge of their clubs, they attacked like a scythe through grass, lines
of twenty and thirty policemen striking out in an arc, their clubs
beating, demonstrators fleeing. Seen from overhead, from the nineteenth floor, it was like a wind blowing dust, or the edge of waves
riding foam on the shore.

The police cut through the crowd one way, then cut through
them another. They chased people into the park, ran them down,

beat them up; they cut through the intersection at Michigan and Balbo like a razor cutting a channel through a head of hair, and then drove columns of new police into the channel who in turn pushed out, clubs flailing, on each side, to cut new channels, and new ones again. As demonstrators ran, they reformed in new groups only to be chased by the police again. The action went on for ten minutes, fifteen minutes, with the absolute ferocity of a tropical storm, and watching it from a window on the nineteenth floor, there was something of the detachment of studying a storm at evening through a glass, the light was a lovely gray-blue, the police had uniforms of sky-blue, even the ferocity had an abstract elemental play of forces of nature at battle with other forces, as if sheets of tropical rain were driving across the street in patterns, in curving patterns which curved upon each other again. Police cars rolled up, prisoners were beaten, shoved into wagons, driven away. The rain of police, maddened by the uncoiling of their own storm, pushed against their own barricades of tourists pressed on the street against the Hilton Hotel, then pressed them so hard—but here is a quotation from J. Anthony Lukas in *The New York Times:*

Even elderly bystanders were caught in the police onslaught. At one point, the police turned on several dozen persons standing quietly behind police barriers in front of the Conrad Hilton Hotel watching the demonstrators across the street.

For no reason that could be immediately determined, the blue-helmeted policemen charged the barriers, crushing the spectators against the windows of the Haymarket Inn, a restaurant in the hotel. Finally the window gave way, sending screaming middle-aged women and children backward through the broken shards of glass.

The police then ran into the restaurant and beat some of the victims who had fallen through the windows and arrested them.

Now another quote from Steve Lerner in *The Village Voice:*

When the charge came, there was a stampede toward the sidelines. People piled into each other, humped over each other's bodies like coupling dogs. To fall down in the crush was just as terrifying as facing the police. Suddenly I realized my feet weren't touching the ground as the crowd pushed up onto the sidewalk. I was grabbing at the army jacket of the boy in front of me; the girl behind me had a stranglehold on my neck and was screaming incoherently in my ear.

Now, a longer quotation from Jack Newfield in *The Village Voice.* (The accounts in *The Voice* of September 5 were superior to any others encountered that week.)

At the southwest entrance to the Hilton, a skinny, long-haired kid of about seventeen skidded down on the sidewalk, and four overweight cops leaped on him, chopping strokes on his head. His hair flew from the force of the blows. A dozen small rivulets of blood began to cascade down the kid's temple and onto the sidewalk. He was not crying or screaming, but crawling in a stupor toward the gutter. When he saw a photographer take a picture, he made a V sign with his fingers.

A doctor in a white uniform and Red Cross arm band began to run toward the kid, but two other cops caught him from behind and knocked him down. One of them jammed his knee into the doctor's throat and began clubbing his rib cage. The doctor squirmed away, but the cops followed him, swinging hard, sometimes missing.

A few feet away a phalanx of police charged into a group of women, reporters, and young McCarthy activists standing idly against the window of the Hilton Hotel's Haymarket Inn. The terrified people began to go down under the unexpected police charge when the plate glass window shattered, and the people tumbled backward through the glass. The police then climbed through the broken window and began to beat people, some of whom had been drinking quietly in the hotel bar.

At the side entrance of the Hilton Hotel four cops were chasing one frightened kid of about seventeen. Suddenly, Fred Dutton, a former aide to Robert Kennedy, moved out from under the marquee and interposed his body between the kid and the police.

"He's my guest in this hotel," Dutton told the cops.

The police started to club the kid.

Dutton screamed for the first cop's name and badge number. The cop grabbed Dutton and began to arrest him, until a Washington *Post* reporter identified Dutton as a former RFK aide.

Demonstrators, reporters, McCarthy workers, doctors, all began to stagger into the Hilton lobby, blood streaming from face and head wounds. The lobby smelled from tear gas, and stink bombs dropped by the Yippies. A few people began to direct the wounded to a makeshift hospital on the fifteenth floor, the McCarthy staff headquarters.

Fred Dutton was screaming at the police, and at the journalists to report all the "sadism and brutality." Richard Goodwin, the ashen nub of a cigar sticking out of his fatigued face, mumbled, "This is just the beginning. There'll be four years of this."

The defiant kids began a slow, orderly retreat back up Michigan Avenue. They did not run. They did not panic. They did not fight back. As they fell back they helped pick up fallen comrades who were beaten or gassed. Suddenly, a plainclothesman dressed as a soldier moved out of the shadows and knocked one kid down with an overhand punch. The kid squatted on the pavement of Michigan Avenue, trying to cover his face, while the Chicago plainclothesman punched him with savage accuracy. Thud, thud, thud. Blotches of blood spread over the kid's face. Two photographers moved in. Several police formed a closed circle around the beating to prevent pictures. One of the policemen then squirted Chemical Mace at the photographers, who dispersed. The plainclothesman melted into the line of police.

Let us escape to the street. The reporter, watching in safety from the nineteenth floor, could understand now how Mussolini's son-in-law had once been able to find the bombs he dropped from his airplane beautiful as they burst, yes, children, and youths, and middle-aged men and women were being pounded and clubbed and gassed and beaten, hunted and driven, sent scattering in all directions by teams of policemen who had exploded out of their restraints like the bursting of a boil, and nonetheless he felt a sense of calm and beauty, void even of the desire to be down there, as if in years to come there would be beatings enough, some chosen, some from nowhere, but it was as if the war had finally begun, and this was therefore a great and solemn moment, as if indeed even the gods of history had come together from each side to choose the very front of the Hilton Hotel before the television cameras of the world and the eyes of the campaign workers and the delegates' wives, yes, there before the eyes of half the principals at the convention was this drama played, as if the military spine of a great liberal party had finally separated itself from the skin, as if, no metaphor large enough to suffice, the Democratic Party had here broken in two before the eyes of a nation like Melville's whale charging right out of the sea.

A great stillness rose up from the street through all the small noise of clubbing and cries, small sirens, sigh of loaded arrest vans as off they pulled, shouts of police as they wheeled in larger circles, the intersection clearing further, then further, a stillness rose through the steel and stone of the hotel, congregating in the shocked centers of every room where delegates and wives and Press and campaign workers innocent until now of the intimate working of social force, looked down now into the murderous paradigm of Vietnam there beneath them at this huge intersection of this great city. Look—a boy was running through the park, and a cop was chasing. There he caught him on the back of the neck with his club! There! The cop is returning to his own! And the boy stumbling to his feet is helped off the ground by a girl who has come running up.

Yes, it could only have happened in a meeting of the Gods, that history for once should take place not on some back street, or some inaccessible grand room, not in some laboratory indistinguishable from others, or in the sly undiscoverable hypocrisies of a committee of experts, but rather on the center of the stage, as if each side had said, "Here we will have our battle. Here we will win."

The demonstrators were afterward delighted to have been man-handled before the public eye, delighted to have pushed and prodded, antagonized and provoked the cops over these days with rocks and bottles and cries of "Pig" to the point where police had charged in a blind rage and made a stage at the one place in the city (besides the Amphitheatre) where audience, actors, and cameras could all convene, yes, the rebels thought they had had a great victory, and perhaps they did; but the reporter wondered, even as he saw it, if the police in that half hour of waiting had not had time to receive instructions from the power of the city, perhaps the power of the land, and the power had decided, "No, do not let them march an-other ten blocks and there disperse them on some quiet street, no, let it happen before all the land, let everybody see that their dissent will soon be equal to their own blood; let them realize that the power is implacable, and will beat and crush and imprison and yet kill before it will ever relinquish the power. So let them see before their own eyes what it will cost to continue to mock us, defy us, and resist. There are more millions behind us than behind them, more millions who wish to weed out, poison, gas, and obliterate every flower whose power they do not comprehend than heroes for their side who will view our brute determination and still be ready to resist. There are more cowards alive than the brave. Otherwise we would not be where we are," said the Prince of Greed.

Who knew. One could thank the city of Chicago where drama was still a property of the open stage. It was quiet now, there was nothing to stare down on but the mules, and the police guarding them. The mules had not moved through the entire fray. Isolated from the battle, they had stood there in harness waiting to be told to go on. Only once in a while did they turn their heads. Their role as actors in the Poor People's March was to wait and to serve. Finally they moved on. The night had come. It was dark. The intersection was now empty. Shoes, ladies' handbags, and pieces of clothing lay on the street outside the hotel.

JAMES BALDWIN

JAMES BALDWIN was born in the Harlem section of New York City on August 2, 1924. The eldest of nine children, his childhood was, in his own words, a "bleak fantasy" of poverty, hopelessness, the violence of Harlem's streets, and—overshadowing it all—the grim religious fanaticism of his father, a lay preacher in an evangelical church. By the time he was fourteen Baldwin saw that only two possible ways lay open to him: either he would sink into the abyss of liquor, sex, drugs, and crime that was already beginning to claim many of his friends; or he would find himself a "gimmick," some role or position that would make him less susceptible to the frustrations of Harlem. The gimmick he found was religion, and for the next three years Baldwin was a Young Minister in a store-front church. He finally abandoned religion as a result of the books he was reading, especially Dostoevsky, and his growing confidence that what he most wanted to do was write.

Following his graduation from DeWitt Clinton High School in 1942, Baldwin began that succession of odd jobs that characterizes the modern, moneyless writer learning his craft. Then, in 1945, he received his first grant, a Saxton Fellowship for an unfinished novel, and since that time he has had to do very little nonliterary work. (Baldwin is a good example of the twentieth century artist who is supported by foundations: between the years 1948 and 1959 he received grants or fellowships from the *Partisan Review*, the National Institute of Arts and Letters, and the Rosenwald, Guggenheim, and Ford Foundations.)

In 1948 he left America for Europe, and for the next nine years lived mainly in Paris on the fringe of a colony of Negro artists that included Richard Wright and Chester Himes. Gradually he began to publish essays in magazines such as *Commentary*, *Harper's*, and *Partisan Review*, and in 1953 his first novel, *Go Tell It On the Mountain*, was published. Largely autobiographical, it describes a climactic day in the life of a Harlem family, during which each of the principal characters reviews his life at the same time that the oldest son of the family is experiencing his soul's salvation. In

1955 Baldwin published *Notes of a Native Son,* a collection of essays, and, in the following year, a second novel, *Giovanni's Room.* The latter is interesting primarily for the way in which it reveals Baldwin's attempt to follow Ralph Ellison's advice that he not confine himself to writing about Negroes (there are none in the book), and in the fact that it deals with homosexuality without capitalizing on its more sensational aspects.

Upon returning to the United States in 1958, Baldwin took up residence in Greenwich Village (where he had lived before going to Europe), and since then has published another collection of essays, *Nobody Knows My Name* (1961), a novel, *Another Country* (1962), and a long essay prophesying racial conflict in America, *The Fire Next Time* (1963). In 1964 his play, *Blues for Mister Charlie,* was produced by the Actor's Studio in New York, and a year later an earlier play, *The Amen Corner* (written in 1953), was produced on Broadway. Although Baldwin has published a number of books in recent years—among them his first collection of short stories, *Going to Meet the Man* (1965); another novel, *Tell Me How Long the Train's Been Gone* (1968); and a long, autobiographical essay on his involvement in black militancy, *No Name In the Street* (1972) —none of it has been as good as his early essays.

It is impossible to know what readers one or two generations from now will think of James Baldwin, whether he will still be read or simply dismissed as a minor novelist and interesting polemicist during a special period of our history, for nothing is more transitory than social-political issues. At the same time, *all* works of art reflect the age in which they are written, and everything, in a sense, is political. Those which survive do so because they manage to transcend the purely temporal aspects of their subjects: they reveal problems—relationships between people—that exist from generation to generation and from nation to nation. Thus, if an essay such as "Notes of a Native Son" lasts beyond our own time, it will most likely be not solely because of what it tells us about Black–White relations, but rather, for what it says about the relationship between fathers and sons. And surely this is what Baldwin had in mind when he said that he did not wish to become "merely a Negro writer." He added, "I wanted to find out in what way the *specialness* of my experience could be made to connect me with other people instead of dividing me from them."

Fortunately, as an essayist Baldwin has developed a style that is both clear and forceful, that draws its strength not from eccentricities but from its combination of candor and a strict adherence to logic. Baldwin recognizes both its strengths and weaknesses when he describes his style as being a mixture of "the King James Bible, the rhetoric of the store-front church, something ironic and violent and perpetually understated in Negro speech—and something of Dickens' love of bravura." It seems perfectly suited to the things he writes about: bitterness, self-pity, rage, and—above all—the struggle to be a man.

STRANGER IN THE VILLAGE

FROM ALL available evidence no black man had ever set foot in this tiny Swiss village before I came. I was told before arriving that I would probably be a "sight" for the village; I took this to mean that people of my complexion were rarely seen in Switzerland, and also that city people are always something of a "sight" outside of the city. It did not occur to me—possibly because I am an American—that there could be people anywhere who had never seen a Negro.

It is a fact that cannot be explained on the basis of the inaccessibility of the village. The village is very high, but it is only four hours from Milan and three hours from Lausanne. It is true that it is virtually unknown. Few people making plans for a holiday would elect to come here. On the other hand, the villagers are able, presumably, to come and go as they please—which they do: to another town at the foot of the mountain, with a population of approximately five thousand, the nearest place to see a movie or go to the bank. In the village there is no movie house, no bank, no library, no theater; very few radios, one jeep, one station wagon; and, at the moment, one typewriter, mine, an invention which the woman next door to me here had never seen. There are about six hundred people living here, all Catholic—I conclude this from the fact that the Catholic church is open all year round, whereas the Protestant chapel, set off on a hill a little removed from the village, is open only in the summertime when the tourists arrive. There are four or five hotels, all closed now, and four or five *bistros*, of which, however, only two do any business during the winter. These two do not do a great deal, for life in the village seems to end around nine or ten o'clock. There are a few stores, butcher, baker, *épicerie*, a hardware store, and a money-changer—who cannot change travelers' checks, but must send them down to the bank, an operation which takes two or three days. There is something called the *Ballet Haus*, closed in the winter and used for God knows what, certainly not ballet, during the summer. There seems to be only one schoolhouse in the village, and this for the quite young children; I suppose this to mean that their older brothers and sisters at some point descend from these mountains in order to complete their education—possibly, again, to the town just below. The landscape is absolutely forbidding, mountains towering on all four sides, ice and snow as far as the eye can reach. In this white wilderness, men and women and children move all day, carrying washing, wood, buckets of milk or water, sometimes skiing on Sunday afternoons. All week long boys and young men are to be seen shoveling snow off the rooftops, or dragging wood down from the forest in sleds.

The village's only real attraction, which explains the tourist season, is the hot spring water. A disquietingly high proportion of these tourists are cripples, or semi-cripples, who come year after year—from other parts of Switzerland, usually—to take the waters. This lends the village, at the height of the season, a rather terrifying air of sanctity, as though it were a lesser Lourdes. There is often something beautiful, there is always something awful, in the spectacle of a person who has lost one of his faculties, a faculty he never questioned until it was gone, and who struggles to recover it. Yet people remain people, on crutches or indeed on deathbeds; and wherever I passed, the first summer I was here, among the native villagers or among the lame, a wind passed with me—of astonishment, curiosity, amusement, and outrage. That first summer I stayed two weeks and never intended to return. But I did return in the winter, to work; the village offers, obviously, no distractions whatever and has the further advantage of being extremely cheap. Now it is winter again, a year later, and I am here again. Everyone in the village knows my name, though they scarcely ever use it, knows that I come from America—though, this, apparently, they will never really believe: black men come from Africa—and everyone knows that I am the friend of the son of a woman who was born here, and that I am staying in their chalet. But I remain as much a stranger today as I was the first day I arrived, and the children shout *Neger! Neger!* as I walk along the streets.

It must be admitted that in the beginning I was far too shocked to have any real reaction. In so far as I reacted at all, I reacted by trying to be pleasant—it being a great part of the American Negro's education (long before he goes to school) that he must make people "like" him. This smile-and-the-world-smiles-with-you routine worked about as well in this situation as it had in the situation for which it was designed, which is to say that it did not work at all. No one, after all, can be liked whose human weight and complexity cannot be, or has not been, admitted. My smile was simply another unheard-of phenomenon which allowed them to see my teeth—they did not, really, see my smile and I began to think that, should I take to snarling, no one would notice any difference. All of the physical characteristics of the Negro which had caused me, in America, a very different and almost forgotten pain were nothing less than miraculous—or infernal—in the eyes of the village people. Some thought my hair was the color of tar, that it had the texture of wire, or the texture of cotton. It was jocularly suggested that I might let it all grow long and make myself a winter coat. If I sat in the sun for more than five minutes some daring creature was certain to come along and gingerly put his fingers on my hair, as though he were afraid of an electric shock, or put his hand on my hand, astonished that the color did not rub off. In all of this, in which it must be conceded there was the charm of genuine wonder and in which there was certainly no element of intentional unkindness, there was yet no suggestion that I was human: I was simply a living wonder.

I knew that they did not mean to be unkind, and I know it now; it is necessary, nevertheless, for me to repeat this to myself each time that I walk out of the chalet. The children who shout *Neger!* have no way of knowing the echoes this sound raises in me. They are brimming with good humor and the more daring swell with pride when I stop to speak with them. Just the same, there are days when I cannot pause and smile, when I have no heart to play with them; when, indeed, I mutter sourly to myself, exactly as I muttered on the streets of a city these children have never seen, when I was no bigger than these children are now: *Your* mother *was a nigger*. Joyce is right about history being a nightmare—but it may be the nightmare from which no one *can* awaken. People are trapped in history and history is trapped in them.

There is a custom in the village—I am told it is repeated in many villages—of "buying" African natives for the purpose of converting them to Christianity. There stands in the church all year round a small box with a slot for money, decorated with a black figurine, and into this box the villagers drop their francs. During the *carnaval* which precedes Lent, two village children have their faces blackened —out of which bloodless darkness their blue eyes shine like ice— and fantastic horsehair wigs are placed on their blond heads; thus disguised, they solicit among the villagers for money for the missionaries in Africa. Between the box in the church and the blackened children, the village "bought" last year six or eight African natives. This was reported to me with pride by the wife of one of the *bistro* owners and I was careful to express astonishment and pleasure at the solicitude shown by the village for the souls of black folk. The *bistro* owner's wife beamed with a pleasure far more genuine than my own and seemed to feel that I might now breathe more easily concerning the souls of at least six of my kinsmen.

I tried not to think of these so lately baptized kinsmen, of the price paid for them, or the peculiar price they themselves would pay, and said nothing about my father, who having taken his own conversion too literally never, at bottom, forgave the white world (which he described as heathen) for having saddled him with a Christ in whom, to judge at least from their treatment of him, they themselves no longer believed. I thought of white men arriving for the first time in an African village, strangers there, as I am a stranger here, and tried to imagine the astounded populace touching their hair and marveling at the color of their skin. But there is a great difference between being the first white man to be seen by Africans and being the first black man to be seen by whites. The white man takes the astonishment as tribute, for he arrives to conquer and to convert the natives, whose inferiority in relation to himself is not even to be questioned; whereas I, without a thought of conquest, find myself among a people whose culture controls me, has even, in a sense, created me, people who have cost me more in anguish and rage than they will ever know, who yet do not even know of my existence. The astonishment with which I might have greeted them, should they have stumbled into my African village a few hundred years ago, might have rejoiced their hearts. But the astonishment with which they greet me today can only poison mine.

And this is so despite everything I may do to feel differently, despite my friendly conversations with the *bistro* owner's wife, despite their three-year-old son who has at last become my friend, despite the *saluts* and *bonsoirs* which I exchange with people as I walk, despite the fact that I know that no individual can be taken to task for what history is doing, or has done. I say that the culture of these people controls me—but they can scarcely be held responsible for European culture. America comes out of Europe, but these people have never seen America, nor have most of them seen more of Europe than the hamlet at the foot of their mountain. Yet they move with an authority which I shall never have; and they regard me, quite rightly, not only as a stranger in their village but as a suspect latecomer, bearing no credentials, to everything they have—however unconsciously—inherited.

For this village, even were it incomparably more remote and incredibly more primitive, is the West, the West onto which I have been so strangely grafted. These people cannot be, from the point of view of power, strangers anywhere in the world; they have made the modern world, in effect, even if they do not know it. The most illiterate among them is related, in a way that I am not, to Dante, Shakespeare, Michelangelo, Aeschylus, Da Vinci, Rembrandt, and Racine; the cathedral at Chartres says something to them which it cannot say to me, as indeed would New York's Empire State Building, should anyone here ever see it. Out of their hymns and dances come Beethoven and Bach. Go back a few centuries and they are in their full glory—but I am in Africa, watching the conquerors arrive.

The rage of the disesteemed is personally fruitless, but it is also absolutely inevitable; this rage, so generally discounted, so little understood even among the people whose daily bread it is, is one of the things that makes history. Rage can only with difficulty, and never entirely, be brought under the domination of the intelligence and is therefore not susceptible to any arguments whatever. This is a fact which ordinary representatives of the *Herrenvolk*, having never felt this rage and being unable to imagine it, quite fail to understand. Also, rage cannot be hidden, it can only be dissembled. This dissembling deludes the thoughtless, and strengthens rage and adds, to rage, contempt. There are, no doubt, as many ways of coping with the resulting complex of tensions as there are black men in the world, but no black man can hope ever to be entirely liberated from this internal warfare—rage, dissembling, and contempt having inevitably accompanied his first realization of the power of white men. What is crucial here is that, since white men represent in the black man's world so heavy a weight, white men have for black men a reality which is far from being reciprocal; and hence all black men have toward all white men an attitude which is designed, really, either to rob the white man of the jewel of his naïveté, or else to make it cost him dear.

The black man insists, by whatever means he finds at his disposal, that the white man cease to regard him as an exotic rarity and recognize him as a human being. This is a very charged and difficult moment, for there is a great deal of will power involved in the white man's naïveté. Most people are not naturally reflective any more than they are naturally malicious, and the white man prefers to keep the black man at a certain human remove because it is easier for him thus to preserve his simplicity and avoid being called to account for crimes committed by his forefathers, or his neighbors. He is inescapably aware, nevertheless, that he is in a better position in the world than black men are, nor can he quite put to death the suspicion that he is hated by black men therefor. He does not wish to be hated, neither does he wish to change places, and at this point in his uneasiness he can scarcely avoid having recourse to those legends which white men have created about black men, the most usual effect of which is that the white man finds himself enmeshed, so to speak, in his own language which describes hell, as well as the attributes which lead one to hell, as being as black as night.

Every legend, moreover, contains its residuum of truth, and the root function of language is to control the universe by describing it. It is of quite considerable significance that black men remain, in the imagination, and in overwhelming numbers in fact, beyond the disciplines of salvation; and this despite the fact that the West has been "buying" African natives for centuries. There is, I should hazard, an instantaneous necessity to be divorced from this so visibly unsaved stranger, in whose heart, moreover, one cannot guess what dreams of vengeance are being nourished; and, at the same time, there are few things on earth more attractive than the idea of the unspeakable liberty which is allowed the unredeemed. When, beneath the black mask, a human being begins to make himself felt one cannot escape a certain awful wonder as to what kind of human being it is. What one's imagination makes of other people is dictated, of course, by the laws of one's own personality and it is one of the ironies of black-white relations that, by means of what the white man imagines the black man to be, the black man is enabled to know who the white man is.

I have said, for example, that I am as much a stranger in this village today as I was the first summer I arrived, but this is not quite true. The villagers wonder less about the texture of my hair than they did then, and wonder rather more about me. And the fact that their wonder now exists on another level is reflected in their attitudes and in their eyes. There are the children who make those delightful, hilarious, sometimes astonishing grave overtures of friendship in the unpredictable fashion of children; other children, having been taught that the devil is a black man, scream in genuine anguish as I approach. Some of the older women never pass without a friendly greeting, never pass, indeed, if it seems that they will be able to engage me in conversation; other women look down or look away or rather contemptuously smirk. Some of the men drink with me and suggest that I learn how to ski—partly, I gather, because they cannot imagine what I would look like on skis—and want to know if I am married, and ask questions about my *métier*. But some of the men have accused *le sale nègre*—behind my back—of stealing wood and there is already in the eyes of some of them that peculiar, intent, paranoiac malevolence which one sometimes surprises in the eyes of American white men when, out walking with their Sunday girl, they see a Negro male approach.

There is a dreadful abyss between the streets of this village and the streets of the city in which I was born, between the children who shout *Neger!* today and those who shouted *Nigger!* yesterday— the abyss is experience, the American experience. The syllable hurled behind me today expresses, above all, wonder: I am a stranger here. But I am not a stranger in America and the same syllable riding on the American air expresses the war my presence has occasioned in the American soul.

For this village brings home to me this fact: that there was a day, and not really a very distant day, when Americans were scarcely Americans at all but discontented Europeans, facing a great un- conquered continent and strolling, say, into a marketplace and seeing black men for the first time. The shock this spectacle afforded is suggested, surely, by the promptness with which they decided that these black men were not really men but cattle. It is true that the necessity on the part of the settlers of the New World of reconciling their moral assumptions with the fact—and the necessity—of slavery enhanced immensely the charm of this idea, and it is also true that this idea expresses, with a truly American bluntness, the attitude which to varying extents all masters have had toward all slaves.

But between all former slaves and slave-owners and the drama which begins for Americans over three hundred years ago at James- town, there are at least two differences to be observed. The Ameri- can Negro slave could not suppose, for one thing, as slaves in past epochs had supposed and often done, that he would ever be able to wrest the power from his master's hands. This was a supposition which the modern era, which was to bring about such vast changes in the aims and dimensions of power, put to death; it only begins, in unprecedented fashion, and with dreadful implications, to be resur- rected today. But even had this supposition persisted with un- diminished force, the American Negro slave could not have used it to lend his condition dignity, for the reason that this supposition rests on another: that the slave in exile yet remains related to his past, has some means—if only in memory—of revering and sustaining the forms of his former life, is able, in short, to maintain his identity.

This was not the case with the American Negro slave. He is unique among the black men of the world in that his past was taken from him, almost literally, at one blow. One wonders what on earth the first slave found to say to the first dark child he bore. I am told that there are Haitians able to trace their ancestry back to African kings, but any American Negro wishing to go back so far will find his journey through time abruptly arrested by the signature on the bill of sale which served as the entrance paper for his ancestor. At the time—to say nothing of the circumstances—of the enslavement of the captive black man who was to become the American Negro, there was not the remotest possibility that he would ever take power from his master's hands. There was no reason to suppose that his situation would ever change, nor was there, shortly, anything to indicate that his situation had ever been different. It was his necessity, in the words of E. Franklin Frazier, to find a "motive for living under American culture or die." The identity of the American Negro comes out of this extreme situation, and the evolution of this identity was a source of the most intolerable anxiety in the minds and the lives of his masters.

For the history of the American Negro is unique also in this: that the question of his humanity, and of his rights therefore as a human being, became a burning one for several generations of Americans, so burning a question that it ultimately became one of those used to divide the nation. It is out of this argument that the venom of the epithet *Nigger!* is derived. It is an argument which Europe has never had, and hence Europe quite sincerely fails to understand how or why the argument arose in the first place, why its effects are so frequently disastrous and always so unpredictable, why it refuses until today to be entirely settled. Europe's black possessions remained—and do remain—in Europe's colonies, at which remove they represented no threat whatever to European identity. If they posed any problem at all for the European conscience, it was a problem which remained comfortingly abstract: in effect, the black man, *as a man*, did not exist for Europe. But in America, even as a slave, he was an inescapable part of the general social fabric and no American could escape having an attitude toward him. Americans attempt until today to make an abstraction of the Negro, but the very nature of these abstractions reveals the tremendous effects the presence of the Negro has had on the American character.

When one considers the history of the Negro in America it is of the greatest importance to recognize that the moral beliefs of a person, or a people, are never really as tenuous as life—which is not moral—very often causes them to appear; these create for them a frame of reference and a necessary hope, the hope being that when life has done its worst they will be enabled to rise above themselves and to triumph over life. Life would scarcely be bearable if this hope did not exist. Again, even when the worst has been said, to betray a belief is not by any means to have put oneself beyond its power; the betrayal of a belief is not the same thing as ceasing to believe. If this were not so there would be no moral standards in the world at all. Yet one must also recognize that morality is based on ideas and that all ideas are dangerous—dangerous because ideas can only lead to action and where the action leads no man can say. And dangerous in this respect: that confronted with the impossibility of remaining faithful to one's beliefs, and the equal impossibility of becoming free of them, one can be driven to the most inhuman excesses. The ideas on which American beliefs are based are not, though Americans often seem to think so, ideas which originated in America. They came out of Europe. And the establishment of democracy on the American continent was scarcely as radical a break with the past as was the necessity, which Americans faced, of broadening this concept to include black men.

This was, literally, a hard necessity. It was impossible, for one thing, for Americans to abandon their beliefs, not only because these beliefs alone seemed able to justify the sacrifices they had endured and the blood that they had spilled, but also because these beliefs afforded them their only bulwark against a moral chaos as absolute as the physical chaos of the continent it was their destiny to conquer.

But in the situation in which Americans found themselves, these beliefs threatened an idea which, whether or not one likes to think so, is the very warp and woof of the heritage of the West, the idea of white supremacy.

Americans have made themselves notorious by the shrillness and the brutality with which they have insisted on this idea, but they did not invent it; and it has escaped the world's notice that those very excesses of which Americans have been guilty imply a certain, unprecedented uneasiness over the idea's life and power, if not, indeed, the idea's validity. The idea of white supremacy rests simply on the fact that white men are the creators of civilization (the present civilization, which is the only one that matters; all previous civilizations are simply "contributions" to our own) and are therefore civilization's guardians and defenders. Thus it was impossible for Americans to accept the black man as one of themselves, for to do so was to jeopardize their status as white men. But not so to accept him was to deny his human reality, his human weight and complexity, and the strain of denying the overwhelmingly undeniable forced Americans into rationalizations so fantastic that they approached the pathological.

At the root of the American Negro problem is the necessity of the American white man to find a way of living with the Negro in order to be able to live with himself. And the history of this problem can be reduced to the means used by Americans—lynch law and law, segregation and legal acceptance, terrorization and concession—either to come to terms with this necessity, or to find a way around it, or (most usually) to find a way of doing both these things at once. The resulting spectacle, at once foolish and dreadful, led someone to make the quite accurate observation that "the Negro-in-America is a form of insanity which overtakes white men."

In this long battle, a battle by no means finished, the unforeseeable effects of which will be felt by many future generations, the white man's motive was the protection of his identity; the black man was motivated by the need to establish an identity. And despite the terrorization which the Negro in America endured and endures sporadically until today, despite the cruel and totally inescapable ambivalence of his status in his country, the battle for his identity has long ago been won. He is not a visitor to the West, but a citizen there, an American; as American as the Americans who despise him, the Americans who fear him, the Americans who love him—the Americans who became less than themselves, or rose to be greater than themselves by virtue of the fact that the challenge he represented was inescapable. He is perhaps the only black man in the world whose relationship to white men is more terrible, more subtle, and more meaningful than the relationship of bitter possessed to uncertain possessor. His survival depended, and his development depends, on his ability to turn his peculiar status in the Western world to his own advantage and, it may be, to the very great advantage of that world. It remains for him to fashion out of his experience that which will give him sustenance, and a voice.

The cathedral at Chartres, I have said, says something to the people of this village which it cannot say to me; but it is important to understand that this cathedral says something to me which it cannot say to them. Perhaps they are struck by the power of the spires, the glory of the windows; but they have known God, after all, longer than I have known him, and in a different way, and I am terrified by the slippery bottomless well to be found in the crypt, down which heretics were hurled to death, and by the obscene, inescapable gargoyles jutting out of the stone and seeming to say that God and the devil can never be divorced. I doubt that the villagers think of the devil when they face a cathedral because they have never been identified with the devil. But I must accept the status which myth, if nothing else, gives me in the West before I can hope to change the myth.

Yet, if the American Negro has arrived at his identity by virtue of the absoluteness of his estrangement from his past, American white men still nourish the illusion that there is some means of recovering the European innocence, of returning to a state in which black men do not exist. This is one of the greatest errors Americans can make. The identity they fought so hard to protect has, by virtue of that battle, undergone a change: Americans are as unlike any other white people in the world as it is possible to be. I do not think, for example, that it is too much to suggest that the American vision of the world—which allows so little reality, generally speaking, for any of the darker forces in human life, which tends until today to paint moral issues in glaring black and white—owes a great deal to the battle waged by Americans to maintain between themselves and black men a human separation which could not be bridged. It is only now beginning to be borne in on us—very faintly, it must be admitted, very slowly, and very much against our will—that this vision of the world is dangerously inaccurate, and perfectly useless. For it protects our moral high-mindedness at the terrible expense of weakening our grasp of reality. People who shut their eyes to reality simply invite their own destruction, and anyone who insists on remaining in a state of innocence long after that innocence is dead turns himself into a monster.

The time has come to realize that the interracial drama acted out on the American continent has not only created a new black man, it has created a new white man, too. No road whatever will lead Americans back to the simplicity of this European village where white men still have the luxury of looking on me as a stranger. I am not, really, a stranger any longer for any American alive. One of the things that distinguishes Americans from other people is that no other people has ever been so deeply involved in the lives of black men, and vice versa. This fact faced, with all its implications, it can be seen that the history of the American Negro problem is not merely shameful, it is also something of an achievement. For even when the worst has been said, it must also be added that the perpetual challenge posed by this problem was always, somehow, perpetually met. It is precisely this black-white experience which may prove of indispensable value to us in the world we face today. This world is white no longer, and it will never be white again.

NOTES OF A NATIVE SON

On the 29th of July, in 1943, my father died. On the same day, a few hours later, his last child was born. Over a month before this, while all our energies were concentrated in waiting for these events, there had been, in Detroit, one of the bloodiest race riots of the century. A few hours after my father's funeral, while he lay in state in the undertaker's chapel, a race riot broke out in Harlem. On the morning of the 3rd of August, we drove my father to the graveyard through a wilderness of smashed plate glass.

The day of my father's funeral had also been my nineteenth birthday. As we drove him to the graveyard, the spoils of injustice, anarchy, discontent, and hatred were all around us. It seemed to me that God himself had devised, to mark my father's end, the most sustained and brutally dissonant of codas. And it seemed to me, too, that the violence which rose all about us as my father left the world had been devised as a corrective for the pride of his eldest son. I had declined to believe in that apocalypse which had been central to my father's vision; very well, life seemed to be saying, here is something that will certainly pass for an apocalypse until the real thing comes along. I had inclined to be contemptuous of my father for the conditions of his life, for the conditions of our lives. When his life had ended I began to wonder about that life and also, in a new way, to be apprehensive about my own.

I had not known my father very well. We had got on badly, partly because we shared, in our different fashions, the vice of stubborn pride. When he was dead I realized that I had hardly ever spoken to him. When he had been dead a long time I began to wish I had. It seems to be typical of life in America, where opportunities, real and fancied, are thicker than anywhere else on the globe, that the second generation has no time to talk to the first. No one, including my father, seems to have known exactly how old he was, but his mother had been born during slavery. He was of the first generation of free men. He, along with thousands of other Negroes, came North after 1919 and I was part of that generation which had never seen the landscape of what Negroes sometimes call the Old Country.

He had been born in New Orleans and had been a quite young man there during the time that Louis Armstrong, a boy, was running errands for the dives and honky-tonks of what was always presented to me as one of the most wicked of cities—to this day, whenever I think of New Orleans, I also helplessly think of Sodom and Gomorrah. My father never mentioned Louis Armstrong, except to forbid us to play his records; but there was a picture of him on our wall for a long time. One of my father's strong-willed female relatives had placed it there and forbade my father to take it down. He never did, but he eventually maneuvered her out of the house and when, some years later, she was in trouble and near death, he refused to do anything to help her.

He was, I think, very handsome. I gather this from photographs and from my own memories of him, dressed in his Sunday best and on his way to preach a sermon somewhere, when I was little. Handsome, proud, and ingrown, "like a toe-nail," somebody said. But he looked to me, as I grew older, like pictures I had seen of African tribal chieftains: he really should have been naked, with war-paint on and barbaric mementos, standing among spears. He could be chilling in the pulpit and indescribably cruel in his personal life and he was certainly the most bitter man I have ever met; yet it must be said that there was something else in him, buried in him, which lent him his tremendous power and, even, a rather crushing charm. It had something to do with his blackness, I think—he was very black—with his blackness and his beauty, and with the fact that he knew that he was black but did not know that he was beautiful. He claimed to be proud of his blackness but it had also been the cause of much humiliation and it had fixed bleak boundaries to his life. He was not a young man when we were growing up and he had already suffered many kinds of ruin; in his outrageously demanding and protective way he loved his children, who were black like him and menaced, like him; and all these things sometimes showed in his face when he tried, never to my knowledge with any success, to establish contact with any of us. When he took one of his children on his knee to play, the child always became fretful and began to cry; when he tried to help one of us with our homework the absolutely unabating tension which emanated from him caused our minds and our tongues to become paralyzed, so that he, scarcely knowing why, flew into a rage and the child, not knowing why, was punished. If it ever entered his head to bring a surprise home for his children, it was, almost unfailingly, the wrong surprise and even the big watermelons he often brought home on his back in the summertime led to the most appalling scenes. I do not remember, in all those years, that one of his children was ever glad to see him come home. From what I was able to gather of his early life, it seemed that this inability to establish contact with other people had always marked him and had been one of the things which had driven him out of New Orleans. There was something in him, therefore, groping and tentative, which was never expressed and which was buried with him. One saw it most clearly when he was facing new people and hoping to impress them. But he never did, not for long. We went from church to smaller and more improbable church, he found himself in less and less demand as a minister, and by the time he died none of his friends had come to see him for a long time. He had lived and died in an intolerable bitterness of spirit and it frightened me, as we drove him to the graveyard through those unquiet, ruined streets, to see how powerful and overflowing this bitterness could be and to realize that this bitterness now was mine.

When he died I had been away from home for a little over a year. In that year I had had time to become aware of the meaning of all my father's bitter warnings, had discovered the secret of his proudly pursed lips and rigid carriage: I had discovered the weight of white people in the world. I saw that this had been for my ancestors and now would be for me an awful thing to live with and that the bitterness which had helped to kill my father could also kill me.

He had been ill a long time—in the mind, as we now realized, reliving instances of his fantastic intransigence in the new light of his affliction and endeavoring to feel a sorrow for him which never, quite, came true. We had not known that he was being eaten up by paranoia, and the discovery that his cruelty, to our bodies and our minds, had been one of the symptoms of his illness was not, then, enough to enable us to forgive him. The younger children felt, quite simply, relief that he would not be coming home anymore. My mother's observation that it was he, after all, who had kept them alive all these years meant nothing because the problems of keeping children alive are not real for children. The older children felt, with my father gone, that they could invite their friends to the house without fear that their friends would be insulted or, as had sometimes happened with me, being told that their friends were in league with the devil and intended to rob our family of everything we owned. (I didn't fail to wonder, and it made me hate him, what on earth we owned that anybody else would want.)

His illness was beyond all hope of healing before anyone realized that he was ill. He had always been so strange and had lived, like a prophet, in such unimaginably close communion with the Lord that his long silences which were punctuated by moans and hallelujahs and snatches of old songs while he sat at the living-room window never seemed odd to us. It was not until he refused to eat because, he said, his family was trying to poison him that my mother was forced to accept as a fact what had, until then, been only an unwilling suspicion. When he was committed, it was discovered that he had tuberculosis and, as it turned out, the disease of his mind allowed the disease of his body to destroy him. For the doctors could not force him to eat, either, and, though he was fed intravenously, it was clear from the beginning that there was no hope for him.

In my mind's eye I could see him, sitting at the window, locked up in his terrors; hating and fearing every living soul including his children who had betrayed him, too, by reaching towards the world which had despised him. There were nine of us. I began to wonder what it could have felt like for such a man to have had nine children whom he could barely feed. He used to make little jokes about our poverty, which never, of course, seemed very funny to us; they could not have seemed very funny to him, either, or else our all too feeble response to them would never have caused such rages. He spent great energy and achieved, to our chagrin, no small amount of success in keeping us away from the people who surrounded us, people who had all-night rent parties to which we listened when we should have been sleeping, people who cursed and drank and flashed razor blades on Lenox Avenue. He could not understand why, if they had so much energy to spare, they could not use it to make their lives better. He treated almost everybody on our block with a most uncharitable asperity and neither they, nor, of course, their children were slow to reciprocate.

The only white people who came to our house were welfare workers and bill collectors. It was almost always my mother who dealt with them, for my father's temper, which was at the mercy of his pride, was never to be trusted. It was clear that he felt their very presence in his home to be a violation: this was conveyed by his carriage, almost ludicrously stiff, and by his voice, harsh and vindictively polite. When I was around nine or ten I wrote a play which was directed by a young, white schoolteacher, a woman, who then took an interest in me, and gave me books to read and, in order to corroborate my theatrical bent, decided to take me to see what she somewhat tactlessly referred to as "real" plays. Theatergoing was forbidden in our house, but, with the really cruel intuitiveness of a child, I suspected that the color of this woman's skin would carry the day for me. When, at school, she suggested taking me to the theater, I did not, as I might have done if she had been a Negro, find a way of discouraging her, but agreed that she should pick me up at my house one evening. I then, very cleverly, left all the rest to my mother, who suggested to my father, as I knew she would, that it would not be very nice to let such a kind woman make the trip for nothing. Also, since it was a schoolteacher, I imagine that my mother countered the idea of sin with the idea of "education," which word, even with my father, carried a kind of bitter weight.

Before the teacher came my father took me aside to ask *why* she was coming, what *interest* she could possibly have in our house, in a boy like me. I said I didn't know but I, too, suggested that it had something to do with education. And I understood that my father was waiting for me to say something—I didn't quite know what; perhaps that I wanted his protection against this teacher and her "education." I said none of these things and the teacher came and we went out. It was clear, during the brief interview in our living room, that my father was agreeing very much against his will and that he would have refused permission if he had dared. The fact that he did not dare caused me to despise him: I had no way of knowing that he was facing in that living room a wholly un-precedented and frightening situation.

Later, when my father had been laid off from his job, this woman became very important to us. She was really a very sweet and generous woman and went to a great deal of trouble to be of help to us, particularly during one awful winter. My mother called her by the highest name she knew: she said she was a "christian." My father could scarcely disagree but during the four or five years of our relatively close association he never trusted her and was always trying to surprise in her open, Midwestern face the genuine, cunningly hidden, and hideous motivation. In later years, particu-larly when it began to be clear that this "education" of mine was going to lead me to perdition, he became more explicit and warned me that my white friends in high school were not really my friends and that I would see, when I was older, how white people would do anything to keep a Negro down. Some of them could be nice, he admitted, but none of them were to be trusted and most of them were not even nice. The best thing was to have as little to do with them as possible. I did not feel this way and I was certain, in my innocence, that I never would.

But the year which preceded my father's death had made a great change in my life. I had been living in New Jersey, working in defense plants, working and living among southerners, white and black. I knew about the south, of course, and about how southerners treated Negroes and how they expected them to behave, but it had never entered my mind that anyone would look at me and expect *me* to behave that way. I learned in New Jersey that to be a Negro meant, precisely, that one was never looked at but was simply at the mercy of the reflexes the color of one's skin caused in other people. I acted in New Jersey as I had always acted, that is as though I thought a great deal of myself—I had to *act* that way— with results that were, simply, unbelievable. I had scarcely arrived before I had earned the enmity, which was extraordinarily ingenious, of all my superiors and nearly all my co-workers. In the beginning, to make matters worse, I simply did not know what was happening. I did not know what I had done, and I shortly began to wonder what *anyone* could possibly do, to bring about such unanimous, active, and unbearably vocal hostility. I knew about jim-crow but I had never experienced it. I went to the same self-service restaurant three times and stood with all the Princeton boys before the counter, waiting for a hamburger and coffee; it was always an extraordinarily long time before anything was set before me; but it was not until the fourth visit that I learned that, in fact, nothing had ever been set before me: I had simply picked something up. Negroes were not served there, I was told, and they had been waiting for me to realize that I was always the only Negro present. Once I was told this, I determined to go there all the time. But now they were ready for me and, though some dreadful scenes were subsequently enacted in that restaurant, I never ate there again.

It was the same story all over New Jersey, in bars, bowling alleys, diners, places to live. I was always being forced to leave, silently, or with mutual imprecations. I very shortly became notorious and children giggled behind me when I passed and their elders whispered or shouted—they really believed that I was mad. And it did begin to work on my mind, of course; I began to be afraid to go anywhere and to compensate for this I went places to which I really should not have gone and where, God knows, I had no desire to be. My reputation in town naturally enhanced my reputation at work and my working day became one long series of acrobatics designed to keep me out of trouble. I cannot say that these acrobatics succeeded. It began to seem that the machinery of the organization I worked for was turning over, day and night, with but one aim: to eject me.

I was fired once, and contrived, with the aid of a friend from New York, to get back on the payroll; was fired again, and bounced back again. It took a while to fire me for the third time, but the third time took. There were no loopholes anywhere. There was not even any way of getting back inside the gates.

That year in New Jersey lives in my mind as though it were the year during which, having an unsuspected predilection for it, I first contracted some dread, chronic disease, the unfailing symptom of which is a kind of blind fever, a pounding in the skull and fire in the bowels. Once this disease is contracted, one can never be really carefree again, for the fever, without an instant's warning, can recur at any moment. It can wreck more important things than race relations. There is not a Negro alive who does not have this rage in his blood—one has the choice, merely, of living with it consciously or surrendering to it. As for me, this fever has recurred in me, and does, and will until the day I die.

My last night in New Jersey, a white friend from New York took me to the nearest big town, Trenton, to go to the movies and have a few drinks. As it turned out, he also saved me from, at the very least, a violent whipping. Almost every detail of that night stands out very clearly in my memory. I even remember the name of the movie we saw because its title impressed me as being so patly ironical. It was a movie about the German occupation of France, starring Maureen O'Hara and Charles Laughton and called *This Land Is Mine*. I remember the name of the diner we walked into when the movie ended: it was the "American Diner." When we walked in the counterman asked what we wanted and I remember answering with the casual sharpness which had become my habit: "We want a hamburger and a cup of coffee, what do you think we want?" I do not know why, after a year of such rebuffs, I so completely failed to anticipate his answer, which was, of course, "We don't serve Negroes here." This reply failed to discompose me, at least for the moment. I made some sardonic comment about the name of the diner and we walked out into the streets.

This was the time of what was called the "brown-out," when the lights in all American cities were very dim. When we re-entered the streets something happened to me which had the force of an optical illusion, or a nightmare. The streets were very crowded and I was facing north. People were moving in every direction but it seemed to me, in that instant, that all of the people I could see, and many more than that, were moving toward me, against me, and that everyone was white. I remember how their faces gleamed. And I felt, like a physical sensation, a *click* at the nape of my neck as though some interior string connecting my head to my body had been cut. I began to walk. I heard my friend call after me, but I ignored him. Heaven only knows what was going on in his mind, but he had the good sense not to touch me—I don't know what would have happened if he had—and to keep me in sight. I don't know what was going on in my mind, either; I certainly had no conscious plan. I wanted to do something to crush these white faces, which were crushing me. I walked for perhaps a block or two until I came to an enormous, glittering, and fashionable restaurant in which I knew not even the intercession of the Virgin would cause me to be served. I pushed through the doors and took the first vacant seat I saw, at a table for two, and waited.

I do not know how long I waited and I rather wonder, until today, what I could possibly have looked like. Whatever I looked like, I frightened the waitress who shortly appeared, and the moment she appeared all my fury flowed towards her. I hated her for her white face, and for her great, astounded, frightened eyes. I felt that if she found a black man so frightening I would make her fright worth-while.

She did not ask me what I wanted, but repeated, as though she had learned it somewhere, "We don't serve Negroes here." She did not say it with the blunt, derisive hostility to which I had grown so accustomed, but, rather, with a note of apology in her voice, and fear. This made me colder and more murderous than ever. I felt I had to do something with my hands. I wanted her to come close enough for me to get her neck between my hands.

So I pretended not to have understood her, hoping to draw her closer. And she did step a very short step closer, with her pencil poised incongruously over her pad, and repeated the formula: ". . . don't serve Negroes here."

Somehow, with the repetition of that phrase, which was already ringing in my head like a thousand bells of a nightmare, I realized that she would never come any closer and that I would have to strike from a distance. There was nothing on the table but an ordinary water-mug half full of water, and I picked this up and hurled it with all my strength at her. She ducked and it missed her and shattered against the mirror behind the bar. And, with that sound, my frozen blood abruptly thawed, I returned from wherever I had been, I *saw*, for the first time, the restaurant, the people with their mouths open, already, as it seemed to me, rising as one man, and I realized what I had done, and where I was, and I was frightened. I rose and began running for the door. A round, pot-bellied man grabbed me by the nape of the neck just as I reached the doors and began to beat me about the face. I kicked him and got loose and ran into the streets. My friend whispered, *"Run!"* and I ran.

My friend stayed outside the restaurant long enough to misdirect my pursuers and the police, who arrived, he told me, at once. I do not know what I said to him when he came to my room that night. I could not have said much. I felt, in the oddest, most awful way, that I had somehow betrayed him. I lived it over and over and over again, the way one relives an automobile accident after it has happened and one finds oneself alone and safe. I could not get over two facts, both equally difficult for the imagination to grasp, and one was that I could have been murdered. But the other was that I had been ready to commit murder. I saw nothing very clearly but I did see this: that my life, my *real* life, was in danger, and not from anything other people might do but from the hatred I carried in my own heart.

[2]

I had returned home around the second week in June—in great haste because it seemed that my father's death and my mother's confinement were both but a matter of hours. In the case of my mother, it soon became clear that she had simply made a miscalculation. This had always been her tendency and I don't believe that a single one of us arrived in the world, or has since arrived anywhere else, on time. But none of us dawdled so intolerably about the business of being born as did my baby sister. We sometimes amused ourselves, during those endless, stifling weeks, by picturing the baby sitting within in the safe, warm dark, bitterly regretting the necessity of becoming a part of our chaos and stubbornly putting it off as long as possible. I understood her perfectly and congratulated her on showing such good sense so soon. Death, however, sat as purposefully at my father's bedside as life stirred within my mother's womb and it was harder to understand why he so lingered in that long shadow. It seemed that he had bent, and for a long time, too, all of his energies towards dying. Now death was ready for him but my father held back.

All of Harlem, indeed, seemed to be infected by waiting. I had never before known it to be so violently still. Racial tensions throughout this country were exacerbated during the early years of the war, partly because the labor market brought together hundreds of thousands of ill-prepared people and partly because Negro soldiers, regardless of where they were born, received their military training in the south. What happened in defense plants and army camps had repercussions, naturally, in every Negro ghetto. The situation in Harlem had grown bad enough for clergymen, policemen, educators, politicians, and social workers to assert in one breath that there was no "crime wave" and to offer, in the very next breath, suggestions as to how to combat it. These suggestions always seemed to involve playgrounds, despite the fact that racial skirmishes were occurring in the playgrounds, too. Playground or not, crime wave or not, the Harlem police force had been augmented in March, and the unrest grew—perhaps, in fact, partly as a result of the ghetto's instinctive hatred of policemen. Perhaps the most revealing news item, out of the steady parade of reports of muggings, stabbings, shootings, assaults, gang wars, and accusations of police brutality, is the item concerning six Negro girls who set upon a white girl in the subway because, as they all too accurately put it, she was stepping on their toes. Indeed she was, all over the nation.

I had never before been so aware of policemen, on foot, on horseback, on corners, everywhere, always two by two. Nor had I ever been so aware of small knots of people. They were on stoops and on corners and in doorways, and what was striking about them, I think, was that they did not seem to be talking. Never, when I passed these groups, did the usual sound of a curse or a laugh ring out and neither did there seem to be any hum of gossip. There was certainly, on the other hand, occurring between them communication extraordinarily intense. Another thing that was striking was the unexpected diversity of the people who made up these groups. Usually, for example, one would see a group of sharpies standing on the street corner, jiving the passing chicks; or a group of older men, usually, for some reason, in the vicinity of a barber shop, discussing baseball scores, or the numbers, or making rather chilling observations about women they had known. Women, in a general way, tended to be seen less often together—unless they were church women, or very young girls, or prostitutes met together for an unprofessional instant. But that summer I saw the strangest combinations: large, respectable, churchly matrons standing on the stoops or the corners with their hair tied up, together with a girl in sleazy satin whose face bore the marks of gin and the razor, or heavy-set, abrupt, no-nonsense older men, in company with the most disreputable and fanatical "race" men, or these same "race" men with the sharpies, or these sharpies with the churchly women. Seventh Day Adventists and Methodists and Spiritualists seemed to be hobnobbing with Holyrollers and they were all, alike, entangled with the most flagrant disbelievers; something heavy in their stance seemed to indicate that they had all, incredibly, seen a common vision, and on each face there seemed to be the same strange, bitter shadow.

The churchly women and the matter-of-fact, no-nonsense men had children in the Army. The sleazy girls they talked to had lovers there, the sharpies and the "race" men had friends and brothers there. It would have demanded an unquestioning patriotism, happily as uncommon in this country as it is undesirable, for these people not to have been disturbed by the bitter letters they received, by the newspaper stories they read, not to have been enraged by the posters, then to be found all over New York, which described the Japanese as "yellow-bellied Japs." It was only the "race" men, to be sure, who spoke ceaselessly of being revenged—how this vengeance was to be exacted was not clear—for the indignities and dangers suffered by Negro boys in uniform; but everybody felt a directionless, hopeless bitterness, as well as that panic which can scarcely be suppressed when one knows that a human being one loves is beyond one's reach, and in danger. This helplessness and this gnawing uneasiness does something, at length, to even the toughest mind. Perhaps the best way to sum all this up is to say that the people I knew felt, mainly, a peculiar kind of relief when they knew that their boys were being shipped out of the south, to do battle overseas. It was, perhaps, like feeling that the most dangerous part of a dangerous journey had been passed and that now, even if death should come, it would come with honor and without the complicity of their countrymen. Such a death would be, in short, a fact with which one could hope to live.

It was on the 28th of July, which I believe was a Wednesday, that I visited my father for the first time during his illness and for the last time in his life. The moment I saw him I knew why I had put off this visit so long. I had told my mother that I did not want to see him because I hated him. But this was not true. It was only that I *had* hated him and I wanted to hold on to this hatred. I did not want to look on him as a ruin: it was not a ruin I had hated. I imagine that one of the reasons people cling to their hates so stubbornly is because they sense, once hate is gone, that they will be forced to deal with pain.

We traveled out to him, his older sister and myself, to what seemed to be the very end of a very Long Island. It was hot and dusty and we wrangled, my aunt and I, all the way out, over the fact that I had recently begun to smoke and, as she said, to give my-self airs. But I knew that she wrangled with me because she could not bear to face the fact of her brother's dying. Neither could I endure the reality of her despair, her unstated bafflement as to what had happened to her brother's life, and her own. So we wrangled and I smoked and from time to time she fell into a heavy reverie. Covertly, I watched her face, which was the face of an old woman;

it had fallen in, the eyes were sunken and lightless; soon she would be dying, too.

In my childhood—it had not been so long ago—I had thought her beautiful. She had been quick-witted and quick-moving and very generous with all the children and each of her visits had been an event. At one time one of my brothers and myself had thought of running away to live with her. Now she could no longer produce out of her handbag some unexpected and yet familiar delight. She made me feel pity and revulsion and fear. It was awful to realize that she no longer caused me to feel affection. The closer we came to the hospital the more querulous she became and at the same time, naturally, grew more dependent on me. Between pity and guilt and fear I began to feel that there was another me trapped in my skull like a jack-in-the-box who might escape my control at any moment and fill the air with screaming.

She began to cry the moment we entered the room and she saw him lying there, all shriveled and still, like a little black monkey. The great, gleaming apparatus which fed him and would have compelled him to be still even if he had been able to move brought to mind, not beneficence, but torture; the tubes entering his arm made me think of pictures I had seen, when a child, of Gulliver, tied down by the pygmies on that island. My aunt wept and wept, there was a whistling sound in my father's throat; nothing was said; he could not speak. I wanted to take his hand, to say something. But I do not know what I could have said, even if he could have heard me. He was not really in that room with us, he had at last really embarked on his journey; and though my aunt told me that he said he was going to meet Jesus, I did not hear anything except that whistling in his throat. The doctor came back and we left, into that unbearable train again, and home. In the morning came the telegram saying that he was dead. Then the house was suddenly full of relatives, friends, hysteria, and confusion and I quickly left my mother and the children to the care of those impressive women, who, in Negro communities at least, automatically appear at times of bereavement armed with lotions, proverbs, and patience, and an ability to cook. I went downtown. By the time I returned, later the same day, my mother had been carried to the hospital and the baby had been born.

[3]

For my father's funeral I had nothing black to wear and this posed a nagging problem all day long. It was one of those problems, simple, or impossible of solution, to which the mind insanely clings in order to avoid the mind's real trouble. I spent most of that day at the downtown apartment of a girl I knew, celebrating my birthday with whiskey and wondering what to wear that night. When planning a birthday celebration one naturally does not expect that it will be up against competition from a funeral and this girl had anticipated taking me out that night, for a big dinner and a night club afterwards. Sometime during the course of that long day we decided that we would go out anyway, when my father's funeral service was over. I imagine I decided it, since, as the funeral hour approached, it became clearer and clearer to me that I would not know what to do with myself when it was over. The girl, stifling her very lively concern as to the possible effects of the whiskey on one of my father's chief mourners, concentrated on being conciliatory and practically helpful. She found a black shirt for me somewhere and ironed it and, dressed in the darkest pants and jacket I owned, and slightly drunk, I made my way to my father's funeral.

The chapel was full, but not packed, and very quiet. There were, mainly, my father's relatives, and his children, and here and there I saw faces I had not seen since childhood, the faces of my father's one-time friends. They were very dark and solemn now, seeming somehow to suggest that they had known all along that something like this would happen. Chief among the mourners was my aunt, who had quarreled with my father all his life; by which I do not mean to suggest that her mourning was insincere or that she had not loved him. I suppose that she was one of the few people in the world who had, and their incessant quarreling proved precisely the strength of the tie that bound them. The only other person in the world, as far as I knew, whose relationship to my father rivaled my aunt's in depth was my mother, who was not there.

It seemed to me, of course, that it was a very long funeral. But it was, if anything, a rather shorter funeral than most, nor, since there were no overwhelming uncontrollable expressions of grief, could it be called—if I dare to use the word—successful. The minister who preached my father's funeral sermon was one of the few my father had still been seeing as he neared his end. He presented to us in his sermon a man whom none of us had ever seen—a man thoughtful, patient, and forbearing, a Christian inspiration to all who knew him, and a model for his children. And no doubt the children, in their disturbed and guilty state, were almost ready to believe this; he had been remote enough to be anything and, anyway, the shock of the incontrovertible, that it was really our father lying up there in that casket, prepared the mind for anything. His sister moaned and this grief-stricken moaning was taken as corroboration. The other faces held a dark, non-committal thoughtfulness. This was not the man they had known, but they had scarcely expected to be confronted with *him*; this was, in a sense deeper than questions of fact, the man they had not known, and the man they had not known may have been the real one. The real man, whoever he had been, had suffered and now he was dead: this was all that was sure and all that mattered now. Every man in the chapel hoped that when his hour came he, too, would be eulogized, which is to say forgiven, and that all of his lapses, greeds, errors, and strayings from the truth would be invested with coherence and looked .upon with charity. This was perhaps the last thing human beings could give each other and it was what they demanded, after all, of the Lord. Only the Lord saw the midnight tears, only He was present when one of His children, moaning and wringing hands, paced up and down the room. When one slapped one's child in anger the recoil in the heart reverberated through heaven and became part of the pain of the universe. And when the children were hungry and sullen and distrustful and one watched them, daily, growing wilder, and further away, and running headlong into danger, it was the Lord who knew what the charged heart endured as the strap was laid to the backside; the Lord alone who knew what one *would* have said if one had had, like the Lord, the gift of the living word. It was the Lord who knew of the impossibility every parent in that room faced: how to prepare the child for the day when the child would be despised and how to *create* in the child—by what means?—a stronger antidote to this poison than one had found for oneself. The avenues, side streets, bars, billiard halls, hospitals, police stations, and even the playgrounds of Harlem —not to mention the houses of correction, the jails, and the morgue— testified to the potency of the poison while remaining silent as to the efficacy of whatever antidote, irresistibly raising the question of whether or not such an antidote existed; raising, which was worse, the question of whether or not an antidote was desirable; perhaps poison should be fought with poison. With these several schisms in the mind and with more terrors in the heart than could be named, it was better not to judge the man who had gone down under an impossible burden. It was better to remember: *Thou knowest this man's fall; but thou knowest not his wrassling.*

While the preacher talked and I watched the children—years of changing their diapers, scrubbing them, slapping them, taking them to school, and scolding them had had the perhaps inevitable result of making me love them, though I am not sure I knew this then— my mind was busily breaking out with a rash of disconnected impressions. Snatches of popular songs, indecent jokes, bits of books I had read, movie sequences, faces, voices, political issues—I thought I was going mad; all these impressions suspended, as it were, in the solution of the faint nausea produced in me by the heat and liquor. For a moment I had the impression that my alcoholic breath, inefficiently disguised with chewing gum, filled the entire chapel. Then someone began singing one of my father's favorite songs and, abruptly, I was with him, sitting on his knee, in the hot, enormous, crowded church which was the first church we attended. It was the Abyssinia Baptist Church on 138th Street. We had not gone there long. With this image, a host of others came. I had forgotten, in the rage of my growing up, how proud my father had been of me when I was little. Apparently, I had had a voice and my father had liked to show me off before the members of the church. I had forgotten what he had looked like when he was pleased but now I remembered that he had always been grinning with pleasure when my solos ended. I even remembered certain expressions on his face when he teased my mother—had he loved her? I would never know. And when had it all begun to change? For now it seemed that he had not always been cruel. I remembered being taken for a haircut and scraping my knee on the footrest of the barber's chair and I remembered my father's face as he soothed my crying and applied the stinging iodine. Then I remembered our fights, fights which had been of the worst possible kind because my technique had been silence.

I remembered the one time in all our life together when we had really spoken to each other.

It was on a Sunday and it must have been shortly before I left home. We were walking, just the two of us, in our usual silence, to or from church. I was in high school and had been doing a lot of writing and I was, at about this time, the editor of the high school magazine. But I had also been a Young Minister and had been preaching from the pulpit. Lately, I had been taking fewer engagements and preached as rarely as possible. It was said in the church, quite truthfully, that I was "cooling off."

My father asked me abruptly, "You'd rather write than preach, wouldn't you?"

I was astonished at his question—because it was a real question. I answered, "Yes."

That was all we said. It was awful to remember that that was all we had *ever* said.

The casket now was opened and the mourners were being led up the aisle to look for the last time on the deceased. The assumption was that the family was too overcome with grief to be allowed to make this journey alone and I watched while my aunt was led to the casket and, muffled in black, and shaking, led back to her seat. I disapproved of forcing the children to look on their dead father, considering that the shock of his death, or, more truthfully, the shock of death as a reality, was already a little more than a child could bear, but my judgment in this matter had been overruled and there they were, bewildered and frightened and very small, being

led, one by one, to the casket. But there is also something very
gallant about children at such moments. It has something to do
with their silence and gravity and with the fact that one cannot help
them. Their legs, somehow, seem *exposed*, so that it is at once
incredible and terribly clear that their legs are all they have to hold
them up.

I had not wanted to go to the casket myself and I certainly had
not wished to be led there, but there was no way of avoiding either
of these forms. One of the deacons led me up and I looked on my
father's face. I cannot say that it looked like him at all. His blackness had been equivocated by powder and there was no suggestion
in that casket of what his power had or could have been. He was
simply an old man dead, and it was hard to believe that he had
ever given anyone either joy or pain. Yet, his life filled that room.
Further up the avenue his wife was holding his newborn child. Life
and death so close together, and love and hatred, and right and
wrong, said something to me which I did not want to hear concerning man, concerning the life of man.

After the funeral, while I was downtown desperately celebrating
my birthday, a Negro soldier, in the lobby of the Hotel Braddock,
got into a fight with a white policeman over a Negro girl. Negro
girls, white policemen, in or out of uniform, and Negro males—in
or out of uniform—were part of the furniture of the lobby of the
Hotel Braddock and this was certainly not the first time such an
incident had occurred. It was destined, however, to receive an un-
precedented publicity, for the fight between the policeman and the
soldier ended with the shooting of the soldier. Rumor, flowing
immediately to the streets outside, stated that the soldier had been
shot in the back, an instantaneous and revealing invention, and that
the soldier had died protecting a Negro woman. The facts were
somewhat different—for example, the soldier had not been shot in
the back, and was not dead, and the girl seems to have been as
dubious a symbol of womanhood as her white counterpart in
Georgia usually is, but no one was interested in the facts. They
preferred the invention because this invention expressed and cor-
roborated their hates and fears so perfectly. It is just as well to
remember that people are always doing this. Perhaps many of those

legends, including Christianity, to which the world clings began their conquest of the world with just some such concerted surrender to distortion. The effect, in Harlem, of this particular legend was like the effect of a lit match in a tin of gasoline. The mob gathered before the doors of the Hotel Braddock simply began to swell and to spread in every direction, and Harlem exploded.

The mob did not cross the ghetto lines. It would have been easy, for example, to have gone over Morningside Park on the west side or to have crossed the Grand Central railroad tracks at 125th Street on the east side, to wreak havoc in white neighborhoods. The mob seems to have been mainly interested in something more potent and real than the white face, that is, in white power, and the principal damage done during the riot of the summer of 1943 was to white business establishments in Harlem. It might have been a far bloodier story, of course, if, at the hour the riot began, these establishments had still been open. From the Hotel Braddock the mob fanned out, east and west along 125th Street, and for the entire length of Lenox, Seventh, and Eighth avenues. Along each of these avenues, and along each major side street—116th, 125th, 135th, and so on—bars, stores, pawnshops, restaurants, even little luncheonettes had been smashed open and entered and looted—looted, it might be added, with more haste than efficiency. The shelves really looked as though a bomb had struck them. Cans of beans and soup and dog food, along with toilet paper, corn flakes, sardines, and milk tumbled every which way, and abandoned cash registers and cases of beer leaned crazily out of the splintered windows and were strewn along the avenues. Sheets, blankets, and clothing of every description formed a kind of path, as though people had dropped them while running. I truly had not realized that Harlem *had* so many stores until I saw them all smashed open; the first time the word *wealth* ever entered my mind in relation to Harlem was when I saw it scattered in the streets. But one's first, incongruous impression of plenty was countered immediately by an impression of waste. None of this was doing anybody any good. It would have been better to have left the plate glass as it had been and the goods lying in the stores.

It would have been better, but it would also have been intolerable, for Harlem had needed something to smash. To smash something is the ghetto's chronic need. Most of the time it is the members of the ghetto who smash each other, and themselves. But as long as the ghetto walls are standing there will always come a moment when these outlets do not work. That summer, for example, it was not enough to get into a fight on Lenox Avenue, or curse out one's cronies in the barber shops. If ever, indeed, the violence which fills Harlem's churches, pool halls, and bars erupts outward in a more direct fashion, Harlem and its citizens are likely to vanish in an apocalyptic flood. That this is not likely to happen is due to a great many reasons, most hidden and powerful among them the Negro's real relation to the white American. This relation prohibits, simply, anything as uncomplicated and satisfactory as pure hatred. In order really to hate white people, one has to blot so much out of the mind—and the heart—that this hatred itself becomes an exhausting and self-destructive pose. But this does not mean, on the other hand, that love comes easily: the white world is too powerful, too complacent, too ready with gratuitous humiliation, and, above all, too ignorant and too innocent for that. One is absolutely forced to make perpetual qualifications and one's own reactions are always canceling each other out. It is this, really, which has driven so many people mad, both white and black. One is always in the position of having to decide between amputation and gangrene. Amputation is swift but time may prove that the amputation was not necessary—or one may delay the amputation too long. Gangrene is slow, but it is impossible to be sure that one is reading one's symptoms right. The idea of going through life as a cripple is more than one can bear, and equally unbearable is the risk of swelling up slowly, in agony, with poison. And the trouble, finally, is that the risks are real even if the choices do not exist.

"But as for me and my house," my father had said, "we will serve the Lord." I wondered, as we drove him to his resting place, what this line had meant for him. I had heard him preach it many times. I had preached it once myself, proudly giving it an interpretation different from my father's. Now the whole thing came back to me, as though my father and I were on our way to Sunday school and

I were memorizing the golden text: *And if it seem evil unto you to serve the Lord, choose you this day whom you will serve; whether the gods which your fathers served that were on the other side of the flood, or the gods of the Amorites, in whose land ye dwell: but as for me and my house, we will serve the Lord.* I suspected in these familiar lines a meaning which had never been there for me before. All of my father's texts and songs, which I had decided were meaningless, were arranged before me at his death like empty bottles, waiting to hold the meaning which life would give them for me. This was his legacy: nothing is ever escaped. That bleakly memorable morning I hated the unbelievable streets and the Negroes and whites who had, equally, made them that way. But I knew that it was folly, as my father would have said, this bitterness was folly. It was necessary to hold on to the things that mattered. The dead man mattered, the new life mattered; blackness and whiteness did not matter; to believe that they did was to acquiesce in one's own destruction. Hatred, which could destroy so much, never failed to destroy the man who hated and this was an immutable law.

It began to seem that one would have to hold in the mind forever two ideas which seemed to be in opposition. The first idea was acceptance, the acceptance, totally without rancor, of life as it is, and men as they are: in the light of this idea, it goes without saying that injustice is a commonplace. But this did not mean that one could be complacent, for the second idea was of equal power: that one must never, in one's own life, accept these injustices as commonplace but must fight them with all one's strength. This fight begins, however, in the heart and it now had been laid to my charge to keep my own heart free of hatred and despair. This intimation made my heart heavy and, now that my father was irrecoverable, I wished that he had been beside me so that I could have searched his face for the answers which only the future would give me now.

[1960]

FIFTH AVENUE, UPTOWN:

A Letter from Harlem

THERE IS a housing project standing now where the house in which we grew up once stood, and one of those stunted city trees is snarling where our doorway used to be. This is on the rehabilitated side of the avenue. The other side of the avenue—for progress takes time—has not been rehabilitated yet and it looks exactly as it looked in the days when we sat with our noses pressed against the window-pane, longing to be allowed to go "across the street." The grocery store which gave us credit is still there, and there can be no doubt that it is still giving credit. The people in the project certainly need it—far more, indeed, than they ever needed the project. The last time I passed by, the Jewish proprietor was still standing among his shelves, looking sadder and heavier but scarcely any older. Farther down the block stands the shoe-repair store in which our shoes were repaired until reparation became impossible and in which, then, we bought all our "new" ones. The Negro proprietor is still in the window, head down, working at the leather.

These two, I imagine, could tell a long tale if they would (perhaps they would be glad to if they could), having watched so many, for so long, struggling in the fishhooks, the barbed wire, of this avenue.

The avenue is elsewhere the renowned and elegant Fifth. The area I am describing, which, in today's gang parlance, would be called "the turf," is bounded by Lenox Avenue on the west, the Harlem River on the east, 135th Street on the north, and 130th Street on the south. We never lived beyond these boundaries; this is where we grew up. Walking along 145th Street—for example—familiar as it is, and similar, does not have the same impact because I do not know any of the people on the block. But when I turn east on 131st Street and Lenox Avenue, there is first a soda-pop joint, then a shoeshine "parlor," then a grocery store, then a dry cleaners', then the houses. All along the street there are people who watched me grow up, people who grew up with me, people I watched grow up along with my brothers and sisters; and, sometimes in my arms, sometimes underfoot, sometimes at my shoulder—or on it—their children, a riot, a forest of children, who include my nieces and nephews.

When we reach the end of this long block, we find ourselves on wide, filthy, hostile Fifth Avenue, facing that project which hangs over the avenue like a monument to the folly, and the cowardice, of good intentions. All along the block, for anyone who knows it, are immense human gaps, like craters. These gaps are not created merely by those who have moved away, inevitably into some other ghetto; or by those who have risen, almost always into a greater capacity for self-loathing and self-delusion; or yet by those who, by whatever means—War II, the Korean war, a policeman's gun or billy, a gang war, a brawl, madness, an overdose of heroin, or, simply, unnatural exhaustion—are dead. I am talking principally about the young. What are they doing? Well, some, a minority, are fanatical church-goers, members of the more extreme of the Holy Roller sects. Many, many more are "moslems," by affiliation or sympathy, that is to say that they are united by nothing more—and nothing less—than a hatred of the white world and all its works. They are present, for example, at every Buy Black street-corner meeting—meetings in which the speaker urges his hearers to cease trading with white men and establish a separate economy. Neither the speaker nor his hearers can possibly do this, of course, since Negroes do not own General Motors or RCA or the A & P, nor, indeed, do they own more than a wholly insufficient fraction of anything else in Harlem (those who *do* own anything are more interested in their profits than in their fellows). But these meetings nevertheless keep alive in the participators a certain pride of bitterness without which, however futile this bitterness may be, they could scarcely remain alive at all. Many have given up. They stay home and watch the TV screen, living on the earnings of their parents, cousins, brothers, or uncles, and only leave the house to go to the movies or to the nearest bar. "How're you making it?" one may ask, running into them along the block, or in the bar. "Oh, I'm TV-ing it"; with the saddest, sweetest, most shame-faced of smiles, and from a great distance. This distance one is com-pelled to respect; anyone who has traveled so far will not easily be dragged again into the world. There are further retreats, of course, than the TV screen or the bar. There are those who are simply sitting on their stoops, "stoned," animated for a moment only, and hideously, by the approach of someone who may lend them the money for a "fix." Or by the approach of some one from whom they can purchase it, one of the shrewd ones, on the way to prison or just coming out.

And the others, who have avoided all of these deaths, get up in the morning and go downtown to meet "the man." They work in the white man's world all day and come home in the evening to this fetid block. They struggle to instill in their children some private sense of honor or dignity which will help the child to survive. This means, of course, that they must struggle, stolidly, incessantly, to keep this sense alive in themselves, in spite of the insults, the in-difference, and the cruelty they are certain to encounter in their working day. They patiently browbeat the landlord into fixing the heat, the plaster, the plumbing; this demands prodigious patience; nor is patience usually enough. In trying to make their hovels habit-able, they are perpetually throwing good money after bad. Such frus-tration, so long endured, is driving many strong, admirable men and women whose only crime is color to the very gates of paranoia.

One remembers them from another time—playing handball in the playground, going to church, wondering if they were going to be promoted at school. One remembers them going off to war—gladly, to escape this block. One remembers their return. Perhaps one remembers their wedding day. And one sees where the girl is now—vainly looking for salvation from some other embittered, trussed, and struggling boy—and sees the all-but-abandoned children in the streets.

Now I am perfectly aware that there are other slums in which white men are fighting for their lives, and mainly losing. I know that blood is also flowing through those streets and that the human damage there is incalculable. People are continually pointing out to me the wretchedness of white people in order to console me for the wretchedness of blacks. But an itemized account of the American failure does not console me and it should not console anyone else. That hundreds of thousands of white people are living, in effect, no better than the "niggers" is not a fact to be regarded with complacency. The social and moral bankruptcy suggested by this fact is of the bitterest, most terrifying kind.

The people, however, who believe that this democratic anguish has some consoling value are always pointing out that So-and-So, white, and So-and-So, black, rose from the slums into the big time. The existence—the public existence—of, say, Frank Sinatra and Sammy Davis, Jr. proves to them that America is still the land of opportunity and that inequalities vanish before the determined will. It proves nothing of the sort. The determined will is rare—at the moment, in this country, it is unspeakably rare—and the inequalities suffered by the many are in no way justified by the rise of a few. A few have always risen—in every country, every era, and in the teeth of regimes which can by no stretch of the imagination be thought of as free. Not all of these people, it is worth remembering, left the world better than they found it. The determined will is rare, but it is not invariably benevolent. Furthermore, the American equation of success with the big times reveals an awful disrespect for human life and human achievement. This equation has placed our cities among the most dangerous in the world and has placed our youth among the most empty and most bewildered. The situation of our youth is not mysterious. Children have never been very good at listening to their elders, but they have never failed to imitate them. They must, they have no other models. That is exactly what our children are doing. They are imitating our immorality, our disrespect for the pain of others.

All other slum dwellers, when the bank account permits it, can move out of the slum and vanish altogether from the eye of persecution. No Negro in this country has ever made that much money and it will be a long time before any Negro does. The Negroes in Harlem, who have no money, spend what they have on such gimcracks as they are sold. These include "wider" TV screens, more "faithful" hi-fi sets, more "powerful" cars, all of which, of course, are obsolete long before they are paid for. Anyone who has ever struggled with poverty knows how extremely expensive it is to be poor; and if one is a member of a captive population, economically speaking, one's feet have simply been placed on the treadmill forever. One is victimized, economically, in a thousand ways—rent, for example, or car insurance. Go shopping one day in Harlem—for anything—and compare Harlem prices and quality with those downtown.

The people who have managed to get off this block have only got as far as a more respectable ghetto. This respectable ghetto does not even have the advantages of the disreputable one—friends, neighbors, a familiar church, and friendly tradesmen; and it is not, moreover, in the nature of any ghetto to remain respectable long. Every Sunday, people who have left the block take the lonely ride back, dragging their increasingly discontented children with them. They spend the day talking, not always with words, about the trouble they've seen and the trouble—one must watch their eyes as they watch their children—they are only too likely to see. For children do not like ghettos. It takes them nearly no time to discover exactly why they are there.

The projects in Harlem are hated. They are hated almost as much as policemen, and this is saying a great deal. And they are hated for the same reason: both reveal, unbearably, the real attitude of the white world, no matter how many liberal speeches are made, no matter how many lofty editorials are written, no matter how many civil-rights commissions are set up.

The projects are hideous, of course, there being a law, apparently respected throughout the world, that popular housing shall be as cheerless as a prison. They are lumped all over Harlem, colorless, bleak, high, and revolting. The wide windows look out on Harlem's invincible and indescribable squalor: the Park Avenue railroad tracks, around which, about forty years ago, the present dark community began; the unrehabilitated houses, bowed down, it would seem, under the great weight of frustration and bitterness they contain; the dark, the ominous schoolhouses from which the child may emerge maimed, blinded, hooked, or enraged for life; and the churches, churches, block upon block of churches, niched in the walls like cannon in the walls of a fortress. Even if the administration of the projects were not so insanely humiliating (for example: one must report raises in salary to the management, which will then eat up the profit by raising one's rent; the management has the right to know who is staying in your apartment; the management can ask you to leave, at their discretion), the projects would still be hated because they are an insult to the meanest intelligence.

Harlem got its first private project, Riverton—which is now, naturally, a slum—about twelve years ago because at that time Negroes were not allowed to live in Stuyvesant Town. Harlem watched Riverton go up, therefore, in the most violent bitterness of spirit, and hated it long before the builders arrived. They began hating it at about the time people began moving out of their condemned houses to make room for this additional proof of how thoroughly the white world despised them. And they had scarcely moved in, naturally, before they began smashing windows, defacing walls, urinating in the elevators, and fornicating in the playgrounds. Liberals, both white and black, were appalled at the spectacle. I was appalled by the liberal innocence—or cynicism, which comes out in practice as much the same thing. Other people were delighted to be able to point to proof positive that nothing could be done to better the lot of the colored people. They were, and are, right in one respect: that nothing can be done as long as they are treated like colored people. The people in Harlem know they are living there because white people do not think they are good enough to live anywhere else. No amount of "improvement" can sweeten this fact. Whatever money is now being earmarked to improve this, or any other ghetto, might as well be burnt. A ghetto can be improved in one way only: out of existence.

Similarly, the only way to police a ghetto is to be oppressive. None of the Police Commissioner's men, even with the best will in the world, have any way of understanding the lives led by the people they swagger about in twos and threes controlling. Their very presence is an insult, and it would be, even if they spent their entire day feeding gumdrops to children. They represent the force of the white world, and that world's real intentions are, simply, for that world's criminal profit and ease, to keep the black man corraled up here, in his place. The badge, the gun in the holster, and the swinging club make vivid what will happen should his rebellion become overt. Rare, indeed, is the Harlem citizen, from the most circumspect church member to the most shiftless adolescent, who does not have a long tale to tell of police incompetence, injustice, or brutality. I myself have witnessed and endured it more than once. The businessmen and racketeers also have a story. And so do the prostitutes. (And this is not, perhaps, the place to discuss Harlem's very complex attitude toward black policemen, nor the reasons, according to Harlem, that they are nearly all downtown.)

It is hard, on the other hand, to blame the policeman, blank, good-natured, thoughtless, and insuperably innocent, for being such a perfect representative of the people he serves. He, too, believes in good intentions and is astounded and offended when they are not taken for the deed. He has never, himself, done anything for which to be hated—which of us has?—and yet he is facing, daily and nightly, people who would gladly see him dead, and he knows it. There is no way for him not to know it: there are few things under heaven more unnerving than the silent, accumulating contempt and hatred of a people. He moves through Harlem, therefore, like an occupying soldier in a bitterly hostile country; which is precisely what, and where, he is, and is the reason he walks in twos and threes. And he is not the only one who knows why he is always in company: the people who are watching him know why, too. Any street meeting, sacred or secular, which he and his colleagues uneasily cover has as its explicit or implicit burden the cruelty and injustice of the white domination. And these days, of course, in terms increasingly vivid and jubilant, it speaks of the end of that domination. The white policeman standing on a Harlem street corner finds himself at the very center of the revolution now occurring in the world. He is not prepared for it—naturally, nobody is—and, what is possibly much more to the point, he is exposed, as few white people are, to the anguish of the black people around him. Even if he is gifted with the merest mustard grain of imagination, something must seep in. He cannot avoid observing that some of the children, in spite of their color, remind him of children he has known and loved, perhaps even of his own children. He knows that he certainly does not want *his* children living this way. He can retreat from his uneasiness in only one direction: into a callousness which very shortly becomes second nature. He becomes more callous, the population becomes more hostile, the situation grows more tense, and the police force is increased. One day, to everyone's astonishment, someone drops a match in the powder keg and everything blows up. Before the dust has settled or the blood congealed, editorials, speeches, and civil-rights commissions are loud in the land, demanding to know what happened. What happened is that Negroes want to be treated like men.

Negroes want to be treated like men: a perfectly straightforward statement, containing only seven words. People who have mastered Kant, Hegel, Shakespeare, Marx, Freud, and the Bible find this statement utterly impenetrable. The idea seems to threaten profound, barely conscious assumptions. A kind of panic paralyzes their features, as though they found themselves trapped on the edge of a steep place. I once tried to describe to a very well-known American intellectual the conditions among Negroes in the South. My recital disturbed him and made him indignant; and he asked me in perfect innocence, "Why don't all the Negroes in the South move North?" I tried to explain what *has* happened, unfailingly, whenever a significant body of Negroes move North. They do not escape Jim Crow: they merely encounter another, not-less-deadly variety. They do not move to Chicago, they move to the South Side; they do not move to New York, they move to Harlem. The pressure within the ghetto causes the ghetto walls to expand, and this expansion is always violent. White people hold the line as long as they can, and in as many ways as they can, from verbal intimidation to physical violence. But inevitably the border which has divided the ghetto from the rest of the world falls into the hands of the ghetto. The white people fall back bitterly before the black horde; the landlords make a tidy profit by raising the rent, chopping up the rooms, and all but dispensing with the upkeep; and what has once been a neighborhood turns into a "turf." This is precisely what happened when the Puerto Ricans arrived in their thousands—and the bitterness thus caused is, as I write, being fought out all up and down those streets.

Northerners indulge in an extremely dangerous luxury. They seem to feel that because they fought on the right side during the Civil War, and won, they have earned the right merely to deplore what is going on in the South, without taking any responsibility for it; and that they can ignore what is happening in Northern cities because what is happening in Little Rock or Birmingham is worse. Well, in the first place, it is not possible for anyone who has not endured both to know which is "worse." I know Negroes who prefer the South and white Southerners, because "At least there, you haven't got to play any guessing games!" The guessing games referred to have driven more than one Negro into the narcotics ward, the madhouse, or the river. I know another Negro, a man very dear to me, who says, with conviction and with truth, "The spirit of the South is the spirit of America." He was born in the North and did his military training in the South. He did not, as far as I can gather, find the South "worse"; he found it, if anything, all too familiar. In the second place, though, even if Birmingham *is* worse, no doubt Johannesburg, South Africa, beats it by several miles, and Buchenwald was one of the worst things that ever happened in the entire history of the world. The world has never lacked for horrifying examples; but I do not believe that these examples are meant to be used as justification for our own crimes. This perpetual justification empties the heart of all human feeling. The emptier our hearts become, the greater will be our crimes. Thirdly, the South is not merely an embarrassingly backward region, but a part of this country, and what happens there concerns every one of us.

As far as the color problem is concerned, there is but one great difference between the Southern white and the Northerner: the Southerner remembers, historically and in his own psyche, a kind of Eden in which he loved black people and they loved him. Historically, the flaming sword laid across this Eden is the Civil War.

Personally, it is the Southerner's sexual coming of age, when, without any warning, unbreakable taboos are set up between himself and his past. Everything, thereafter, is permitted him except the love he remembers and has never ceased to need. The resulting, indescribable torment affects every Southern mind and is the basis of the Southern hysteria.

None of this is true for the Northerner. Negroes represent nothing to him personally, except, perhaps, the dangers of carnality. He never sees Negroes. Southerners see them all the time. Northerners never think about them whereas Southerners are never really thinking of anything else. Negroes are, therefore, ignored in the North and are under surveillance in the South, and suffer hideously in both places. Neither the Southerner nor the Northerner is able to look on the Negro simply as a man. It seems to be indispensable to the national self-esteem that the Negro be considered either as a kind of war (in which case we are told how many Negroes, comparatively, bought Cadillacs last year and how few, comparatively, were lynched), or as a victim (in which case we are promised that he will never vote in our assemblies or go to school with our kids). They are two sides of the same coin and the South will not change—*cannot* change—until the North changes. The country will not change until it re-examines itself and discovers what it really means by freedom. In the meantime, generations keep being born, bitterness is increased by incompetence, pride, and folly, and the world shrinks around us.

It is a terrible, an inexorable, law that one cannot deny the humanity of another without diminishing one's own: in the face of one's victim, one sees oneself. Walk through the streets of Harlem and see what we, this nation, have become.

An Appendix on Style

[1640]

BEN JONSON

Of Style

FOR A MAN to write well, there are required three neces-
saries—to read the best authors, observe the best speakers, and much
exercise of his own style. In style, to consider what ought to be
written, and after what manner, he must first think and excogitate
his matter, then choose his words, and examine the weight of either.
Then take care, in placing and ranking both matter and words,
that the composition be comely; and to do this with diligence and
often. No matter how slow the style be at first, so it be labored and
accurate; seek the best, and be not glad of the forward conceits or
first words that offer themselves to us, but judge of what we invent,
and order what we approve. Repeat often what we have formerly
written; which beside that it helps the consequence, and makes the
juncture better, it quickens the heat of imagination, that often cools
in the time of setting down, and gives it new strength, as if it grew
lustier by the going back. As we see in the contention of leaping,
they jump farthest that fetch their race largest; or, as in throwing a
dart or javelin, we force back our arms to make our loose the
stronger. Yet, if we have a fair gale of wind, I forbid not the
steering out of our sail, so the favor of the gale deceive us not. For
all that we invent doth please us in the conception of birth, else we
would never set it down. But the safest is to return to our judgment, and handle over again those things the easiness of which
might make them justly suspected. So did the best writers in their
beginnings; they imposed upon themselves care and industry; they
did nothing rashly: they obtained first to write well, and then custom made it easy and a habit. By little and little their matter showed
itself to them more plentifully; their words answered, their composi-

tion followed; and all, as in a well-ordered family, presented itself in the place. So that the sum of all is, ready writing makes not good writing, but good writing brings on ready writing. Yet, when we think we have got the faculty, it is even then good to resist it, as to give a horse a check sometimes with a bit, which doth not so much stop his course as stir his mettle. Again, whether a man's genius is best able to reach, thither it should more and more contend, lift and dilate itself; as men of low stature raise themselves on their toes, and so oft-times get even, if not eminent. Besides, as it is fit for grown and able writers to stand of themselves, and work with their own strength, to trust and endeavor by their own faculties, so it is fit for the beginner and learner to study others and the best. For the mind and memory are more sharply exercised in comprehending another man's things than our own; and such as accustom themselves and are familiar with the best authors shall ever and anon find somewhat of them in themselves, and in the expression of their minds, even when they feel it not, be able to utter something like theirs, which hath an authority above their own. Nay, sometimes it is the reward of a man's study, the praise of quoting another man fitly; and though a man be more prone and able for one kind of writing than another, yet he must exercise all. For as in an instrument, so in style, there must be harmony and consent of parts.

[1720]

JONATHAN SWIFT

from *A Letter to a Young
Gentleman*
LATELY ENTERED INTO
HOLY ORDERS
By a Person of QUALITY

January 9, 1720

Sir,

Although it was against my knowledge or advice, that you entered
into holy orders, under the present dispositions of mankind toward
the Church, yet since it is now supposed too late to recede (at least
according to the general practice and opinion), I cannot forbear
offering my thoughts to you upon this new condition of life you are
engaged in.

I could heartily wish that the circumstances of your fortune had
enabled you to have continued some years longer in the university,
at least until you were ten years' standing; to have laid in a com-
petent stock of human learning, and some knowledge in divinity,
before you attempted to appear in the world: for I cannot but
lament the common course, which at least nine in ten of those who
enter into the ministry are obliged to run. When they have taken a
degree, and are consequently grown a burden to their friends, who
now think themselves fully discharged, they get into orders as soon
as they can (upon which I shall make no remarks), first solicit a
readership, and if they be very fortunate, arrive in time to a curacy
here in town; or else are sent to be assistants in the country, where
they probably continue several years (many of them their whole

lives), with thirty or forty pounds a year for their support, until some bishop, who happens to be not overstocked with relations, or attached to favorites, or is content to supply his diocese without colonies from England, bestows upon them some inconsiderable benefice, when it is odds they are already encumbered with a numerous family. I would be glad to know what intervals of life such persons can possibly set apart for improvements of their minds; or which way they could be furnished with books, the library they brought with them from their college being usually not the most numerous, or judiciously chosen. If such gentlemen arrive to be great scholars, it must, I think, be either by means supernatural, or by a method altogether out of any road yet known to the learned. But I conceive the fact directly otherwise, and that many of them lose the greatest part of the small pittance they received at the university.

I take it for granted, that you intend to pursue the beaten track, and are already desirous to be seen in a pulpit; only I hope you will think it proper to pass your quarantine among some of the desolate churches five miles round this town, where you may at least learn to *read* and to *speak* before you venture to expose your parts in a city congregation; not that these are better judges, but because, if a man must needs expose his folly, it is more safe and discreet to be so before few witnesses, and in a scattered neighborhood. And you will do well if you can prevail upon some intimate and judicious friend to be your constant hearer, and allow him with the utmost freedom to give you notice of whatever he shall find amiss either in your voice or gesture; for want of which early warning, many clergymen continue defective, and sometimes ridiculous, to the end of their lives; neither is it rare to observe among excellent and learned divines, a certain ungracious manner, or an unhappy tone of voice, which they never have been able to shake off.

I could likewise have been glad, if you had applied yourself a little more to the study of the English language, than I fear you have done; the neglect whereof is one of the most general defects among the scholars of this kingdom, who seem to have not the least conception of a style, but run on in a flat kind of phraseology, often mingled with barbarous terms and expressions, peculiar to the nation. Neither do I perceive that any person either finds or acknowledges his wants upon this head, or in the least desires to have them supplied. Proper words in proper places, makes the true definition of a style. But this would require too ample a disquisition to be now dwelt on: however, I shall venture to name one or two faults, which are easy to be remedied, with a very small portion of abilities.

The first is the frequent use of obscure terms, which by the women are called *hard words*, and by the better sort of vulgar, *fine language*; than which I do not know a more universal, inexcusable, and unnecessary mistake, among the clergy of all distinctions, but especially the younger practitioners. I have been curious enough to take a list of several hundred words in a sermon of a new beginner, which not one of his hearers among a hundred could possibly understand; neither can I easily call to mind any clergyman of my own acquaintance who is wholly exempt from this error, although many of them agree with me in the dislike of the thing. But I am apt to put myself in the place of the vulgar, and think many words difficult or obscure, which the preacher will not allow to be so, because those words are obvious to scholars. I believe the method observed by the famous Lord Falkland in some of his writings, would not be an ill one for young divines: I was assured by an old person of quality who knew him well, that when he doubted whether a word was perfectly intelligible or no, he used to consult one of his lady's chambermaids (not the waiting woman, because it was possible she might be conversant in romances), and by her judgment was guided whether to receive or reject it. And if that great person thought such a caution necessary in treatises offered to the learned world, it will be sure at least as proper in sermons, where the meanest hearer is supposed to be concerned, and where very often a lady's chambermaid may be allowed to equal half the congregation, both as to quality and understanding. But I know not how it comes to pass, that professors in most arts and sciences are generally the worst qualified to explain their meanings to those who are not of their tribe. A common farmer shall make you understand in three words, *that his foot is out of joint, or his collarbone broken*, wherein a surgeon, after a hundred terms of art, if you are not a scholar, shall leave you to seek. It is frequently the same case in law, physic, and even many of the meaner arts.

And upon this account it is, that among *hard words*, I number likewise those which are peculiar to divinity as it is a science; because I have observed several clergymen, otherwise little fond of obscure terms, yet in their sermons very liberal of those which they find in ecclesiastical writers, as if it were our duty to understand them; which I am sure it is not. And I defy the greatest divine to produce any law either of God or man, which obliges me to comprehend the meaning of *omniscience, omnipresence, ubiquity, attribute, beatific vision*, with a thousand others so frequent in pulpits, any more than that of *eccentric, idiosyncracy, entity*, and the like. I believe I may venture to insist further, that many terms used in Holy Writ, particularly by St. Paul, might with more discretion be changed into plainer speech, except when they are introduced as part of a quotation.

I am the more earnest in this matter, because it is a general complaint, and the justest in the world. For a divine has nothing to say to the wisest congregation of any parish in this kingdom, which he may not express in a manner to be understood by the meanest among them. And this assertion must be true, or else God requires from us more than we are able to perform. However, not to contend whether a logician might possibly put a case that would serve for an exception, I will appeal to any man of letters, whether at least nineteen in twenty of those perplexing words might not be changed into easy ones, such as naturally first occur to ordinary men, and probably did so at first to those very gentlemen who are so fond of the former.

We are often reproved by divines from the pulpits, on account of our ignorance in things sacred, and perhaps with justice enough. However, it is not very reasonable for them to expect, that *common men* should understand expressions which are never made use of in *common life*. No gentleman thinks it safe or prudent to send a servant with a message, without repeating it more than once, and endeavoring to put it into terms brought down to the capacity of the bearer. Yet after all this care, it is frequent for servants to mistake, and sometimes to occasion misunderstandings between friends, although the common domestics in some gentlemen's families may have more opportunities of improving their minds than the ordinary sort of tradesmen.

It is usual for clergymen who are taxed with this learned defect, to quote Dr. Tillotson, and other famous divines, in their defense, without considering the difference between elaborate discourses upon important occasions, delivered to princes or parliaments, written with a view of being made public, and a plain sermon intended for the middle or lower size of people. Neither do they seem to remember the many alterations, additions, and expungings, made by great authors in those treatises which they prepare for the public. Besides, that excellent prelate above-mentioned, was known to preach after a much more popular manner in the city congregations: and if in those parts of his works he be anywhere too obscure for the understandings of many who may be supposed to have been his hearers, it ought to be numbered among his omissions.

The fear of being thought pedants hath been of pernicious consequence to young divines. This hath wholly taken many of them off from their severer studies in the university, which they have exchanged for plays, poems, and pamphlets, in order to qualify them for tea tables and coffee-houses. This they usually call *polite conversation; knowing the world;* and *reading men instead of books.* These accomplishments when applied in the pulpit, appear by a quaint, terse, florid style, rounded into periods and cadences, commonly without either propriety or meaning. I have listened with my utmost attention for half an hour to an orator of this species, without being able to understand, much less to carry away one single sentence out of a whole sermon. Others, to show that their studies have not been confined to sciences, or ancient authors, will talk in the style of a gaming ordinary, and Whitefriars, where I suppose the hearers can be little edified by the terms of *palming, shuffling, biting, bamboozling,* and the like, if they have not been sometimes conversant among pickpockets and sharpers. And truly, as they say, a man is known by his company, so it should seem that a man's company may be known by his manner of expressing himself, either in public assemblies, or private conversation.

It would be endless to run over the several defects of style among us; I shall therefore say nothing of the *mean* and *paltry* (which are usually attended by the *fustian*), much less of the *slovenly* or *indecent*. Two things I will just warn you against: the first is the frequency of flat unnecessary epithets; and the other is the folly of using old threadbare phrases, which will often make you go out of your way to find and apply them, are nauseous to rational hearers, and will seldom express your meaning as well as your own natural words.

Although, as I have already observed, our English tongue is too little cultivated in this kingdom, yet the faults are nine in ten owing to affectation, and not to the want of understanding. When a man's thoughts are clear, the properest words will generally offer themselves first, and his own judgment will direct him in what order to place them, so as they may be best understood. Where men err against this method, it is usually on purpose, and to show their learning, their oratory, their politeness, or their knowledge of the world. In short, that simplicity without which no human perform-ance can arrive to any great perfection, is nowhere more eminently useful than in this. . . .

[1 8 2 1]

WILLIAM HAZLITT

Of Familiar Style

IT IS NOT easy to write a familiar style. Many people mis-take a familiar for a vulgar style, and suppose that to write without affectation is to write at random. On the contrary, there is nothing that requires more precision, and, if I may so say, purity of expression, than the style I am speaking of. It utterly rejects not only all unmeaning pomp, but all low, cant phrases, and loose, unconnected, *slipshod* allusions. It is not to take the first word that offers, but the best word in common use; it is not to throw words together in any combinations we please, but to follow and avail ourselves of the true idiom of the language. To write a genuine familiar or truly English style, is to write as any one would speak in common conversation, who had a thorough command and choice of words, or who could discourse with ease, force, and perspicuity, setting aside all pedantic and oratorical flourishes. Or to give another illustration, to write naturally is the same thing in regard to common conversation, as to read naturally is in regard to common speech. It does not follow that it is an easy thing to give the true accent and inflection to the words you utter, because you do not attempt to rise above the level of ordinary life and colloquial speaking. You do not assume indeed the solemnity of the pulpit, or the tone of stage declamation: neither are you at liberty to gabble on at a venture, without emphasis or discretion, or to resort to vulgar dialect or clownish pronunciation. You must steer a middle course. You are tied down to a given and appropriate articulation, which is determined by the habitual associations between sense and sound, and which you can only hit by entering into the author's meaning, as you must find the proper words and style to express yourself by fixing your thoughts on the subject you have to write about. Any one may mouth out a passage with a theatrical cadence, or get upon stilts to tell his thoughts: but to speak or write with propriety and simplicity is a more difficult task. Thus it is easy to affect a pompous style, to use a word twice as big as the thing you want to express: it is not so easy to pitch upon the very word that exactly fits it. Out of eight or ten words equally common, equally intelligible, with nearly equal pretensions, it is a matter of some nicety and discrimination to pick out the very one, the preferableness of which is scarcely perceptible, but decisive. The reason why I object to Dr. Johnson's style is, that there is no discrimination, no variety in it. He uses none but "tall, opaque words," taken from the "first row of the rubric": words with the greatest number of syllables, or Latin phrases with merely English terminations. If a fine style depended on this sort of arbitrary pretension, it would be fair to judge of an author's elegance by the measurement of his words, and the substitution of foreign circumlocutions (with no precise associations) for the mother tongue. How simple it is to be dignified without ease, to be pompous without meaning! Surely, it is but a mechanical rule for avoiding what is low to be always pedantic and affected. It is clear you cannot use a vulgar English word, if you never use a common English word at all. A fine tact is shown in adhering to those which are perfectly common, and yet never falling into any expressions which are debased by disgusting circumstances, or which owe their signification and point to technical or professional allusions. A truly natural or familiar style can never be quaint or vulgar, for this reason, that it is of universal force and applicability, and that quaintness and vulgarity arise out of the immediate connection of certain words with coarse and disagreeable, or with confined ideas. The last form what we understand by *cant* or *slang* phrases. To give an example of what is not very clear in the general statement, I should say that the phrase *To cut with a knife*, or *To cut a piece of wood*, is perfectly free from vulgarity, because it is perfectly common: but to *cut an acquaintance* is not quite unexceptionable, because it is not perfectly common or intelligible, and has hardly yet escaped out of the limits of slang phraseology. I should hardly therefore use the word in this sense without putting it in italics as a license of expression, to be received *cum grano salis*. All provincial or bye-phrases come under the same mark of reprobation— all such as the writer transfers to the page from his fireside or a particular *coterie*, or that he invents for his own sole use and convenience. I conceive that words are like money, not the worse for being common, but that it is the stamp of custom alone that gives them circulation or value. I am fastidious in this respect, and would almost as soon coin the currency of the realm as counterfeit the King's English. I never invented or gave a new and unauthorized meaning to any word but one single one (the term *impersonal* applied to feelings) and that was in an abstruse metaphysical discussion to express a very difficult distinction. I have been (I know) loudly accused of reveling in vulgarisms and broken English. I cannot speak to that point: but so far I plead guilty to the determined

use of acknowledged idioms and common elliptical expressions. I am
not sure that the critics in question know the one from the other,
that is, can distinguish any medium between formal pedantry and
the most barbarous solecism. As an author, I endeavor to employ
plain words and popular modes of construction, as were I a chap-
man and dealer, I should common weights and measures.

The proper force of words lies not in the words themselves, but in
their application. A word may be a fine-sounding word of an unusual
length, and very imposing from its learning and novelty, and yet in
the connection in which it is introduced, may be quite pointless and
irrelevant. It is not pomp or pretension, but the adaptation of the
expression to the idea that clenches a writer's meaning: as it is not
the size or glossiness of the materials, but their being fitted each to
its place, that gives strength to the arch; or as the pegs and nails
are as necessary to the support of the building as the large timbers,
and more so than the mere showy, unsubstantial ornaments. I hate
any thing that occupies more space than it is worth. I hate to see a
load of band-boxes go along the street, and I hate to see a parcel of
big words without any thing in them. A person who does not
deliberately dispose of all his thoughts alike in cumbrous draperies
and flimsy disguises, may strike out twenty varieties of familiar
everyday language, each coming somewhat nearer to the feeling he
wants to convey, and at last not hit upon that particular and only
one, which may be said to be identical with the exact expression
in his mind. This would seem to show that Mr. Cobbett is hardly
right in saying that the first word that occurs is always the best. It
may be a very good one; and yet a better may present itself on reflection or from time to time. It should be suggested naturally, however,
and spontaneously, from a fresh and lively conception of the subject.
We seldom succeed by trying at improvement, or by merely sub-
stituting one word for another that we are not satisfied with, as we
cannot recollect the name of a place or person by merely plaguing
ourselves about it. We wander farther from the point by persisting
in a wrong scent, but it starts up accidentally in the memory when
we least expected it, by touching some link in the chain of previous
association.

There are those who hoard up and make a cautious display of nothing but rich and rare phraseology: ancient medals, obscure coins, and Spanish pieces of eight. They are very curious to inspect; but I myself would neither offer nor take them in the course of exchange. A sprinkling of archaisms is not amiss; but a tissue of obsolete expressions is more fit *for keep than wear*. I do not say I would not use any phrase that had been brought into fashion before the middle or the end of the last century; but I should be shy of using any that had not been employed by any approved author during the whole of that time. Words, like clothes, get old-fashioned, or mean and ridiculous, when they have been for some time laid aside. Mr. Lamb is the only imitator of old English style I can read with pleasure; and he is so thoroughly imbued with the spirit of his authors, that the idea of imitation is almost done away. There is an inward unction, a marrowy vein both in the thought and feeling, an intuition, deep and lively, of his subject, that carries off any quaintness or awkwardness arising from an antiquated style and dress. The matter is completely his own, though the manner is assumed. Perhaps his ideas are altogether so marked and individual, as to require their point and pungency to be neutralized by the affectation of a singular but traditional form of conveyance. Tricked out in the prevailing costume, they would· probably seem more startling and out of the way. The old English authors, Burton, Fuller, Coryate, Sir Thomas Browne, are a kind of mediators between us and the more eccentric and whimsical modern, reconciling us to his peculiarities. I do not, however, know how far this is the case or not, till he condescends to write like one of us. I must confess that what I like best of his papers under the signature of Elia (still I do not presume, amidst such excellence, to decide what is most excellent) is the account of *Mrs. Battle's Opinions on Whist*, which is also the most free from obsolete allusions and turns of expressions—

A well of native English undefiled.

To those acquainted with his admired prototypes, these *Essays* of the ingenious and highly gifted author have the same sort of charm and relish that Erasmus's *Colloquies* or a fine piece of modern Latin have to the classical scholar. Certainly, I do not know any borrowed pencil that has more power or felicity of execution than the one of which I have here been speaking.

It is as easy to write a gaudy style without ideas as it is to spread a pallet of showy colors, or to smear in a flaunting transparency. "What do you read?"—"Words, words, words."—"What is the matter?"—"*Nothing*," it might be answered. The florid style is the reverse of the familiar. The last is employed as an unvarnished medium to convey ideas; the first is resorted to as a spangled veil to conceal the want of them. When there is nothing to be set down but words, it costs little to have them fine. Look through the dictionary, and cull out a *florilegium*, rival the *tulipomania*. *Rouge* high enough, and never mind the natural complexion. The vulgar, who are not in the secret, will admire the look of preternatural health and vigor; and the fashionable, who regard only appearances, will be delighted with the imposition. Keep to your sounding generalities, your tinkling phrases, and all will be well. Swell out an unmeaning truism to a perfect tympany of style. A thought, a distinction is the rock on which all this brittle cargo of verbiage splits at once. Such writers have merely *verbal* imaginations, that retain nothing but words. Or their puny thoughts have dragon-wings, all green and gold. They soar far above the vulgar failing of the *Sermo humi obrepens*—their most ordinary speech is never short of an hyperbole, splendid, imposing, vague, incomprehensible, magniloquent, a cento of sounding commonplaces. If some of us, whose "ambition is more lowly," pry a little too narrowly into nooks and corners to pick up a number of "unconsidered trifles," they never once direct their eyes or lift their hands to seize on any but the most gorgeous, tarnished, threadbare patchwork set of phrases, the left-off finery of poetic extravagance, transmitted down through successive generations of barren pretenders. If they criticize actors and actresses, a huddled phantasmagoria of feathers, spangles, floods of light, and oceans of sound float before their morbid sense, which they paint in the style of Ancient Pistol. Not a glimpse can you get of the merits or defects of the performers: they are hidden in a profusion of barbarous epithets and willful rhodomontade. Our hypercritics are not thinking of these little fantoccini beings—

> That strut and fret their hour upon the stage—

but of tall phantoms of words, abstractions, *genera* and *species*, sweeping clauses, periods that unite the Poles, forced alliterations, astounding antitheses—

> And on their pens *Fustian* sits plumed.

If they describe kings and queens, it is an Eastern pageant. The Coronation at either House is nothing to it. We get at four repeated images—a curtain, a throne, a scepter, and a footstool. These are with them the wardrobe of a lofty imagination; and they turn their servile strains to servile uses. Do we read a description of pictures? It is not a reflection of tones and hues which "nature's own sweet and cunning hand laid on," but piles of precious stones, rubies, pearls, emeralds, Golconda's mines, and all the blazonry of art. Such persons are in fact besotted with words, and their brains are turned with the glittering, but empty and sterile phantoms of things. Personifications, capital letters, seas of sunbeams, visions of glory, shining inscriptions, the figures of a transparency, Britannia with her shield, or Hope leaning on an anchor, make up their stock in trade. They may be considered as *hieroglyphical* writers. Images stand out in their minds isolated and important merely in themselves, without any groundwork of feeling—there is no context in their imaginations. Words affect them in the same way, by the mere sound, that is, by their possible, not by their actual application to the subject in hand. They are fascinated by first appearances, and have no sense of consequences. Nothing more is meant by them than meets the ear: they understand or feel nothing more than meets their eye. The web and texture of the universe, and of the heart of man, is a mystery to them: they have no faculty that strikes a chord in unison with it. They cannot get beyond the daubings of fancy, the varnish of sentiment. Objects are not linked to feelings, words to things, but images revolve in splendid mockery, words represent themselves in their strange rhapsodies. The categories of such a mind are pride and ignorance—pride in outside show, to which they sacrifice every thing, and ignorance of the true worth and hidden structure both of words and things. With a sovereign contempt for what is familiar and natural, they are the slaves of vulgar affection— of a routine of highflown phrases. Scorning to imitate realities, they are unable to invent any thing, to strike out one original idea. They are not copyists of nature, it is true; but they are the poorest of all plagiarists, the plagiarists of words. All is farfetched, dear-bought, artificial, oriental in subject and allusion: all is mechanical, con-ventional, vapid, formal, pedantic in style and execution. They startle and confound the understanding of the reader, by the remote-ness and obscurity of their illustrations: they soothe the ear by the monotony of the same everlasting round of circuitous metaphors. They are the *mock-school* in poetry and prose. They flounder about between fustian in expression, and bathos in sentiment. They tantalize the fancy but never reach the head nor touch the heart. Their Temple of Fame is like a shadowy structure raised by Dullness to Vanity, or like Cowper's description of the Empress of Russia's palace of ice, as "worthless as in show 'twas glittering"—

It smiled, and it was cold!

[1863]

ALEXANDER SMITH

from *On the Writing of Essays*

. . . GIDDY PEOPLE may think the life I lead here staid and humdrum, but they are mistaken. It is true, I hear no concerts, save those in which the thrushes are performers in the spring mornings. I see no pictures, save those painted on the wide sky-canvas with the colors of sunrise and sunset. I attend neither rout nor ball; I

have no deeper dissipation than the tea-table; I hear no gossip. Yet
I enjoy my concerts more than I would the great London ones. I
like the pictures I see, and think them better painted, too, than
those which adorn the walls of the Royal Academy; and the village
gossip is more after my turn of mind than the scandals that convulse
the clubs. It is wonderful how the whole world reflects itself in the
simple village life. The people around me are full of their own
affairs and interests; were they of imperial magnitude, they could
not be excited more strongly. Farmer Worthy is anxious about the
next market; the likelihood of a fall in the price of butter and eggs
hardly allows him to sleep o' nights. The village doctor—happily
we have only one—skirrs hither and thither in his gig, as if man
could neither die nor be born without his assistance. He is continually standing on the confines of existence, welcoming the new
comer, bidding farewell to the goer-away. And the robustious fellow
who sits at the head of the table when the Jolly Swillers meet at
the Blue Lion on Wednesday evenings is a great politician, sound
of lung metal, and wields the village in the taproom, as my Lord
Palmerston wields the nation in the House. His listeners think him
a wiser personage than the Premier, and he is inclined to lean to
that opinion himself. I find everything here that other men find
in the big world. London is but a magnified Dreamthorp.

    And just as the Rev. Mr. White took note of the ongoings of
the seasons in and around Hampshire Selborne, watched the colonies
of the rooks in the tall elms, looked after the swallows in the cottage
and rectory eaves, played the affectionate spy on the private lives
of chaffinch and hedge-sparrow, was eavesdropper to the solitary
cuckoo; so here I keep eye and ear open; take note of man, woman,
and child; find many a pregnant text imbedded in the commonplace of village life; and, out of what I see and hear, weave in my
own room my essays as solitarily as the spider weaves his web in
the darkened corner. The essay, as a literary form, resembles the
lyric, in so far as it is molded by some central mood—whimsical,
serious, or satirical. Give the mood, and the essay, from the first
sentence to the last, grows around it as the cocoon grows around
the silkworm. The essay writer is a chartered libertine, and a law

unto himself. A quick ear and eye, an ability to discern the infinite suggestiveness of common things, a brooding meditative spirit, are all that the essayist requires to start business with. Jacques, in "As You Like It," had the makings of a charming essayist. It is not the essayist's duty to inform, to build pathways through metaphysical morasses, to cancel abuses, any more than it is the duty of the poet to do these things. Incidentally he may do something in that way, just as the poet may, but it is not his duty, and should not be expected of him. Skylarks are primarily created to sing, although a whole choir of them may be baked in pies and brought to table; they were born to make music, although they may incidentally stay the pangs of vulgar hunger. The essayist is a kind of poet in prose, and if questioned harshly as to his uses, he might be unable to render a better apology for his existence than a flower might. The essay should be pure literature as the poem is pure literature. The essayist wears a lance, but he cares more for the sharpness of its point than for the pennon that flutters on it, than for the banner of the captain under whom he serves. He plays with death as Hamlet plays with Yorick's skull, and he reads the morals—strangely stern, often, for such fragrant lodging—which are folded up in the bosoms of roses. He has no pride, and is deficient in a sense of the congruity and fitness of things. He lifts a pebble from the ground, and puts it aside more carefully than any gem; and on a nail in a cottage door he will hang the mantle of his thought, heavily brocaded with the gold of rhetoric. He finds his way into the Elysian fields through portals the most shabby and commonplace.

The essayist plays with his subject, now in whimsical, now in grave, now in melancholy mood. He lies upon the idle grassy bank, like Jacques, letting the world flow past him, and from this thing and the other he extracts his mirth and his moralities. His main gift is an eye to discover the suggestiveness of common things; to find a sermon in the most unpromising texts. Beyond the vital hint, the first step, his discourses are not beholden to their titles. Let him take up the most trivial subject, and it will lead him away to the great questions over which the serious imagination loves to brood—fortune, mutability, death—just as inevitably as the runnel, trickling among the summer hills, on which sheep are bleating, leads you to the sea; or as, turning down the first street you come to in the city, you are led finally, albeit by many an intricacy, out into the open country, with its waste places and its woods, where you are lost in a sense of strangeness and solitariness. The world is to the meditative man what the mulberry plant is to the silkworm. The essay writer has no lack of subject matter. He has the day that is passing over his head; and, if unsatisfied with that, he has the world's six thousand years to depasture his gay or serious humor upon. I idle away my time here, and I am finding new subjects every hour. Everything I see or hear is an essay in bud. The world is everywhere whispering essays, and one need only be the world's amanuensis. The proverbial expression which last evening the clown dropped as he trudged homeward to supper, the light of the setting sun on his face, expands before me to a dozen pages. The coffin of the pauper, which today I saw carried carelessly along, is as good a subject as the funeral procession of an emperor. Craped drum and banner add nothing to death; penury and disrespect take nothing away. Incontinently my thought moves like a slow-paved hearse with sable nodding plumes. Two rustic lovers, whispering between the darkening hedges, is as potent to project my mind into the tender passion as if I had seen Romeo touch the cheek of Juliet in the moonlight garden. Seeing a curly-headed child asleep in the sunshine before a cottage door is sufficient excuse for a discourse on childhood; quite as good as if I had seen infant Cain asleep in the lap of Eve with Adam looking on. A lark cannot rise to heaven without raising as many thoughts as there are notes in its song. Dawn cannot pour its white light on my village without starting from their dim lair a hundred reminiscences; nor can sunset burn above yonder trees in the west without attracting to itself the melancholy of a lifetime. When spring unfolds her green leaves I would be provoked to indite an essay on hope and youth, were it not that it is already writ in the carols of the birds; and I might be tempted in autumn to improve the occasion, were it not for the rustle of the withered leaves as I walk through the woods. Compared with that simple music, the saddest-cadenced words have but a shallow meaning.

The essayist who feeds his thoughts upon the segment of the world which surrounds him cannot avoid being an egotist; but then his egotism is not unpleasing. If he be without taint of boastfulness, of self-sufficiency, of hungry vanity, the world will not press the charge home. If a man discourses continually of his wines, his plate, his titled acquaintances, the number and quality of his horses, his men-servants and maid-servants, he must discourse very skillfully indeed if he escapes being called a coxcomb. If a man speaks of death—tells you that the idea of it continually haunts him, that he has the most insatiable curiosity as to death and dying, that his thought mines in churchyards like a "demon-mole"—no one is specially offended, and that this is a dull fellow is the hardest thing likely to be said of him. Only, the egotism that over-crows you is offensive, that exalts trifles and takes pleasure in them, that suggests superiority in matters of equipage and furniture; and the egotism is offensive, because it runs counter to and jostles your self-complacency. The egotism which rises no higher than the grave is of a solitary and a hermit kind—it crosses no man's path, it disturbs no man's *amour propre*. You may offend a man if you say you are as rich as he, as wise as he, as handsome as he. You offend no man if you tell him that, like him, you have to die. The king, in his crown and coronation robes, will allow the beggar to claim that relationship with him. To have to die is a distinction of which no man is proud. The speaking about one's self is not necessarily offensive. A modest, truthful man speaks better about himself than about anything else, and on that subject his speech is likely to be most profitable to his hearers. Certainly, there is no subject with which he is better acquainted, and on which he has a better title to be heard. And it is this egotism, this perpetual reference to self, in which the charm of the essayist resides. If a man is worth knowing at all, he is worth knowing well. The essayist gives you his thoughts, and lets you know, in addition, how he came by them. He has nothing to conceal; he throws open his doors and windows, and lets him enter who will. You like to walk round peculiar or important men as you like to walk round a building, to view it from different points, and in different lights. Of the essayist, when his mood is

communicative, you obtain a full picture. You are made his contemporary and familiar friend. You enter into his humors and his
seriousness. You are made heir of his whims, prejudices, and play-
fulness. You walk through the whole nature of him, as you walk
through the streets of Pompeii, looking into the interior of stately
mansions, reading the satirical scribblings on the walls. And the
essayist's habit of not only giving you his thoughts, but telling you
how he came by them, is interesting, because it shows you by what
alchemy the ruder world becomes transmuted into the finer. We like
to know the lineage of ideas, just as we like to know the lineage of
great earls and swift race horses. We like to know that the discovery of the law of gravitation was born of the fall of an apple
in an English garden on a summer afternoon. Essays written after
this fashion are racy of the soil in which they grow, as you taste
the lava in the vines grown on the slopes of Etna, they say. There
is a healthy Gascon flavor in Montaigne's Essays; and Charles
Lamb's are scented with the primroses of Covent Garden.

The essayist does not usually appear early in the literary history
of a country: he comes naturally after the poet and the chronicler.
His habit of mind is leisurely; he does not write from any special
stress of passionate impulse; he does not create material so much as
he comments upon material already existing. It is essential for him
that books should have been written, and that they should, at least
to some extent, have been read and digested. He is usually full of
allusions and references, and these his reader must be able to follow
and understand. And in this literary walk, as in most others, the
giants came first: Montaigne and Lord Bacon were our earliest
essayists, and, as yet, they are our best. In point of style, these
essays are different from anything that could now be produced. Not
only is the thinking different—the manner of setting forth the
thinking is different also. We despair of reaching the language. We
can no more bring back their turns of sentence than we can bring
back their tournaments. Montaigne, in his serious moods, has a
curiously rich and intricate eloquence; and Bacon's sentence bends
beneath the weight of its fruit. Bacon seems to have written his
essays with Shakespeare's pen. There is a certain want of ease about

the old writers which has an irresistible charm. The language flows like a stream over a pebbled bed, with propulsion, eddy, and sweet recoil—the pebbles, if retarding movement, giving ring and dimple to the surface, and breaking the whole into babbling music. There is a ceremoniousness in the mental habits of these ancients. Their intellectual garniture is picturesque, like the garniture of their bodies. Their thoughts are courtly and high-mannered. A singular analogy exists between the personal attire of a period and its written style. The peaked beard, the starched collar, the quilted doublet, have their correspondences in the high sentence and elaborate ornament (worked upon the thought like figures upon tapestry) of Sidney and Spenser. In Pope's day men wore rapiers, and their weapons they carried with them into literature, and frequently unsheathed them too. They knew how to stab to the heart with an epigram. Style went out with the men who wore knee breeches and buckles in their shoes. We write more easily now; but in our easy writing there is ever a taint of flippancy: our writing is to theirs, what shooting coat and wideawake are to doublet and plumed hat.

Montaigne and Bacon are our earliest and greatest essayists, and likeness and unlikeness exist between the men. Bacon was constitutionally the graver nature. He writes like one on whom presses the weight of affairs, and he approaches a subject always on its serious side. He lives amongst great ideas, as with great nobles, with whom he dare not be too familiar. In the tone of his mind there is ever something imperial. When he writes on building, he speaks of a palace with spacious entrances, and courts, and banqueting halls; when he writes on gardens, he speaks of alleys and mounts, waste places and fountains, of a garden "which is indeed princelike." To read over his table of contents, is like reading over a roll of peers' names. We have, taking them as they stand, essays treating *Of Great Place, Of Boldness, Of Goodness, and Goodness of Nature, Of Nobility, Of Seditions and Troubles, Of Atheism, Of Superstition, Of Travel, Of Empire, Of Counsel*—a book plainly to lie in the closets of statesmen and princes, and designed to nurture the noblest natures. Bacon always seems to write with his ermine on. Montaigne was different from all this. His table of contents reads in comparison like a medley, or a catalogue of an auction. He was quite as wise as Bacon; he could look through men quite as clearly and search them quite as narrowly; certain of his moods were quite as serious, and in one corner of his heart he kept a yet profounder melancholy; but he was volatile, a humorist, and a gossip. He could be dignified enough on great occasions, but dignity and great occasions bored him. He could stand in the presence with propriety enough, but then he got out of the presence as rapidly as possible. When, in the thirty-eighth year of his age, he—somewhat world-weary, and with more scars on his heart than he cared to discover—retired to his chateau, he placed his library "in the great tower overlooking the entrance to the court," and over the central rafter he inscribed in large letters the device—"I DO NOT UNDERSTAND; I PAUSE; I EXAMINE." When he began to write his Essays he had no great desire to shine as an author; he wrote simply to relieve teeming heart and brain. The best method to lay the specters of the mind is to commit them to paper. Speaking of the Essays, he says, "This book has a domestic and private object. It is intended for the use of my relations and friends; so that, when they have lost me, which they will soon do, they may find in it some features of my condition and humors; and by this means keep up more completely, and in a more lively manner, the knowledge they have of me." In his Essays he meant to portray himself, his habits, his modes of thought, his opinions, what fruit of wisdom he had gathered from experience sweet and bitter; and the task he has executed with wonderful fidelity. He does not make himself a hero. Cromwell would have his warts painted; and Montaigne paints his, and paints them too with a certain fondness. He is perfectly tolerant of himself and of everybody else. Whatever be the subject, the writing flows on easy, equable, self-satisfied, almost always with a personal anecdote floating on the surface. Each event of his past life he considers a fact of nature; creditable or the reverse, there it is; sometimes to be speculated upon, not in the least to be regretted. If it is worth nothing else, it may be made the subject of an essay, or, at least, be useful as an illustration. . . .

. . . Bacon is the greatest of the serious and stately essayists—Montaigne the greatest of the garrulous and communicative. The one gives you his thoughts on Death, Travel, Government, and the like, and lets you make the best of them; the other gives you his on the same subjects, but he wraps them up in personal gossip and reminiscence. With the last it is never Death or Travel alone; it is always Death one-fourth, and Montaigne three-fourths. He pours his thought into the water of gossip, and gives you to drink. He gilds his pill always, and he always gilds it with himself. The general characteristics of his Essays have been indicated, and it is worth while inquiring what they teach, what positive good they have done, and why for three centuries they have charmed, and still continue to charm.

The Essays contain a philosophy of life, which is not specially high, yet which is certain to find acceptance more or less with men who have passed out beyond the glow of youth, and who have made trial of the actual world. The essence of his philosophy is a kind of cynical common sense. He will ask nothing in life; he will keep to the beaten track; he will not let passion blind or enslave him; he will gather around him what good he can; and will therewith endeavor to be content. He will be, as far as possible, self-sustained; he will not risk his happiness in the hands of man, or of woman either. He is shy of friendship, he fears love, for he knows that both are dangerous. He knows that life is full of bitters, and he holds it wisdom that a man should console himself, as far as possible, with its sweets, the principal of which are peace, travel, leisure, and the writing of essays. He values obtainable Gascon bread and cheese more than the unobtainable stars. He thinks crying for the moon the foolishest thing in the world. He will remain where he is. He will not deny that a new world may exist beyond the sunset, but he knows that to reach the new world there is a troublesome Atlantic to cross; and he is not in the least certain that, putting aside the chance of being drowned on the way, he will be one whit happier in the new world than he is in the old. For his part he will embark with no Columbus. He feels that life is but a sad thing at best; but as he has little hope of making it better, he accepts it, and will not make it worse by murmuring. When the chain galls him, he can at least revenge himself by making jests on it. He will temper the despotism of nature by epigrams. He has read Aesop's fable, and is the last man in the world to relinquish the shabbiest substance to grasp at the finest shadow.

Of nothing under the sun was Montaigne quite certain, except that every man—whatever his station—might travel farther and fare worse; and the playing with his own thoughts, in the shape of essay writing, was the most harmless of amusements. . . .

. . . And on style depends the success of the essayist. Montaigne said the most familiar things in the finest way. Goldsmith could not be termed a thinker; but everything he touched he brightened, as after a month of dry weather, the shower brightens the dusty shrubbery of a suburban villa. The world is not so much in need of new thoughts as that when thought grows old and worn with usage it should, like current coin, be called in, and, from the mint of genius, reissued fresh and new. Love is an old story enough, but in every generation it is reborn, in the downcast eyes and blushes of young maidens. And so, although he fluttered in Eden, Cupid is young today. If Montaigne had lived in Dreamthorp, as I am now living, had he written essays as I am now writing them, his English Essays would have been as good as his Gascon ones. Looking on, the country cart would not for nothing have passed him on the road to market, the setting sun would be arrested in its splendid colors, the idle chimes of the church would be translated into a thoughtful music. As it is, the village life goes on, and there is no result. My sentences are not much more brilliant than the speeches of the clowns; in my book there is little more life than there is in the market place on the days when there is no market.

F. L. LUCAS

On the Fascination of Style

WHEN IT was suggested to Walt Whitman that one of his works should be bound in vellum, he was outraged—"Pshaw!" he snorted, "—hangings, curtains, finger bowls, chinaware, Matthew Arnold!" And he might have been equally irritated by talk of style; for he boasted of "my barbaric yawp"—he would *not* be literary; his readers should touch not a book but a man. Yet Whitman took the pains to rewrite *Leaves of Grass* four times, and his style is unmistakable. Samuel Butler maintained that writers who bothered about their style became unreadable but he bothered about his own. "Style" has got a bad name by growing associated with precious and superior persons who, like Oscar Wilde, spend a morning putting in a comma, and the afternoon (so he said) taking it out again. But such abuse of "style" is misuse of English. For the word means merely "a way of expressing oneself, in language, manner, or appearance"; or, secondly, "a *good* way of so expressing oneself"— as when one says, "Her behavior never lacked style."

Now there is no crime in expressing oneself (though to try to *im*press oneself on others easily grows revolting or ridiculous). Indeed one cannot help expressing oneself, unless one passes one's life in a cupboard. Even the most rigid Communist, or Organization-man, is compelled by Nature to have a unique voice, unique fingerprints, unique handwriting. Even the signature of the letters on your breakfast table may reveal more than their writers guess. There are blustering signatures that swish across the page like cornstalks bowed before a tempest. There are cryptic signatures, like a scrabble of lightning across a cloud, suggesting that behind is a lofty divinity whom all must know, or an aloof divinity whom none is worthy to know (though, as this might be highly inconvenient, a docile typist sometimes interprets the mystery in a bracket underneath). There are impetuous squiggles implying that the author is a sort of strenuous Sputnik streaking round the globe every eighty minutes. There are florid signatures, all curlicues and danglements and flamboyance, like the youthful Disraeli (though these seem rather out of fashion). There are humble, humdrum signatures. And there are also, sometimes, signatures that are courteously clear, yet mindful of a certain simple grace and artistic economy—in short, of style.

Since, then, not one of us can put pen to paper, or even open his mouth, without giving something of himself away to shrewd observers, it seems mere common sense to give the matter a little thought. Yet it does not seem very common. Ladies may take infinite pains about having style in their clothes, but many of us remain curiously indifferent about having it in our words. How many women would dream of polishing not only their nails but also their tongues? They may play freely on that perilous little organ, but they cannot often be bothered to tune it. And how many men think of improving their talk as well as their golf handicap?

No doubt strong silent men, speaking only in gruff monosyllables, may despise "mere words." No doubt the world does suffer from an endemic plague of verbal dysentery. But that, precisely, is bad style. And consider the amazing power of mere words. Adolf Hitler was a bad artist, bad statesman, bad general, and bad man. But largely because he could tune his rant, with psychological nicety, to the exact wave length of his audiences and make millions quarrelsome-drunk all at the same time by his command of windy nonsense, skilled statesmen, soldiers, scientists were blown away like chaff, and he came near to rule the world. If Sir Winston Churchill had been a mere speechifier, we might have lost the war; yet his speeches did quite a lot to win it.

No man was less of a literary aesthete than Benjamin Franklin; yet this tallow-chandler's son, who changed world history, regarded as "a principal means of my advancement" that pungent style which he acquired partly by working in youth over old *Spectators*; but mainly by being Benjamin Franklin. The squinting demagogue,

John Wilkes, as ugly as his many sins, had yet a tongue so winning that he asked only half an hour's start (to counteract his face) against any rival for a woman's favor. "Vote for you!" growled a surly elector in his constituency, "I'd sooner vote for the devil!" "But in case your friend should not stand . . . ?" Cleopatra, that ensnarer of world conquerors, owed less to the shape of her nose than to the charm of her tongue. Shakespeare himself has often poor plots and thin ideas; even his mastery of character has been questioned; what does remain unchallenged is his verbal magic. Men are often taken, like rabbits, by the ears. And though the tongue has no bones, it can sometimes break millions of them.

"But," the reader may grumble, "I am neither Hitler, Cleopatra, nor Shakespeare. What is all this to me?" Yet we all talk—often too much; we all have to write letters—often too many. We live not by bread alone but also by words. And not always with remarkable efficiency. Strikes, lawsuits, divorces, all sorts of public nuisance and private misery, often come just from the gaggling incompetence with which we express ourselves. Americans and British get at cross-purposes because they use the same words with different meanings. Men have been hanged on a comma in a statute. And in the valley of Balaclava a mere verbal ambiguity, about *which* guns were to be captured, sent the whole Light Brigade to futile annihilation.

Words can be more powerful, and more treacherous, than we sometimes suspect; communication more difficult than we may think. We are all serving life sentences of solitary confinement within our own bodies; like prisoners, we have, as it were, to tap in awkward code to our fellow men in their neighboring cells. Further, when A and B converse, there take part in their dialogue not two characters, as they suppose, but six. For there is A's real self—call it A_1; there is also A's picture of himself—A_2; there is also B's picture of A—A_3. And there are three corresponding personalities of B. With six characters involved even in a simple tête-a-tête, no wonder we fall into muddles and misunderstandings.

Perhaps, then, there are five main reasons for trying to gain some mastery of language:

We have no other way of understanding, informing, misinforming, or persuading one another.

Even alone, we think mainly in words; if our language is muddy, so will our thinking be.

By our handling of words we are often revealed and judged. "Has he written anything?" said Napoleon of a candidate for an appointment. "Let me see his *style*."

Without a feeling for language one remains half-blind and deaf to literature.

Our mother tongue is bettered or worsened by the way each generation uses it. Languages evolve like species. They can degenerate; just as oysters and barnacles have lost their heads. Compare ancient Greek with modern. A heavy responsibility, though often forgotten.

Why and how did I become interested in style? The main answer, I suppose, is that I was born that way. Then I was, till ten, an only child running loose in a house packed with books, and in a world (thank goodness) still undistracted by radio and television. So at three I groaned to my mother, "Oh, I *wish* I could read," and at four I read. Now travel among books is the best travel of all, and the cheapest. (Not that I belittle ordinary travel—which I regard as one of the three main pleasures in life.) One learns to write by reading good books, as one learns to talk by hearing good talkers. And if I have learned anything of writing, it is largely from writers like Montaigne, Dorothy Osborne, Horace Walpole, Johnson, Goldsmith, Montesquieu, Voltaire, Flaubert and Anatole France. Again, I was reared on Greek and Latin, and one can learn much from translating Homer or the Greek Anthology, Horace or Tacitus, if one is thrilled by the originals and tries, however vainly, to recapture some of the thrill in English.

But at Rugby I could *not* write English essays. I believe it stupid to torment boys to write on topics that they know and care nothing about. I used to rush to the school library and cram the subject, like a python swallowing rabbits; then, still replete as a postprandial python, I would tie myself in clumsy knots to embrace those accursed themes. Bacon was wise in saying that reading makes a full man; talking, a ready one; writing, an exact one. But writing from an empty head is futile anguish.

At Cambridge, my head having grown a little fuller, I suddenly found I *could* write—not with enjoyment (it is always tearing oneself in pieces)—but fairly fluently. Then came the War of 1914-18; and though soldiers have other things than pens to handle, they learn painfully to be clear and brief. Then the late Sir Desmond McCarthy invited me to review for the *New Statesman*; it was a useful apprenticeship, and he was delightful to work for. But I think it was well after a few years to stop; reviewers remain essential, but there are too many books one *cannot* praise, and only the pugnacious enjoy amassing enemies. By then I was an ink-addict—not because writing is much pleasure, but because not to write is pain; just as some smokers do not so much enjoy tobacco as suffer without it. The positive happiness of writing comes, I think, from work well done—decently, one hopes, and not without use—and from the letters of readers which help to reassure, or delude, one that so it is.

But one of my most vivid lessons came, I think, from service in a war department during the Second War. Then, if the matter one sent out was too wordy, the communication channels might choke; yet if it was not absolutely clear, the results might be serious. So I emerged, after six years of it, with more passion than ever for clarity and brevity, more loathing than ever for the obscure and the verbose.

For forty years at Cambridge I have tried to teach young men to write well, and have come to think it impossible. To write really well is a gift inborn; those who have it teach themselves; one can only try to help and hasten the process. After all, the uneducated sometimes express themselves far better than their "betters." In language, as in life, it is possible to be perfectly correct—and yet perfectly tedious, or odious. The illiterate last letter of the doomed Vanzetti was more moving than most professional orators; Eighteenth Century ladies, who should have been spanked for their spelling, could yet write far better letters than most professors of English; and the talk of Synge's Irish peasants seems to me vastly more vivid than the later style of Henry James. Yet Synge averred that his characters owed far less of their eloquence to what he invented for them than to what he had overheard in the cottages of Wicklow and Kerry:

"*Christy.* 'It's little you'll think if my love's a poacher's, or an earl's itself, when you'll feel my two hands stretched around you,

and I squeezing kisses on your puckered lips, till I'd feel a kind of
pity for the Lord God is all ages sitting lonesome in His golden
chair.'

"*Pegeen*. 'That'll be right fun, Christy Mahon, and any girl would
walk her heart out before she'd meet a young man was your like for
eloquence, or talk at all.' "

Well she might! It's not like that they talk in universities—more's
the pity.

But though one cannot teach people to write well, one can
sometimes teach them to write rather better. One can give a certain
number of hints, which often seem boringly obvious—only experience shows they are not.

One can say: Beware of pronouns—they are devils. Look at even
Addison, describing the type of pedant who chatters of style without having any: "Upon enquiry I found my learned friend had
dined that day with Mr. Swan, the famous punster; and desiring
him to give me some account of Mr. Swan's conversation, *he* told
me that *he* generally talked in the Paronomasia, that *he* sometimes
gave in to the Plocé, but that in *his* humble opinion *he* shone most
in the Antanaclasis." What a sluttish muddle of *he* and *him* and *his*!
It all needs rewording. Far better repeat a noun, or a name, than
puzzle the reader, even for a moment, with ambiguous pronouns.
Thou shalt not puzzle thy reader.

Or one can say: Avoid jingles. The B.B.C. news bulletins seem
compiled by earless persons, capable of crying round the globe: "The
enemy is re*port*ed to have seized this im*port*ant *port*, and reinforce-
ments are hurrying up in sup*port*." Any fool, once told, can hear
such things to be insupportable.

Or one can say: Be sparing with relative clauses. Don't string
them together like sausages, or jam them inside one another like
Chinese boxes or the receptacles of Buddha's tooth. Or one can say:
Don't flaunt jargon, like Addison's Mr. Swan, or the type of modern
critic who gurgles more technical terms in a page than Johnson used
in all his *Lives* or Sainte-Beuve in thirty volumes. But dozens of
such snippety precepts, though they may sometimes save people from
writing badly, will help them little toward writing well. Are there
no general rules of a more positive kind, and of more positive use?

Perhaps. There *are* certain basic principles which seem to me observed by many authors I admire, which I think have served me and which may serve others. I am not talking of geniuses, who are a law to themselves (and do not always write a very good style, either); nor of poetry, which has different laws from prose; nor of poetic prose, like Sir Thomas Browne's or De Quincey's, which is often more akin to poetry; but of the plain prose of ordinary books and documents, letters and talk.

The writer should respect truth and himself; therefore honesty. He should respect his readers; therefore courtesy. These are two of the cornerstones of style. Confucius saw it, twenty-five centuries ago; "The Master said, The gentleman is courteous, but not pliable: common men are pliable, but not courteous."

First, honesty. In literature, as in life, one of the fundamentals is to find, and be, one's true self. One's true self may indeed be unpleasant (though one can try to better it); but a false self, sooner or later, becomes disgusting—just as a nice plain woman, painted to the eyebrows, can become horrid. In writing, in the long run, pretense does not work. As the police put it, anything you say may be used as evidence against you. If handwriting reveals character, writing reveals it still more. You cannot fool *all* your judges *all* the time.

Most style is not honest enough. Easy to say, but hard to practice. A writer may take to long words, as young men to beards—to impress. But long words, like long beards, are often the badge of charlatans. Or a writer may cultivate the obscure, to seem profound. But even carefully muddied puddles are soon fathomed. Or he may cultivate eccentricity, to seem original. But really original people do not have to think about being original—they can no more help it than they can help breathing. They do not need to dye their hair green. The fame of Meredith, Wilde or Bernard Shaw might now shine brighter, had they struggled less to be brilliant; whereas Johnson remains great, not merely because his gifts were formidable but also because, with all his prejudice and passion, he fought no less passionately to "clear his mind of cant."

Secondly, courtesy—respect for the reader. From this follow several other basic principles of style. Clarity is one. For it is boorish to make your reader rack his brains to understand. One should aim at being impossible to misunderstand—though men's capacity for misunderstanding approaches infinity. Hence Molière and Po Chu-i tried their work on their cooks; and Swift his on his men servants— "which, if they did not comprehend, he would alter and amend, until they understood it perfectly." Our bureaucrats and pundits, unfortunately, are less considerate.

Brevity is another basic principle. For it is boorish, also, to waste your reader's time. People who would not dream of stealing a penny of one's money turn not a hair at stealing hours of one's life. But that does not make them less exasperating. Therefore there is no excuse for the sort of writer who takes as long as a marching army corps to pass a given point. Besides, brevity is often more effective; the half can say more than the whole, and to imply things may strike far deeper than to state them at length. And because one is particularly apt to waste words on preambles before coming to the substance, there was sense in the Scots professor who always asked his pupils—"Did ye remember to tear up that fir-r-st page?"

Here are some instances that would only lose by lengthening:

It is useless to go to bed to save the light, if the result is twins. (Chinese proverb.)

My barn is burnt down—
Nothing hides the moon. (Complete Japanese poem.)

Je me regrette. (Dying words of the gay Vicomtesse d'Houdetot.)

I have seen their backs before. (Wellington, when French marshals turned their backs on him at a reception.)

Continue until the tanks stop, then get out and walk. (Patton to the Twelfth Corps, halted for fuel supplies at St. Dizier, 8/30/44.)

Or there is the most laconic diplomatic note on record: when Philip of Macedon wrote to the Spartans that, if he came within their borders, he would leave not one stone of their city, they wrote back the one word—"If."

Clarity comes before even brevity. But it is a fallacy that wordiness is necessarily clearer. Metternich when he thought something he had written was obscure would simply go through it crossing out everything irrelevant. What remained, he found, often became clear. Wellington, asked to recommend three names for the post of Commander-in-Chief, India, took a piece of paper and wrote three times—"Napier." Pages could not have been clearer—or as forcible. On the other hand the lectures, and the sentences, of Coleridge became at times bewildering because his mind was often "wigglewaggle"; just as he could not even walk straight on a path.

But clarity and brevity, though a good beginning, are only a beginning. By themselves, they may remain bare and bleak. When Calvin Coolidge, asked by his wife what the preacher had preached on, replied "Sin," and, asked what the preacher had said, replied, "He was against it," he was brief enough. But one hardly envies Mrs. Coolidge.

An attractive style requires, of course, all kinds of further gifts—such as variety, good humor, good sense, vitality, imagination. Variety means avoiding monotony of rhythm, of language, of mood. One needs to vary one's sentence length (this present article has too many short sentences; but so vast a subject grows here as cramped as a djin in a bottle); to amplify one's vocabulary; to diversify one's tone. There are books that petrify one throughout, with the rigidly pompous solemnity of an owl perched on a leafless tree. But ceaseless facetiousness can be as bad; or perpetual irony. Even the smile of Voltaire can seem at times a fixed grin, a disagreeable wrinkle. Constant peevishness is far worse, as often in Swift; even on the stage too much irritable dialogue may irritate an audience, without its knowing why.

Still more are vitality, energy, imagination gifts that must be inborn before they can be cultivated. But under the head of imagination two common devices may be mentioned that have been the making of many a style—metaphor and simile. Why such magic power should reside in simply saying, or implying, that A is like B remains a little mysterious. But even our unconscious seems to love symbols; again, language often tends to lose itself in clouds of vaporous abstraction, and simile or metaphor can bring it back to concrete solidity; and, again, such imagery can gild the gray flats of prose with sudden sun-glints of poetry.

If a foreigner may for a moment be impertinent, I admire the native gift of Americans for imagery as much as I wince at their fondness for slang. (Slang seems to me a kind of linguistic fungus; as poisonous, and as short-lived, as toadstools.) When Matthew Arnold lectured in the United States, he was likened by one newspaper to "an elderly macaw pecking at a trellis of grapes"; he observed, very justly, "How lively journalistic fancy is among the Americans!" General Grant, again, unable to hear him, remarked: "Well, wife, we've paid to see the British lion, but as we can't hear him roar, we'd better go home." By simile and metaphor, these two quotations bring before us the slightly pompous, fastidious, inaudible Arnold as no direct description could have done.

Or consider how language comes alive in the Chinese saying that lending to the feckless is "like pelting a stray dog with dumplings," or in the Arab proverb: "They came to shoe the pasha's horse, and the beetle stretched forth his leg"; in the Greek phrase for a perilous cape—"stepmother of ships"; or the Hebrew adage that "as the climbing up a sandy way is to the feet of the aged, so is a wife full of words to a quiet man"; in Shakespeare's phrase for a little England lost in the world's vastness—"in a great Poole, a Swan's nest"; or Fuller's libel on tall men—"Ofttimes such who are built four stories high are observed to have little in their cockloft"; in Chateaubriand's "I go yawning my life"; or in Jules Renard's portrait of a cat, "well buttoned in her fur." Or, to take a modern instance, there is Churchill on dealings with Russia: "Trying to maintain good relations with a Communist is like wooing a crocodile. You do not know whether to tickle it under the chin or beat it over the head. When it opens its mouth, you cannot tell whether it is trying to smile or preparing to eat you up." What a miracle human speech can be, and how dull is most that one hears! Would one hold one's hearers, it is far less help, I suspect, to read manuals on style than to cultivate one's own imagination and imagery.

I will end with two remarks by two wise old women of the civilized eighteenth Century.

The first is from the blind Mme. du Deffand (the friend of

Horace Walpole) to that Mlle. De Lespinasse with whom, alas, she was to quarrel so unwisely: "You must make up your mind, my queen, to live with me in the greatest truth and sincerity. You will be charming so long as you let yourself be natural, and remain without pretension and without artifice." The second is from Mme. de Charrière, the Zélide whom Boswell had once loved at Utrecht in vain, to a Swiss girl friend: "Lucinde, my clever Lucinde, while you wait for the Romeos to arrive, you have nothing better to do than become perfect. Have ideas that are clear, and expressions that are simple." ("Ayez des idées nettes et des expressions simples.") More than half the bad writing in the world, I believe, comes from neglecting those two very simple pieces of advice.

In many ways, no doubt, our world grows more and more complex; Sputniks cannot be simple; yet how many of our complexities remain futile, how many of our artificialities false. Simplicity too can be subtle—as the straight lines of a Greek temple, like the Parthenon at Athens, are delicately curved, in order to look straighter still.

2 3 4 5 6 7 8 9 10 11 12 13 14 15   88 87 86 85 84 83 82 81 80 79 78 77 76 75 74